Random memories of a chequered lifetime

BITS AND PIECES

By BRAD FLEMING

For Mary —
with Best Wishes.
Enjoy! — Brad

PROLOGUE

This is the story of a life – my life. How boring is that? Please don't be alarmed though; these little tales are not intended to be taken too seriously, or be read by the public at large. I'm by no means certain that I have the right to inflict them on anyone, not least my long-suffering family, and the few friends I have left. Please note that reading them isn't compulsory; you can stop at any time - or not bother to start at all.

On reflection, it's perhaps presumptuous to call it a life story in the first place. After all, I haven't lived all my life yet, even if the final clarion could sound at any time. I know it's the accepted thing for politicians, sportsmen and so called personalities to cash in by writing their memoirs while still at the height of their fame.

In my case, however, fame clearly doesn't come into it at all. But, on the whole, I've rather enjoyed treading this little bit of earth for more than four-score years. I've done one or two things I'm reasonably proud of, and a great many more I wish I hadn't. Looking back, there's not a lot I'd change – even if I could – except perhaps that I wish I'd treated some folk more kindly than I have.

But take heart, my little band of brothers and sisters; if by chance you do summon the curiosity, or indeed the courage, to delve more deeply into these pages, it's just possible that you'll discover something of interest. Who knows, you may even find yourself lurking somewhere within.

If what you read produces a talking point or two, or raises a question here or there, then that's a fair start. If it offends, then I apologise belatedly, but I'm afraid it's too late to make changes now.

Some of these events took place a long time ago and my memory isn't what it was. I don't pretend to have recorded every conversation verbatim, but I have endeavoured, to the best of my ability, to capture the essence of what words were said, and by whom.

To this end, I was aided by being able to consult a number of notes and diaries I've kept intermittently throughout the years. I regret not having been a more assiduous diarist.

Remembering faces has never been a problem for me; recalling names is another matter entirely. In the main, I've followed the old maxim, if in doubt, leave out.

If then, you chance upon this little book, and read your pearls of wisdom attributed to someone else, please be charitable. I meant no disrespect. Conversely, if you're misquoted, but are pleased by what you're supposed to have said, then accept it as a well-earned plaudit from an old friend.

One final thought. This book is not for everyone – goodness knows, it may not be for anyone – but if it gives even one reader a moment's fleeting enjoyment, then the writing of it was worthwhile.

Brad Fleming

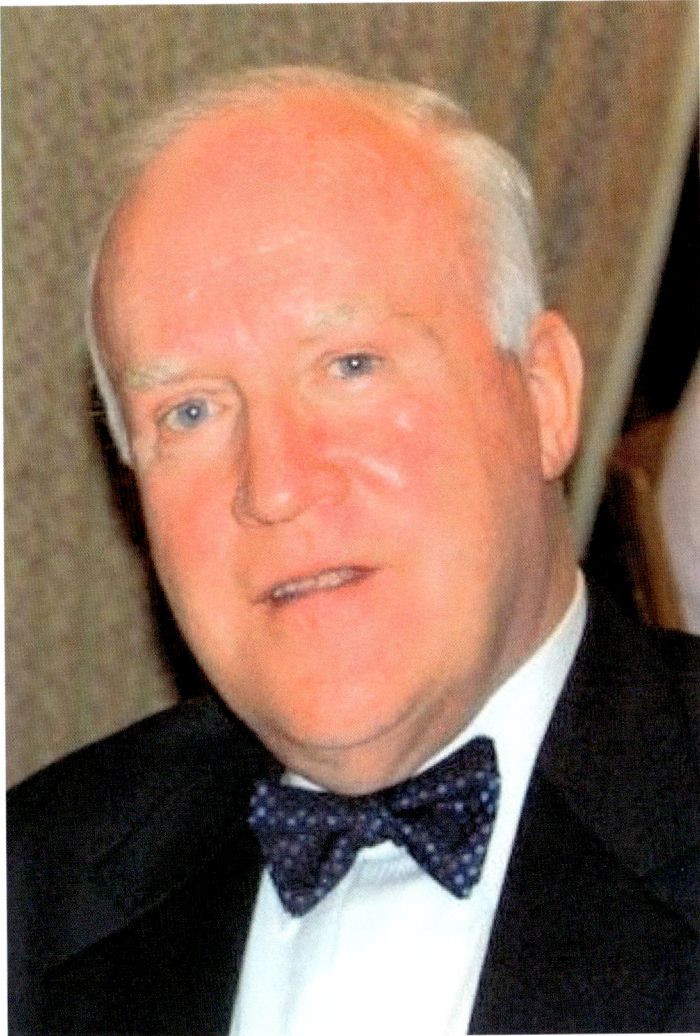

Dedication

For my family and my friends.

Family group. (from left, back) Brad, Val and John Crawford, Mollie Fleming. (front) Philip Crawford, Nip Fleming and Jonathan Crawford

That's me on the left with the curls, aged one and a bit. Note the family likeness with daughter Valerie (right) with mum, Mollie.

Schooldays

I don't remember my first day at school. For one thing, it was a long time ago, and for another, my memory for unpleasant things has never been particularly good. I do remember the second day though; I was given two strokes of the cane for doing something I shouldn't. I can't remember what heinous crime I committed, but, knowing me, I probably deserved the whacking.

Corporal punishment was allowed in those days, even encouraged. I believe the theory was that it would make men – and presumably women – of us. As I recollect, it was comparatively rare for any of the girls to merit a slapping. Their punishment was usually a stern talking to, or a short period of detention after class.

Now, alas, having noted the behaviour of some of the modern generation of schoolgoers, I'm old and curmudgeonly enough to reflect that a return of the bamboo punisher might be no bad thing.

I was never a subscriber to the adage that schooldays are the happiest days of one's life. As with any other time of life there were fairly equal shares of the good, the bad and the ugly. Fortunately for most of us I believe we tend to remember the happier times.

My first small-town primary school was much like any other in the Northern Ireland of the immediate post-World War II period. There were three classrooms – Junior, Intermediate and Senior – all uniformly nondescript, each with a charcoal-grey pot-bellied stove to provide heating in winter. Sometimes, when well stoked up, they glowed red hot. Those unfortunate enough to have desks positioned too close to them got gently cooked on one side. They stood out from the rest of us with their blotched and reddened legs. In winter there was always a scramble to grab a desk on the other side of the classroom.

There were no playing-fields or grassy areas. A narrow, concrete-covered yard ran the entire length of the rear of the building and it was there we had out breaks and ate our lunchtime sandwiches. We clustered in little bunches, chatting with our particular pals, or played tig, touch rugby, or rough-and-tumble football matches with an old tennis ball.

The toilet block stood at the far end of the yard. It was grey and unwelcoming and stank of stale urine. Girls used the door on the left, the boys the one on the right. Never the twain shall meet. There was no hot water and the solitary roller-towel probably concealed more germs than you'd find in the Amazonian jungle.

It was there that the more adventurous of us were introduced to the delights and dangers of tobacco. One day somebody produced a slim green packet of Woodbine cigarettes. You could buy a pack of five for as many pence in the old pre-decimal money. Of course he'd forgotten to buy matches, so one of our number was dispatched to Murphy's general store across the street.

Solemnly we tore the unfiltered cigarettes in half and ten of us lit up. It was not a pretty sight. As I recall, most of us collapsed into paroxysms of coughing and spluttering and immediately began picking flecks of the demon weed off our lips and tongues. I have no doubt that, through time, some of us mastered the dubious art of smoking a fag. For my part, it was a good few years before I tried another cigarette.

The master

In due time, when we'd worked our way through the junior and intermediate classes, we took our seats in the Headmaster's room. It was a chastening experience. We'd heard rumours of course, and some of the seniors had alarmed us with dire warnings about what "He" was like. We figured they were just trying to frighten us with tall stories. We were wrong. There was rarely a day when the long, evil-looking cane, hanging on a nail beside the blackboard, didn't beat a tattoo on some luckless pupil's backside or palms.

We'd seen him many times of course. At morning assembly, sports days, the beginning of a new term and the like. Sharing a small classroom with him, up close and personal, was a horse of an entirely different colour. I quickly learned to keep my head down, avoid eye-contact and speak only when I was spoken to. I didn't escape my fair share of whippings, even if the passing years have allowed me to acknowledge that the majority of them were probably well deserved.

A native-born Dubliner who had lived and taught in the North for many years, he rejoiced in the name of Harley Lyle Sleith. It's a name not easily forgotten and those he taught are never likely to forget him. An MA and PhD from Trinity bespoke his abilities, but it was a fair few years later when I came fully to appreciate and be grateful for his work. Quite simply, he was the best teacher I ever knew.

In later years, long after he'd retired, I got to know him better. It would be presumptuous to say we'd become friends, but I was ridiculously pleased when he proffered the odd compliment. I couldn't recall many of those in my student days. The closest I ever got to it – even if it was a kind of backhanded one – was one day when I answered a particularly difficult question almost correctly.

"Fleming," he said, with the closest he ever got to a twinkle, "of all my pupils, sometimes I think you are something of a genius . . . (the pause was a lengthy one) . . . with the emphasis on the ass!"

He instilled in his pupils a healthy respect, sometimes bordering on real fear. When he spoke we listened. If we didn't we could expect trouble ahead. I remember an occasion when, as a 10 year-old, I was walking down main street with my father and noticed Mr Sleith coming towards us. Without thinking, I instinctively moved position so that my Dad was between us. Mr Sleith, ever the gentleman, touched the brim of his hat and stopped for a word with my father, giving me only the curtest of nods.

When we walked on Dad looked down and flashed me a wry smile. "I noticed you taking shelter there," he said. "I'm glad someone seems to be able to put the fear of God in you."

I remember thinking *I'm not sure about God, but I'm not taking any chances with Mr Sleith.*

Freddy

Freddy was what we called a Bernardo Boy and came from a Charitable Home only a stone's throw from the school. Originally from Belfast, he was one of a number of refugee children sent out of the city during the wartime blitz. I never got to know him all that well; he was simply one of the gang.

He was a tough little nut though, as one youngster who picked a fight with him in the playground discovered to his cost. As far as I knew, Freddy was an orphan who was well used to fending for himself.

Bernardo boy or not, he neither received nor expected any favours from Mr Sleith. One day, for whatever reason, he was called up to the front of the class and received the standard punishment of four strokes of the cane. Having been on the receiving end of several of these lashings, Freddy had my sympathy. He accepted his caning stoically before being brusquely ordered back to his desk.

Mr Sleith turned back to the blackboard, picked up a piece of chalk and began to write. A second later we heard a dull thud and saw a brown-handled throwing knife quivering in the board a scant six inches from the teacher's hand. I wouldn't presume to say you could cut the atmosphere with a knife, but I can think of no better description.

I snatched a glance at Freddy's expressionless face before watching our teacher stretch out a languid hand, wrest the knife from the blackboard, close it and put it in his pocket. Pointing at the door he barked an order at the culprit. "Leave my classroom. Now."

Freddy obeyed. We never saw him again.

Dermot

No one could ever accuse our teacher of playing favourites. His son Dermot was in my class and I always felt he was given a much rougher time by his father than any of the rest of us. He was caned more than most and spent an inordinate amount of time in detention after school. Once, when I mentioned this to him and offered sympathy he shrugged and gave a watery smile as if to say That's how the cookie crumbles.

There came a day when Mr Sleith definitely went too far, and perhaps for the only occasion during my time with him, he plummeted in my estimation. During the first lesson that particular morning Dermot was caught out in a lie. It was only a little white lie, but it was a lie nonetheless.

In addition to receiving four of the best he was made to sit all that day, even though lunchtime, on a three-legged stool in the corner with a large placard round his neck bearing the legend I AM A LIAR in large capital letters.

Had that happened to me I believe I'd have broken the placard over his father's head.

My saddest memory

I suppose for most of us memories of our early childhood are little more than ephemeral, fleeting snapshots, frozen in time and embellished and coloured afterwards by repeated flashbacks throughout the years which follow. That's certainly how it was with me.

To this day I can recall an image of my father standing just outside the front door of our home in Kilkeel, looking down at a small white casket he was holding in his arms. My three-year-old brain was completely unable to comprehend that inside that little box was my younger brother, Clifford, who had died of diphtheria having just attained his first birthday. There was simply no way I could understand that I would never see him again.

Two years later, as a five-year-old, I do remember Dad standing outside that same front door. For whatever reason, I hadn't been home for some time and had been looked after by my aunt and uncle. My father raised me up in his arms, and childlike, I hugged him and said, "Where's my Mummy?"

His next words hit me like a truck. "Your Mummy's dead, son!"

Of course, I had known for some months that Mum was ill. The doctor had become a frequent visitor to the house and there were weekly trips to hospital, but I had no notion of how serious things were. I suppose I accepted blindly that my Mum had always been there for me – and always would be. It took a long time for the realisation to dawn that she was never coming back.

Dad never spoke of it much to me afterwards, but I came to understand that he must have missed Mum even more than I did. I do know that he never ever contemplated marrying again.

A tale of two aunts and a grandma

I have few standout memories of the next few years. Dad was working away from home a lot of the time and I was billeted, in turn, with two aunts, his sisters, Minnie and Maud, and my maternal grandmother, Agnes. I had no favourites; they were all generous and good to me in their different ways. I didn't see a lot of my respective uncles. They were all busy with their own work and were content to let the womenfolk get on with keeping an eye on me.

Aunt Minnie owned two shops, one of them a newsagents and book store. She and my cousin, Bobby, who managed it, were kindly folk and as soon as I was old enough to help behind the scenes in the back room, unpacking cartons of books, sweeping up, and assembling regular orders for newspapers and magazines, that became my regular after-school job for a couple of hours most days.

It didn't normally run to pay or pocket money, but to my mind, it provided something much more valuable to a growing boy. After all my chores were done, I was allowed to retreat to the back office and read whatever I wanted, providing I kept it clean and returned it to the shop undamaged.

I was in seventh heaven. Starting off with picture comic books, I progressed steadily to printed comics such as the Wizard, Hotspur, Adventure and Rover. I'm sure older UK readers will remember those. Short stories and serials full of tales of derring do. I devoured them as quickly as they came into the shop.

In time I moved on to the well-stocked shelves of hardbacks –

Treasure Island, Robinson Crusoe, Tom Sawyer, Black Beauty, The Coral Island and many more. Encouraged by my aunt, I tackled their stock of classics – Wilde, Austen, Conan Doyle, Dickens, Mark Twain, Jules Verne, the Brontes and Blackmore. I stopped short of Shakespeare though – too difficult for me then, and besides, he reminded me too much of school. I can still quote reams of his work today though – it was drummed into me by my English teacher, who was a huge fan. That said, his sonnets and some of the Bard's soliloquies are writings of exquisite beauty.

Looking back on that period of my life in later years, I came to realize how remarkably fortunate I'd been. Had my aunt paid me in coin I would have eaten more sweets, drank more pop and watched more movies, but I would unquestionably have missed out on a unique opportunity of acquiring an appreciation of, and love for, the English language I still enjoy today.

It isn't cricket

Perhaps unusually for an Irishman, Harley Lyle Sleith had an enduring and abiding love for the game of cricket. I discovered this quite late in our association and often wished I had known of it earlier in order that I might somehow have been able to turn it to my advantage. As it was, I was able to make use of it on at least two occasions during my final year at school.

Mr Sleith was President and principal umpire of the town cricket club and he took both these duties extremely seriously. He rarely missed a match or a practice session at the local ground and was an avid follower of England's Test Matches through the newspapers and the BBC's radio commentaries. He was mildly surprised, but I think quite pleased, when I became a member of the club as an aspiring spin bowler.

This sets the scene for one early summer afternoon when I had been awarded half an hour's detention for some minor misdemeanour. I was the only captive that day and Mr. Sleith, marking homework at his desk, instructed me to write a short essay on whatever subject took my fancy.

Fearing the worst, but determined to play the percentages, I penned a short critique on the shortcomings and inadequacies of an education system which dared to incarcerate young students in a stuffy schoolroom after normal hours when otherwise they could have been outdoors in God's good fresh air following useful pursuits such as improving their bowling at cricket practice.

Beckoned forward to hand in my offering, I waited, not without a certain trepidation, for the threatened storm to break.

Was that an angry tremor of his upper lip? Surely that couldn't be the glimmer of a twinkle in those cold grey eyes?

"Hmmm," he said, then glanced at his watch. "If you cut along sharpish you can still manage an hour's practice at the ground before tea!"

A month or so later, just before the long summer holidays and before I moved on to another school, I was given my first game for the town First XI. As a newbie, I batted number eleven and was not unduly displeased when my services were not called upon.

The opposition went in to bat and were soon going well. Things were looking bleak for us when our skipper, probably in desperation, threw the ball to me with a "have a go young'un and good luck!"

As fortune had it my friend Mr Sleith, umpiring at my end, maintained an indifferent and neutral silence, ignoring me completely until he gave the batsman his guard and called "Play." His presence did absolutely nothing to ease my nervousness.

I'll never be quite sure how, but I managed to take four wickets for two runs and we won the match by a distance. As the players trooped off to the pavilion Mr Sleith walked alongside me. "Well done Brad," he said. He'd never used my first name before, but I guessed it was because we were outside school hours. "Thank you very much," I replied.

My first passport picture. I was recovering from a black-eye, the result of a smack from a cricket ball for not paying attention while fielding in the slips.

The classroom demeanour wasn't long in returning. "That being said, that last delivery of yours, the lbw, was just about the worst

I've seen this season."

"Oh I don't know sir, "I responded. "at least it must have been pretty straight, otherwise an excellent umpire like you would never have given it out!"

He stopped dead in his tracks. Perhaps I had gone a bit far – but what the hell, we had won the match, I was starting a new school, and I would never have to sit in his classroom again.

The old firelighter of long, long ago

Robert had been caretaker and janitor long before I ever started school. An affable old pensioner, I would sometimes come down to the deserted building before anyone else arrived to enjoy a little chat and to help him prepare kindling and coal for the three pot-bellied stoves. He lived alone in a small terraced house almost directly opposite the school and always smelled of paraffin oil and coal dust.

I loved listening to his stories about the local fishing fleet and the old town he had grown up in. He was a grand old man and he always thanked me for what little assistance I was able to give him.

One day I had just finished reading a book of sea stories and it occurred to me that it was exactly the sort of thing Robert would enjoy. I presented it to him next morning and was surprised when he burst out laughing.

"Bless your heart lad and thank you, but hold on to your book. It would be no use to me at all, at all. I never learned to read you see."

He laughed again, loud and long. "It's funny when you think about it. I've been to school every day for the last fifteen years and I still never learned to read or write!"

Jimmy's last day at school

Jimmy was the quietest lad in our class. Not shy exactly, but he never joined in any of our knockabout games in the school yard. He didn't care for football, or cricket, or any other sport. He wasn't the brightest, but you wouldn't call him stupid either. He rarely initiated a conversation but would always respond cheerfully enough when approached. I can never remember him getting into trouble of any kind. He was the only lad I never saw getting a taste of the cane.

I sat in the next desk to his on his last morning, although neither of us knew then that he wouldn't be back. He was one of those who habitually went home for lunch. When we resumed our lessons we noticed his desk was empty. About half an hour into the afternoon session the headmaster answered a knock on the door. He opened it and we heard a muffled conversation.

He returned silently to the front of the room and said quietly. "I'm sorry to have to tell you that our friend Jimmy has passed away at home this lunchtime."

The entire class attended Jimmy's funeral but no one ever told us what had happened to him.

A visit to the dentist

We had an officially appointed school dentist who visited twice a year, usually about a week apart. First time around he would line us up in a row, prise open our mouths with a plastic spatula thingamajig and dictate his findings to the nurse who accompanied him to inscribe the details on a set of postcards. Between each inspection he would sanitise the spatula by swirling it around in a glass in some sort of disinfectant. I don't know what it was but it tasted absolutely foul.

He was a gruff, humourless, heavy-handed individual whose bedside manner, or more accurately, his classroom manner, was sadly lacking in either sympathy or politeness. In short, it would have ensured him a job with the Spanish Inquisition, or in the torture chambers of the Gestapo. His inspection over, he would read out the names of those victims he had earmarked for further attention and warn them solemnly of the fate awaiting them if they failed to appear for treatment at his next visit on whatever date he indicated.

I have to say that many disregarded this threat and chickened out anyway. Sadly, he appeared to take this as a personal affront and their torture was all the greater when he finally caught up with them.

I was fortunate in having to endure his administrations only once, when I needed two injections while he filled a back tooth. As if disappointed that I was escaping so lightly, he applied the drill before the injections had time to take effect. The memory lives with me still, and although dentistry has improved out of sight since those far off days, I can't honestly say I look forward to taking my seat in that dreaded chair.

The loudest cheer I can ever remember at school came when it was announced that school dental visits were being suspended and that henceforth we would have to sign on with our parents at our local health centre.

The challenge

We had a sort of league table in senior school. Marks were awarded each week according to how well, or how badly, we had done in English, Maths, History, Geography and so on. The swots and the bright lads and lasses had desks in the front two rows, occasionally moving up or down a notch or two depending on how they performed.

There was no way my mates and I wanted to be up there in the spotlight, right under the Sleith proboscis, and in close proximity to the cane hanging by the blackboard. No, we knew our place – which was somewhere between the halfway line and the back wall. There we could pass the odd scribbled note to one another, crib an answer from one of the brighter kids whenever a difficult question was posed and generally bluff our way through our lessons.

Imagine my discomfiture then when one day, down at cricket practice; while we were sheltering in the pavilion from a sudden rainsquall, my esteemed headmaster beckoned me over to where he was sitting alone in the farthest corner.

"Fleming," he began sternly, and I wondered what in hell I had done now, "I have been watching you in school for some time and I have come to the conclusion that you are in grave danger of becoming an idle waster."

Wait a minute, I thought. Thanks a bunch, we're not in school now, we're meant to be playing cricket. This is supposed to be my free time.

"You are stumbling along, doing just enough to get by. When you put your mind to it – something I have observed on only rare occasions – you are by far the best student of English in the school. Your Geography and History are more than adequate, your basic Arithmetic is sound, but your grasp of Algebra is non-existent. Tell me, why is this?"

"I'm sorry, but I do not like Algebra."

"That much is evident. I want to know why."

"Because, while I have no idea what I am going to do when I leave school, I know it isn't going to involve Algebra."

"I say again, why?"

"Because I find it difficult to grasp. Anyway, I understand by using Algebra it can be proved conclusively that two equals zero. What's the point of that?

"Don't be flippant. It doesn't suit you. I am trying to have a serious conversation with you. I'm trying to help you. I want to help you, do you understand. You have a talent and I don't want to see it wasted."

Not to put too fine a point on it, I was gobsmacked; although I'm not sure I knew the meaning of the word back then. Was I hearing right? Was the dreaded Harley Lyle Sleith actually paying me a compliment? Was he really genuinely concerned about my future once my schooldays were over? He'd thrown me completely – and what's more he knew it. He'd intended to do exactly that.

He was leaning forward in his chair, speaking again. "Ah, I see I have your attention."

He certainly had. I was all ears.

"Now listen carefully. I have a little challenge for you. I believe you're the sort of chap who will accept and respond to a challenge. Am I right?"

I paused for a moment. "I suppose it depends on the challenge."

He fixed me with his stare. "Oh the challenge is simple enough. The question is are you man enough, ambitious enough, to go for it?"

"And the challenge is?"

"I want you to work harder than you ever have before. I want you to come top of our school merit table for three successive weeks. Do you accept?"

I sat in silence for a long time, thinking hard. Was I up for this? Did I really want to be up there with the swots at the top of the class? Maybe he was just trying to slap me down again, or was he using the old carrot and stick technique to make me stir my stumps. Whatever? Damn him, I'd show the beggar.

I nodded. "I accept. I'll give it a go."

"Good man," he exclaimed enthusiastically. "Today's Tuesday. That gives you three days to prepare. The challenge starts on Monday. I'll expect to see you in the front row beginning the following week."

He rose, shook my hand and glanced out the window. "I do believe the rain's over. Let's get out there."

Later my mates laughed out loud when I told them of the conversation.

"You're mad," "What's the point?" "You'll never do it," "You haven't a pup's chance," were typical rejoinders. "I just want to prove the old beggar wrong," was all I could say.

I doubt I've ever worked as hard at anything as I did in the weeks that followed. I studied, I swotted, I revised, I even spent time battling with the dreaded Algebra. I skipped going to the pictures some nights. I was almost glad when the rain ruled out cricket practice. I spent time on my weaker subjects. I sweated blood. I was shattered. I knew I couldn't have done any more. If it wasn't good enough, then to hell with it!

That first Monday morning arrived and I took my customary seat beside my mates, around halfway back. The usual suspects sat up front, primed and ready for business as usual.

Mr Sleith stood up, cleared his throat, and began to read. "The Merit Table for this week is as follows. Number one . . ."

Not daring to catch his eye, I embarked on an intensive scrutiny of my desktop, the blot-stained inkwell, my exercise books, a couple of sharpened pencils. Keep your head down man. Steady the ship.

"We have a change at number one this week . . . something of a surprise if I may say so . . . Brad Fleming."

The atmosphere in the room could have been cut with a chain-saw. The swots in the front desks swung round and gazed towards me, their faces masks of disbelief. Surely this could not be. There must have been a mistake. My mate at the next desk jabbed a sharp elbow into my ribs. "You cunning old git. You only went and did it!"

There was a buzz of animated conversation as the list continued to be read out. I don't know if anyone was listening. I know I wasn't.

As I advanced to take my unaccustomed seat there was a smattering of muffled applause from my fellow denizens in the back benches. Several girls smiled and cooed, "Well done." Even a couple of male swots smiled their congratulations. Fergus, the previous week's incumbent, who had now been deposed to third spot, sat stony-faced and cut me dead. There's always at least one sore loser, I reflected.

I can't claim I fancied my new exalted position. Being within cane-stroke of Master Sleith positively bristled with potential disasters. As it turned out, I needn't have worried. Perhaps the old devil was so chuffed with the success of his ruse in stirring me into productivity that he was happy enough to let the hare sit for now.

I have to admit to being rather less surprised when I topped the charts again in the two succeeding weeks. I'd done it, and I took a degree of modest satisfaction from the fact. Looking back on it now, I suppose the exercise gave me the kick up the backside I richly deserved. Sleith was right. I'd been coasting. He had known it and now I knew it too. The penny had dropped; the lesson had been well and truly taken on board.

Predictably, I never rose to such dizzy heights again. I never wanted to and was happy to be back with my friends. I knew I had it in me to do it and that was enough. Thank you, you crafty old Dubliner. I owe you a lot.

School holidays

The memory plays tricks. It can be selective. Looking back down those years with the aid of the old rose-tinted spectacles it's easy to imagine that school holidays dragged on forever, that the sun always shone and that it rained only occasionally. Of course it wasn't like that; only our memories make it so.

As the wise old Bard of Avon had it, each year had its seasons and every one of them held its own special attractions. The main benefit of being on holiday, of course, was that we could put away our satchels, pencils, erasers and exercise books and forget all about school for weeks on end. *Hooorrraaay!*

Easter was the first real holiday to come along. Sad to say, its religious significance was almost entirely lost on us. It was a time for picnics out in the countryside – Easter Feasts we would call them. The plan was to gather up a few dozen eggs and a battered old saucepan or two and head off to a favourite spot, usually close to a steam or river – with an abundance of whin blossom nearby.

For the benefit of later, less easily pleased generations, I should, perhaps, explain that the purpose of the beautiful yellow blossoms was to colour our eggs while they were boiled hard as iron over an open fire. Why so hard, you enquire? So we could roll them of course, down a grassy hill, until the shells cracked and they could be peeled away to reveal the treasure beneath.

I'm not sure if kids still have Easter feasts, but if not I can assure them they're missing a rare, if simple, treat.

Next came the big summer holiday, which stretched from mid-July into the first week of September. Schools shut down for all of that time. No wonder I flirted with the notion of becoming a teacher.

The annual Orange Order Twelfth of July parade, with its flute and pipe bands, Lambeg drums, lodges and banners, and besashed Brethren resplendent in their bowler hats, rolled umbrellas and white gloves, was always worth a look, especially when us kids arrived at *The Field* to enjoy our fill of ice-cream, lemonade, sandwiches and sticky buns. The grave solemnity of the many speeches, usually given from the back of a Union Jack bedecked lorry, was entirely lost on us, and best left to the adults in any case.

Those particular festivities over and done with, there were still oodles of things to keep us happily occupied. When the weather got too hot for football or cricket, we'd grab our swimming togs and head for the beach, or the local harbour.

The term 'swimming togs' is a bit of a misnomer for, in actual fact, as seven or eight year-olds none of us could swim. That handicap was soon resolved, however, by a few of the older boys. They kitted each of us out with a bandolier of fishing-net corks strung on a length of rope. Fitted around our scrawny little chests and secured under the armpits, they, coupled with the salty sea-water, provided sufficient buoyancy to keep our heads above water. To be fair to them, while they chucked us in off the pier with fierce shrieks of savage glee, they made sure to keep a brotherly eye on us to note how we were faring. In all the years I spent growing up in Kilkeel, I can recall only one instance of a young lad being drowned in the harbour, and even then there were several extenuating circumstances.

Anyhow, once recovered from the initial panic of our first ducking, we quickly came to terms with our new environment – and we loved it. With increasing confidence, we struck out in every variety of swimming stroke. The universal favourite was the doggy paddle, so called because that's how our canine friends did it. It was never going to turn us into a Johnny Weissmuller, of Tarzan fame, but at least it propelled us about at a moderately sedate rate of knots.

In time we were able to dispense with our cork brassieres and doggy paddles and progress to proper swimming strokes like the breaststroke backstroke and crawl. I can still recall with modest pride the first time we made it all the way across the harbour mouth to Meany's Pier, about forty yards away. Even more satisfying was the journey back, after a brief rest to regain our breath.

Years later, having enjoyed my first swim in a splendid fifty-metre freshwater pool, I was surprised to discover how much less buoyant it was than the salty, diesel oil-streaked waters of Kilkeel harbour.

The long stint between summer and Christmas was broken by a fortnight's break in October. It was known locally as potato-gathering time. We welcomed it, not simply as a holiday and an escape from school, but because it afforded a rare opportunity of making some decent money.

As I've tried to explain, the world, including our little part of it, was a vastly different place in those days. Money was tight – indeed, when is it ever otherwise? – and our weekly pocket-money was counted in copper rather than silver coin. What if it cost only sixpence in pre-decimal coinage to take a fellow to the local fleapit a couple of times a week; some of us had to do a six-day paper-round to garner that amount.

The first year I went potato-gathering the going rate was five shillings a day. The better farms would provide a hot dinner, or a lunch of tea and sandwiches on top of that. By the time I left school and went on to other things,

the rate had doubled to ten shillings. An improvement, but still a pitiful amount by today's standards. Still, as I say, we appreciated the chance to earn a few bob that would provide funds for some visits to the pictures, a comic book or two, or a fish supper and lemonade in one of the local chippies.

It was hard backbreaking work too, even if we were young and fit. We worked in pairs, each with a wicker basket in which to toss the spuds before carrying them to a pit to be covered over for a period before they were bagged and moved on to their final destination. When I first started, the potato diggers were all horse-drawn, which enabled the gatherers to grab a short breather while the digger was manoeuvred around before starting another run.

Gradually though, as tractors and more modern equipment replaced the old ploughshares and wonderful big shire horses, the increasing speed of operations placed more and more pressure on the luckless potato gatherers, until in the end they could no longer keep up. I'm not sure how it is today, but I assume it's completely mechanised.

That's probably no bad thing. The children of today could neither do it, nor endure it.

I became friendly with one of the old farmers. Sam was a decent, simple, hard-working soul. One of the few who allowed us into his big farmhouse kitchen where his wife served up excellent broth or Irish stew. A massive old mahogany-encased valve wireless occupied a table in one corner, beside the open hearth. Lunch was timed to coincide with the midday news and weather forecast. He told me this would be repeated at six o'clock,

"What programmes do you enjoy most?" I wanted to know.

"I only listen to the news and weather, son," he informed me. First thing in the morning, at dinner time, tea time and last thing at night."

I couldn't believe it. "Don't you listen to anything else? What sort of things do you like?"

He thought for a moment or two. "I like to hear a good band playing," he replied. "but I can hear that on the Twelfth or now and then on the odd Sunday on the bandstand down in Newcastle."

The collectors

Money was usually in short supply, and potato gathering occupied only two or three short weeks of the year. I have to say that Dad was really decent in that connection. I never remember receiving a fixed amount of pocket-money, but he would often put his hand in his trouser-pocket, hand me a shilling or half-a-crown and say, "Away you go to the pictures, or wherever."

I could be quite crafty too. I worked out that if I sat on the chair opposite him in the kitchen while he was reading the paper, or listening to the radio, and I stared fixedly into the fire he would take the hint and proffer a coin. In the end, I think he just wanted to get rid of me.

There were accepted ways of earning a few pence. Running a paper round was probably the most common of these, but it involved quite a lot of work and demanded a steady commitment. Other possibilities included carrying out odd jobs such as gardening, cutting firewood, sweeping backyards, washing cars and running errands. Some local shops paid as much as threepence for a dozen empty jam jars, which would be sent back to the manufacturers for recycling, and this sum was enough to admit one person to the front three rows of the local fleapits.

Dennis, clearly a more entrepreneurial spirit than the rest of us, seemed to be onto a winner when he developed his own window cleaning round. I'm not sure how much he charged, but I remember seeing him traipsing around, toting a bucket and sponge and with an extending ladder slung over his shoulder.

Sadly, the promising business hit the buffers when the incumbent window-washer, whose patch Dennis had invaded, grabbed the young man by the ear and marched him round to his parents, accompanied by a grim warning of the fate likely to befall him if he ever transgressed again.

The new bicycle

The one thing I wanted more than anything else in the world was a new bicycle. I'd had my eye on the very job down in Quinn's cycle shop at the bottom of our street for the past three months. It was a gleaming, maroon-coloured Rudge Whitworth Roadster, complete with five-speed gear, dropped handlebars, silvered front light, tool-bag, pump and even a clip on flask for holding a cold drink. In short, all the bells and whistles any twelve-year old would ever desire.

Mr Quinn himself assured me this was the very prince of pedal cycles. I believed him. After all, I could see as much for myself. He even offered to take a pound off the asking price of £22 19 shillings. Sadly, he didn't do hire purchase, and he couldn't guarantee to hold the beautiful machine until I had raised the necessary.

Not having a bike was a total drag. Nearly all my friends had their own bikes and several had even been kind enough to let me borrow theirs. All well and good, but I wanted – I needed -- my own personal bicycle.

To be fair, it wasn't that Dad was unwilling to fork out the readies. Goodness knows, he'd been more than generous in the past. No, the fact was he was dead scared that I'd be involved in an accident, and possibly come to a grim and gristly end. I'd tried every single ruse I could think of, but he wouldn't budge.

We were sitting by the fire one evening about a week before my birthday. I'm not certain if I was even trying to put on my usual, hangdog, down in the dumps expression. Unusually for me, I even had enough change in my pocket to take in a movie and enjoy a fish supper and lemonade afterwards. I was just sitting there feeling sorry for myself, dreaming dreams of a shiny new bicycle which would always be beyond my grasp.

The newspaper rustled as he set it to one side and reached for his pipe and tobacco-pouch. "Your heart's set on this bicycle isn't it?"

I nodded. "Yes Dad."

"You will be careful on it, won't you?"

I sat up and took notice. "Yes Dad, of course I will." Heart pounding. Breathing quickening.

"Well then, we'd better go down and have a word with Mr Quinn in the morning, hadn't we?"

I don't remember a great deal after that. I do remember leaping out of my chair and giving him the most tremendous hug.

I knew it was going to be a wonderful birthday. I also knew I had the best Dad in the world!

Tony

Tony Heaney was the best friend I ever had – our relationship endured for well over fifty years until his untimely death on Christmas Day, 2002.

My great pal, Tony Heaney, at his Linotype machine in the *Mourne Observer*.

To an outsider we must have seemed an unlikely pair. For a start – in the vernacular of Northern Ireland – we kicked with different feet, we each belonged on the other side, we went to different schools, different churches, hailed from different cultures and were supposed to want different futures for the tiny piece of earth we shared. He was Catholic, I was Protestant, and in the crazy, outdated overhyped and senseless tradition of the times, the twain should never meet. We hadn't even heard of Rudyard Kipling, but, to bastardise one of his better-known lines, we treated those twin imposters just the same.

Even if we'd had the slightest comprehension of Ireland's troubled past, I know it wouldn't have mattered a jot to either of us. Down the years Tony and I debated just about every topic under the sun, often agreeing to differ, yet never having to utter an angry word.

Carrying on from the story about my new bicycle, I shared my first cycle ride with Tony, through the beautiful Mourne country we both loved. In the years that followed we shared a whole lot more. Life took us to different continents, different countries. At times we were apart for years on end. We always kept in touch, and when we met again we simply picked up the threads and resumed where we'd left off. It was almost as if we'd never been away.

Tony and I always seemed to operate on the same wavelength. It was as though we shared a certain telepathy, ESP or sixth sense – call it what you will. I don't think either of us believed in that sort of stuff, yet sometimes you have to wonder.

I believe it was a mutual interest in photography that first drew us together. We strove to outdo one another in an endless friendly rivalry. When he made a makeshift filter for his camera by fitting am orange sweet-wrapper in front of the lens to make the clouds more prominent, I improved on it by using the yellow cellophane wrapper from a Lucozade bottle. He added blue dye to his developer to give a nice tone to his prints. Using a home chemistry set, I managed to produce photographic paper which could be activated by direct sunlight. I have to admit though, that the results were less that satisfactory.

And so it went on. I was the first to break the bond when I went to London for a year or two. We corresponded regularly. He took to always using green ink, simply, he said, to make me feel homesick so that I would come back to Ireland. Eventually I did and on that first evening we went to see John Ford's epic *The Quiet Man,* which, forever afterwards, remained our favourite movie. I'm not sure how many times we've watched it - separately and together – but we could quote entire sections of the script from memory and often did so on our walks.

We shared many a laugh when we recalled that first showing in the old Mourne Cinema back in 1952. We went to the second of two screenings and were standing in a queue when the first house exited. An old farmer emerged and spotted a friend waiting to enter.

"Hello Jamsie," he said. "Are you going to the pictures?"

"I am indeed, Willie John. Were you at it?"

There'll be some more about Tony later.

The monthly fair

The last Tuesday of the month was about as close as the town ever got to having a *Red Letter Day.* The farmers liked it for the chance it provided to buy and sell their sheep, cattle, horses and pigs. The housewives appreciated the opportunity of picking up a bargain or two from the dozens of stalls, which seemed to offer everything from toothbrushes to tea-cosies and sandals to schoolbags. Even the shopkeepers enjoyed it because it brought strangers and country folk into town and increased the possibility of making a sale.

The only people who weren't too keen were the council road sweepers who had to clean up the mess afterwards. The fellow who drew the short straw and was allocated the top of the town, where the livestock were penned, must have grimaced whenever it was a particularly busy day for heifers and cows. When the wind blew in from the south-west the rest of the townsfolk weren't exactly delighted either.

Perhaps the few farmers' sons among the pupils had a passing interest in the livestock sales; I'm not sure, but for the rest of us it was a matter of supreme indifference, What really attracted us was when a novelty act would set up camp. By novelty act I mean a magician, a strong man, or an escapologist. I was especially keen on the last named for I'd just finished reading a book about Harry Houdini the Handcuff King. I'd been so impressed by it, I'd forked out some of my precious pocket-money on a Boy's Conjuring Kit and was seriously considering abandoning my ambition to be a Canadian Mountie and become a world-famous illusionist and escape artist instead.

On the day I have in mind the chief attraction turned out to be the Strong Man. To us he cut an impressive enough figure, if a tad on the geriatric side. He stood bare-footed and bare-chested, clad in what I took to be imitation leopard-skin trousers. His overlong, mousey-brown hair was swept back off his forehead and secured at the nape of his neck by a leather thong. His left bicep was adorned with a wide silver band.

He began his act by passing round a selection of 6-inch nails and demanding we check their authenticity. Taking them back, he bent one into the shape of a hairpin with his bare hands. Wrapping another in a grotty-looking rag, he clenched it in his teeth and twisted until it became a right-angle. There was a smattering of applause which grew louder when he wrapped the cloth round his hand and bludgeoned a nail through a solid-looking plank of wood,

He gave full value for money, I'll grant him that. He hoisted a well-padded gentleman at arm's length above his head, juggled with three cannonballs, raised a blacksmith's anvil with his teeth, and allowed two three-man teams to play tug-of-war with his neck in a noose in the middle of the rope.

His grand finale was to lie down on a bed of nails, clutching a concrete building block to his chest and have a burly local smash it in pieces with a sledgehammer. The dramatic effect was lessened only slightly when, halfway through the downswing, a wag in the audience shouted "For God's sake Billy. Mind you don't hit him below the belt!"

Fortunately, the artiste himself appeared to see the funny side of it. At least he was smiling as he scooped up the generous number of coins in his cap and bowed to the assembled company.

The hoaxer

Not every performer at the fair provided such good value for money. We had only just arrived one day when we were drawn to the exceptionally large throng around one of the stalls. We could hear the loud voice of the vendor, but so dense was the crowd that it took us some time to squeeze through to the front.

The fellow's patter was bright and breezy, and to judge by the rapidity with which his assistant was dealing with customers, handing over little cardboard boxes in exchange for cash, it was certainly proving effective.

"Ladies and gentlemen," he crooned, "I can't begin to describe how delighted I am to be able to bring you this opportunity today – the opportunity of a lifetime. Many of you have been fortunate enough to have secured a bottle already, and I regret to inform the remainder of you that we now have only a few bottles left. Of course, more will be available from the manufacturers in due course, but my commitments are such and my schedule so busy that it may be some time before I am able to pass this way again."

"This ingenious product is in use in every civilised country of the world – North and South America, Australia, South Africa, even as far away as Russia and China. As I understand it, it's a particular favourite amongst the crowned heads of Europe. Please permit me to give you one more little demonstration of what this incredible creation can accomplish."

At last! I was going to find out what it was all about, what was the mysterious and wonderful thing this garrulous man was selling.

"Please watch very carefully ladies and gentlemen, seeing is believing."

He reached into a container and produced what looked like a faded little snuff box. He poured something form a bottle onto a linen cloth and began to polish. In a matter of seconds, he held the box aloft. The transformation was amazing. It had turned a glistening silver and sparkled brilliantly in the sunlight.

I'd never seen anything like it. I couldn't believe my eyes. It was a miracle. Inside the next few minutes he had repeated the feat with a cigarette case and a dinner knife. My jaw must have gaped open for he smiled and said. "Here sonny, do you possess a penny by any chance?"

Dumbly, I handed him one. "Walla!" he exclaimed and returned it with a flourish. "You may keep that sonny. There's absolutely no charge."

My new silver coin was a thing of beauty. The King's head gleamed in the sunlight.

"Now don't go trying to pass that off as half a crown, young fella, or the police will be after the pair of us!"

He turned to address the crowd at large. "Now ladies and gentlemen. I would be well within my rights to offer you a bottle of this miraculous potion for a one-pound note – and it would be excellent value at that, an absolute steal. But I have no intention of doing that. I'm not even asking you to give me a ten-shilling note, Not at all ladies and gentlemen, not at all. Would you think five shilling about right? What about half-a-crown then?"

He paused and looked round the crowd, holding up the bottle in one hand, the gleaming cigarette-case in the other.

"I really like you good folk," he continued, "and I like your nice little town. I'm doing myself no favours here, but you can take home your very own bottle of this famous elixir for a miserly florin, a paltry two-shilling piece. Now I can't say fairer than that, can I?"

I was almost swept aside in the rush, but I managed to hang on long enough to buy a bottle. I was staying in my aunt's at the time and I couldn't wait to get back and demonstrate my new discovery.

I was congratulated warmly and feted in triumph. But not for long. Within 48 hours the silver had completely disappeared, gone like a thief in the night. The cutlery I had so lovingly treated had resumed its former state. Even my beautiful silver penny was just a plain copper again.

I did find out the name of the liquid, some oxide or other. But I've long forgotten it. I don't think I'll ever forget the smiling scoundrel who duped me and a fair few of the folk who attended Kilkeel Fair that day.

Blackie

I suppose Blanche was the first girl I ever had a schoolboy crush on. She was a vivacious little tomboy who popped in and out of my life at irregular intervals. She had radiant black hair, an attractive, carefree laugh and was always up for a bit of fun. For obvious reasons, everybody called her Blackie and I seem to have known her and her family since I was in short pants. Of course I ought to have done something about taking things a stage farther, but I'm sure you must be beginning to realise what I'm like by now.

It's not as if there weren't chances aplenty. Maybe one small example will illustrate what I mean. I've already mentioned that there were two cinemas in town, the Vogue and the Mourne. Both changed their programmes three times a week, so in theory, it was possible to see a different movie every night.

Usually I'd go with a few mates, but on this particular Tuesday I was alone. Alone that is until I literally bumped into Blackie in the foyer. We sat together. I ought to have slipped my arm round her but the thought never entered my head. I may have bought her an ice-cream but I can't be sure. I had the decency to walk her home afterwards. I ought to have treated her in the café on the way but, sadly, funds didn't permit. I ought to have kissed her goodnight, but I didn't do that either.

It was raining Wednesday and I made a late decision to take in a movie – in the Mourne this time. Ten yards from the entrance I overtook Blackie. She turned round, saw me and we both laughed. "Snap!" she said.

I hadn't enough change for ice-creams, never mind treat her to a ticket. I felt really bad about that. I'd have scraped together a few dozen jam jars if only time permitted. As on the previous night, I walked her home. Happily, it had stopped raining.

They saw that good, and bad, things happen in threes. Without tossing a coin, I opted for the Vogue that Thursday evening. There weren't too many cinemagoers about. I turned away from studying the billboard and Blackie was standing there, doubled over with laughter.

"I don't believe it," I said.

"You're stalking me," she replied.

"Kismet," I told her. I'd been reading a better class of book recently.

"What an incredible coincidence. We'd better go in I suppose."

I nodded. "Blackie, I'm sorry. I really should buy you a ticket, but I'm flat broke I'm afraid."

"Not at all, Brad. After all, it's not like we're on a date, is it?"

There were so many things I could – perhaps should have – said then. As so often before, I let the moment pass. I felt I'd forfeited the right to even think about putting my arm around her. I did walk her home though.

Friday evening came. Dad was still away so I couldn't tap him for the price of two tickets. It would have had to be two, plus, hopefully, enough left over for a couple of fish suppers. I stayed home, wondering which cinema Blackie might have gone to.

It was a long time afterwards that I left for London. Tony had given me a new camera and I made good use of it. I took several pictures of Blackie, and her big sister took a couple of us, with her hand hooked round my arm. I still treasure them.

The evening before I caught the cross-channel steamer for Liverpool I finally asked her for a date. "Thank you", she said. "Pity it took you so long."

I decided to give the cinema a miss. I'd probably have picked the wrong one anyway. The circus was in town and I took her there instead. "Like to come out for a last supper? I asked. "I seem to remember I owe you at least three."

She smiled, no doubt remembering out chance meetings. "Thanks, but Mum said I was to make sure I brought you home for a bite to eat."

The supper was great – but the lingering goodbye kiss from Blackie was special.

Down on the farm

Boyd's farm stood only a matter of yards from where I lived, just off Bridge Street, on the way round to the Presbyterian Church graveyard. The family could best be described as good God-fearing folk and Sam, their only son, two years older than me, was a long-time friend.

It was Sam who taught me to ride a bicycle, milk a cow, churn buttermilk, muck out a cowshed and feed the chickens. He would lift me up onto the broad backs of Dick and Nora, the two working shire horses they owned. A great reader, he let me borrow his books. Agatha Christie was his special favourite and I remember well the savage twist at the end of *The Murder of Roger Ackroyd,* the first of her novels I ever read.

He taught me to play a one-handed version of Beethoven's Minuet in G on the family's grand piano. The fact that I could only play it in the key of C is purely co-incidental. Even today when I amuse myself on the keyboard for an hour or so everything is usually in C. It's the only chords I understand you see. His speciality was a rousing boogie-woogie version of *In the Mood* and he liked nothing better than when I joined him in a four-handed attack on the number. I have to point out, however, that mine was very much the secondary role.

At certain times our gang was allowed to play football, rugby or cricket on the farm and we shared many a vigorous knock-about game in one of the fields. A small river meandered its way along the bottom of the field on its journey from the foothills of the Mournes to the sea, and here we loved to catch spricks and sticklebacks and carry them home in a jam-pot.

Kids being kids, we would try our hands at more adventurous and dangerous pastimes. When no one was looking and when the big horses Dick and Nora were turned into the field to graze, as many as four of us would scramble up on their backs, one behind other in Indian file, hold on like grim death and go charging down the hill towards the river.

I don't think the horses fancied it much though. They were big and strong and were used to plodding rather than galloping. Halfway down the hill Dick decided he'd had enough of the nonsense and stopped abruptly. The four of us went sailing forwards, ass over tip, to land on the grass in a tangled heap. Worse still, Norman, riding tail-end-Charlie, had his ankle broken by a sturdy hoof. All eight of us were summarily banned from entering the farm for a month. Norman made a full recovery, but it was a long time before he could play football – and I don't believe he ever went horse-riding again.

On another occasion half a dozen of us were fortunate to escape an even more serious accident. There was a large red hayshed in the top corner of the farmyard which could be entered through two huge sliding doors. We were allowed to use it on wet days on the proviso that we didn't muss up the large piles of hay and straw. As anything was preferable to being outside in the teeming rain we acquiesced readily enough.

Of course, we needed something to keep us entertained, so we rigged up a makeshift swing with four lengths of rope and lashed the tailboard of an old cart to it as a makeshift seat. The whole apparatus was suspended from a girder just inside the open door.

Time passed quickly and we were all having tremendous fun, changing places every five minutes or so. My turn came round again and five of us scrambled aboard our chariot. With the aid of forceful shoves from the others we soared higher and higher, the swing creaking and groaning in protest. We yelled in delight.

Suddenly there was a crack like a pistol shot. The rope snapped and we were sent hurtling through the air. We hung suspended for what seemed minutes, but was only a split second, before landing with a muffled clump in a pile of soft straw, breathless but unhurt.

We dusted ourselves down and stood giggling. It was only afterwards that realisation dawned and we looked out through the open doorway into the concreted farmyard chock-a-block with heavy farm machinery, much of it bristling with sharp blades and pointed metal prongs. I knew I wasn't the only one thinking what would have happened if the rope had given way when we were swinging in that direction?

Ghosts and goblins

As mentioned above, the laneway that ran beyond Boyd's farm led to the graveyard of the local Presbyterian Church. It was a place we tended to avoid, and when we happened to pass that way we would be ultra-quiet and scurry by as fast as possible. I'm not sure why – maybe we'd seen too many scary movies, or heard too many ghost stories. Not one of us would have gone anywhere near it on a dark winter's night - not even for all the pocket-money in the world.

One year – it was just after Hallowe'en and we'd had our share of tales of ghosts and goblins and banshees – an event occurred that is still talked about today, although the story has certainly not lost anything in the telling.

It all began one November evening just as dusk was settling in. Half a dozen of us were leaving Boyd's farm and heading home for tea when we were brought up short by the sound of piercing screams and the thump of running feet. Two youngsters, aged perhaps five or six, came racing towards from the direction of the graveyard, caterwauling shrilly and obviously in a high state of panic.

They were really frightened and clung to us as we tried to calm them down. It was some time before we could get any sense out of them, but eventually the older lad was able to speak. "There's a ghost in the graveyard," he blurted. Out. "One of them banshee things. It came after us. It was terrible."

Plainly this youngster had taken the Hallowe'en stories he'd been told a bit too seriously, although being only a few years older ourselves, we hesitated to debunk his account entirely. Still, there's safety in numbers, so they say. With a display of confidence I can't say I felt inside, I attempted to reassure him.

"There's no such thing as banshees. They're only stories the grown-ups make up to frighten us." I ought to have had my fingers crossed behind my back, but I wasn't aware of that old trick at the time. "Come and show us what you saw. We'll all go with you."

The pair of them cowered back and one began to blubber. The message was clear – there was no way they were going anywhere near that graveyard.

What were we going to do? A couple of us thought we should go and explore, a few more wanted us to tell our folks, or Farmer Boyd about it; the majority just wanted to forget it and go home for their dinners.

As it happened, the matter was taken out of our hands. Old Willie John, universally known as *The Black Fella* from his work with a coal-delivery firm, which left him more or less permanently smothered in coaldust, stopped by us on his way home. A bachelor, he lived alone in his wee cottage about one-hundred yards on the far side of the graveyard.

He listened as we blurted out our story, before muttering, "Boys-a-boys. I don't like the sound of that. I suppose we'd best have a wee look though. Are you coming with me?"

Fortified by his presence, we trooped behind him like a gaggle of geese after their mother, minus of course, the two youngsters who'd scurried off on their way. Night was really drawing in by the time we reached the heavy wrought-iron gates of the graveyard. The *Black Fella* grabbed two of the bars and peered inside. We did likewise. About halfway down we saw a stooping, black-clad figure crouching over one of the graves.

"Bejasus, it's a bloody banshee!" he screamed and without another word took to his heels in the direction of his home, and disappeared at a high rate of knots. We followed his example and scooted off like billy-o in the other direction.

The mystery would probably have remained with us for the rest of our lives, except that next morning we met Sam Boyd and couldn't wait to tell him all about it. He smiled, stroked his chin, and said. "We'd better go and have a look-see." It took a bit of persuading, but he was taking the lead and the darkness of the night before had given way to a bright, sunny morning.

We arrived at the gate and peered in. The dark figure of the banshee was still there, maintaining its ghostly vigil over the same grave. We were about to inform Sam we'd told him so, but he simply opened the gate and beckoned us through. We shuffled in nervously and he led us down the gravelled pathway towards the dark figure.

As we drew nearer realisation dawned. "There you are, ye eejits," snorted Sam. "Someone has been painting gold lettering on the tombstone's inscription and tied an old coat round it to protect it from the weather. That's all it was."

We shuffled our feet, emitted feeble laughs, then stuck our chests out as if to say we'd known that all the time. But inside we were hugely relieved. As the Yanks would say "Shucks. Banshees! Who needs them?"

The fair sex

The middle years of the last century belong to a gentler, more innocent age – at least that's how it was as far as most of my mates and I were concerned. We knew all about girls of course. At least we thought we knew all about them. They were all right in their own way, even if they preferred hockey and netball to proper games like football and cricket.

It was our friend Austin who tossed a cat among the pigeons. We were debating which of the two local cinemas we'd go to that evening when he observed quietly. "You'll have to count me out I'm afraid. I won't be going."

"Why not?" we wanted to know.

"I just can't, he whispered, a trifle sheepishly.

"But why ever not," we persisted. "You're not sick, are you?"

"It's nothing like that." Long pause. "I've got a date if you must know!"

"A date! You don't mean a date with a girl, do you? A proper date. Wow!"

None of us had ever had a date before, although we'd speculated once or twice about what going out with a girl would be like. Let's say simply that it was something which didn't rate all that high on our *Things to do List*. Now one of us – and Austin was only a couple of months older than me – was taking that first brave, faltering step into the unknown.

"Good for you," I congratulated him. "I'll see you tomorrow and you can let me know how you got on."

"I will," he whispered, "but I want you to promise you won't tell the others. They'll only laugh and poke fun at me."

"I promise," I agreed readily. "Not a word."

We met as planned next day. "Well then, I enquired eagerly, "how did it go with your date last night?"

"It was all right."

"What do you mean all right? Did you go to the pictures? What film did you see?"

"We went to the Vogue. James Cagney in *White Heat*. The short was a Johnny Mac Brown western."

"Go on then Austin, what happened?"

"It was a really good gangster movie. Cagney got killed in the end. Blew himself up. You should go and see it tonight."

"Never mind the movie. Tell me what happened. Did you put your arm round her? Did you kiss her?"

He actually blushed. "Course not. She grabbed my arm when the explosion came, and we held hands for a while. That's all."

"Good man," I said encouragingly. "Well done. You going to tell me her name?"

"You'll find out anyway. It was Hazel from our class in school. You know Hazel?"

"Of course I do. Nice girl Hazel. You going to see her again?"

"Absolutely. Friday night. We're going to the Mourne this time. It's some romantic film she wants to see."

"Excellent. You seem to be well in there. You're a star Austin."

He paused and looked at me in a peculiar way. "Actually, I've been asked to give you a message. It's from her sister Vera. You know Vera, don't you. She left school last year and is a trainee nurse in the hospital."

"Sure, I know Vera. What's the message?" Vera was a bubbly brunette, perhaps a year or two older than me.

"Well, she says she likes you and she wants you to join us and make up a foursome. Will you come?"

It was as simple as that. I was about to embark on my first proper date. "Thank you Austin. Please tell Vera I'd love to." I left him and waltzed down the street on a cushion of air.

Austin and I were playing football with the gang the following Saturday afternoon. News of our double-date had already leaked out. I was besieged by the crowd who demanded a full account of proceedings.

I decided that honesty was the best policy. If I didn't come clean, the small-town grapevine would soon make it public anyway, even if Austin, who'd been sworn to secrecy, held his tongue.

"It was going just fine," I informed then. The four of us had seats in the back stalls. When the film started I saw Austin put his arm around Hazel, so I decided to do likewise with Vera. She didn't seem to mind, so I few minutes later I decided to give her a kiss. Unfortunately, just as I bent forward she lifted her head and my forehead caught her smack on the nose. It took ten minutes to stop the bleeding, her brand new blouse was saturated and we all had to leave early to walk her home. She says she never wants to see me again, so I don't think we'll be having another date any time soon.

The gang laughed for a solid five minutes, and looking back on it now, I can't say I blame them.

Better luck second time around

Mildred was a strikingly lovely girl. No, more than that, she was absolutely beautiful, a proper stunner. As members of the same local youth club our paths crossed several evenings a week. We'd played the occasional game of table tennis or badminton together and I'd noticed how she'd cut a dashing figure on court with her trim figure and long tanned ballet-dancer legs. That was as far as it went. I considered her way out of my league, and as events transpired, so she was.

So, it was a major surprise when, on the night of the annual club social, she walked straight across the floor to where I was chatting to a couple of the lads and enquired if I'd like to dance.

As it happened, I'd just finished a course of dance lessons, so at least I didn't tramp all over her feet. You must understand I'm talking about proper dancing here – waltzes, foxtrots, quicksteps and all that good stuff – none of your shuffling and gyrating modern rubbish. At least, in those days you got to hold a girl in your arms and could chat without fear of your voices been drowned out by what the moderns call disco music.

I have to concede that I was a painfully shy lad in those days. I found it easy enough stringing sentences together on paper; but verbal communication, especially with a girl, was an entirely different matter. I never seemed able to find the right thing to say, so consequently I tended to lapse into long periods of silence. It wasn't like that with Mildred, possibly because we knew each other through the club.

Still, it was an even greater surprise when she approached me again half an hour later and asked if she might have another dance. At least it was a lady's choice on that occasion. We sat the next one out and shared glasses of orange juice from the bar. It was a church hall and they didn't serve alcohol. Anyway we were both much too young.

Sometime later I reckoned it was high time I sought her out and returned the favour of a dance, but she wasn't to be found anywhere. Then, twenty minutes before the social was due to end, I looked up and there she was, asking if I'd please dance with her again. It was a slow number and I held her close. Her cheek was soft against mine and the scent of her perfume was intoxicating. It was the last dance of the evening. She'd sought me out not once but three times. And I hadn't once asked her to dance. She must think me a proper wimp. When the last waltz finished I thanked her and apologised for not having had the courtesy of instigating a dance. "I did look for you," I said, "but you weren't to be found."

"I'm sorry; I had to step out for a little while."

"Well, thank you for a wonderful evening, Mildred. As it's now too late to invite you to dance, the least I can do is walk you home."

"Thank you, I'd like that," she said.

We got our coats, said goodnight to our friends and set off walking into a crystal-clear starry night. Mildred's home was just under a mile outside town. When she took my arm, I wished it had been ten times that distance.

On the outskirts of town, she complained of a stone in her shoe and I steadied her while she fished it out. She stared up at me and kissing her seemed the most natural thing in the world. It was the kind of long, lingering kiss that deserved another, and another one after that. After a while we laughed and lost count of the kisses we shared along the way.

The final kiss, outside her front gate, was the most special of all. Again I thanked her for the evening and asked if I might see her again.

She shook her golden head, smiled a touch sadly and said. "I'm so sorry Brad, but I'm afraid that won't be possible. I like you very much. I really am sorry."

"Someone else?"

She nodded. "We hope to get engaged next year."

My smile was forced and must have appeared a trifle crooked. "I wish you well, Mildred. When you see him again tell him I said he's an extremely fortunate man."

I didn't see a lot of Mildred after that. One day I glimpsed her being driven through town in an expensive-looking open sports car, her blonde curls blowing in the wind. Surprisingly enough, I wasn't the least bit jealous of the darkly handsome young man behind the wheel, with his designer sunglasses and the sleeves of a white cricket sweater knotted carelessly about his throat.

My only mode of transport was a bicycle - and I was intensely envious of his shiny new sports car. I wouldn't have minded owning one of those. But now and again I still smile at the thought of how I borrowed his girlfriend for that one memorable evening.

The gentle art of pipe smoking

Dad smoked a pipe, and some years after my unfortunate experience with the cheap Woodbines in the school yard, I decided it was high time I learned the art.

It wasn't as if I had an addiction for the dreaded weed, but simply that it seemed to be the next logical step in my ascent into adulthood. At that time the majority of adults smoked; mostly unfiltered cigarettes, straight or curved briar pipes or, occasionally, a cheroot or cigar. Even a few of the old, beshawled women of the town would lean out over their half-doors with a stained clay pipe clenched between whatever teeth they possessed, as they enjoyed a bit of craic with their next-door neighbours.

One day Bertie, John and I decided it was time we made a start. Knowing full well it would result in a clip round the ear if our parents found out, we embarked on a cycle safari to the next village and purchased three white clay pipes, an ounce of St Bruno tobacco and a box of Swan Vesta matches. I think our entire outlay came to one shilling and tuppence. An instant cancer kit came cheap in those days.

The next half hour was painful. We opened the tobacco, filled our pipes, sat on a convenient wall and lit up. All this produced was billowing clouds of smoke, frenzied bouts of spluttering and coughing and three emerald green complexions. We shook our heads sadly and gave up. Pipe smoking, we decided, was not for us. Chastened and downcast, we solemnly pitched our cancer kits over the wall, mounted our bikes and headed for home.

In the years that followed I essayed two more abortive attempts at mastering the pipe, this time with my father's permission. I think he agreed only because he knew that once I'd failed he'd acquire a couple of new pipes. Or perhaps he simply wanted me to learn the lesson the hard way.

I hadn't given up entirely though and I'll be returning to the subject of pipe-smoking in a later chapter.

The Twelfth of July and all that

Mr Sleith had fixed ideas about many things, Ireland's troubled history amongst them. I've never forgotten his particular version of the famous, or infamous, Battle of the Boyne on the 1st of July, 1690, when the Protestant King William of Orange routed the forces of the Catholic King James on the banks of that little river.

Mr Sleith made it plain that he was neither an Orangeman, nor a supporter of James. His version of events ran something like this: "I will never understand why Irishmen, of whatever creed or political affiliation, get so agitated over what was little more than a minor skirmish," he would inform us. "The fact that it took place In Ireland at all was purely coincidental. It might just as easily have occurred anywhere in the United Kingdom."

"The central issue was to determine whether William or James would occupy the English throne. The two men were actually connected by marriage, but they didn't allow a mere detail like that to deter them.

"As always, religion was at the root of it. Dutchman William was Protestant and the vast bulk of his officer corps was German. Catholic King James relied almost entirely on officers drawn from France. The foot-soldiers on both sides were a motley assortment of mercenaries from England, Ireland, Scotland and Wales, with a sprinkling of Europeans thrown in for good measure."

"It's even claimed that the Pope of the day was a supporter of the Williamite cause and the sole purpose of the affray was to determine which of the monarchs would occupy the English throne. The battle – if indeed it might be called a battle – actually took place on July the first, not the twelfth, so the Orange Order, which in any case, wasn't formed until long afterwards, couldn't even get that right.

"Now, can any of you make sense of all that?"

Off to work we go

My schooldays came to an end suddenly and quite unexpectedly. I went home as usual one Friday afternoon, fully intent on resuming classroom hostilities on the Monday, but it was not to be. The course of my life changed on the intervening Sunday.

Without possessing what might be called a religious disposition, I did go to church most Sunday mornings; there wasn't a great deal else to do in our sleepy little town. So I was on my way there, walking through the town, when I heard someone call my name. I looked round and saw a man waving at me from the front door of his house. I knew him as Davy McConville, who was in business as an electrician.

"You're young Fleming, aren't you?" he said when I approached. "And your headmaster tells me you're a bit of a bright spark."

I was to discover he had a penchant for making what he considered to be little jokes like that. Electricians were usually referred to as sparks, and probably still are for all I know.

Having established that I was indeed young Fleming, he waved me to a wooden summer-seat beside him and continued. "As I say, he has a good word of you and thinks you are exactly the type of lad I'm looking for."

All this was news to me and my face must have revealed as much. Things became clearer, however, as Davy explained to me that he was looking for an assistant, or apprentice. His business was picking up and he needed to take on more staff. Later I discovered that the existing staff consisted of Ellen, who was in charge of his small shop and kept the firm's books. Ellen and Davy got married a few months later, but that, as they say, is another story.

I sat there in a state of minor shock as he sketched in how my immediate future would unravel. I was being offered a golden opportunity to learn a solid professional trade from a leading authority. I wasn't entirely certain if he was joking or boasting. With Davy, it was sometimes difficult to work out if he was being serious, or simply pulling your leg.

It was all a bit much to take in. Apart from my childish fantasies of becoming an international sportsman, a film star, a Canadian Mountie or a world famous magician, I wasn't at all certain of what I wanted to do, other than that it wouldn't involve Algebra. The vague notion of embracing something to do with writing and English still lurked in the back of my head, but hadn't crystalized. Becoming a sparks, even a bright one, hadn't figured at all.

"You needn't make up your mind right away," Davy was saying. "Go away and think about it, talk it over with your dad and pop back in to see me before six o'clock. If you don't appear by then I'll take it you aren't interested. If you are, I'll start you tomorrow at one pound a week."

I had a lot to think about, so I thanked him for the offer, shook his hand, and instead of turning right at the crossroads and going to church as intended, I hung a left and headed in the direction of the harbour. Being Sunday it was almost deserted. I flung myself down on a grassy slope and lay in the sunshine pondering what to do.

Still undecided after an hour, I did what I ought to have done in the first place and went home to talk it over with my dad. He listened patiently, drew on his pipe, and said "Well son, to be truthful, I'd like you to stay on at school a bit longer. You know the old saying a little bit of learning is easily carried. Why don't you go over and have a chat with your Uncle Jim and see what he has to say? At the end of the day only you can decide what you want."

Uncle Jim, my mother's brother, was Principal of Ballymartin Primary School, some three miles outside Kilkeel. I agreed to go and see him, but I already knew very well what his advice would be. We'd talked about it often enough. He'd encourage me to go on to Newry Grammar, and hopefully University, just as he had done. And so it turned out. He was horrified at the prospect of me, as he put it, "spending your life replacing light bulbs and mending fuses."

I literally hadn't a clue what to do for the best. I knew my uncle's advice was the sensible option. I wish I had been able to seek the advice of old Harley Lyle Sleith, but sadly, that wasn't possible. Anyway, deep down inside, I knew what he'd have said.

It was a fifty-fifty call, the toss of a coin. In the end that's exactly what I did, and flicked a penny into the air. Heads for going to work for Davy, tails for staying on at school. It came down heads.

The tyro electrician

Working for Davy was something else again and nothing like I'd expected. I'd been ordered to report for duty at nine o'clock on the Monday morning. Anxious to make a good impression I got there early. Ellen was just opening up and I introduced myself. She'd been aware the boss was taking on an apprentice but hadn't known it was me. I already knew her family, especially her younger brother Sam, who'd been in my class at school and had played in the town football and cricket teams with me.

Davy appeared about a quarter past nine and was greeted by a "You're early" from Ellen. I was soon to discover what lay behind her observation. By no stretch of the imagination could the boss claim to be an early riser, so his relative promptness that morning was due entirely to my arrival. I discovered he normally surfaced at any time between ten and eleven, unless we were on a job which required an earlier start. Even then, as I gained experience and became more useful, it was expected that I was to proceed straight to where the job was and do what I could until he deigned to appear when the streets were well aired, as Ellen put it.

For most of that morning Davy held forth about what being an electrician was all about. He seemed gratified that I already knew how to mend a fuse. I thought back to Uncle Jim's disparaging remark the previous day. He explained the differences between alternating and direct current and ran through the finer points of things like ohms and amps and watts. He presented me with a little leather case containing three assorted screwdrivers, a pair of pliers with insulated handles and a little gadget for stripping the ends of cables so they could slot into where they were needed.

The little lecture concluded when he instructed me to lift my feet off the concrete floor of the shop and shake his hand. Puzzled, I complied and instantly felt a tingling in my fingers and wrist. It was a little like holding an electric drill, only sharper. I noticed his other hand had disappeared behind the counter and was gripping something.

"That's electricity," he announced sagely. "It's a truly marvellous thing, quite useful and only dangerous to those who don't know what they're doing. It's a good servant, but a bad master. Make sure you always treat it with respect, and for God's sake don't touch the floor with your feet and complete the circuit or you'll get a shock that will send you flying through that plate-glass window!"

The lesson was brought home to me quite forcibly a few months later when a gypsy woman, clad in a tartan shawl and carrying a large shopping bag, entered the shop and held out her hand, palm upwards. Her heavy brogue was unadulterated County Cork. "Augh, God bless your honours so, but could you ever be sparing a wheen of coppers for a poor ould widda woman to help feed the weans in these hard toimes?"

Davy nudged me to lift my feet off the floor and pass her a couple of pennies from the till. He clasped my left hand and reached under the counter with his other hand. I felt the familiar pins and needles in my wrist and knew what was coming. The instant the woman touched the coppers the tingle throbbed in my right wrist and the gypsy seemed to jump a foot off the floor, sending the coins flying ceilingwards.

She glared at us balefully and released a tirade of what we assumed was Irish. The last few words were intelligible enough though. "You bloody, f...... b.......s. Bad cess to you and yours. May all the evils of Ireland curse you and may you never rest easy in your beds!"

She stormed out of the shop, slamming the door viciously in her wake.

"That was really naughty, Davy," Ellen said.

"I know, I know, but it was fun. Wasn't it Brad?"

He stooped, picked up the two pennies which were still lying on the floor and returned them to the till with a smirk.

Learning the trade

The work was varied and interesting, and at my lowly level, relatively easy to pick up. I was able to walk, or use my bicycle, to carry out small jobs around town on my own. In most cases Davy demanded that I request payment immediately the job was completed.

One morning I answered a call to a little terraced house halfway up Newry Street where I found a little apron-clad woman in some distress. "I can't make my breakfast, son," she complained. The electric cooker won't start."

As I suspected, it was nothing more serious than a blown fuse, which I repaired in a couple of minutes.

"Thank you very much son, you're very smart. How much do I owe you?"

"Nothing at all," I told here, "you sit down and enjoy your breakfast."

She smiled. "You'll have a wee drop of tay in your hand before you go, won't you?"

It would have been churlish to refuse.

Davy was up by the time I got back to the shop and asked what sort of job it had been.

He was a tad miffed when told it had been a freebie and gave me a stern talking to, based on the text that the labourer is worthy of his hire.

"It only took a couple of inches of fuse wire and a minute's work," I exclaimed indignantly. She was just a poor wee woman who couldn't have her breakfast."

He wagged an accusatory finger in front of my nose and emphasised that there was a principle involved here. He was running a business, not a charity. I could never expect people to respect me, if I didn't respect myself. "You were providing a service, doing a job she couldn't do herself. You should have charged her something – even if it was only a shilling."

I gave a snort and tossed a shilling coin into the petty cash box.

Behind Davy's back Ellen smiled broadly and gave me a massive wink.

Parting with that shilling was more than just an idle gesture, although I never regretted it for a moment. During the twelve months or so I stayed with the firm my wages remained stuck on one pound a week. To add insult to injury I never got to take home the whole pound note. Two shillings and eleven pence of it went to pay my National Insurance stamp. I was clearly going to have to work for a long time to make my first million.

After about six months of being tolerably happy and content in my work, things took a turn for the worse. The Northern Ireland Government embarked on a scheme of building a host of what were called advance factories all over the country and Kilkeel was awarded its share. Davy applied for and was given the contract for installing the wiring and all the electrical fittings; enough work to keep us more than fully occupied for at least a couple of years.

It transpired that we were expected to begin the work of installing all the electrics immediately the builders had finished. This included rows of fluorescent lights and a designated number of wall switches and plugs for the plant and machinery. All well and good so far, we believed. Unfortunately, it emerged that all the conduit piping for the wires had to be concealed. This required a huge number of tracks to be cut into the walls to accommodate the pipes. Even more unfortunately, that task fell to yours truly.

In vain I asked Davy to have this work done by the builders. Surely it was a task for a stonemason or a labourer rather than an apprentice electrician? Surely it ought to have been done by the firm which built the factories in the first place? Davy was sympathetic, but said the buck stopped with us. Sadly, he couldn't afford to employ anyone else to do the work. Perhaps in a week or two.

I should have chucked my hand in there and then, but for some reason I stayed on and stuck it out for nearly six months. After countless hours up a ladder, battering away at solid block walls with a sledgehammer and cold-chisel, I'd dug what seemed like several miles of tracks and boasted biceps that would have done credit to a young Arnold Schwarzenegger.

Finally, with no apparent end in sight, and seeing my prospects of either becoming a proper electrician, or earning a decent wage, diminishing by the minute, I handed in my notice. Davy said he was sorry to see me go. No doubt he was, as a labourer they didn't come much cheaper than me. I don't know which budding young apprentice took my place, but I'll wager he learnt a damn sight more about wielding a hammer and chisel than he ever did about becoming an electrician.

If you go down to the woods . . .

To clear the concrete dust out of my lungs, I decided to apply for a job as a forestry officer with the Ministry of Agriculture. The prospect of an outdoor job appealed and the 150 per cent increase in pay was an added attraction, even though as a trainee, I took home only about a quarter of what the general labourers did.

I rolled up at Tollymore Forest Park, just outside Newcastle, on my first Monday morning and was told I'd been allocated to Bob Robinson's gang. This meant nothing to me at the time. It was only afterwards I discovered he had the reputation of being a harsh taskmaster, who, in the vernacular, took no prisoners.

Our gang were thinning out that particular week, which meant we were tasked with sawing down trees which had been specifically marked with a blob of white paint. I was told they were destined to become pit-props, among other things. I detected a few sniggers among the rest of the gang when Robinson issued his instructions and I was teamed up with a brawny taciturn character called Barney. He wore a cloth cap and a waistcoat over a well-worn collarless shirt and had arms like your typical village blacksmith.

43

I soon discovered the reason for my colleagues' ill-disguised merriment when Robinson handed Barney a hefty cross-cut saw and indicated I was to attach myself to the other end of it. "I want all those marked trees cut down as low to the ground as you can manage," he grated. "I don't want any high stumps left behind. The other six of you lop off the branches. And mind you do a neat job of it. I expect to see a good clean finish."

Without a word, Barney set off for the nearest tree, dragging me after him on the other end of the saw. With a curt nod, he picked his spot on the trunk and bent his back. I followed suit and in what seemed only seconds the tree bit the dust and we were attacking another. My partner, no doubt with years of practise behind him, maintained an even rhythm which I did my best to match. He was setting a furious pace, clearly designed to make me buckle and cry "enough," but I believe I'd have died before giving him and the giggling brood behind that satisfaction.

We scarcely drew breath until 12:30, when we stopped for our 40-minute lunchbreak. I was gratified that we'd built up a decent lead on the guys with the machetes. The giggling had stopped a long time back and I fancied I was beginning to sense a muted respect from the gang. Barney was definitely breathing a lot harder than when we'd started. I even caught Robinson shooting several surprised glances in my direction from beneath his peaked cap.

Sure, I was bloody tired and my right arm and shoulder throbbed achingly. If it came to that, there weren't many parts of me that didn't. I took my lunch of milk and sandwiches standing up and pacing slowly up and down. If I'd lain down, even for a minute or two, I wasn't at all certain I'd be able to get up again. My one consolation was that Barney appeared to be in no better shape. Even the others looked every bit as knackered as I felt.

The pace slowed markedly in the afternoon but Robinson made sure it didn't flag too much. Barney and I sawed away steadily and had no difficulty in keeping comfortably ahead of our workmates.

I think everyone was glad when 5:30pm arrived and we downed tools for the day. Even our foreman had a grimly satisfied look as he recorded our output for the day in a little black notebook. It was a good feeling when Barney straightened his back, parked the cross-cut against a tree, produced his first smile of the day and stuck out a hand. "You're a tight'un" was all he said - but it meant a hell of a lot.

Later that night, as I lay soaking my wounds in a relaxing Radox bath, I reflected on the rigors of my first day in the new job.

I believed it had gone all right and I allowed myself a grin of smug satisfaction. You see, I knew something my new workmates didn't – that I'd spent the last six months knocking seven bells out of a series of concrete walls with a sledgehammer and cold chisel. Not bad training for handling a cross-cut. They didn't know – and I was never going to tell them.

Having earned the respect of the forest workers, I was accepted as a fully-fledged member of the gang. They reverted to their usual system of work so that my time was now divided evenly between the cross-cut and the machete, making life easier and fairer all round. I was told I would have to wait for three to six months before being sent to an agricultural college in Wales to learn some of the finer points of the job. They didn't say so, but it soon became clear that, I was regarded as little more than cheap labour, for, although I was doing exactly the same work as the others, my take-home pay was only about a quarter of theirs.

At the start of my second week, having apparently passed my initiation as a budding lumberjack, I was taken off thinning out and moved to a vast patch of ground which had been planted out with tiny seedlings. These little fellows had to be protected, nurtured and kept free of weeds and other nasties in order that they might one day turn into decorative and useful trees. My simple task was to ensure they would achieve this goal by obliterating anything around them that looked remotely like a weed. My heart sank. There were acres and acres and acres of the little perishers, all lined up in rows like soldiers on parade. I was instructed that everything in the area that wasn't a sapling was to be dispensed with post haste, and as our American cousins have it, stricken from the record.

It was like potato gathering all over again – only much worse. I spent most of the time on my knees, grovelling around, yanking at bits of vegetation. There was no one to talk to and I was expected to toil away in all but the foulest of weather. It would have been ideal preparation for training for the SAS or some other elite force. It probably accounts for the fact that, to this day, I detest gardening with a passion.

A new job and back to school

Relief came from a totally unexpected quarter. You may recall my friend Austin, the bloke who set me up on my first disastrous date with the unfortunate Vera? I knew he'd gone off about six months previously to work in England, so I was surprised to bump into him in town one day.

"The very man," he greeted me. "I've got an offer for you that you simply won't be able to refuse." We repaired at once to our favourite café where he put me in the picture.

"You know I'm over in London with Sainsbury's, the big chain store. I'm a trainee manager and I have to tell you they're a brilliant firm. They pay decent wages, look after their staff and opportunities for promotion are good. We go up to college in London two days a week for special courses and we get every Wednesday afternoon off to play football. The thing is, they're having a big recruiting drive for trainee managers here in Northern Ireland, starting next week. Are you interested?"

"You sound like a recruiting sergeant," I laughed.

"Of course not," he smiled, "I'm just home on a week's holiday. "Haven't you seen their advertisement in the *Telegraph*?"

I said I hadn't, but it sounded a lot more exciting than exterminating seemingly endless acres of weeds.

"Besides," Austin continued, "The Festival of Britain is on in London and that's well worth seeing."

I'm not sure if that was the clincher, but I decided it was worth finding out some more. Interviews were being held in Kilkeel the following Wednesday, so I took the day off work and went to have a look. The interviewing panel certainly painted an attractive picture of life in the Sainsbury Empire. At that time the firm operated only in the midlands and southern England. It was only later that they expanded throughout the whole United Kingdom.

There was a short initial written examination which I found ridiculously easy. This was followed by a series of aptitude tests which were equally straightforward. I discovered that my starting salary would be on a par with my current earnings. Beyond that, from what I was told and from what Austin had said, the prospect looked good. It was probably the prospect of seeing the festival and the bright lights of London that tipped the balance. I handed in my notice at the end of the week.

I have to say the Forestry Division of the Ministry of Agriculture didn't exactly throw a tantrum when told of my imminent departure. I don't suppose there was a critical shortage of either tree-fellers or weed-gatherers at the time, but at all events, I wasn't even required to work the statutory months' notice.

A letter from Sainsbury's instructed me to report for duty at their Headquarters in Blackfriars, London, in five weeks' time. This left me with a month to kill before I headed for the Liverpool boat. I could have reverted to type and simply lazed about the place, but it happened that most of my friends had moved on to continue their education at the local Technical College. Why not join them? I had a word with the Principal, Mr Cecil Baxter, and it was all arranged. It didn't exactly qualify as further education and I can't claim to have done any real work or learnt a great deal. I did, however, have a whale of a time.

I played a couple of football matches and competed in the annual school sports. I brought in my camera a few days and took lots of pictures of the boys and girls and the teachers. All in all, it was by far the happiest of all my schooldays. If school had always been so good I might well have stayed on forever.

The bright lights of London

Having bidden farewell to family and friends, I caught the bus for Belfast where I was to meet up with the rest of the party who'd been singled out by Sainsbury's as potential managerial material.

Tony came to see me off and we spent that last twenty minutes debating which of us would miss the other the most. We swore an oath to keep in touch no matter what and I promised to write just as soon as I knew my new address.

A little incident that day might give a glimmer of the kind of relationship we shared. I reckoned I owed him a couple of quid for printing off some photographs I'd taken at the Tech', so I placed the notes in an envelope with a scribbled note of thanks. He wasn't to open it until after I'd gone.

"That's odd," he said, handing me an envelope. "I've written a few words for you to read on the bus. Nothing important, just shove it in your pocket until you're on your way."

I slit open the envelope as the bus cleared the town boundary. It contained two crisp pound notes. The accompanying note read:

"I had a feeling you were going to do that. So here's your two pounds back. You'll probably need it in London more than I will! Good luck and all the best."

We spoke about it when I came home for a few days the following Christmas. I recalled the incident and thanked him again.

"You were lucky," he said with a twinkle. "Things are so tight over here just now you'd have no chance of getting that two quid back!"

"Don't worry Tony," I countered, "after what its cost me to travel over here for this break, you wouldn't have got the lolly in the first place!"

But I digress. You'll find I do that quite a lot, especially when I'm looking back down the years. Arriving in Belfast, I was met by a representative of the firm and five other lads who had thrown in their lot with Sainsbury's. Ian, Owen, Pat, Ronnie and Willie were all about my own age and hailed from Counties Down and Armagh.

I hadn't met any of them before but we developed a firm bond during the time we spent together.

Our guide outlined the plan of campaign. Initially we would be based in a hostel above one of the firm's shops in Surbiton, Surrey. We'd have the weekend to settle in before commencing our two weeks' introductory course on the Monday. We had the weekend to ourselves.

The short passage across the Irish Sea was uneventful, as was the train journey from Liverpool to London's Euston Station. A short thirty-minute jaunt from Waterloo took us on to Surbiton, a busy satellite and commuter town on the banks of the Thames.

We were greeted cordially enough by Mrs Renoir, the friendly housekeeper, who gave us dinner and directed us to our respective rooms. I was pleased to note that the hostel's large games-room boasted a table-tennis table, a draughtboard and a dartboard. There was also a reasonably well-stocked library.

House rules were simple enough. We were expected to be indoors by 10:30pm and in bed by eleven. We could only be out later than that with Mrs Renoir's express permission. As the outer door was locked at eleven o'clock precisely, this required our being issued with a key.

This was a facility we availed of only rarely. Our little party was well content. After dinner we all took a stroll down by the Thames, almost as far as Kingston, before calling it a night.

A blast from the past

An odd thing happened the following afternoon. Ronnie, Owen and I decided to take the train and tube to Highbury to watch Arsenal play West Bromwich Albion in the old English First Division. Other than international matches in Belfast's Windsor Park, it was the first time I'd seen that standard of football. Fans stood on the terraces in those days and we had an excellent position almost on the half-way line.

Arsenal were a goal up at half-time and the majority of the almost-fifty thousand strong crowd were as happy as sand-boys.

Suddenly I felt a violent push in the small of my back and turned angrily to find a familiar face leering down at me. It was a bloke called Bertie Law, who only a fortnight before, playing against me for Newry Town in my last game for Kilkeel United, had knocked seven bells out of me for most of the ninety minutes!

We chuckled at the coincidence of it. Fifty-thousand people there and he had to be standing right behind me. What's more he'd just committed a blatant foul on me again – and the only referee in the ground was in the dressing-room, no doubt enjoying a refreshing cup of tea. Bertie told me he was holidaying in London for a week.

Our paths never crossed again. Probably just as well – he wasn't the sort of defender who took any prisoners.

An Introduction to Sainsbury's

I've no idea how Sainsbury's operate these days, but back in the early Fifties they ran a slick and tight ship, at least as far as their trainee managers were concerned. Although the war had been over for more than six years, commodities like butter, cheese and eggs were still rationed and customers had to produce a ration card to secure their meagre weekly allocation.

In Blackfriars that first Monday morning the six of us joined perhaps another thirty would-be managers to be welcomed by some of the top brass, given a brief history of the firm and to pick up some idea of what was expected of us. The rest of the fortnight was filled by a busy programme aimed at demonstrating what the provisions business was all about.

We visited farms and factories, many of which were owned by Sainsbury's themselves, watched cows being milked and butter being churned, (shades of Sam Boyd's farm back home). We saw pigs being slaughtered, chickens being plucked, eggs being candled to detect bloodspots, and biscuits and cakes being baked. A lot of our time was spent at the College of Distributive Trades in Charing Cross Road and later we learnt that we would spend two days there every week, studying everything from the countries where various goods came from to the advertising and the mechanics of selling them. On a day at the docks we saw bananas being imported from the West Indies, cheese from France and Italy and best butter all the way from New Zealand. It was certainly a lot more practical and interesting than anything I learnt at the old school in Kilkeel. I'm sure Mr Sleith would have approved.

On our final day we were allocated to the branches where we would start work. Pat and I were lucky to draw the shop in Surbiton just below our hostel. This meant we could spend an extra relaxing fifteen minutes over breakfast, to ease our way into the day. The rest of the lads were sent to shops in Kingston, Hook and other surrounding towns. We were each allocated a number of spotless white tunics and aprons. The former were expected to last for two days, the aprons had to be changed every day.

Feeling more than a little self-conscious in our sparkling new gear, Pat and I reported downstairs to the manager, Mr Huggett, promptly at 8:30 the following Monday morning. He seemed affable enough as he shook hands and bade us welcome. Pat was sent to work on the cooked meats counter; I was allocated to dairy and introduced to the section manager Mrs Munday and her staff.

Now, while the dairy counter was up in the main shop, all the real work was carried out below decks in the spacious and well-stocked basement. While two or three of us manned the counter and served customers, the remainder beavered away downstairs, doing clever stuff like patting chunks of butter into handy quarter-pound and half pound rectangles which were then wrapped in greaseproof paper bearing the firm's name. Eggs were candled and borne up the spiral stairway to the shop in large wicker baskets. Because of rationing they were always sold loose in brown paper bags. No little shaped cardboard cartons in those days.

My first job, under the hawk-like gaze of Mrs Munday, was to peel the wrapping and corded skin off a 50 lb Cheddar cheese and cut it into serviceable v-shaped chunks for display on the counter. This was done with a length of strong wire strung between two wooden handles which would have made an ideal weapon for an expert garrotter. Each piece had to be labelled and priced according to weight. After a fortnight of this I could gauge a four, eight or twelve-ounce wedge with uncanny accuracy.

"You're a natural, Brad," said a beaming Mrs Munday.

"Beginner's luck," I answered modestly.

In my third week I was allowed to serve on the counter, under supervision. I enjoyed this hugely, especially the opportunity it afforded to talk to and share the odd joke with the customers. The first three days of the week were moderately slack. Things began to pick up by Thursday and Friday, and Saturday was absolute bedlam, with all hands to the pumps and both electric tills on the dairy counter ringing continually like the Bells of St Mary's.

While Cheddar was rationed, most of the other cheeses were

not, and as time went on, more and more of them became available for sale. The customers didn't seem to mind the expense. They would snap up pieces of Stilton, Cheshire, Brie, Edam, Gorgonzola and Primula when they could get them to supplement the few ounces of proper cheese rationing allowed.

Some of the customers could be quite humorous. One Friday regular would purchase his portion of Cheddar; swallow it in two bites and say. "Don't bother wrapping it son; it's not worth taking it home."

One little old lady, who was almost blind, would hold out a handful of loose change and invite me to take the right money. It was wrong, I know, but as often as not I wouldn't charge her the full amount, and usually gave her a little over the odds as well. I reckoned that what Mr Sainsbury didn't know wouldn't cost him any sleep. What's the worst they could have done to me? Given me fifty lashes with a wet noodle!

One chilly December Friday Mrs Munday and half the staff in dairy came down with 'flu. A worried Mr Huggett asked if I were sure I could manage the counter on my own. "Not a problem," I said bravely, forbearing to tell him of my exploits with the redoubtable Barney and his crosscut-saw in Tollymore Park all that time ago.

"I'll see you're relieved at lunchtime," he promised, "and if the going gets too rough give me a shout and I'll see what I can do."

It was a hectic day, but the time simply flew by and I managed to keep one jump ahead of the steady queue at the counter. At close of play Mr Huggett came round as usual to collect the takings and the reels of paper from the tills which listed all the transactions.

Next morning, he called me aside and said. "Well done. Your counter took in over £1500 yesterday and it was correct to the last halfpenny!"

Genuinely surprised I asked "But surely the till should always be correct."

"Of course it should," he told me, "but it very rarely is. There's usually a discrepancy of several shillings and sometimes pounds, so well done indeed."

I thanked him again and went back to work. It was only afterwards I thought I should have asked him for a raise, or at least an extra half-day off.

The customer isn't always right

Writing these little reminiscences can jog the memory and bring to mind events which have lain dormant and forgotten for years. I recall the day when Mr Huggett approached me in the shop, accompanied by a corpulent middle-aged woman, resplendent in a full-length fur coat, stylish hat and carrying an expensive-looking leather handbag.

"This is Mrs Blenkinsop, a valued customer," he announced, before turning back to her and continuing, "Mr Fleming here will be happy to assist you with your purchases Madam, and if I can be of further assistance, please do not hesitate to call upon me."

Mrs Blenkinsop acknowledged this announcement with a gracious wave of a gloved hand before indicating that I should select one of our largest trolleys and follow in her wake.

"Best be on my best behaviour here," I reflected and screwed my features into the sort of fixed smile that would have done credit to a high-kicking chorus girl on the stage of the London Palladium. For the next forty minutes I shadowed Mrs B on several laps of the store, more than once retracing our steps to collect something she'd overlooked on an earlier circuit.

Between forays into different departments, she explained to me that she was shopping in preparation for a party to celebrate her daughter Cynthia's twenty-first birthday.

A number of important guests were expected and her husband was away on business. "Not that he'd been of much use in any case," she confided, "He hasn't the remotest idea about that sort of thing. He leaves everything to me and I have absolutely no help. One simply cannot get proper help these days."

I clucked sympathetically and reflected silently that her hubby was well out of it.

All things do come to an end eventually and I propelled Mrs B's heavily-laden trolley to a vacant checkpoint, passed everything through the till, packaged items as required before replacing them in the trolley and presenting her with the print-out bill. From memory, it came to seventy-eight pounds and some odd pence – a considerable amount in those days.

I was about to suggest pushing her trolley out to her car for her when she broke off from perusing the bill, while absentmindedly withdrawing a shilling from her purse and handing it to me with a "Thank you, young man. That will not be necessary. I must have a word with Mr Huggett before I go."

I thanked her for the tip and returned to my duties. You can imagine my surprise when she returned to my counter a few minutes later, an anxious looking Manager pushing her trolley alongside.

Mr Huggett frowned and announced, "Mr Fleming, Mrs Blenkinsop has complained of being overcharged. I want you to recheck her order please."

The three of us trooped off to the register I'd used earlier and both of them watched intently as I repeated my action of ringing up all the items and handing the itemised list to Mr Huggett.

He compared the two print-outs before showing them to Mrs B. "These are identical," he said. "They tally to the last penny."

The customer straightened, arched an eyebrow and mumbled some words I took to be an apology. The Manager flicked his head to indicate I should return to my counter. Before leaving I reached in my pocket and placed a shilling in Mrs Blenkinsop's elegantly kid-gloved palm. "I believe this is yours, Madam."

I didn't wait to note her expression but Mr Huggett had a word a short time later. "That was very naughty, Brad," he said.

"Not at all, sir," I replied. "She obviously needs it more than I do!"

Deja vu all over again

If I thought I'd left my schooldays behind me I was sadly mistaken. On Tuesdays and Thursdays we'd take the train to Waterloo and catch the tube to Charing Cross. From there a short walk took us to the tall greystone edifice that housed the LCC College.

Our principal instructor was a Mr Crook, a fiery Scotsman with a strong Highland accent, a shock of flaming red hair and a hair-trigger temper. He knew his stuff though; we had to give him that. He encouraged questions, providing he deemed them sensible and proper, and he would go to considerable lengths to ensure we grasped the fundamentals of our chosen trade.

There were other teachers to cover English, Geography and Maths. It's fair to say that the six of us found these lessons almost ridiculously easy. I understand the curriculum was based on the system then in force in the Home Counties and South of England, but we reckoned it lagged at least a year behind what we had been used to in Northern Ireland. I mean, apart from my untypical three-week class-topping spell for dear old Mr Sleith, I didn't consider myself much of a student. As Tony used to put it "Fleming, sometimes I think you know just enough not to eat yourself!"

Whatever. In the end-of-term examinations I came out top of the class:

Business Studies (100 per cent)
English (100 per cent)
Maths (100 per cent)
Geography (96 per cent)
Commodities (100 per cent).

It was plainly ridiculous. Even Mr Crook joked about it. "You'll have to brush up your Geography," he said as he handed me my marks, "or we'll think you're not trying!"

Happily, my five companions from Northern Ireland all found the exam just as easy as I did.

Taking in the Festival

The big attraction in the country in 1951 was the Festival of Britain. With Clement Attlee's Labour Government anxious to show the world how well the country was recovering from the rigors of World War 2, all the stops were pulled out and every effort made to attract visitors from all corners of the globe.

The aim was to demonstrate Britain's contribution to science, technology, industrial design, architecture and the arts. The centrepiece was the Royal Festival Hall and various exhibitions on the South Bank of the Thames. Over ten million people attended during the five months of the festival, which cost £10.5 million, or £250m in today's money.

Interestingly enough, when Sir Winston Churchill's Conservatives were re-elected later that year, the entire show was demolished, with the exception of the Royal Festival Hall. Crafty old Winnie didn't want any lasting reminders of a Labour Party initiative.

Personally, I enjoyed the two visits I made to the festival. Looking back on it now, I'm tempted to quote Dr Johnson's comment on the Giant's Causeway – that it was *"worth seeing, but not worth going to see."*

Incidentally, a casual remark I made to Mrs Renoir in the hostel one evening landed me in hot water with the Sainsbury management. We were chatting about the festival and I remarked that one of the reasons I'd come to London was to see it.

Imagine my discomfiture when, a few days later, I was summoned to Blackfriars for an interview without coffee with the Personnel Officer Mr Powis. The only time we'd met prior to that was when he'd been one of the speakers the day we'd arrived.

He had my file opened on the desk in front of him and he cut to the chase right away. "I have to say, Brad, that I'm rather disappointed in you," was his opening salvo.

My face must have shown my surprise. I hadn't a clue what he was on about, or what I was supposed to have done wrong. His next remark provided clarification. He ran a forefinger down my file and peered at me over his horn-rim glasses. "I see from your record that you've been doing exceptionally well since you joined us. Your work in the shop and at college has been excellent and your manager, Mr Huggett, speaks well of you. Yet I'm given to understand that the principal reason you joined us is so that you could visit the Festival of Britain."

The penny dropped with a loud clink. Clearly Mrs Renoir had been doing her Mata Hari act. Worse, she had added up two and two to make five, and had shopped me to the Gestapo.

It was so utterly ridiculous I almost smiled, but I was also quite angry.

"Ah, I see now where this has come from, Mr Powis. However, I'm afraid Mrs Renoir has got the wrong end of the stick. Some of us visited the festival the other day and we were chatting about it later in the hostel. I can remember saying that being able to see the festival was part of the attraction of living in London. It's quite ridiculous to suggest I'd sign up with Sainsbury's just so I could see the Festival of Britain. I could have jumped on a plane or boat and gone to see it any time."

"Brad, there's no need to get upset about this." He was on the back foot now.

"Of course there is," I replied sharply. "I wonder exactly what sort of cretin you and Mrs Renoir think I am. Do you honestly believe I'd be so stupid, Mr Powis?"

I felt better for that little outburst and the interview simmered down a notch or two after that. Mr Powis apologised for the misunderstanding, did his best to placate me and said some nice things about how well I was doing and how pleased they were with my progress. I never raised the matter with Mrs Renoir again, but I was extremely careful what I said in her presence.

London life

The great thing about attending college in Central London was the opportunity it provided for visiting famous buildings and landmarks I'd only heard of or read about previously. Either alone or with some of the lads, I went sightseeing to inspect Buckingham Palace, Big Ben and the Houses of Parliament, St Paul's Cathedral, Madame

Tusnad's Waxworks, Trafalgar Square, Hyde Park, the Albert Hall, the Tower of London and a host of other places.

As an enthusiastic reader of the Sir Arthur Conan Doyle Sherlock Holmes stories, I particularly enjoyed my trip to his headquarters at 221b Baker Street. One day I walked down Fleet Street to call at the shop of the famous cricketer Sir Jack Hobbs, passing the splendid offices of the *Daily Express, The Times* and the *Telegraph,* little realising that one day I would join the serried ranks of the mighty Fourth Estate, albeit it at a much more humble level.

Foyle's bookshop, on the corner of Charing Cross and Tottenham Court roads, became a regular port of call and I still possess many of the books I bought there. The helpful assistants never seemed to mind how much time I spent browsing their shelves.

We usually lunched each day in a Lyons' Corner House, of which there were a great many in the capital at that time. It was cheap and clean and the service was brisk. A typical meal of liver and onions, chips and two veg, followed by apple tart and custard and a pot of tea cost only four shillings and two pence in the old pre-decimal coinage.

As far as I can remember, I had no problems with balancing my own little budget at that time. The firm deducted a small amount from my weekly wage to cover board and lodging at the hostel, the rest was mine to spend as I wished. Although Dad had never asked me to, I always sent something home each week. I felt it was the right thing to do. Years later I discovered he'd never spent a penny of it, but had lodged it in a Post Office account he'd opened in my name. It was typical of the sort of man he was.

I have to admit, that at that stage of my life, I didn't give a lot of consideration to putting something by for a rainy day. If it rained, the sensible thing to do was to stay indoors. That said, the firm paid our rail and tube fare to and from London. Travel was much cheaper then and two old pennies would take us several stops on the Underground.

We soon settled in to the weekly routine. Monday, Wednesday morning, Friday and Saturday in the shop; Tuesday and Thursday at the college. We had Wednesday afternoon off to do as we pleased. One of my co-workers, Jock, a cheery Glaswegian and even more of a football fanatic than I was, on discovering I played, speedily arranged a trial and I was co-opted onto his local team. We actually finished runners-up in the Surrey League that season.

I got to know and like many of the staff. Mrs Laws, from dairy, invited me to dinner and to watch show jumping from White City on their little 14-inch black and white television. TV sets were still a comparative rarity in those days and the hostel didn't possess one. Her husband, Alf, a convivial soul, often took me on his motorcycle to Wimbledon Stadium for a night's speedway racing. I can still remember the distinctive smell of mixed shale and petrol fumes.

I also played a few times for the firm's darts team, but I was hopeless at the game and they only called on my services when they were absolutely desperate. At lunchtime the dartboard and table tennis table were in great demand and I had a number of stirring encounters on the latter with a jovial cockney character I knew only as Mac, who ruled the bacon department. I'll have more to say about him later.

The youth club

I recall that Tony and Pat, as good Irish Catholics, attended Mass on the first Sunday after we arrived in England. I'm ashamed to say we four Protestants didn't. I may be doing the pair an injustice, but I believe they rarely went again, although they may well have gone to Confession without our knowledge.

I mention this only to say how surprised we were a few weeks later when the vicar of one of the neighbouring Church of England parishes called one evening to introduce himself and invite us to visit his church. Even if we decided not to, he smiled, we were welcome to join the youth club, entirely without obligation.

The following week Willie and I decided to take him up on his offer. The church hall was not unlike the one I remembered from Kilkeel, with facilities for table tennis, badminton, board games and the like. There were about two dozen boys and girls of our own age present and we were welcomed warmly enough. The vicar introduced us and explained that we were new to the area.

Shortly before the club closed at about 9:45pm, I noticed two of the better looking girls talking together in a corner and shooting occasional glances in our direction. They'd been introduced to us as Evelyn Carstairs and Sandra Burdett. They walked across to where we were sitting and it was the former who spoke. "Hello again," she said with a smile which showed almost every one of her sparkling white teeth. "Sandra has agreed to walk me home. I live in Kingston, it's just less than two miles. We were wondering if you gentlemen would be kind enough to accompany us?"

Now here was a thing. I couldn't have imagined it happening back in my home town. There the guys generally sat along one side of the room and the gals on the other. I glanced at Willie whose face remained blank. To be fair it was his normal expression. As it happened we'd taken the precaution of securing a late pass, so I rose like a proper gentleman and said. "It will be our pleasure." Willie simply shrugged his shoulders and followed suit.

Immediately we were outside Evelyn linked her arm in mine, as though claiming possession. Sandra took up station on my other side and Willie, even more bashful than I was, loped along a yard to her left.

There were lots of questions about us, most of them from Evelyn. How did we like England? Had we been to the festival? What was it like being a manager in Sainsbury's? Were we going to stay on at the club? I fielded all of them, Willie simply walked along, seemingly lost in his own little world, from time to time idly kicking a foot out at an imaginary football.

Eventually I got the chance to ask a question or two of my own. The girls had gone to the same school and had been friends for a long time. Both of them seemed inordinately proud of the fact that one of their classmates had been Petula Clark, by then already a prodigy in the entertainment world and who later became a singer of international repute.

Upon arriving in Kingston, Evelyn kissed me softly on the cheek and thanked me for chaperoning her home, and barely acknowledging poor Willie, bade us all goodnight and skipped off, carolling shrilly over her shoulder to Sandra that she'd see her as usual the following day.

As the three of retraced our steps along the silent Thames, I was surprised to learn that Sandra lived in Surbiton, little more than a stone's throw from the hostel.

Puzzled, I enquired if she usually escorted her friend home from the club. She mumbled a quiet apology before whispering "Do you mind if I take your hand, please Brad?"

Of course I didn't mind. If truth be told and it came down to a choice, I much preferred Sandra to Evelyn. I'm not sure I fancied a particular type of female, but if I did, then Sandra's black hair, sparkling smile and petite athletic figure was exactly it.

Now it isn't often I get the chance to escort two pretty girls home on the same night, and separately at that. I was grateful that Willie was still doing his own thing several yards to port, seemingly quite content to play gooseberry.

Sandra's fingers were soft and cool and she spoke quietly as she explained what had occurred in the club earlier. "Evelyn usually takes the bus home, but tonight she asked me to walk with her so that she could invite you to escort us. I probably shouldn't have agreed, but anyhow I did. I'm truly sorry. The thing is, I think she's attracted to you!"

I gave Sandra's hand a gentle squeeze, reflecting that Surbiton was a whole world apart from sleepy Kilkeel.

It would have made life a whole lot easier and less complicated if I'd come out with it then and there that, while Evelyn was a wonderful girl and I hoped we could become good friends, it was Sandra whom I really wanted to get to know. As usual, however, shrinking violet that I was then, I kept my mouth firmly closed and the opportunity slipped by.

One step forward . . . two back

I was disappointed when Sandra didn't turn up at the club the following Wednesday. Evelyn was there, of course, and we spent a lot of time together during several games of table tennis and badminton. She even steered me to a corner table during an interval while she went to fetch two cups of tea.

As closing time approached I helped her on with her coat and we stepped out the door together. She looked expectantly up into my face, her look radiating the unspoken question. "Yes, of course I'll walk you home, Evelyn." Willie had taken the hint and scarpered.

Our route down by the Thames was that of the previous week. She took my arm again and chattered away about her school – a private one of course, not that that bothered me at all – about her mother, who didn't work, but who spent much of her time doing numerous good works for several charitable causes; her younger brother, still at prep school, and her father, who was something in the city. It wasn't the first time I'd heard that expression, with all that it implied. In short, Evelyn was as much out of my league as Manchester United are from Tiddlywink Wanderers.

I have to say, there's not a hint of inverted snobbery in the above remark. The folk who live in the fashionable stockbroker belt are doubtless doing an excellent job and are fully entitled to whatever lifestyle and luxuries their money can buy.

It's not a reflection on Evelyn either. She really was a lovely girl, warm and generous to a fault. She was fluent in three languages, always impeccably dressed, and was entertaining company and a wonderful companion. I was happy to accept her suggestion that we should meet on Sunday afternoons so that she could, as she put it, show me around.

We visited Windsor Castle and Hampton Court Palace, tramped around Epsom and Kempton Park racecourses and enjoyed some of London's most wonderful attractions. It sounds dreadfully ungrateful, but it was really Sandra I wanted to get to know.

I met her in town one day and we stood chatting for ten minutes or so. I took the plunge and asked if she'd like to go to the cinema with me one evening. I was over the moon when she smiled and said "Yes please." English girls were so polite.

I arranged to call for her and her mother answered the door. I knew her dad had died some years before and that Sandra was an only child. It was natural her mum would worry about who she went out with.

Mrs Burdette asked the name of the film we were going to see. I said it was called *The Lavender Hill Mob*.

She stiffened noticeably and said "That sounds violent. Are you certain it's a good choice?"

I hastened to reassure her that it wasn't quite what the title implied, but an Ealing comedy, with solid chaps like Alec Guinness and Stanley Holloway in the starring roles. I think Mrs Burdett was mollified, but my discomfiture wasn't helped by the sight of Sandra, lurking in the background, trying desperately to stifle a laugh.

I enjoyed that evening in the cinema immensely – and not only because the film was absolutely hilarious, one of the best comedies ever in my opinion. Mindful of previous lost opportunities, I slipped my arm around Sandra's shoulders at what I judged to be an appropriate moment. She smiled and nestled her face in close to mine. We held hands. I bought some ice-creams. We held hands again.

I walked her home and stopped outside her front door. "Make sure you tell your mum it really was a comedy," I advised.

"Absolutely," she responded, laughing.

I leaned forward to kiss her but she turned her head away about six inches and my lips only brushed her cheek.

I was about to ask if we might repeat our date another time, but she breathed "Thanks for this evening, Brad, I really enjoyed myself." Next second she'd opened the door and was gone. We never had another date.

All three of us went to the club the following Wednesday. It wasn't at all like the previous times I'd been. There was a decided atmosphere I couldn't quite put a finger on, but it would have needed a pickaxe to cut through. It was almost a relief when the time came to leave. Sandra and Evelyn were deep in conversation in one corner. Suddenly Sandra turned and strode across the room to me, her expression totally devoid of emotion.

"Evelyn's waiting for you," she said, "I think she's expecting you to walk her home."

"Of course I will," I replied. "You'll come with us?"

In a voice that was as cold as ice, she whispered. "I don't think so. Goodnight."

With that she turned on her heel and walked straight out the door.

I did walk Evelyn home, along the familiar route to Kingston. She was unusually quiet, even tense, and made no attempt to take my arm. Several times I asked what the matter was, but got no reply. In fact, she said virtually nothing until we arrived at our usual spot and she said. "Thank you for seeing me home, Brad. I'm sorry, but I don't think we'll be going out again."

I never did find out what had transpired between the girls and can only conclude they must have had some kind of falling out concerning me. Willie and I called into the club the following week but neither of the girls was there. I called at Sandra's house twice and rang the doorbell. There was no response. As a last resort I sent her a note via one of the lads at the club, There was no reply. I literally bumped into Evelyn in the street outside the shop some weeks later.

"Oh hello," she gasped. She said she was fine and hoped I was too. I asked if she'd seen Sandra. She shrugged, explained she was in a hurry and had to dash. With a brusque wave of the hand she scurried away. I never saw her – or Sandra – again.

What a strange, jumbled mixture of joy and sadness life can be at times. People enter our world, sometimes to enrich it with the sheer uniqueness and warmth of their personalities; before passing on – usually never to be seen, or heard of again - but leaving us in a brighter and better place.

Ships passing in the night on a deep ocean. How often do we lose friends because we let things slide, refuse to make the effort, are too passive, or simply lack that spark of resolve and initiative to do something about it. Before we realise it the opportunity has gone, and probably gone forever.

I wonder if, like me, you sometimes wish you could step back in time and make a different choice? Alas, for good or ill, that can never be. We pass this way but once.

What was it the wise old poet wrote all those years ago?

"Time, you old gipsy man, will you not stay.
Put up your caravan, just for one day?"

Normal service resumed

After three months I was transferred to the bacon department, which, as I've already explained, was run by the redoubtable Mac. Although right next door to dairy, it was an entirely separate entity and presented a different set of challenges. Sides of bacon, weighing perhaps forty or fifty pounds, were delivered to the shop each week and were suspended on s-shaped hooks from the ceiling behind Mac's boning table.

Those of you who buy your bacon neatly sliced into rashers and packaged in shiny cellophane will have no idea of what I'm talking about. But in those post-war days a lot of things were different. A side of bacon was, quite literally, half a pig, and before being sold it had to be cut into sections to provide cuts such as collar, back, streaky and gammon.

Grabbing a stout pole with a chrome hook on one end, Mac neatly hoisted a side from the ceiling rail and deposited it with a flourish on top of his heavy wooden table. Taking up a sharp, pointed knife with a four-inch blade, he brandished it under my nose.

"This," he said, "is the principal tool of your trade. Treat it with care, guard it and look after it as a soldier would his rifle. It is yours. Don't let anyone else use it, not even me. Ensure it is always perfectly clean and the blade sharp as a razor. Keep it in a safe place, and if you take my advice, never let it out of your sight."

With a courtly little bow, he inserted the knife in a scabbard and solemnly presented it to me. Then, picking up his own blade, he turned to address the waiting cadaver of the late pig. Quickly pointing out the location of the different cuts, he told me the first step was to remove the ribs and a number of other little bones, most of which were completely hidden from view.

"The trick is to work at the right depth. Cut too lightly and you'll have to dig deeper to extricate the bone; cut too deep and you'll make a mess of it. Remember customers don't expect their morning rashers to be sliced up like shredded wheat. It will take time, laddie, but soon, under my tutelage, you'll acquire the skill of a brain surgeon. Pay attention now. Watch."

There was a blur of movement and in little more time than it takes to read this the carcase was stripped of all its bones, which were stacked in a net little pile to one side. The ribs had been picked clean by means of a thin wire, not dissimilar to the one I'd encountered on the cheese counter. Mac stepped and waved a nonchalant hand to draw attention to his work.

I was impressed and said so. "That was bloody marvellous, Mac," I said respectfully. "I'd treat you to a round of applause, only I don't want to embarrass you. I could never hope to be able to do that."

"It takes time, Brad, it takes time." But I could sense he was pleased. "We all have to learn. I've been at it for well over twenty years. Even during the war I couldn't get away from it, I spent most of my service dossing in the cookhouse with the Catering Corps. Never heard a shot fired in anger. Now, see what you can do with this baby."

He flung another side onto the table and watched me labour clumsily through the ritual, interjecting a pointer here and there. In my time in Bacon I operated on a good few deceased pigs, without ever remotely approaching Mac's expertise.

Playing with the big boys

It was through Mac that I took up table tennis again. I've already mentioned our knockabout lunchtime games. Back in the bacon department immediately after one session, Mac said "You know Brad, you're pretty good at this game. You should play in one of the county leagues."

"I used to play a fair bit back home in Ireland," I told him, "but it was just friendly stuff at the local youth club."

"Well I reckon you're a well above average player. I can see you have a lot of shots and have good hand-eye coordination. I happen to know that one of our shop managers is visiting for two days next week. He's a top player and I think you could give him a game. Like me to arrange it?"

"Why not," I said. "I'm always up for a laugh."

Mac was as good as his word. Most of the other lads went out but I stayed in and was introduced to the other manager, a Mr Leach, after dinner. He was a brisk, approachable man, tall and slim with a ready smile. Mac accompanied us to the games room and took a chair while we armed ourselves with a couple of bats.

"Let's not play a game just yet," the stranger said. "Tell me, do you prefer to attack or defend?"

"I don't really mind," I said. "Attack I suppose."

"Right, you have a go with your forehand and I'll defend. Nice and slow, don't go for outright winners, just try to build a good rhythm."

The forehand was probably my strongest stroke and the little white ball was soon whizzing back and forth across the net with satisfying regularity. After ten minutes we switched to backhand attack. I was on less sure ground here and muffed a couple of shots. My opponent simply nodded and we resumed our play. Gradually I started making fewer and fewer errors, helped by the fact that the ball kept being returned in more or less the same place and at uniform height.

This was followed by twenty minutes of defence on both forehand and backhand wings. I'd never practised in this way before and grew in confidence as my returns kept finding the table.

"Good stuff," Mr Leach said. "I enjoyed that Brad. Thank you Mac for introducing me to this lad. Perhaps before I leave tomorrow evening we can have a few proper games?"

"I'd like that, thank you, sir."

Sure enough, after a repeat of the previous night's practise session, we played three games. I was soundly thrashed in every one of them, my opponent scarcely breaking sweat.

Afterwards he thanked me courteously and handed me his card. "I'm a member of this club," he said. "It's not all that far away. Perhaps you'd like to come and visit? Next Tuesday evening would be good if that suits."

He smiled and left after shaking hands with Mac and me.

"That's some player," I said to Mac afterwards.

"So he bloody well should be," my friend said. "Didn't you recognise Johnny Leach? He's only been champion of the world for the past two years. Best player on the bloody planet he is."

I took the World Champ up on his generous offer and became a member of his table tennis club. It was full of good international and county standard players and I was a long way down the pecking order. I played for them all that season and even managed a handful of games for Surrey Seconds. I lost far more games than I won, but I did improve. Try as I might though, I never came remotely close to taking a game off Johnny Leach.

Moving on

After we'd been in England for six months our little gang of six from Northern Ireland was split up. I think we were all sorry about it, but I suppose it was bound to happen eventually. Mrs Renoir threw a farewell party for us before putting us out of her mind and preparing for the next intake. We exchanged group hugs and promised to keep in touch before heading off to take up our new posts.

I was packed off to work in the shop in Barkingside, historically in Essex, but which was to become part of the newly created London Borough of Redbridge in 1965. My new hostel was above the firm's shop in Hook, on the Kingston by-pass. The shop was fine, and like all others in the chain, laid out along similar lines. Sadly, the same could not be said of the hostel.

There were eight of us boarders – I almost said prisoners – and the housekeeper, Miss Mathers, ran what might be called an exceedingly tight ship. As it happens, that's not the worst analogy because she struck me as a hybrid of Dicken's Ebenezer Scrooge and the infamous Captain William Bligh, of HMS Bounty. I gathered from a new friend and fellow inmate, Dennis Higgins, that rumblings of dissatisfaction had been going on below decks for quite some time. If an army marches on its stomach, then it seemed the war had already been lost.

The litany of complaints was a lengthy one, although apparently no one had thus far summoned up sufficient courage to beard the lioness in her den. The quality and quantity of the food dished up to us was well below par, and certainly nothing like we'd been used to in Surbiton. There were unsubstantiated suspicions that she siphoned off some of her housekeeping allocation to boost her personal retirement fund.

There were other irritations as well. It took an inordinate amount of cajoling and wheedling to persuade Miss Mathers to issue any of her prisoners with a late pass. In my own case I need at least two of these each week to fulfil my table tennis commitments, and it was only the threat of reporting the matter to Mr Leach that caused her to grant a grudging approval.

The final straw came when she caught one of the lads reading in bed with the light on at 11:15pm one night. Not content with administering a monumental dressing down to every one of us, she took it upon herself to switch the electricity off at the mains sharp at 11:00 o'clock from that point on. As if this wasn't inconvenient enough, it meant that those of us on a late pass had to use a torch, or undress in the dark.

The eight of us called a council of war and Dennis was deputed to contact personnel in Blackfriars and lodge an official complaint.

Two evenings later my old friend Mr Powis arrived and we all assembled in the lounge. I imagined he'd already had a word with Miss Mathers to elicit her side of events. As he took a seat I fancied he shot me a glance as much as to say *Oh Lord, not you again. I might have known you'd be in the thick of this.*

As it happened I had little to say. Dennis had been elected spokesman and he gave a fair and factual resume of events. Mr Powis then addressed each of us in turn and we all corroborated what had been said. I simply told him that as I was now playing table tennis for Surrey I had no way of controlling what time I could return, especially from away matches. I threw in the name of Johnny Leach, just for good measure.

Mr Powis said he had taken our complaints on board and would see what he could do to address them. In fairness, from that time forward, matters improved considerably. The food was much better, there was no further embargo on the use of electricity and late passes were invariably issued, even if it was difficult to read much into Miss Mather's somewhat stiff and begrudging smile. Dennis had a theory she spent her evenings sticking pins into handmade effigies of the eight of us.

Some bad news

I had been in Barkingside for about six weeks when I received some bad news about an old friend. You'll remember my old school chum, Austin, who fixed me up with my first date and who was largely responsible for my joining Sainsbury's in the first place?

First though, I ought to explain a little about what working in the bacon department in those days involved. Not all stores had a cellar like the one in Surbiton. Instead there was an extra marble-topped bench behind the counter where the sides of bacon were dissected before being displayed on the front counter for sale. Above the bench ran a rail where the bacon was hung on hooks after delivery.

To one side of the serving counter stood a large, manually driven slicing machine, calibrated to carve up the rashers to the precise thickness desired by the customer. This machine had to be cleaned several times each day, a process which entailed removing the curved guard and cleaning the incredibly sharp circular blade with a muslin cloth.

Apparently Austin had been engaged in this cleaning task, and had just removed the guard, when a colleague, standing immediately behind him, lost his footing while taking down a side of bacon from the rail. The full weight of the bacon caught my friend across the back of the head and shoulders, driving his face down on to the unprotected blade. The injuries were horrific as the poor chap was sliced open from forehead to chin, right down the middle of his face! It didn't really bear thinking about.

The firm, as was to be expected, did their absolute best for him, and after surgery and a lengthy spell in hospital, he went on to make a remarkable recovery, although he would carry a scar for the rest of his days. A lasting regret is that I never saw Austin again. Last I heard he had risen to the position of manager in one of their stores.

A steady girlfriend

Dennis Higgins, or Den as most of us called him, became a special friend and he often took me to meet his family in Byfleet at weekends. His parents were lovely people and always made me welcome.

He had a girlfriend, Doreen, whom I hadn't met, and one evening as he was leaving the hostel to meet her to go to the cinema, he popped into my room to say cheerio. I was lying on my bed reading a book and jokingly called after him "Ask her if she's got a friend." It was a throwaway remark and I thought nothing more about it as I returned to my book. But inside five minutes he was back and stuck his head round the door, grinning from ear to ear.

"Your wish is my command, sir," he declared. "Come on, grab your coat. We can't keep the girls waiting."

Outside Den introduce me to his girlfriend, Doreen, and my partner for the evening, a tall, attractive, black-haired girl by the name of Pat Carter. I learned later that she and Doreen were best friends from schooldays.

We caught a bus into Richmond and went to the Odeon to see the recently released *African Queen,* an excellent film starring Humphrey Bogart and Katherine Hepburn. Pat had recently sprained her wrist while playing hockey and had her left arm in a sling.

Den and Doreen were having a gentle cuddle in their seats beside us and Pat nodded her head in their direction and smiled. Nodding towards her sling, I whispered, "I can see I'm going to have to treat you very gently, Pat."

Her smile broadened. "I won't break," she said chirpily, "and I hope it isn't going to stop you putting your arm around me."

It didn't. In the months that followed she became my first steady girlfriend.

The call of home

I suppose it was my old friend Tony who got me thinking about Ireland and home. Now well into my second year in England, I was enjoying life enormously. Work seemed to be going well, I'd had a couple of pay rises, was playing lots of sport, had made a host of new friends, was getting on famously with my steady girlfriend, Pat, and had settled comfortably into all that London suburbia had to offer.

Tony and I exchanged letters regularly, keeping each other abreast of how we were doing. His correspondence, penned in the now familiar green ink, made it plain that my old home town hadn't changed a lot – and wasn't likely to. He was still working with his father in the Mourne Printing Works in Greencastle Street, still riding his bicycle and taking and developing his photographs.

He sent me one he'd taken of Dad, whom he'd met in town one afternoon. But it was his accompanying note which really set me thinking. It ran:

"I'm forwarding a photo of your dad whom I met in town the other day. I've given him a copy as well. We had a nice little chat, mostly about you of course. He's glad you're doing well and liking the job. He didn't say so in as many words, Brad, but it's plain to see he is missing you a lot. I suppose it didn't help much when I told him I missed you too and wished you would come home."

That letter really threw the cat among the pigeons and got me thinking. For the first time I realised that Dad, who had married late in life, and had me even later, wasn't getting any younger, and was, in fact, close to retirement age. I'd only seen him once – during a hectic two-day Christmas holiday – in over a year, and it would be a couple of months before I was due to go back home on annual leave.

I thought about it for a long time and talked it over with Den. He was entirely practical, as I knew he would be, pointing out the obvious that I was enjoying my job, doing well with the firm, and had settled into London life like the proverbial duck to water. "Anyway," he asked, "are job prospects as good back in Ireland?"

That last was a fair point. If Sainsbury's had expanded into

Northern Ireland, things might have been different. I could have applied for a transfer. However, they didn't make that move until many years later. I'd no reason to think that job prospects were any brighter back home than when I'd left. I'd already tried my hand as a trainee electrician, a trainee forestry officer and a trainee chain-store manager. It was high time I made my mind up about what I really wanted to do.

When I raised the matter with Pat she simply threw her arms round my neck and said, "Please Brad, don't go."

But a month later I did. I handed in my notice and had another encounter with Mr Powis in his Blackfriars office. Leaning back behind his desk, he stared at me over folded arms and said. "So it's finally come down to this after all. It's a shame we've no more Festivals of Britain coming up, or you might have stayed with us a while longer. May I ask why you're leaving?"

I wasn't going to give this smug little man the satisfaction of going back over old ground, so I said simply, "Personal reasons."

He tut-tutted severely. "We've spoken about your record before. You do realise you are throwing away a promising career, don't you?"

I shrugged. "Perhaps. There are other careers."

"But you've wasted a year-and-a-half of your time, and ours."

"I wouldn't say I've wasted them, Mr. Powis. I've learnt quite a lot during my time here and I don't believe Sainsbury's have been exactly short-changed either. I've worked hard here."

He smashed his fist on the desk in vexation. "That's my whole point. You have it in you to become one of our best managers. Why throw it away like this?"

"As I've said already, personal reasons."

He leant forward. "You know, I don't understand you Irish lads. Surely there are lots of Roman Catholic Churches and clubs over here you could join. You've been made welcome in this country, but all most of you seem to want to do is to go back to Ireland."

I could have explained to Mr Powis that I wasn't Roman Catholic, not that that mattered a damn anyhow. I could have told him I hadn't taken my decision lightly. I could have explained that personal reasons were precisely that – personal, and therefore of no concern to him. I could have told him a lot of things, but I doubt he'd have understood. You see, he wasn't a particularly good personnel manager.

The exile returns

Farewells are sad affairs, so I won't dwell on them here. Suffice to say I was sorry to leave London and the many good friends I made there. I remember them all with affection. I kept in touch with Pat, and Den and one or two others for a while, before, as is the way of things, we drifted on along our separate ways.

Tony Heaney was waiting at the same depot when my bus pulled in. "What kept you?" he said and embraced me in an enormous bear-hug.

"Put me down," I pleaded, "and before you start, you're not getting that two pounds back. It was spent a long time ago."

"I don't need it. I've had a couple of pay rises while you were away. Seriously though, it's good you're home."

"I had to come, Tony, I was afraid if I'd stayed longer you'd run out of green ink!"

The easy banter had picked up again from where we'd left off eighteen months before. Kilkeel hadn't changed much in that time, and thank God, neither had Tony.

After a couple of weeks settling back in with Dad and doing a round of family and friends, it was time to consider getting a job, even if it were only a temporary one until I sussed out what I really wanted to do. Typically, my Uncle Jim, headmaster to the core, urged that it wasn't too late to resume my education. His brother, Bobby, was more practical. Since being demobbed from the wartime RAF, he'd joined the Civil Service and was an official in the Employment Exchange in Newcastle.

"Murland's Mill, outside Castlewellan, is taking on workers and I've arranged an interview for you with Mr Robinson, the manager," he said. "Turn up there at twelve o'clock next Monday and ask for him. You're expected. Good luck. It's a bit far for you to travel from Kilkeel, so you can stop with us in Newcastle if you like. It'll give you a chance to look around for something better."

Having stayed with Bobby and his wife Ethel overnight, I caught a bus for Murland's in good time for my appointment. Not having the slightest idea where the mill was, I asked the conductor if he would kindly let me know when we reached it. He nodded assent and I relaxed and tried to collect my thoughts as we bowled along through the countryside.

I'd been told the journey was only a few miles, so, when we'd been travelling for half-an-hour or so, I asked the conductor if we were nearly there.

Clamping a hand to his forehead, he exclaimed, "Strewth son, I'm sorry, I totally forgot about you. We're miles past it; almost in Ballynahinch. We can drop you off here and maybe you'll get a lift back."

I climbed out of the bus and started walking back the way we'd come, still not entirely certain of my destination. After ten minutes or so a car appeared heading in the right direction. I turned and stuck up a hopeful thumb, only to withdraw it when I saw the vehicle was a gleaming Rolls Royce – a Silver Ghost or Silver Cloud or something of the sort, as I remember.

To my surprise the car slowed to a halt and the rear window slid down. An elegantly attired figure in the rear seat turned and addressed me in cultured tones.

"May we be of assistance to you, young man?"

I apologised for stopping them and blurted out a garbled account of what had happened.

"I see," he exclaimed casually. "In that case you'd better get in. You might just make it in time for your interview."

I was about to open the back door but the chauffeur, in his grey livery and smart peaked-cap, beat me to it. Gliding round the lustrous bonnet as though he were on ball bearings, he had the door open for me in a trice and ushered me inside. Within seconds he had retaken his place behind the wheel and the Rolls purred away.

As we drove along my host enquired politely about my prospective new job, asked a few questions about my previous career, and as we drew up to the wide entrance of Murland's, wished me good luck in my interview.

Two men were talking just inside the gateway and they both sprang to attention at our approach. My host acknowledged them with a courteous nod and bade me wait until the driver had opened the door for me. In doing so the chauffer bowed slightly and touched his fingers to the brim of his peaked-cap.

"Thank you, sir," I said to the man in the back seat. "I appreciate the lift."

"You are welcome my boy," he smiled "The taller man on the left Is Mr Robinson. Please give him my regards, and, once again, good luck with the interview."

As his companion moved off, Mr Robinson greeted me with a warm handshake and ushered me into his office. It was the shortest interview I've ever had in my life. I can only remember one question. Could I start work the following Monday?

I was provided with tea and biscuits while his secretary looked up the time of the next bus to Newcastle. When I was leaving, Mr Robinson walked me to the front gate and enquired. "Are you a friend of Sir Graeme then?"

My raised eyebrow must have given a fair impression of the film actor Roger Moore. "Sir Graeme . . . ?" I returned blankly.

"Yes, Sir Graeme Lamour, the owner of this establishment."

"Oh, we've only known each other a short time," I said, and crossed the road to the bus stop. If the manager thought Sir Graeme and I were best buddies, I saw no need to disabuse him of the notion.

I quite enjoyed the few months I spent working in the mill. The job was undemanding and my work colleagues all good friendly folk, but I realised it was only a stop-gap. Still undecided as to what I really wanted to do, I began to study the Situations Vacant section of the newspapers.

Yet another new career

Arriving home from work one autumn evening, my aunt announced we were having a guest for dinner. He had just arrived in Newcastle and had taken the house next door. My uncle added that our new neighbour intended launching a weekly newspaper in the area. "You never know, Brad. Play your cards right and there might be a job in it for you!"

A few minutes later I was introduced to Jim Hawthorne for the first time. Neither of us realised it then, but our lives would be closely intertwined for the next thirty-odd years.

Our visitor was a dapper, dark-haired little man. He favoured a striped business suit, white shirt and conservative red tie. I quickly noticed he had a peculiar habit of prefacing almost every sentence with a strange little humming noise, not unlike that made by a distant bumble-bee.

"Mmmm. It's very kind of you to invite me to dinner, Mrs Harper. The rest of the family won't be arriving for about two weeks, so I'm having to fend for myself."

He went on to tell us that he already had a newspaper in Dromore, and believed he had spotted an opportunity for basing another in Newcastle. "I'm going to call it the *Mourne Observer,*" he said. "There are a number of fair-sized towns in this part of County Down and I trust it's a big enough area to carry another paper."

He explained that as well as providing comprehensive coverage of standard events such as courts, councils, farmers' meetings and the like, he hoped to report on all sports and entertainment. He had already appointed a number of local columnists, and with a glance in my direction, added that young readers would not be forgotten.

"In that last connection, Brad," he continued, "I wonder if you could tell me what young fellows of your age would like to read about?"

I wasted no time in rattling off a comprehensive list. He listened intently, nodded his head several times and finished with a soft "Mmmm. Interesting."

We had reached the coffee stage when he asked me if I knew any young fellows who might be interested in coming to work for the paper.

"Would I do?" I said, figuring it could be a lucky day for both of us.

"Come and see me in my office on Saturday morning," he said.

I'm still not sure whether our first meeting was a coincidence, or if he and my uncle had cooked it up in advance. My uncle certainly never admitted to it. I didn't care either way. Given a fair wind on Saturday, it looked like I was going to be a trainee again – this time a trainee journalist.

Starting on the ground floor

Any dreams I might have entertained about being a movie-style investigative reporter - a la James Stewart or Jimmy Cagney – with a fedora on the back of my head, sitting on the corner of the editor's desk and spinning tales of all my scoops – were quickly dispelled. On my first morning I was handed a broom and ordered to sweep out the storeroom floor in preparation for the imminent arrival of a stock of newsprint paper. I suppose there's nothing wrong with starting at the bottom – the only way from there is supposed to be up.

My interview with the Boss on the previous Saturday had gone well enough, I suppose, even if it had made it plain that there was to be no royal road to journalistic stardom. After being set a little test in English grammar, which didn't present too many problems, I was told I'd be expected to learn typing and Pitman's shorthand. This would entail attending evening classes in the local Technical College and a lot of hard work during my free time at home.

Free time? That was a laugh for a start! I don't know where Hawthorne thought my free time was going to come from. Officially, we worked a five-and-a-half-day week. Unofficially, it never quite worked out like that. Wednesday was always a late night, collating and preparing copy. Thursday was print night, which meant finishing sometime between 11pm and one o'clock in the morning There was an early start Friday, when the print run had to be finished and the papers counted, parcelled and delivered. On good days we got cleared up around 6pm. Saturday was nominally a half-day, with a 12:30pm finish.

Throw in a couple of hours on Tuesday and Friday nights to study shorthand and typing at the Tech and you could say my week was a fairly full one. Of course, when I had my interview I thought working a couple of nights a week would be no great hardship. At least the overtime would help soften the blow.

The Boss shook his head vigorously when I brought up that subject. "We don't do overtime," he retorted sharply. "A fair week's pay for a fair week's work is my motto."

That little exchange led on to the next question. What did he consider to be a fair week's pay?"

"Mmmm," he said, steepling his fingers on his desk and leaning back in his chair. "Normally I start apprentices at one pound a week. But, as you're a wee bit older and seem a bright enough lad, I'm prepared to make it thirty bob!"

Now that is £1.50 in today's money, or about 2.5p an hour for my average sixty-hour week. It was considerably less than I'd been earning in England and roughly on a par with my pay-packet when I was knocking down walls as an apprentice electrician for Nicky McConville in Kilkeel. At least I didn't have to pay for a National Insurance stamp.

I must have been mad – but we shook hands on it.

Jack of all trades

In my first few weeks as a junior reporter in the *Mourne Observer* I did precious little reporting. I did lots of other things though, like carting up reams of newsprint from the storeroom, making sure the three linotype machines were supplied with metal in order that the operators could keep on punching their keys without interruption, cleaning off the inky rollers on the big Cosser flatbed printing machine and collating and parcelling the weekly print run of newspapers.

After a month or so, when I had signed up for my night classes at the Tech, I was actually permitted to do a little reporting, if, indeed, it could be called that. I was entrusted with calling on the secretaries of local organisations like the Women's Institute, the Young Farmers' Club and the Unionist Association to elicit details of their meetings, jumble sales and the like. At least it provided a chance to escape the printing works for an hour or so and I was usually offered a cup of tea by the kind ladies who passed on their news.

I was amazed and amused at how people absolutely loved seeing their name in print, unless of course it was because they were up on a charge at one of the local Petty Sessions courts. In that event they would go to almost any length to ensure their name did not appear.

The Boss had a strict rule about that sort of thing. "Mmmm, if you can't face the shame, don't do the crime," was his mantra. He insisted that all such requests were referred directly to him. All the staff had a good belly-laugh when the Boss himself was nabbed for not having a rear light on his bicycle by an over-zealous police constable who was new to the town and didn't know who he was dealing with.

He instructed Stanley Maxwell, our chief reporter, who was covering the court, to make sure his name and fine of 10 shillings was included in the list of Other Cases. Mind you, he did change it from James Hawthorne, to David James and later to D J Hawthorne before its final appearance. Ever afterwards he would delight in informing the luckless culprits who begged that their names be kept out of the paper. "Mmmm. I'm afraid I simply can't do that. Why, I even publicised my own name when I fell foul of the law some time ago!"

There was one particular job I detested with a passion. We had a supply of printed forms to be handed in to households who were about to have a wedding in the family, or who had suffered a bereavement. The former wasn't too bad, but funerals were something else again. I was expected to call on the family concerned, offer condolences and present them with this form to be filled in.

I could either leave it with them to be collected later, or else fill it in myself while they provided whatever details they thought fit. I was sent packing a number of times, but, to be fair, most folk were content enough to provide the information I needed. It was then a matter of returning to the office and typing up a short report on either the dear departed or the happy couple.

Most reports of local nuptials would start with the immortal phrase "The wedding took place of so-and-so and so-and-so in such-and-such church on whatever date it happened to be."

I was told the story of a junior reporter on a local paper, who, having churned out dozens of such reports, each with an identical introduction, was chastised by his editor and instructed to introduce a little variety. "For instance," he was admonished, "you might write something like 'Kilkeel Parish Church was the setting for the wedding of . . .' or 'Miss so-and-so became the bride of Mr so-and-so . . .' or 'A newly-wed Ballynahinch couple will be spending their honeymoon in . . .' "There are lots of alternatives, just use your imagination."

All went well until the young tyro, waxing really lyrical, placed an effort on the editor's desk beginning "The wedding was consummated in Dromore Parish Church . . ."

I understand the aspiring reporter in question is now in another job.

The sporting life

Although working ridiculously long hours, I contrived to continue playing, football, cricket, table tennis, athletics and several other sports whenever I could, although it was difficult to hold down a regular place in any team. When the Boss discovered my sporting interest, he suggested I might write a little account of those matches I was engaged in.

I wasn't keen on this, as you might imagine. I pointed out that we already had a number of correspondents, club secretaries and the like, who provided a lot of these reports. "I wouldn't want to go treading on their toes," I argued. "Besides, I couldn't exactly take a pencil and notebook onto the pitch with me. And if I scored the winning goal, or, more likely, made a total horlicks of something, you could hardly expect me to write about myself, now could you?"

"Mmmm, I don't see why not, as long as you were honest about it."

I drew the line at that particular suggestion, however, reckoning it was bad enough working the hours I did, without having to file reports on my off-duty pursuits.

Back to school – yet again

When the autumn term began I found myself back at school again, though this time there were many differences. The Technical

College was only a stone's throw from the *Observer* office and both shorthand and typing classes were taken by a personable young man by the name of Tom Little, who worked as a clerk for a prominent firm of local solicitors.

I was the only male in a class of about thirty-six would-be secretaries and office workers and initially subject to a lot of good-natured banter. Fortunately, I had lost a good deal of my earlier shyness and actually came to quite enjoy the badinage. Each of us sat at a desk equipped with a stout Remington, Royal or Underwood typewriter and a pile of A4 paper. These venerable machines were a far cry from the lightweight keyboards and word-processors of today and required a fair measure of downward pressure to get satisfactory and uniformly printed results.

To help us develop a good style and rhythm in our typing, Tom would play a selection of old 78 records on a wind-up gramophone. We all found this quite amusing at first, but I have to admit it did help us to attain a consistent tempo. Victor Sylvester and his Ballroom Orchestra were Tom's particular favourite and every time I heard Victor on the radio in later years it took my thoughts right back to the rhythmical clicking of keys in that classroom. When three-dozen keyboards were clattering away in some semblance of unity It must have sounded something like a machine-gun barrage in the trenches of World War 1.

First we had to master the guide keys, which our fingers were expected to return to automatically as a kind of base of operations. From that position it was a matter of training the old grey matter to find the remaining keys without consciously thinking about it. To add to the complexity of this, we weren't permitted to look at our fingers. Surprisingly enough, we all seemed to pick this up reasonably quickly, and after a few weeks, Victor Sylvester's services were able to be dispensed with and his records were returned to the storeroom.

I believed I was progressing quite nicely and was typing away merrily one afternoon in the office I shared with the Boss, when he turned and observed somewhat caustically, "Mmmm, Brad, if you think you can produce that any quicker in longhand, go right ahead. That staccato rattling is driving me mad!"

I like to think my typing skills have improved a little since those days. Typing was one thing; acquiring the niceties of Pitman's Shorthand was a horse of an entirely different colour. Now I stand behind no one in my admiration of old Isaac Pitman, whose system of speed-writing was certainly a revelation in its day, and for many years afterwards. It's a thing of beauty and effectiveness and it has been an undoubted boon to countless thousands of journalists, secretaries, record takers and scribes ever since; even if the modern generation shirk from the hours of study necessary to master it and favour dictaphones, tape-recorders and similar such devices instead.

A further word of explanation might be in order. Pitman is a system of shorthand for the English language developed by an Englishman, Sir Isaac Pitman, in 1837. It is a phonetic system; the symbols do not represent letters, but rather sounds, and words are, for the most part, written as they are spoken. As of 1996, Pitman shorthand was the most popular shorthand system used in the United Kingdom and the second most popular in the United States.

Now for the boring bit. One characteristic feature of Pitman's is that unvoiced and voiced pairs of sounds (such as p and b, or t and d) are represented by strokes which differ only in thickness; the thin stroke representing "light" sounds such as [and t; the thick stroke representing "heavy" sounds such as b and d. Doing this requires a writing instrument responsive to the user's drawing pressure: specialist fountain pens (with fine, flexible nibs) were originally used, but pencils are now more commonly used.

Pitman shorthand uses straight strokes and quarter-circle strokes, in various orientations, to represent consonant sounds. The predominant way of indicating vowels is to use light or heavy dots, dashes, or other special marks drawn close to the consonant. Vowels are drawn before the stroke (or over a horizontal stroke) if the vowel is pronounced ahead of the consonant, and after the stroke (or under a horizontal stroke) if pronounced after the consonant.

Each vowel, whether indicated by a dot for a short vowel or by a dash for a longer, more drawn-out vowel, has its own position relative to its adjacent stroke (beginning, middle, or end) to indicate different vowel sounds in an unambiguous system. However, to increase writing speed, rules of "vowel indication" exist whereby the consonant stroke is raised, kept on the line, or lowered to match whether the first vowel of the word is written at the beginning, middle, or end of a consonant stroke—without actually writing the vowel.

This is often enough to distinguish words with similar consonant patterns. Another method of vowel indication is to choose from among a selection of different strokes for the same consonant. For example, the sound "R" has two kinds of strokes: round, or straight-line, depending on whether there is a vowel sound before or after the R.

I found learning shorthand to be akin to learning a foreign language. In fact, that is what it amounted to. Left to my own devices, I'd probably have given it up as a bad job. With the Boss, that was never an option. During idle moments – not that there were too many of those in the *Observer* – he would sort of sneak up on me and say, "Mmmm, Brad, let's take a minute or two to have a wee look at Sir Isaac."

This was one of his favourite little witticisms. We'd repair to the office, he'd pick up anything that came to hand, like an old newspaper or catalogue, and rattle off a few hundred words, craftily building up speed as he got into his stride. Then he'd have me read it back, pointing out all the errors I'd made. At times I'm not sure whom I hated most – the late Sir Isaac Pitman, or the Boss himself.

Over the subsequent three years my speed at both shorthand and typing improved. Each year we sat Royal Society of Arts examinations. I worked my way up to 60 words per minute for typing and 140wpm for shorthand – and I had the diplomas to prove it. I find the typing still useful today. Sadly though, my shorthand fell by the wayside a long time ago.

This might be a good time to point out that Jim Hawthorne was probably the best and most accurate exponent of shorthand I've ever known. His Pitman's was copperplate – so precise that I could read his notebook as though it were an instruction manual. Indeed, on occasions when he was snowed under with work, He would give me his record of a council meeting or the like and tell me to type a report and leave it on his desk.

His skill owed much, not just to his years in newspapers, but to the time he'd spent as a shorthand writer for Hansard, the agency responsible for maintaining a verbatim record of Parliamentary debates and business. The only trouble was he expected the likes of yours truly to be every bit as proficient as he was. And, in my case, while I managed to get by, I acknowledged that I was never going to attain anything approaching his proficiency.

Jumping ahead a few years, I remember an incident that arose out of a heated debate at a monthly council meeting. During a discussion on which cleaning product the council should order in bulk, a councillor referred to Rinso, the brand name of a leading soap powder of the day, manufactured by Unilever, as a detergent.

Unilever took umbrage, claimed their product was a soap powder, not a detergent, and threatened possible legal action against the councillor and the council. The former claimed that he had been misreported, that he had said washing powder and had never mentioned the word Rinso. He pointed the finger at Hawthorne and the Council Clerk was directed to write and make this clear to Unilever.

Upon learning of this, the Boss was furious. First, he showed me his shorthand notes of the meeting which showed clearly that the word Rinso had been used. When I concurred he insisted on seeking confirmation from my shorthand teacher, Tom Little. Then, armed with our joint corroboration, he accosted the councillor and the clerk with a dire warning of further legal action unless a full apology and retraction was forthcoming. It was, and a shamefaced councillor was left to sort out the dispute with Unilever.

I never got to hear what ultimately transpired, but, to the best of my recollection, nobody ever challenged the validity of Jim Hawthorne's shorthand notetaking again.

More strings to my bow

I wrote earlier about the many and varied jobs which existed in a weekly newspaper in those days. Those entering the profession today can have no conception of how it used to be. The computer has replaced the linotype machine, Lithography and modern printing methods have superseded the cumbersome old printing machines, the laptop has taken over from the steam typewriter and it's now possible to do more with a mobile phone than we could manage with all our ponderous equipment combined.

Yet I don't regret it for an instant. As my old Dad was fond of saying "A little bit of knowledge and experience is easily carried."

So it was no surprise when one day the Boss said to me, "Mmmm, I think it's about time you took a turn on the Intertype."

We had two Linotype machines and one Intertype which were used to set up hot-metal type for the paper and job-printing department. We had three typesetters and the Boss would turn his hand to it when required.

"It will be another string to your bow," he explained, as if he were doing me a huge favour. "You can always stand in if any of the lads are off sick, and if there's a rush you could always set up your copy straight from your shorthand notebook!"

He wasn't joking. I hadn't heard the expression at that time, but if I had, I might well have told him, *"And if you stick a brush up my ass I can always sweep the floor at the same time!"*

In the event, his master plan was a failure for two reasons.

First, the Intertype keyboard had a completely different layout from that of a typewriter – apparently all to do with the time it takes for the little matrix to slip down into the slot to form one line of type. It was a bit like trying to type in English and French at the same time. My fingers had, almost unconsciously, become attuned to my typewriter and I had to keep peering at the Intertype's keys to study the new alignment.

Second, the Intertype's keys had become so worn over the years that the letters were virtually illegible. Not to be deterred, the Boss ordered me to cut out letters from a Letterset card and glue them to the keys. When I complied, it brought howls of protest from Jimmy Martin, the usual operator, who waved his hands under the Boss's nose with most of the cut-out letters adhering to his fingers.

My reprieve didn't last for long. After placating an irate Jimmy, the Boss pulled me to one side and instructed, "Mmmm, that doesn't seem to work, so instead you can spell Sam on the Cosser."

"*Spell*" was his way of saying relieve. Sam Martin, the senior printer and machine man - no relation to Jimmy - was a rather taciturn individual with a dry sense of humour. Overhearing the discourse, he pulled me to one side immediately afterwards and observed. "Well, it will make a nice change to see you working for a living, instead of sitting on your arse, twiddling your thumbs in the Boss's office all day."

"Thanks Sam," I said. "I love you too."

In fact, I was quite fond of Sam, although up to that point our paths hadn't crossed a great deal. To be fair, he gave me a good half-hour's run-down on the workings of the Cosser. In essence, this involved feeding successive individual sheets of newsprint, broadsheet size, into the waiting maw of the press. A ream of five-hundred sheets was laid on a flat wooden board at one end of the machine. These were then flicked up individually to allow a current of air to separate them from the rest, before being slid against a gage to be clamped by rubber grippers and fed round a series of rollers.

Sam had one dire word of warning, however. Pointing at a steel handle to the left of where the operator stood, he intoned gravely, "That's the guard, or brake. If anything goes wrong, if a sheet snags or you can't lift it and get it in position in time, for God's sake pull that handle immediately. If you don't, the sheet will get meshed up in the rollers or get shredded into the type. Either way, it will take ten or fifteen minutes to clean up the mess and *His Nibs* will not be best pleased. For that matter neither will I, or anybody else, for it just means we'll all be fifteen minutes later getting the hell out of this place tonight."

"Point taken," I said, "Don't worry, Sam, you're looking at the bloke with the quickest left-handed draw since Billy the Kid."

I'm pleased to be able to report that in the almost four years that I shovelled newsprint into that big beast of a machine I never once contrived to make a horlicks of a single sheet.

Once mastered, I found feeding the big machine, as we termed it, quite therapeutic. The steady thump, thump, thump of the mechanism was strangely soothing. Besides, although he could see where I was, I was well away from of the Boss's immediate ambit.

As a means of alleviating any possible feelings of boredom, Ian Crosset, one of Sam's young apprentices, who also tended the Cosser on occasion, and I invented a little sporting duel which he engaged in with all due seriousness. This involved seeing how many sheets of paper we could feed through without having to pause to apply the brake.

Not only did this require considerable dexterity, it meant keeping an eye skinned for the Boss, who would occasionally pop down to check the print quality and halt the Cosser if he considered the ink too heavy or too light. Many a record attempt was scuppered by his sticking an inquisitive nose in.

To be fair, there wasn't much to choose between Ian and myself. Gradually our respective records rose higher and higher. Centuries became commonplace, 250 was passed. Ian was the first to reach the 500 mark and wore a smug grin for a fortnight before I overtook him.

It must be said that, as our totals soared higher and higher, we had to take Sam into our confidence so that we could keep our stockpile of paper fully topped up. Finally, as both of us, neared the thousand mark – equivalent, we reckoned, to Roger Bannister's first breaking of the four-minute mile – Sam, showing no favouritism – would daub extra ink on the rollers so that the Boss wouldn't twig on to what we were doing.

In the end I beat Ian to the 1,000 tape by the shortest of short heads. My record stood for only a week. When we finally tired of the sport we had each attained totals of over 1,200, Daft as a pair of brushers we were – but it certainly helped to pass the time.

My first pay rise

On Friday afternoons, usually around three o'clock, the Boss would emerge from his office clutching a pile of little brown envelopes, each with a name scribbled on the front. He would hand one to each of us, usually accompanied by an "Mmmm" and a curt little nod. Part of the mystique of the little ceremony was that none of us was supposed to be aware of what the rest were being paid.

On one such Friday, after I'd been with the paper for a while, I was handed my little envelope as usual. On this occasion, however, the Boss paused for a moment and treated me to one of his rare smiles. "Mmmm, Brad, I want to tell you that you've done very well since you started here six months ago. Keep up the good work. You'll find a wee bit extra in your wage-packet from now on."

That afternoon is one I remember for two reasons.

First, the two extra half-crowns in the little envelope, which boosted my weekly earnings to one pound and seventy-five pence. Second, because it was the only time in all the years I knew him that I can ever remember Jim Hawthorne paying me any sort of compliment.

Things begin to change

Not long after that there was a major change in my fortunes. Stanley Maxwell, the senior reporter, who had moved to the paper with the Boss from the *Dromore Weekly Times,* announced he was taking up a new job in Belfast and was handing in his notice.

To be fair, Stanley had tipped me the wink a day or two earlier and promised to put in a good word for me. "But you'll have to act quickly," he added, "before Jim takes on somebody else."

I talked it over with Ken Purdy, who was slightly senior to me and on hearing that he wasn't interested, decided I had nothing to lose by chucking my hat in the ring. I fancied the Boss looked more than a little surprised when I raised the matter, as much as to say what are you on about, you've only been here five minutes?

"I know I can do it," I said, with more brass neck than confidence. Then I threw in what I considered to be my ace. "Besides, if you take on a reporter with Stanley's experience it's going to cost you a packet."

I fancied I detected that old Scrooge glint in his eye, but perhaps that was only wishful thinking. He "Mmmmed" for a little while, before he said. "Leave it with me until Friday afternoon."

It was well after closing time Friday and the office was deserted when we finally spoke. I knew he had deliberately kept me hanging on and I also knew I could expect no favours. He wasted no time in firing the opening salvo. "Kenny takes a much better shorthand note than you do."

"Granted," I acknowledged, "but he can't type and he writes all his copy in longhand."

"He doesn't type because he spends a lot of time on the Lino (Linotype). It's a different keyboard."

"That's exactly the point I made when you suggested I went on the Intertype a while back. I don't want to be a machine operator; I want to be a journalist. That's why I came here in the first place."

"Kenny wants to be a journalist too. Why should I give you precedence over him?"

"I'm not asking you to do that. Kenny and I have talked about this and he says he isn't interested in the job at the moment. I'm not running him down in any way. He has a lot of fine qualities, but in my opinion, he lacks both the imagination and the writing ability required to be a journalist."

The Boss sat up straight and looked me right in the eye. "That's a bit of a sweeping statement. Perhaps you can give an example of what you're driving at?"

"Certainly. I don't mean this disrespectfully, but Kenny models himself on you."

The Boss's eyebrows shot up and he was about to say something, probably uncomplimentary. But I held up a forestalling hand.

"You've said that Kenny has better shorthand than I do. I agree absolutely. It's what he does with it that I'm talking about."

I turned, picked up a copy of that morning's *Observer,* and opened it at Kenny's report of the last Newcastle Petty Sessions, "That's what I mean."

Hawthorne glanced at the report. "I don't see anything wrong with it. Are you suggesting it isn't accurate?"

"Not at all. I'm saying it reads like one of your old Hansard reports, accurate in every detail. It's how you yourself might have recorded a debate in Parliament when you worked there. It begins with the first word spoken and finishes with the last. Let me ask you, would *The Times* or the *Daily Telegraph* have written it that way?" I picked up the paper and read the first paragraph aloud. From memory it ran something like this:

'Newcastle Petty Sessions was held in the Annesley Hall on

Friday of last week, Mr J O H Long, RM, presiding. In attendance were Capt. W Hunter, CPS, RUC Superintendent W S Smyth, prosecuting officer. The following solicitors were also present.'

There followed the names of ten or twelve members of the legal profession. Next under a sub-heading "Minor Offences" there was a list of perhaps twenty or so unfortunates who had been fined sums ranging from ten shillings to five pounds for minor motoring, cycling, or lighting offences.

I pointed a finger at a subheading halfway down the second-long column of grey type. "There's the most interesting case of the day," I said. "It's about a cow that jumped over a hedge and landed on the bonnet of this fellow's car, which then swerved into a bus! That's the most readable case and just look where it's buried. Halfway down the page under a pile of rubbish. I'm sorry, but I don't call that good journalism."

The silence lasted quite a while and the Boss sucked his teeth.

"That's not Kenny's fault, it's my fault. You're right, I ought to have changed that."

I thought it best to maintain a discreet silence.

"I suppose you'd have done it differently?"

"It's probably not my place to tell you, but I would. My Dad has been taking the *Daily Express* for years and I look at it most days. I know it's a national as opposed to a

Mourne Observer colleague, Ken Purdy, and I acting the fool.

weekly paper, but the principle is no different. To go back to Newcastle Court, are the readers really interested in that bunch of officials at the beginning? I don't think so. If they appear in cases later on they can be mentioned then, when they have something to say. Why give them free publicity by listing them all? The same goes for the RM and the prosecutor. They can be mentioned when they come out with something worth reporting."

We continued the conversation and I said the same thing applied to the different council meetings we reported. Sometimes these ran to several long columns of grey type interspersed with the occasional subheading. Why couldn't the more important stories be printed individually and given more prominence? Nothing need be excluded but smaller and less important business could be treated accordingly. In short, I suggested the *Observer* could use a complete update.

Finally, the Boss stroked his chin and said. "I can see you've been giving this a lot of thought. There may be something in what you say. I tell you what I'm going to do. You can have a shot at this for a month and we'll see how you get on. After that we'll take stock and have another chat. Agreed?"

I nodded and he continued. "Stanley isn't leaving for a month, so he can take you to the courts and council meetings and help you learn the ropes. You'll have to learn to drive the van too, but I can teach you that at weekends. I can put you on the firm's insurance but you'll have to get a driving licence."

In those days driving tests had yet to be introduced, but I have to say the thought of getting behind the wheel of the *Observer*'s Morris van was appealing.

"Anything else?" he said, getting to his feet.

"There is one thing. With all this extra work, I think a pay rise might be in order."

There was a long "Mmmm," and I could almost hear the cogs grinding round in his brain. "Let me see. You had a rise not long ago and you're on one pound, fifteen shillings. I suppose we could make it the even two pounds."

"Three would be better. I know Stanley is on eight."

There was a loud spluttering noise. "How did you know that? He recovered himself quickly. "Stanley has served his time and is an experienced reporter."

We settled on two pounds, ten shillings, to be reviewed after a month's trial period. After all the years, I still think the crafty old so and so got much the better of the deal. Mind you, he usually did.

The driving lesson

With time of the essence, the Boss decided I might as well have my first driving lesson the following morning. Clearly he was determined I should earn my extra fifteen bob a week.

I climbed into the passenger seat of the van; he got behind the wheel and spent a few minutes explaining how to operate the accelerator, clutch and brake pedals, and the art of changing gear. He emphasised the necessity of releasing the clutch gently while gradually increasing pressure on the accelerator, but other than warning me to keep a good watch on the road ahead at all times, I can't recall his mentioning much else with regard to road safety.

He drove to the wide open spaces of Donard Park, then boasting much less traffic than is the case today, and had me practise a few starts. After only a few lurches and judders we moved on to driving round in a wide circle while increasing speed and changing up through the gears. This was thrilling stuff and I was delighted when he suggested we go out onto the road and drive up to Bryansford, a couple of miles away.

There was little traffic about and I accomplished this feat without any undue alarms. Determined not to blot my copybook, or give the Boss anything approaching a white-knuckle ride, I concentrated on the road and in keeping my speed within moderate limits.

As we approached the T-junction leading into Bryansford village, not far from where I'd worked as a trainee forester, the Boss suggested I should stop and change seats. "I think it best if I execute this manoeuvre," he advised. "It's a wee bit tricky. I'll turn the van and head back towards Newcastle and then you can take over again."

This accomplished, he restarted the van and turned left in the direction of the Mournes. I noticed a lorry approaching, heavily laden with pit props. "I think we've time to reverse and then turn in front of it," he declared. It was a mistake. Realising the lorry was much closer than he'd originally thought, he abandoned his original notion and decided to pull into the verge and allow the lorry to pass. In doing so, however, he swung the wheel too soon and the back of the van ran full-tilt into a drystone wall with a tremendous thump!

The situation was scarcely helped by the lorry-driver's assistant leaning out of the passenger window and unleashing a mighty bellow of appreciative applause as his vehicle drove on towards Newcastle. I thought silence was the best policy as we scrambled out to inspect the damage, which, thankfully, was minimal.

"Mmmm," the Boss exclaimed sagely, "It's a good job you didn't do that or I might have had to dock that new pay rise you're getting!"

The smoking ban

A smoking ban had been imposed in the office and printing works, and while I wasn't a smoker myself at that time, a lot of the lads would slip out the back or into the yard for a crafty drag whenever they thought the coast was clear. Working a fourteen or fifteen-hour day, I suppose they thought it keep them sane.

The Boss, as a confirmed non-smoker, showed absolutely no sympathy in this regard. He had a nose like a bloodhound's for sniffing the faintest trace of smoke and he would deal harshly with any transgressors. The smoking apart, he deeply resented the few minutes' loss of time which he felt might have been spent on more productive work. The hardened smokers among the crew would occasionally take the risk and either nip out to the street or into the work's toilet for a quick drag.

One afternoon, Hawthorne emerged from the house in time to catch a glimpse of Harry Poland, one of the young printers, disappearing into the cloakroom leading to the loo at a high rate of knots. Always suspicious, he scuttled after him and stood for some seconds outside the toilet door, which had a twelve inch opening at top and bottom.

Even from the far end of the works we could hear him give a number of heavy snuffles as he strove to detect the tell-tale smell of a cigarette. Not certain, but not prepared to give up, he finally called out. "Is that you in there, Harry?"

"Yes it is," came the reply.

"What are you up to? Are you smoking?"

"No, I'm not smoking. If you must know, I'm shitting!"

The Boss stepped back a pace. "That's all right then. At least you're not wasting your time entirely. But don't take all day about it. We have a paper to get out."

Stepping up

Having spent a month accompanying Stanley Maxwell on his rounds of courts, councils and various other meetings, I was quite sorry to see him go. At the same time, I was eager to flex my reporting muscles on my own. So I was more than a little miffed when, just as I about to climb into the van to drive to my first solo appearance at Kilkeel Petty Sessions, the Boss announced he was coming with me. "But you can drive," he declared, as if by way of consolation.

On the way, he explained he had some calls to make in the town afterwards. He added that he would take a note of the court proceedings as a check, but I was to write it up and leave the copy on his desk. *Looking for bloomers in my report, you mean,* I reflected bitterly. *Look away then. It's up to me to make sure you don't find any.*

He didn't find any, although I'm certain he double-checked every line. I reported it in my own way too, highlighting a few of the more interesting cases separately, and deliberately ignoring any mention of lawyers and officials unless they had taken an active part. I half expected him to have a moan about this and was prepared to argue my corner, but he never mentioned it. I'm not sure he ever trusted me entirely, but at least he didn't volunteer to ride shotgun on me again.

Derick

Derick Moore had been in the *Observer* for over a year by the time I arrived. A linotype operator to trade, he was a great character, full of Irish wit and charm. He and I were to become special friends.

We worked together in local newspapers for years, I as a reporter and he as a linotype operator. He had a saying – one of several hundred – "You bring in the news Fleming and I'll set it up in print." On print night – Thursday for release the following day – it was a case of all hands to the pumps and Derick and I joined the rest of the crew in collating and parcelling up the papers and carting them off to the bus station for delivery.

That job usually finished at any time between midnight and three in the morning. I had only a short walk home. He lived out in the country and would walk with me to my house, pushing his enormous and ancient bicycle, before heading homewards. Notwithstanding our tiredness or the lateness of the hour, we would habitually stop and natter for twenty minutes or more, sorting out the events of the day.

I recall one summer night, clammier and stickier than usual, when we exited the works and he made a suggestion. "You know Brad, it's bloody hot. What do you say we nip up to the pool and have a nice refreshing dip?"

In those days Newcastle had an enclosed seawater pool.

"But it'll be locked up and we have no togs."

He smiled the impish smile I knew so well. "We can skip round the back and climb over the wall. And don't be afraid of me seeing your Willie. I've seen it lots of times."

I smiled in return; what else could I do? I scrambled on the crossbar of his bike and we set off. Getting into the pool was no bother. He parked the cycle in a shaded corner and within minutes we were in the cool, refreshing water, which sparkled and rippled in the moonlight. After long hours of toiling in the sweaty print works it was sheer bliss.

We splashed one another, swam a few leisurely lengths and were floating on our backs, chatting idly about how good life could be at times like this, when we were picked out by the beam of a powerful flashlight.

"All right lads, the show's over now. You know the rules. Out you come!" A couple of flicks of the torch ushered us towards the steps and we clambered out, standing meekly side by side in our birthday suits.

"Not a pretty sight, I have to say," the voice continued good-humouredly. "I suppose you could do with a couple of towels? Can't have you dying of hypothermia on council property. You wouldn't want me to lose my job now, would you? Besides, I'm the bloke who'd be left to clean up the mess."

Derick and I had both recognised the voice instantly. It belonged to Tom Fagan, the town's jovial homespun philosopher, who appeared to divide his time by working for the council, reading learned tomes from the library and drawing unemployment benefit on the dole.

We handed the towels back to Tom who chucked them in a corner. "There'll be no charge for those," he laughed, "the city fathers can well afford it."

"You're working late tonight Tom," Derick said. "The overtime must be good, eh?"

"Overtime my arse," came the reply. "I was riding past on my bicycle when I heard you buggers splashing and laughing your heads off. I just didn't want anything to happen to you, that's all."

I think it was later that summer that Derick and I shared a week's holiday on a large estate outside Groomsport. Having no transport of our own, we borrowed the paper's delivery van, loaded it up with a ridge tent and our personal gear and deposited it on site before returning to collect our bicycles and cycle back to our campsite.

Far more worldly wise than I, Derick decreed that we should break our journey outside Killyleagh for a drink at a wayside pub.

"I'm having a Guinness," he proclaimed as we approached the counter. "What do you fancy?"

Now I have to admit that in those days I probably didn't qualify even as a modest drinker. Frankly, I hadn't a clue what to order. I searched around frantically in desperation, before finally coming out with "Can I have a bottle of lacquer please?"

Derick took a pace backwards and exclaimed in mock amazement "Gordon Bennet, what kind of drinking company have I got myself into now!"

He and the landlord hugely enjoyed my embarrassment. "Best settle for a lager instead," Derick advised.

The campsite was a good one, conveniently situated on the edge of the village. There was fresh milk and home baked bread from the farm kitchen, and my companion had brought with him a veritable larder load of goodies, including a large square biscuit tin of fresh eggs, each individually wrapped in a piece of newspaper. "At last I've found a good use for the old paper at last," he joked.

It was Derick's custom each morning, before crawling out of his sleeping bag, to open the biscuit tin, select an egg, unwrap it, crack the shell on the edge of the tin, and swallow the contents whole in one massive gulp. He offered me an opportunity to share in this procedure. I declined as gracefully and tactfully as I could, pointing out that I preferred my eggs boiled, fried or scrambled.

One morning, midway through the week, Derick awoke, opened his tin and commenced his now familiar egg-swallowing routine. Just as it disappeared down his gullet I became aware of a horrible, pungent stench. The egg was rancid. Poor Derick, trapped within the confines of his sleeping bag, retched, coughed and spluttered, before becoming violently ill.

It took some time for him to recover and when he eventually did, I advised, not unkindly, "Well, I guess that's the end of the raw eggs?"

"Certainly not," he asserted sternly, "but from now on I'll make sure to crack the bloody things into a cup before I swallow them!"

Derick was lightning quick with his repartee and rarely missed the chance to score a point. A member of the local pigeon club, he was once trying to sell their raffle tickets to the rest of us. The first prize was a massive Christmas hamper.

"Is it a really good one?" one sceptic enquired.

"Good," sneered Derick. "I tell you boy, if Napoleon had had a hamper like this on the retreat from Moscow there'd be a French government in the Kremlin today!"

Raymond was an occasional visitor to the works on print nights. He would usually stay for a bit of craic, before grabbing a paper and catching the late bus home.

"I haven't seen you in a while Ray," Derick declared, "Where were you last week?"

"I had a great time man. I rode a woman from Dublin."

"At least it makes a change from walking," Derick replied laconically.

Puppies for sale

I would always bring a couple of papers home when the print run was finished on Thursday nights, and at breakfast one Friday my uncle pointed to the classified advertisements' page and said "I see there are puppies for sale in Kilkeel. Your Aunt Ethel and I were thinking we might like one. What do you think?"

"I'll be up that way Monday," I told him, "and if you like I'll see if I can pick one up for you. Want me to bring it home if I find one I think you'd like?"

They both agreed to this, so I called at a little bungalow on the Monday afternoon. The woman of the house answered my knock, looking slightly harassed and dusting flour from her hands. "As you can see, I'm up to my neck just now," she said in answer to my inquiry, "but if you go round to the shed at the back you'll find five of them in there. Pick whichever one you fancy. There'll be no charge. We just want them to go to a good home. You'll see an old tramp fellow dossing down in the straw. Pay him no mind and just let him sleep away there."

Sure enough, even before I had opened the shed door I could heard the sound of loud snoring coming from inside. A ragged old boy lay huddled in a pile of straw, clad in a khaki army greatcoat and floppy felt hat. Sharing his quarters were five mostly black and tan coloured mongrel pups. They looked to be six or seven weeks old.

They all appeared much of a muchness, but I remembered being told that, when selecting a new pup, always choose the one which comes towards you. This is said to indicate that he's bolder and brighter than the rest of the litter. I hunkered down, and sure enough, one of the little fellows waddled up to me, tail wagging furiously, clearly intent on sussing out this newcomer and possibly hoping for a morsel of food.

"You'll do," I said, and scooped him up in my arms. Scanning the shed, I found an empty cardboard shoebox on a bench and popped him into it. Shouting my thanks to the housewife through the open kitchen window I retreated to the van. Tearing an old copy of the *Observer* into shreds, I made my little friend as comfortable as I could and set the box on the passenger seat where I could keep an eye on him.

I'd promised to stop by the office and show the lads the puppy before taking him home. They all made a great fuss of him but dispersed when the Boss put in an appearance. I explained the situation and he picked the little dog up and set him on his desk, petting him and chatting away to him in the daft way folk do.

Obviously overwhelmed by all this unaccustomed attention, the pup wiggled his rear end, spread his little legs and unleashed a stream of pee right in the middle of the Boss's desk!

I was mortified, thinking I was in for a right bollocking. Instead my employer snatched up the animal and held him over the wastebasket until the flood subsided. Replacing him in his box, he somehow forced a smile and muttered something to the effect that accidents will happen.

Typically though, he reverted to type as I was carting the culprit out of the office. "The sooner that little customer is house-trained the better for all concerned!"

"Practise makes perfect"

Jim Hawthorne was always urging Ken and me to practise (or, as he pronounced it, *prac-tize)* our shorthand at every opportunity. "There's a lot of truth in the old saying that *practize* makes perfect. You can't beat it."

So, it was no real surprise, when one Friday afternoon, he called me over and said that some new bells were being dedicated at a service in St John's Parish Church the following Sunday morning. "Dean Jones is giving the address. You know him of course. He's a fine preacher and doesn't speak too quickly. We might as well give him a good show so take a verbatim note of his sermon and we can find space for it all next week."

It may soundly faintly ridiculous today, but at that time it was not uncommon for some of the more old-fashioned weeklies to report church sermons in full, especially if there was a scarcity of other news. And the *Mourne Observer* was as old-fashioned as they come.

Being familiar with the Boss's ways by this time, I took particular care over my report, even going so far as to correct two or three small grammatical errors the Dean had made. The story was published exactly as I had written it.

You can no doubt imagine my trepidation then, when the Boss

approached me, stern-faced, in the middle of the following Friday afternoon and announced that Dean Jones was sitting in his office and wanted a word with me. *Bloody hell,* I thought, as I fell into step behind him, *what have I got myself into this time?*

The Dean rose, shook hands and the three of us sat down, yours truly waiting for the inevitable axe to fall.

The Dean coughed and shook his head a little sadly.

"I read your account of last Sunday's service of dedication in St John's over breakfast this morning," he said, "and I've just been explaining to James here that I felt I had to call to thank you personally and to commend you, not only on your accuracy, but also for correcting a few little mistakes of my own. I'm afraid my grammar isn't quite what it used to be."

Turning to the Boss, he continued. "I believe you are fortunate in having such an accomplished man of letters in your employ. I look forward to reading more of your reports in the future, Brad. Thank you once again."

I thanked the Dean and left the office, feeling distinctly taller than when I'd entered it. I remember thinking, what a great opportunity for demanding a pay-rise. I didn't of course and the Boss never mentioned the matter again.

A new girlfriend

I'd been in the *Mourne Observer* for almost four years, still working too many hours for too little pay, but generally being fairly content with my lot. I enjoyed journalism, I loved meeting people and writing about them. I'd even started sending little snippets of news to the Belfast dailies and the BBC. In fact, more than a third of my meagre income came from that quarter.

I remember in particular one Saturday afternoon in June, 1956. I'd returned from playing an away match for Newcastle Cricket Club and intended catching the evening bus to Kilkeel to spend the weekend with Dad and to catch up with Tony, who, by this time, had gone to work as a typesetter with the *Irish News* in Belfast.

The bus was waiting in the depot and was already well filled with passengers. I took a vacant seat beside an attractive black-haired girl whom I knew was called Rita Cunningham, and who worked in the office of one of the town's most prominent stores. I'd seen her there on a number of occasions I'd called to talk to her boss, who was a leading figure in Unionist Party circles. She had just finished work for the week and I explained I was on my home to Kilkeel.

We chatted away quite happily while the bus filled with passengers. An elderly woman, laden with a heavy shopping bag, entered and stood in the aisle right behind us, and much as I didn't want to, etiquette demanded I should do the gentlemanly thing. With apologies to Rita I rose and offered the woman my seat. On the outskirts of town, a seat became vacant farther up the bus and I took it. To my surprise I was joined in a few minutes by a smiling Rita.

First love, Rita. A star-crossed affair that couldn't work out in the Northern Ireland of the times.

We spent perhaps ten minutes together before the bus reached her stop at Glassdrumman. By that time, and to my surprise, my offer of a date, same place, same time the following Saturday, had been accepted with a warm smile. You may have gathered by now that, in matters concerning the fair sex, I didn't usually move so swiftly.

For most of the following week I thought of little else but my incipient date with Rita. Since I'd returned from England and started working in the paper, there hadn't been a lot of time for girls – not much time for anything, other than work and study, to be honest. I was looking forward to it immensely, hoping that no last-minute problem would chuck a spanner in the works.

I had a home cricket match that Saturday afternoon and I prayed for an early finish. I was lucky and had just enough time to nip home, change out of my whites, and be at the station on the dot of 6:30pm. The town was choc-a-bloc with holidaymakers and visitors but I had no difficulty in picking out Rita walking up the street towards me.

Having established that she'd already eaten, I asked if she'd like to go to the cinema. "Yes please, Brad. If you want me to," she said with a smile which momentarily took me back to a night in Surbiton and a date with another raven-haired beauty five years before. I hoped for better luck with the relationship this time.

As it happened, the Palace Cinema was showing *Love is a Many Splendored Thing,* a popular romantic movie starring Jennifer Jones and William Holden, and the title sequence and now-famous introductory music was just beginning as we took our seats.

Rita smiled up at me and said "An excellent smoochy film, Mr Fleming, if I may say so. Was this mere chance, or did you choose it deliberately?"

"These things are not easy to arrange," I said non-committedly, "but I thought it might be appropriate. I hope you enjoy it."

Going steady

Rita and I saw as much of one another as we possibly could during that first month. With my work commitments it wasn't always easy, but I tried to wangle things as best I could, even to the extent of dodging a few evening classes at the Tech, and keeping my fingers crossed *His Nibs* didn't find out. I even managed to borrow the van on a few occasions, and when I couldn't manage that, she'd either come into Newcastle on the bus, or else I'd ride out her way on my bicycle and we'd go for walks along by the shore.

I guess you could say I was well and truly smitten. Rita was everything I could ever have wanted in a girlfriend – bright, witty, agreeable, utterly attractive in my eyes, and perhaps most important of all, she possessed an impish sense of humour that was a delight.

In short, we got along famously together; so much so that, when the first storm cloud appeared on the horizon, it made the blow all that much harder to take.

I believe I've made it clear already that someone else's religious belief has never mattered a jot to me. It simply didn't enter the scheme of things. To be blunt, I couldn't give a damn whether a person was of a particular religion - or none at all. I know it seems to matter much more in Ireland than in other parts of the world, but look about you and ask what discrimination and religious bigotry has ever done for this country, apart from setting it back centuries.

Of course I knew that Rita was Catholic, just as my best friend, Tony, was. We never discussed it; we didn't need to. At that time it simply didn't matter to either of us. Sadly, all that was to change after we'd been going out together for about a month.

I was walking her to the bus station one evening after we'd been to the movies and she suddenly squeezed my arm. "Oh oh," she whispered. "I think I'm in trouble."

"What's wrong?" I enquired anxiously. "What's the matter, love?"

"It's my brother, Jim," she breathed, "I think he's just seen us."

"Does that bother you, Rita? Surely you aren't doing anything wrong. Let's go and speak to him and I'll explain."

Her grip on my arm tightened even more. "Oh please no, Brad. You don't understand. You mustn't do that."

Then, very patiently, she explained it all to me. "You know my father died some time ago. There's just my Mum, my brother, Jim, and me. He's very protective of me – and I'm afraid he's also very traditional about these things."

Picking up on my puzzled look, she hurried on. "I hate having to say this, but you must know it's not how I feel. Jim will go straight back home and tell Mum he's seen me out with you, a Protestant, and there's going to be an almighty row!"

I was thunderstruck. Surely this couldn't be happening. Taking Rita in my arms, I said, "This can't be right, love. You know how I feel about you. Look, let us both go and talk to your Mum, it's high time I got to know her in any case, and I'll make her understand."

But Rita was shaking her head, even before I'd finished. "I knew you wouldn't understand, darling. Mum simply wouldn't listen – and she would never change her mind."

Anxious now, I held Rita tightly and managed to say, "So what are we going to do about this? Is it over? Are you going to pack me in?"

She clung to me. "I don't want to do that, Brad. I really don't. But I have to think this through. I'm going to get a broadside when I get home, and that's for sure. Will you leave it with me please, and trust me to try to work something out?"

I felt as if I'd been hit by a truck. "If that's the only chance we have I'll just have to hope you can do something about it."

Undercover courtship

I didn't see Rita for four or five days after that. My mind was in turmoil. I couldn't concentrate on anything else and I found myself snapping at people for no reason whatsoever. Several times I was on the point of calling into her office to see her, but thought better of it. Finally, I received a message from her suggesting we meet after work that evening. She explained that, as she had feared, her brother had told her mother about seeing us together and she had been given a severe talking to by both of them. She explained how she hadn't tried to answer back, but had simply sat there meekly and tried to let it wash over her.

"So that's it then," I said when she'd finished. "It's over for us."

She kissed me fiercely and shook her head. "No, Brad, it isn't over. I don't want it to be. I'm not going to stop seeing you. We're just going to have to be more careful, that's all."

My spirits soared. I couldn't believe this girl shared the sort of feelings I had for her. I just stood there and held her tightly for a long time. I didn't stop to think that I was storing up trouble for her with her family. It was enough that she still wanted to see me. Looking back on it now, down all the years, I can see it was never going to work. Not in the Ireland of those days. But we were young, and in love, and I had all the selfishness, and brashness, of youth.

Our being careful worked for a while. We'd snatch a few minutes before going to work in the mornings, or at lunchtime, or on her way home after work. We even managed to take in a few movies, but always we were looking over our shoulders, fearful our secret would be discovered; yet somehow drawing even closer to one another because of all the difficulties and complications.

More than once I suggested going to talk to her mother or Jim, but the very idea made her so frightened I was forced to abandon the notion. We endured this unsatisfactory state of affairs for several months, until, as was bound to happen, Jim discovered Rita and I were still seeing each other. Another major dust up followed and there was talk of her being banned from Newcastle altogether and possibly being sent somewhere else to work.

It was my first real brush with religious discrimination. Small wonder that I have continued to detest that particular blight on this wonderful country of ours all my life.

We decided to stop meeting completely for a number of weeks. Even then, we'd exchange letters and little notes, usually delivered via my workmate, Harry Poland, who was a cousin of Rita's, and in on our little secret. Once she sent me a lock of her hair, tied in a blue silk ribbon. Talk about youthful infatuation!

Through Harry, we arranged to meet a few days before the Christmas holidays and kissed and cuddled in our little shelter in Downes Road by the sea. We exchanged gifts and shared expectations of a better and more hopeful New Year. I can't say I was anticipating a happy Christmas, but I certainly didn't foresee what lay in store.

A new light on the situation

Christmas 1956 endures in my memory for a number of reasons. First, because what passed for my love life was in tatters. Second, Northern Ireland was struck by one of the fiercest storms in its history. In Newcastle there was a total black out, caused by a power failure which lasted almost 48 hours. Far from being a White Christmas, it was the blackest one on record – in more than one respect.

Gale force winds disrupted the electricity supply in many parts of the country. Power lines were down and hundreds of Christmas dinners were ruined. Dad came down from Kilkeel and stayed over for a few days. My aunt coped wonderfully well on a little gas cooker, and a host of candles and an old oil lantern made it seem like a throwback to Christmases long ago. In the absence of television and radio, we sat huddled round the fire, yarning and telling stories.

By nightfall on Boxing Day the power still hadn't been reconnected. Having had enough of this enforced idleness, I decided to venture down town to see if anything was going on. The town centre made an eerie sight. It was pitch black, apart from the lights of passing cars and an occasional glimmer from behind curtained windows.

Passing the Palace Cinema, I bumped into Patrick, one of the *Observer's* apprentice printers, who earned some extra cash by doubling as assistant projectionist He bemoaned the fact that his employers had insisted he hung around in case the current came back on and they could open for business. "Bloody nuisance," he complained. "I probably won't even get paid and I could have been back home with the family instead of hanging around here."

Patrick lived with his parents in Aticall, outside Kilkeel, He was a cheery, affable, big fellow, standing well over six feet tall and built in proportion. A Catholic himself; like everyone else in the paper he knew how things were with Rita and me.

He suggested a stroll along the promenade and I was glad of his company. Our conversation centred on the Rita situation and he voiced his sympathy. He agreed with me that Ireland was a backward old country and that religion probably caused more problems than it cured. He told me he intended leaving shortly to join the Metropolitan Police in London.

I was genuinely sorry to hear that. He had once taken me to meet his elderly parents who lived in a humble little cottage on the lower slopes of the Mournes. It was a long way from anywhere and we'd ridden there on our bicycles. He was their only son.

"Your folks will miss you terribly, Patrick," I said. "Why the London police? Couldn't you stay here and join the RUC instead?"

He gave me an old fashioned look. "Brad, Brad, what have we just been talking about? This is Ireland. Join the RUC. My folk could never live down the disgrace!"

He was deadly serious. I didn't know whether to laugh or cry.

We walked on. Halfway along the prom the streetlights suddenly came on, lighting up the whole town. I blinked. Walking towards us, not half-a-dozen yards away, was Rita, smiling happily, arm-in-arm with a tall, good-looking black-haired fellow!

Our eyes met. The streetlights flickered and went off again.

We walked on. I looked at Patrick. "Now there's a thing," I said."

He looked at me. "It's fate," he said solemnly.

I saw Rita on the Kilkeel bus a few days later. She was alone and I eased into the seat beside her. "Hello," I said.

"Hello, Brad."

The silence dragged. I didn't know what else to say, so I let it hang.

"I'm sorry, but I won't be seeing you again."

"I've gathered as much," I replied drily. "Goodbye then."

I rose, walked to the front of the bus, and took a seat on my own.

I saw Rita only once after that, maybe six years later. I was married and I'd heard she'd married the bloke I'd seen her with on the promenade that night. I believe he was a bartender in Kilkeel. We almost literally bumped into each other in town one day. She was pushing a baby in a pram and had two other toddlers hanging on her coattails. She looked tired, and older, and had put on a little weight.

I nodded and she smiled. But it wasn't the smile I remembered.

Another parting of the ways

Tony and I were enjoying a fish supper and an orange juice in Annett's Café one Saturday. We'd been to the Vogue Cinema and were rounding the evening off in our habitual style.

"Cheer up," he said, when I'd brought him up to date on the Rita affair. "You know what they say about there being plenty more fish in the sea. I know you were fond of her, but these things happen. You'll get over it. Chalk it up to experience. It's all part of life's rich tapestry!"

"All right, all right, mate," I said. "Stop waxing lyrical, I get the message."

"A word to the wise old lad," he continued, tapping the side of his nose with a forefinger. "Stick to your own side of the house next time. Leave our lot alone. We're nothing but trouble anyway. I thought you'd have worked that out by now and have more sense."

I knew he was simply trying to cheer me up. He was a real friend. More than once, during the time Rita was banned from seeing me, he'd driven me to meet her somewhere, then make himself scarce so that we might have the car to ourselves for an hour.

"Anyway," he said, "I've something much more important than that to tell you about."

"What's that then?"

"Only that the family and I are off to Australia, lock, stock and barrel. We're going to forge a new life in the Antipodes, land of the free and of opportunity."

"What?"

"It's the honest truth. I can hardly wait. I'll be sorry to lose you, of course, but we can keep in touch. Who knows, you might even come out and join me one of these days. God knows, there's not much to keep you here."

"When is all this happening?" I asked, feeling that life had just kicked me in the teeth yet again. First my girl, now my best friend. In some ways the prospect of his leaving hurt even more.

"Not sure yet. Two, three months maybe. There's a lot of paperwork still to be done, but Dad is handling most of that. My brother, Jim, and the two girls are going as well. Jim's a joiner, as you know, and Oz is crying out for skilled tradesmen. Wages are much better than here, housing is cheap and you know what the weather is like."

My face must have shown what I was thinking, for he stopped and put a hand on my shoulder. "Come on, come on, buck up. I've already had one of my brilliant ideas. When I get out there I'm going to buy a good tape-recorder. You can buy one as well and we can record stuff and send it back and forth. It only takes four or five weeks by boat. We're going to have a ball. I'll also take stacks of photos and send them to you by airmail. That reminds me, I must get a new bottle of green ink!"

Slow, slow, quick quick, slow

I was in the café again a few evenings later with Charlie McCullough, another friend who was a teacher in a local school. He commiserated with me over the Rita affair. How I wished people would stop doing that; they meant well but it didn't help.

"I wanted to ask you something," he said. "I'm thinking of taking up ballroom dancing. Not the posh stuff, I just want to learn enough to get by at the local dances."

"Good for you, Charlie," I said, "that sounds like a plan."

"I've checked it out," he continued, "There's a Mrs Avril Shannon who runs classes in the WI Hall in Newcastle on Tuesday nights. She's supposed to be really good and her prices are reasonable. What do you say we go together?"

"That's kind of you Charlie old son, but you're not my type."

He sniggered. "Not like that, you idiot. There'll be lots of people there. Lots of nice girls. And if there isn't, once we pick up the steps we'll be able to go to dances anywhere."

"And pick up a couple of nice girls you mean?"

"Why the hell not, man. That's what life's all about."

I was about to decline Charlie's offer, but something in his last remark made me pause. "Why the hell not?" he'd said. I thought about it. I couldn't spend the long winter nights simply working and playing table tennis, and I'd finished my shorthand and typing classes long ago. Up to that time I'd never considered dancing as a pastime. Why not give it a go.

"Okay Charlie, you're on. When do we start?"

Charlie did the necessary spadework and we started two weeks later.

Getting into the swing

Charlie was the first to admit that, when it came to dancing, he had two left feet. He was a slow learner. On the other hand, all modesty aside, I fancy I took to it rather well. Perhaps it was because I'd played a lot of sports and had reasonable coordination, or maybe it was a throwback to typing practise to the strains of Victor Sylvester. Strangely enough, Victor and his Orchestra's strict tempo recordings formed a large part of our dancing programme.

By the mid-fifties modern dancing - that is waltzes, quicksteps, tangos, foxtrots and the like - was all the rage. The rock-and-roll era was about to dawn and change all that forever, but in those days, thank God, you still got to hold a girl in your arms as you sashayed round the floor.

There were two other blokes besides Charlie and myself, eight assorted girls and Miss Shannon's petite and charming assistant, Bridget. On our opening session, Mrs S, after welcoming the class and setting the scene, announced that she intended beginning with the waltz. "It's perhaps the most graceful of all the dances, when executed properly," she explained, "and it has the added merit of being the easiest to learn. If you can count to three – one, two-three – you can learn the waltz. Bridget and I will demonstrate the basic steps. You should have no difficulty in mastering them."

Pausing only to put on a record of the aforementioned Mr Sylvester, she and Bridget glided round the floor for thirty seconds in perfect harmony. While the record continued to play, Mrs Shannon approached me like a Spanish galleon under full sail, spread her arms wide and indicated I was to join her on the floor.

I barely had time to whisper to Charlie, "I knew this was going to happen," when I felt myself being whisked around in circles while Mrs S shrilled "One-two-three, one-two-three," in my ear. This was soon replaced by "Good-good-good, good-good-good." as she began to hit her straps. I was relieved, when the music stopped, to find myself still in one piece. I'd done my best, but I must have looked like an elephant on roller skates.

"That was excellent, Brad, really excellent for someone who

has never danced before," she gushed. "You will do very well, I can tell. You have a true sense of rhythm, hasn't he Bridget?"

From the corner of my eye I glimpsed Bridget giving a dutiful nod. But was that a hint of laughter I detected in her expression? The evening progressed and eventually it was my turn to dance with her.

"I saw that look of yours when Mrs Shannon asked you about my waltzing prowess," I chided her gently. "I know I'm totally useless at the moment, but I will learn. I promise. One day you and I will have a proper dance."

"Oh, I'm sorry. I certainly wasn't laughing at you. It's just how Mrs Shannon goes on. Please don't mind her, she's a dear, really. As a matter of fact, you're quite good for a beginner, easily the best dancer in the class in fact, and I do look forward to that proper dance with you one day."

It's good to talk

Surprisingly enough, I found myself looking forward with keen anticipation to the Tuesday evening lessons and I know Charlie was enjoying them too. We encouraged one another and planned that it wouldn't be too long before we sallied forth to proper dances together.

The other members of the class were a happy bunch and Mrs Shannon, who hailed from the north of England and hadn't quite lost her Yorkshire accent, was a first class teacher.

For whatever reason, Charlie wasn't able to make it to the third class. I danced with Bridget a fair bit and once she invited me onto the floor in a ladies' choice. She was encouraging and said I was progressing very nicely. During one dance I referred to her as Smithy, then immediately apologised.

"I don't mind in the least," she said. "In fact I rather like it. No one else has ever called me Smithy." From that moment onwards she was always Smithy to me.

As that dance was about to end she said, "Do you mind if I ask you a personal question?"

"Not at all."

"Why do you come here? Why do you want to learn to dance?"

I looked at her and thought, *Gosh, I don't really want to go into all that again. Why can't people just let it drop?*

"I just want to forget someone."

I hadn't meant it to sound so abrupt. Her brow puckered into a frown and I fancied I saw something in her eyes that hadn't been there before.

"I'm sorry, Smithy, I didn't mean it to come out like that. It's a really long story. Perhaps another time."

She gave a faint nod as I escorted back to her seat. "Another time then," she said softly.

By the time the lesson finished and we were due to leave, the heavens had opened and the rain was streaming down in torrents. Some of the girls were picked up in cars and the two blokes made a run for it, until only Smithy, another girl named Mildred and I were left, huddled in the shelter of the small porch.

"Where do you live?" I asked them.

"King Street, up near the harbour."

"You can't possibly go out in that. Wait here, I'll be back inside five minutes."

Pulling my jacket up about my ears, I sprinted for the printing works, where I knew the van was kept overnight. I also knew where the key was and I took it, not caring too much whether the Boss minded or not. To be on the safe side though, I left a scribbled note on his desk.

Smithy got into the passenger seat, Mildred scrambled into the back. In King Street Smithy pointed. "Mildred lives up at the top end. You can turn there and drop me off on the way back if you like."

"Thanks Brad, you're a lifesaver." Mildred waved as she scurried indoors. I drove back and stopped outside Bridget's house. "Thank you, Sir Lancelot, for rescuing two damsels in distress. You're a kind man."

"You're entirely welcome, Smithy. I could hardly leave the pair of you to tramp home in this deluge. Goodnight, and thank you for the dancing lessons. I enjoyed them."

I started to reach across to open the passenger door for her, but she made no move to go. "Are you in a hurry, Brad?"

"Not at all. I just assumed you would want to get indoors out of the wet and cold."

"Thanks to you I'm neither wet nor cold. So, if you're not in a rush and it's not a huge secret, perhaps you could tell me what it is that you're trying to forget?"

"Oh, I apologise about that. I'm afraid I was rather rude."

"You weren't in the least rude. It was I who was dreadfully nosey. I'm genuinely interested – and curious. You said it's a long story. Well, I'm up for that. Take all the time you need.""

She pulled up her knees and snuggled down into the seat. I

grabbed a tartan travel rug from the back and fixed it around her shoulders. Then I told her all about Rita and me from first meeting to last. It took a long time, as I knew it would. Apart from a couple of questions here and there, she remained silent and listened attentively throughout.

"Wow," she mused softly when I'd finished. "What a story. I've read worse books than that."

I laughed out loud. "Perhaps I will write about it one day."

"Well, I'll certainly buy it, if you do."

We chatted on for a long time after that, until finally she asked "You know I'm Catholic, don't you?"

"With a first name like Bridget, I think I could manage to work that out."

She laughed. "If you keep on calling me Smithy, nobody will ever know what I am. Please don't stop doing that though. As I said earlier, I do rather like it. Bridget is such a plain old Irish name, and Bridie or Bridge is even worse."

I promise to never call you anything but Smithy, at least when we're alone. "I'm sure Mrs. Shannon wouldn't approve if I called you that in class."

"I really don't think she'd mind. She's not as stuffy as you might think. But let me just say one thing to you, in all seriousness. I believe I'm as staunch a Catholic as the next woman, but I would never have treated anyone the way this Rita treated you. It's, it's a blooming disgrace and if I ever meet her I'll tell her so."

"Thank you for that. But, as I said, it's over now and all water under the bridge. Thanks for listening too. It's helped and it means a lot that you did. And as for her brother and her mother, well . . ."

In a strange sort of way, spelling it out in detail to Smithy had served to clarify my thinking on the subject of Rita. As Tony had advised, the whole affair was best chalked up to experience. It was still raw, of course, but it was over and done with. As the Boss would have no doubt put it, there was no use crying over spilled milk.

Smithy cut into my reverie. "You know Brad, you're well out of it. If that girl had been worth anything at all, she'd have stood by you, even if it meant defying her family. With ingrained attitudes like theirs, it's no wonder this poor country of ours is the way it is."

I treated her to a wry little smile. "If only everyone was as tolerant as you, my dear, Ireland would be a far better and happier place. Here endeth the lesson."

She smiled. I looked at my watch and gave a start. "Gracious, Smithy, do you realise it's 4:20 in the morning and we've been chatting here for over five hours! You're missing out on your beauty sleep and I have to get this old van back to base before the Boss thinks it's been nicked."

"I'm so sorry Brad, I had no idea it was so late. But your story was so interesting and I'm not in the least sleepy. Thank you for driving me home and for a wonderful evening, or should I say morning. Perhaps we can do it again sometime?"

"I'd like that, Smithy, I really would, and next time may we please talk about you for a change?"

"We'll have to see. Goodnight now. I look forward to seeing you next Tuesday. Make sure you save a dance for me."

Long hours and low prospects

It was around this time that I began to think seriously about my career. I was quite enjoying working in the *Observer,* but, frankly, the pay was ridiculous and the long hours even more so. It wasn't uncommon for me to log between seventy and eighty hours a week. If I'd been on a decent wage, with proper overtime, I'd have been significantly better off. What was even worse was my growing conviction that things were unlikely to get better any time soon.

I'd raised the matter with Hawthorne several times to no avail. He was adamant that he'd never allow a union to be established in his newspaper and he declared that he saw no need to pay for overtime.

On one occasion this topic became quite heated. I'd just logged up a 78-hour week for a take-home wage of four pounds ten shillings. We're still talking old money here; that would be £4.50 today.

It had all started calmly enough. I'd just worked nine nights out of ten, including an annual meeting of the East Down Unionist Association the previous Saturday. I typed out a list, detailed and accurate to the last minute, and handed it to him at his desk.

He read down it before handing it back. "A fair bit of work," he declared.

"I think so too," I replied mildly. "Now tell me, do you think £4.10 is fair payment for it?

He threw down the pen he had been using and swivelled in his chair to face me. "And how many hours do you think I've worked in that time? A damn sight more than 78 I can tell you!"

I cracked at that. I rarely lost my temper, but this was too much. "And how much did you earn for that?" I snapped. " A damn sight more than you paid me, I'll be bound!"

He had a real good go at me then, citing how hard he'd worked, how he'd scrimped and saved every penny until he had enough to purchase the *Dromore Weekly Times* and launch the *Observer*. How I'd no idea what he'd been through, or of what hard work was. How he'd taken me on and given me a job when he didn't have to.

"Instead of constantly carping and complaining, and expecting to be paid for doing a wee bit of overtime, you should be thankful to have a good secure job on my newspaper."

I hadn't uttered a word since he'd started his harangue. I hadn't had a chance to. But his last comment had left the door open. I smarted at the rank injustice of his outburst. I'd seldom felt so angry.

"You hit the nail smack on the head there," I yelled. "Of course you work hard. Everybody here does, including me. But you're entitled to. As you just said, it's your bloody paper, not mine – and you're taking home a damn sight more than four-and-a-half pounds every week!"

I stormed out of the office, slamming the door behind me as hard as I could.

Cooling off

I stalked straight through the printing works and was out in the street before I knew it. I was angrier than I'd ever been, literally trembling with rage. It was mid-morning but there was no way I was going back in the office. The miserable old sod could do what he liked about it. At that moment I didn't give a stuff if he sacked me or not.

I wandered up Valentia Place, cut across Main Street and began walking down the promenade. The sea was as dull and grey as my spirits. I realised I hadn't taken my jacket and the wind was biting. When I came abreast of the Broadway Café I decided a nice hot coffee was the order of the day.

I took a long time over it, then ordered a refill. I didn't feel like lunch. I didn't feel like anything much. As my anger abated, I turned my thoughts to where I stood with the Boss and what, if anything, I was going to do about this new situation. One thing was for sure – I'd be damned if I was going to apologise.

I asked myself what he might do about it. I'm sure none of his staff had ever talked to him like that before. Maybe if someone had I wouldn't be in my present predicament. Whatever. Halfway through my second coffee I decided I'd go home for lunch and report back to the office as usual at two o'clock.

The Boss was pulling on his overcoat as I opened the door.

"Mmmm, Ah," he said, in what I recognised as his normal intonation, "I've left some copy on your desk for you to go through. There's also a few proofs to check, I have to make a few calls, but I should be back before five."

Situation normal. It was as if the morning row had never been.

Smithy again

"Hello there," Smithy said while we were having our first dance of the evening. "What have you been up to since last Tuesday? Something nice I trust?"

"You don't want to know, believe me."

"Oh dear, not something else you want to forget, surely? Sounds intriguing. Going to tell me all about it later?"

"You're closer to the mark than you realise. And you wouldn't be angling for another ride home by any chance?"

She smiled. "You know you're simply dying to tell me all about it. I can tell. Alright then, you've talked me into it. Is it okay if we give Mildred a lift as well? Don't worry, she won't cramp our style. We can drop her off first, same as last week. Then you can have me all to yourself."

I looked hard into her laughing face. "Smithy, you're not flirting with me, are you?"

She wrinkled her pretty nose and winked. "As if I would. I'm already spoken for; didn't you know? I'll explain later, if we've time after you tell me about your latest adventure."

During a break Charlie asked me if I fancied a coffee in the Broadway when the class finished.

"Sorry Charlie, not this time. I promised to run Smithy home."

"Smithy?"

"Yes, you know, Bridget."

Charlie flashed a knowing grin. "Smithy is it? You crafty old basket. You don't waste any time, do you?"

"It's not like that, Charlie. I'm giving a lift to Mildred as well."

"So, something happened when I wasn't here last week. Did it?"

"Nothing happened, you suspicious sod. It was pouring with rain and I gave the girls a lift home, that's all."

Charlie glanced across the hall to where the girls were sitting. "Hmmm, pity Mildred wasn't a bit better looking. I'd make up a foursome."

"Down boy, we're not playing golf!"

"It's not golf I was thinking about. Anyway, Good luck with Smithy and behave yourself. I know what you're like."

Apart from an absence of rain, it was a virtual re-run of the previous Tuesday. We dropped Mildred off as before and parked in the same spot.

"This is getting to be a habit," I observed, as she huddled up in her seat and leant forward so I could slip the rug round her shoulders.

"Maybe. But it's a nice habit. I'm beginning to look forward to our little chats. And thank you for bringing me home too. As I said last time, you're a gentleman."

"I'm not sure I agree with you, so let's pass on that one for now."

She rubbed her hands together briskly and made a face at the night outside. "Well, perhaps not then, a real gentleman would put his arm around me and help me keep warm."

"Smithy! You must stop this flirting. I like you very much, I think you know that, but you've already told me you're spoken for. And even if you weren't, I've already had my fingers burnt with this Catholic - Protestant thing.

She was suddenly contrite. "Oh Brad, I am so sorry. How thoughtless of me. I like you too, quite a lot in fact, but I am going out with someone, have been for some time in fact. You'd like him. His name's Brendan. I'd like you to meet him one day. I wasn't flirting with you, and certainly not trying to lead you on. I would never do that. But it is cold, and if things run true to form, we're likely to be here for some time."

"Hopefully not as long as last week," I smiled. "but, if you want me to, of course I'll put my arm around you."

So I did and she eased across and snuggled into my shoulder. "It's just like dancing," she said, "except that we're not moving."

We were snug as the proverbial bugs in a rug. I told her about the row at work and how I was considering making a change. She talked about Brendan, her schoolteacher boyfriend of two years, her job as a buyer for Wadsworth's, the town's biggest fashion store, and her love of dancing, modestly glossing over the medals I'd heard she'd won. It was another late night - early morning when I walked her to her door and felt her soft lips brush my cheek.

Breaking the routine

"I've a special wee job for you tonight," said the Boss, when he buttonholed me on the following Thursday. "It's out at Ballyward,

110

which, as you know, is my old stomping ground. I'd have gone myself if it hadn't been print night, but I can't get away."

He explained the Presbyterian Church there was holding a special memorial service which would be followed by a guest tea and speeches in the adjoining hall. "It will probably be a late night, so we'll have to manage without you here. But bring the van back as soon as you can because we'll need it for deliveries. Here's the official invitation. It's in my name and I've already tendered my apologies, but you can voice them again on my behalf."

I wasn't exactly displeased at the prospect of a print-night away from the works and I was happy to find E T (Edward) Brady, the editor of the *Rathfriland Outlook,* among the guests. The papers were in competition, deadly rivals at least as far as Hawthorne was concerned. In fact, the two men were as different as chalk and cheese. I knew E T quite well, and liked him. We'd opposed one another often on the cricket field and had frequently reported on the same events.

After the service, we sat together at tea and enjoyed an amicable chat. He asked how things were going and I said something to the effect that they could be better. When the speeches were over we sat in his car and engaged in a long conversation, during which I mentioned that I might be moving on to another job before long.

"Are you seriously thinking of moving, Brad," he asked.

"Absolutely," I replied and told him why.

"But that's ridiculous for what you do and the hours you put in. Would you consider coming to work for the *Outlook?* I'm prepared to offer you twice what you're being paid now!"

"Honestly?"

I almost fell off my chair.

"Guaranteed, I had no idea you were working for that sort of salary. I'm surprised you've stuck it as long as you have."

We talked some more. He was aware I did the rounds in Kilkeel on a Monday and invited me to lunch with him in the Kilmorey Arms Hotel.

The lunch was excellent and the meeting which followed it even better. We mostly talked cricket until coffee was served, then E T got down to business.

"Now Brad, I offered you a tenner a week and I will look after your national insurance contributions on top of that. That still stands, but I have an alternative suggestion and you may choose whichever one you wish. We can make it eight pounds a week, clear of insurance, and I'm prepared to pay you forty per cent of all new advertising you bring in. What's it to be? Take your time if you want to think about it."

"I don't need time, Mr Brady. Your offer is most generous and I accept." We stood up and shook hands on it. "Good," he grinned, "I think that calls for a glass of something a little stronger than coffee!"

We toasted each other and the *Outlook* and began to sort out the fine details. He told me he'd draw up a little contract to keep things legal and above board. I'd need transport, so until that could be sorted, I could have the use of one of their vans three days a week. Would it be alright if I brought it back to Rathfriland on Thursdays and gave a hand with putting the paper to bed? One of the staff would run me home afterwards. If I needed to use public transport at any time my expenses would be reimbursed, but hopefully this would be short term until I had a car.

"Now Brad, how much notice are you required to give?"

"I hadn't thought about that, but when Stanley Maxwell left he gave a month's."

"Strictly speaking, as you're paid weekly, you're only obliged to give seven days' notice. I suggest you be more generous than he deserves and make it a fortnight's."

I smiled. I was beginning to enjoy this. I said I'd hand in my notice that coming Friday and added that I could cut down on travelling by dividing my time between living with my uncle in Newcastle and my father in Kilkeel. Things would be a lot easier when I got my own wheels. Mobile phones were still a pipedream in those days so I said I'd call the office every day.

I couldn't wait to tell the family, but took care that everyone was sworn to secrecy until I'd handed in my noticed.

Tony heads Down Under

A lot of things were changing, or were about to change. Tony and I had a last fish and chip supper in Annett's Cosy Café. I couldn't help recalling how I'd felt when I'd left for England. This was somehow more permanent. He said he'd be back one day, if I didn't show up out there first; but neither of us were at all certain we'd meet again.

His folks invited me out to their house for a meal, which ended along the lines of a typically Irish wake, with lots of hugs, and kisses and tears.

I presented them with a little Irish blackthorn shillelagh, complete with a bunch of shamrock, and finally I handed Tony a huge bottle of green ink, a genteel reminder to keep in touch.

"Make sure you buy that reel-to-reel tape recorder," he asserted. "I'll fire you off a tape as soon as we're settled."

We engulfed each other in an enormous bear-hug, the only one we ever shared. I knew I was going to miss him, far more than I can explain here.

Lords and ladies of the dance

The dancing class was cancelled on that Tuesday. Instead Mrs Shannon chaperoned us all to our first proper dance. It was held in the Annesley Hall, where I'd covered many a petty sessions court. There was a proper orchestra and a crowd of several hundred.

Typically, the class members tended to cling together, myself included. Smithy was there of course, looking positively radiant. And at long last I got to meet and be introduced to her boyfriend, Brendan, a tall and darkly handsome fellow, with a pleasant, open manner.

Perhaps I ought to have felt a twinge of the old green-eyed monster, but I didn't. Brendan was a good man, as well as a lucky one.

I told Smithy as much when we had our solitary dance of the evening. "I assume I haven't much chance of driving you home tonight?"

"I'm afraid not. I told you I was spoken for, didn't I? But don't despair, Brad, If all goes well, and you be on you best behaviour tonight, I'll see what I can do when you run me home next Tuesday."

"I guess I'll just have to settle for that then. Take care you."

Notice to quit

I'd been awaiting Friday with mixed feelings. It hadn't been easy keeping my news from the gang. The only one I'd told was Derick, as we walked home from work the previous night. We stopped and talked for a bit longer than usual at our crossroads.

He was philosophical as ever. "I can't say I'm surprised. You work even longer hours than the rest of us. D J will either have to get a new reporter, or let Kenny do it and hire another lino man. To tell the truth, I'm not sure how long I'm prepared to stay here myself."

We shook hands. I always had a lot of time for Derick. "Let's have a jar in the Legion tomorrow night and you can tell me how it went." Then he straddled his huge bike and pedalled away.

The next afternoon I waited my opportunity until the Boss was alone in the office and asked if I might have a word. He was writing at his desk and he didn't lift his head for a few seconds. I waited until I had his attention before saying.

"I'd like to hand in my notice."

"Mmmm. This is a bit sudden, isn't it?"

"Not really. I've been thinking about it for some time."

"Have you indeed. And what brought this on, I suppose it was that little performance the other day when you nearly took the door off its hinges?"

"That was part of it I suppose. You made it pretty plain where I stand. I finally realise there's no future for me here; so it's time to go."

"Is this another way of asking for a rise, Or maybe get paid for overtime. If so it won't work. I've made my position quite clear on that."

I was having trouble maintaining my cool. "You certainly have. My own position is clear too. I won't be asking you again."

"I suppose you've got another job all lined up? Where is it?"

"Yes I have, but that's not your concern. I've given you my notice and that's all I have to say, except that I'm sorry it had to end like this."

He gave a grim little smile and waved a hand towards my chair. "Look Brad, take a seat for a minute and let's see if there's anything to be done about this."

"No thanks, I'm fine here. I'm off in a minute anyway."

"Will you not give me five minutes?"

"I've already given you nearly five years."

He actually grinned and shook his head as if recalling all our ups and downs we'd had. "Very good, very good. You always had a way with words."

"I could say it didn't get me very far, but you know that already."

"Look here, Brad, what is it you actually want?"

"Just my cards in two weeks' time please."

His eyebrows shot up. "Two weeks! The usual notice is a month."

"Not for someone who's paid weekly it isn't. You're actually getting double the entitlement!"

"You've done your homework I see."

"Yes I have."

He stood up. "I tell you what I'll do. Leave this with me for a week and we'll have another chat. We'll see if something can we worked out. What do you say?"

"I'll still be here next Friday and we can talk if you want. But I doubt it will do much good."

"Let's wait and see. You might be surprised."

I bade him goodnight and had almost reached the door when he called after me. "I've got it. You're going to work for that man Brady in Rathfriland, aren't you? I'll bet he was at that meeting in Ballyward. I read his report this morning. I'd be careful of him, if I were you. That would be a bad move, boy, a very bad move."

I should have kept walking and not given him the satisfaction of an acknowledgement. But that last jibe had stung.

I turned, one hand on the door handle. "As a matter of fact he did offer me a job – at more than double the wage I'm on now, plus bonuses and a car. He couldn't understand why I'd worked here for so long for such peanuts. For that matter, neither can I!"

For a moment I thought of telling him about the 40 per cent advertising deal, but I recalled the old adage about revenge being a dish best served cold. He was going to find out soon enough. To coin a phrase, I knew where the bodies were buried! I knew where Hawthorne got his advertising revenue from around the circulation area. I'd collected the ads myself more than once.

My mind was made up. I was going to hit him where it would hurt most – in his wallet!

The lull before . . .

After a busy weekend during which I had the promised couple of jars with Derick and told him the latest; and phoned Brady with an account of my last session with Hawthorne, Monday was a relatively quiet day at work. I spent most of the time going about my usual rounds in Kilkeel. I had thought about telling our advertisers that I was joining the *Outlook,* but thought better of it in case the news reached unfriendly ears. Time enough for that later.

Tuesday passed as usual too and I couldn't wait to get to the class and give Smithy my news. As it turned out she was rather subdued and I could scarcely get a word out of her except. "Tell you all about it later." Having dropped Mildred off, I parked outside Smithy's and said lightly, "Wot's up Doc?"

"I'm afraid I'm in trouble, Brad. Someone's told Brendan you and I are having an affair!"

"What! Who? I don't understand."

"I'm not sure I do either, but I know he's very angry. I can only think that someone from the class has said something and Brendan's got the wrong end of the stick, Charlie wouldn't have made some stupid joke about us at the dance the other night, would he?"

"Of course not. He'd never do that. Do you think Mildred said something out of turn?"

"I've already asked her and she says not."

"Oh Smithy, I'm sorry. Tell you what, why don't I have a word with Brendan and straighten him out?"

"No, Brad. It would only make matters worse if he thought I'd discussed it with you. I'll talk to him myself and make him understand he's just being silly. It's most untypical of him. He's not usually like that."

"Would it help if we stopped seeing each other? I hate the thought of having caused trouble for you."

"Don't be silly. You're a good friend and we've done nothing wrong. He's going to be away on a teaching course for the next two weeks anyway, so it will have to wait until he's back. I'm sorry, I shouldn't have bothered you with it."

"Of course you should. It concerns me too, you know."

"Now, you said you had some good news for me. Come here and tell me all about it."

"Wouldn't you rather go inside; be on your own? My news will keep."

"For goodness sake," she forced a smile. "What does a girl have to do to get a hug around here? Especially when she really needs one."

So I dug out the rug and we cuddled up and I gave her chapter and verse about my new job. She was pleased for me and wanted to know if I'd still be living in Newcastle and if I'd be keeping on with the class.

Having reassured her on those points, I gave her my uncle's telephone number in case she ever needed to get in touch. "If I'm not in, leave a number and I'll ring you back. If that doesn't work ring me in the *Observer*. I'll be there until Friday week. So there you go Smithy, all bases covered."

I could tell she was really upset about the latest developments so we didn't chat as long as usual. I walked her to her door, hugged her warmly and delivered a chaste peck on her nose. Before leaving I said, "If you need anything, anything at all, just phone me. Otherwise, see you Tuesday as usual."

The offer

It was a funny old week – funny peculiar that is. The Boss and I went about our business as usual, keeping out of each other's way as much as possible. There was no mention of my notice, although I told all the other lads that I was leaving.

On the Thursday night I was working the big Cosser, thinking it might well be the last time I'd ever have to do it, and speculating with Ian Crosset about how many pages the pair of us had fed into its hungry maw over the years.

Glancing up, I noticed the Boss greeting a man I recognised as Davy Biggerstaff and escorting him into his office, where they engaged in conversation. I knew that the man hailed from Hawthorne's part of the country and that the pair were old friends, so I thought no more about it. However, about an hour later, when Ian had taken over from me on the machine, Davy came into the works and beckoned me over to a corner with a flick of his head.

The penny dropped when he uttered his first sentence. "I understand you're thinking of leaving the paper?"

The fact that he'd never shown the slightest interest in me, or my career, up to that point was a bit of a giveaway. Devious as ever, Hawthorne had primed his old crony to do his dirty work. Well, fair enough, this was going to be interesting. I might as well play along and listen to what he had to say.

"That's right, Mr Biggerstaff."

I might have asked what the hell it had to do with him, but let it ride.

"It's Davy to you," he continued. "No need for formalities."

"All right, Davy. Thanks."

He dropped his voice and turned his back as if to prevent the rest of the staff from hearing our conversation. "I wouldn't be too hasty about this, Brad. I happen to know Jim thinks a lot of you. In fact, he has some interesting plans in hand which could well involve you."

He hasn't shown much evidence of it so far, I thought. *Steady Fleming. Let's hear what the man has to say.*

"Is that so, Davy? That's interesting. He's never said anything about it to me."

His voice dropped even lower and he leaned forward conspiratorially to whisper into my ear. "That's because it's still all very hush, hush. Negotiations are at a very delicate stage, but there's every indication they'll be completed soon."

"And?"

"And what?"

"What happens when these negotiations are completed?"

Come on Davy, don't tell me you've forgotten your script?

"There will be a big part for you to play, a very important position to be filled."

"I see. And exactly what sort of position are we talking about here, and where is this position?"

"Look Brad," he said, casting a furtive glance over his shoulder to where everyone else was beavering away, heads down, "all I can tell you is that it's in your home town of Kilkeel and you'll be in total charge of it."

"So, I'll be my own boss, will I?"

"Well, Jim will be the owner, of course, but I believe he intends leaving the running of things to you!"

"And he's told you all this himself?"

"He has discussed it with me several times. As a matter of fact, he was just mentioning it a few minutes ago."

I'd heard enough. This was so ridiculous and implausible a blind man could have seen through it.

"Pull the other one, Davy. Do you think I came down the Lagan in a bubble! You're not talking about him buying the old Mourne Printing Works to open as a Kilkeel office, are you? That's old news, there's nothing hush hush about it."

Davy's mouth dropped open until his lower jaw almost rested on his chest. He had no way of knowing that, before leaving for Australia, my friend Tony had explained that the owners of the property intended to sell and that Hawthorne had expressed an interest.

"Davy, I know what you're trying to do. If Jim had any serious thoughts about making me manager of the Kilkeel office, he should have been man enough to tell me himself. God knows, he's had plenty of opportunity. He shouldn't expect you to do his dirty work for him. Did he honestly think I'd be gullible enough to withdraw my notice and soldier on here in the expectation of getting this Kilkeel job? Go back and tell him to catch himself on."

I turned away and went back up the works to help with parcelling the papers. I watched Davy head back to the office and begin chin-wagging with the Boss. Neither of them ever raised the subject with me again.

Late night phone call

My folks were retiring for the night when I got home. My aunt flashed me a conspiratorial smile as she handed me a slip of paper. "A young lady phoned earlier and asked if you would ring this number urgently. She said it didn't matter how late it was. She sounded really nice. Is she your new girlfriend?"

Immediately they left me I phoned Smithy.

"Thanks for calling, Brad."

"It must be important for you to call this late. What's up?"

Her reply was so quiet I could barely hear. "I've had a letter from Brendan. He's broken it off with me. It's over!"

"Aw Smithy, I'm sorry. Have you spoken to him?"

"No, the letter was waiting when I got home from work this evening. He's really angry. I don't' think he'd listen anyway."

I thought for a moment. "Look love, I don't have the van. And in the circumstances, I can't very well go back and ask to borrow it. But, if you like, I could walk up and see you."

No, no. Thanks, but it's much too late. I would like to see you though. Are you free tomorrow?"

"From lunchtime onwards. I was going to Kilkeel but I don't have to. I still won't have any transport, but I'll be glad to meet you."

"I don't finish until six." There was a pause. "I don't suppose you'd like to take me to the dance in the Central, would you?" The Central Ballroom, owned by local businessman, Pat Curran, was the Mecca of dancehalls in the area and, indeed had long been billed as the Best Provincial Dancehall in Ulster.

I hadn't been expecting this. "Of course I would. I'd love to, but do you think it's wise? Suppose Brendan got to hear of it; you'd be in even deeper trouble."

"The way I feel right now, I don't care if he does. I don't think I could face a night alone in the house. He and I have been out together almost every weekend for the last two years."

"Okay love, I know my uncle will let me borrow his car. What do you say I call for you about 8:30pm?"

Thank you, Brad. That would be perfect. I look forward to it."

When is a date not a date?

Over breakfast I was the butt of much good natured banter from my uncle and aunt about the previous night's phone call. When I asked if I might borrow his car, that evening he assented readily enough, but told me to behave myself. I'd given them a partial explanation of why I needed it, but his parting words were "You've already had one unfortunate experience with a young Catholic girl. Make sure you don't have another."

There was no point in trying to explain that it simply wasn't like that. I doubt If I'd have been believed. Anyway, I wasn't the one in trouble. It was Smithy's problem and I had contributed to it. I was determined to sort out this mess if I could.

Nothing untoward arose at work during the day and I drove to Smithy's, arriving on the stroke of 8:30. I got a warm "Thank you" as I handed her into the car. "Well," she said, "I must say this is a decided step up from the *MO's* van."

The dancehall was beginning to fill up as we arrived, and the resident Pioneers' band was already tuning up. I glimpsed a familiar face across the floor and a second later Derick came over. I introduced him to Smithy, remembering to use her proper name. He stayed chatting to us for a few minutes before returning to his friends.

Later in the evening, he snatched a private word with me. "Congratulations mate," he declared. "You certainly don't hang about, do you? Actually I've known Bridget for a few years. She's a lovely girl. I just hope you don't hit the same snag you did with Rita Cunningham!"

I told him it wasn't like that and I'd explain when I had the chance. He just winked in a nudge, nudge, kind of way and went back to his pals.

Dancing with Smithy, and especially having her all to myself, made us, at least temporarily, forget our current problems. She was a magnificent dancer – to this day the best I've ever known - as light as a feather on her feet, and she seemed to know instinctively which direction I was going to turn next, as often as not before I realised it myself. She'd already shown me a lot of new steps and combinations, and whatever progress I was making was almost entirely down to her.

Occasionally we sat out a dance at one of the side tables, sipped our lemonades, and chatted about anything and everything, except what was really on her mind.

It was perhaps an hour later when we finished a quickstep and were close to the hall's large double entrance doors. I had my arm around her waist, prior to leading her back to our table, when I felt her stiffen and heard her faint indrawing of breath. I followed her gaze and there was Brendan, standing with a bunch of men not five yards away, with a countenance that would have halted a charging lion in its tracks.

Our little tableau stood frozen in time for what seemed ages, but which in reality could have been no more than seconds. Smithy threw out her left arm and took a pace towards him, but he turned away abruptly and strode straight out through the door.

By the time we reached our table Smithy was trembling, her face white as chalk. I put my hand over hers but she simply stared at me and whispered. "Well, I guess that's that. He must have decided to come home for the weekend without telling me. There's no way we're getting back together now."

We stayed a little longer, had a few more dances, but I could tell her heart wasn't in it. She didn't demur when I suggested running her home and barely said a word on the drive to King Street. I quite expected her to say goodnight and head straight indoors, but she shifted towards me and said simply, "Just hold me for a minute please, Brad." She remained in my arms for a long time, until I felt her body tremble and realised she was crying.

By the time the tears stopped I'd made up my mind. "Right Smithy. I know Brendan lives in Clough, but I need you to give me his full address."

"What are you going to do? You saw how he looked at us. He'll never forgive me. Anyway, after that dirty look he gave me, I'm not sure I want him to."

"As I told you once before, Brendan needs straightening out. He needs to know the score. Obviously he won't talk to you at the moment, but he's going to listen to me."

"He's got a temper on him and he's more likely to knock your head off. I've never seen him look so angry."

"I'm not prepared to leave things as they are. I presume he'll stay home for the weekend before going back to his course. I'll give him a call tomorrow and let you know how I get on next Tuesday."

We didn't say a lot more after that, simply stayed in a tight cuddle for a long, long time. I remember one thing she did say though, as if it were yesterday. Still in our little clinch, she tilted her head, looked straight into my eyes and said. "There's one thing I want you to know, Brad. I like Brendan, I always have. But I like you too, very much."

She linked her fingers behind my head and gave me a long kiss on the lips. It was the only proper kiss we ever shared.

Straightening out Brendan

Shortly after breakfast next morning, I borrowed the car again, promising my folks a full explanation when I returned, and headed for Clough. On the short journey I kept running over in my head exactly what I wanted to say and wondering about the kind of reception I was likely to get. One thing I must avoid at all costs was to use the name Smithy.

I rang the front door bell and was relieved when the door was opened by the man himself, tall, dark and handsome as ever, in an open-necked spotless white shirt with the sleeves rolled up neatly to just below his elbows.

He stood there, face expressionless, still clutching the door-handle.

"Hello Brendan. I know I'm probably the last person you want to see just now, but I'd like a word please. You and I really do need to talk."

Time seemed to stand still for a while. It looked like an even money bet whether I'd get a reply, or have the door slammed in my face. In the end he gave the slightest of nods, opened the door wide, stepped back and said "You'd better come in."

He ushered me into a comfortable sitting room and waved me to a chair. He didn't take a seat himself, but stood, arms folded, staring down at me. He waited, saying nothing. He certainly wasn't intending to make this easy.

"Thank you for seeing me, Brendan," I began hesitantly. "I'm here because I feel you're owed an explanation. I believe you think I'm trying to snatch your girlfriend, Bridget away from you. I can imagine how it must look like to you, but I assure you that isn't the case."

"It certainly looked like the case when I saw the two of you in the Central last night!"

"I know, and I do understand that and how it must seem to you. But if you'll hear me out, I'd like to explain how all this happened. Bridget has told me all about you two and how you've been together for around two years. I couldn't have cut in on your relationship even if I'd wanted to, and I certainly wouldn't have come here this morning if I'd any designs on Bridget."

Brendan took a seat on the arm of an armchair, arms still folded across his chest. "I'm listening."

"Thank you. I'm afraid it's a rather long story but I'll try to make it as brief as possible. He listened intently, but in silence, while I outlined the events of the last few months - the Rita affair, my friend Tony's departure, my forthcoming change of jobs and my joining Mrs Shannon's dancing academy.

"All told, I was at a pretty low ebb," I finished. "I hadn't been able to confide in anyone until Bridget sensed something was troubling me and was kind and patient enough to listen when I ran her and her friend, Mildred, home one night after class because it was raining. Bridget's a great girl and has become a good and caring friend.

"She has been a tremendous help in getting me through an extremely tough time. I can totally understand what you must have thought about us, but I can assure you that girl loves you very much. I may be her friend, but it's you she loves. Please don't let her go. I'm not any kind of threat to you, Brendan. I never could be."

He looked at me for a long time before getting to his feet with a broad smile and sticking out a hand, which I took.

"Thanks, Brad, for coming here and telling me all this. It took a lot of guts. I can see why Bridget is so fond of you. I admit I was jealous, and angry, especially last night when I thought I had caught the pair of you out. I'll get in touch with Bridget later on, apologise and get things back on an even keel. By the way, you say you're lucky to have Bridget as a friend. I think that works the other way round as well. Now, you'll take a cup of something before you go?"

The final week

Smithy flung her arms around my neck, engulfed me in an enormous hug and said, "Thank you so much for what you did with Brendan. You're quite a man."

"Put me down woman, before Mrs Shannon chucks a bucket of cold water over us."

We both knew it would be the last time I'd drive her home from the class in the *MO's* van; the last time we'd cuddle up against the cold and talk far into the night. It was the end of another chapter in my life. A new page would soon be turned.

She told me how Brendan had been in touch, apologised for being such a clot and for ever doubting her. He related how I'd gone over to see him and explained everything. Things between them were now back in good standing.

I told Smithy I was quitting the class and thanked her for everything she'd helped me with. It was time for this ugly duckling to leave the nest and seek out new fields to explore.

She pouted. "But I'll miss you. You're too good a friend to lose. I meant it the other night when I tried to explain how I felt about you. Besides, I'm well on the way to making a half-decent dancer of you. It would be a shame if I couldn't finish the job."

"You'll never lose me Smithy. The time we've had together was special. But you've got your Brendan back again, and no matter what he says, if I keep on seeing you he's always going to perceive me as a threat. And he's probably right about that. You may not be aware of it, but it was always a struggle for me to be on my best behaviour when I was with you."

She looked at me hard. "You never told me that."

"And now you know why."

Apart from a casual meeting in the street one day, I never saw Smithy again. There is a postscript though. Nearly eighteen months later, on my wedding day, my best man read out a number of congratulatory cards and telegrams. The inscription on one said simply – Best Wishes to you both – Smithy.

A silent departure

To be truthful, I don't remember much about my last week in the *Observer*. The boys had a little whip round for me and a few of us had a drink that Friday night. By unspoken agreement I didn't put in an appearance on the Saturday and took the bus to Kilkeel instead.

I do remember the Boss handing over my last little brown envelope, with a muted "Mmmm" and the slightest of nods – and I do recall that it didn't contain any farewell bonus. But then I hadn't expected one, so I wasn't unduly disappointed.

There had been no further visit from Davy Biggerstaff on the Thursday night and the promised final conversation with Hawthorne never materialised either. I guess matters had gone too far for either of us to change our minds.

Derick and I walked back to the works after our little drinks session, he to collect his king-size bike, I to pick up my portable typewriter and a half-used shorthand notebook I was now going to complete on another newspaper.

Derick and I stopped at our familiar crossroads for the last of perhaps five-hundred conversations.

"I'm not going to say goodbye," he said. "It's not as if you're leaving the country after all. So I'll be seeing you around as usual. We shook hands, wished one another luck and I stood and watched him ride that ridiculous bicycle on his homeward way until he disappeared from sight.

A new paper and a new beginning

I'd love to have spent the weekend in the company of Smithy, or Tony, or Derick. Instead I spent it in Kilkeel with Dad, talking things over, and later jotting down some ideas of how I was going to go about my new job.

Dad, wise and cautious as ever, said he hoped I was doing the right thing. He appreciated the fact that I appeared to have found a more sympathetic and understanding new boss and stood to be better rewarded for my work, but I fear he may have believed it was all a bit too good to be true.

"It's a chance to prove myself, Dad," I told him. "I doubt I was ever fully appreciated in the *Observer,* whereas I believe Mr Brady shares my belief that I can make a go of this. He's certainly giving me every incentive and opportunity to do that. I think you know I want to specialise in journalism; proper journalism that is. In the *Observer* I was expected to do a bit of everything, be a jack of all trades, but basically I just want to write. And if I don't succeed it won't be for any lack of effort on my part."

Dad nodded and said he was going out for a while, leaving me with a pencil and notebook to draw up my plan of campaign.

Essentially this was a matter of attracting new readers and pinching as many of Jim Hawthorne's as I could. I had no illusions it would be easy. There wasn't much I could do about the established sources of news. The courts, councils, police, hospitals, political and farmers' meetings would have to be reported as a matter of routine.

I felt it was important to provide blanket coverage of sport – all sport, from football and cricket, to golf and Gaelic games. Happily, I had a notebook full of contacts from my own playing days and I was determined to add to these as the weeks went by. I drafted a pamphlet which would be printed and distributed to sports clubs and secretaries all over my patch. And much as I hated it, I was also going to ask for a supply of wedding and obituary forms to be made ready.

I made plans to visit every photographer and photo agency in every town on the look-out for material I could use, particularly wedding pictures. Instead of cash payment, I'd guarantee them a tag-line on every picture we published.

With my forty percent cut in mind, I listed every shop and

business I intended approaching for advertising. It wasn't something I was particularly looking forward to doing, but I appreciated a newspaper can't run on sales alone. I also wanted to run a weekly gossip column, although I branded it a human interest corner, and I'd invite contributions. Everybody loves a nice bit of tittle-tattle, and as long as it didn't land either the editor or me in court, I'd be happy to give it to them. The magazine *Private Eye* did much the same thing, on a much larger scale, years later.

There was a lot of other ideas too. My chief concern was how I was going to find the time to fit it all in. I was well used to late nights and long hours, but I was mindful of the old adage - All work and no play can give Jack a dull life.

Local band attacked

On the Saturday night the news swept throughout Kilkeel that the local Glenloughan Flute Band, based on the outskirts of the town, had been attacked by a mob of stone- and bottle-throwing louts while taking part in a parade in Lurgan that afternoon. Thankfully no one was badly hurt, but the incident was untypical during a period of comparative peace in Northern Ireland.

I knew a fair number of the bandsmen and women personally, indeed had been to primary school with several of them. I got on the phone and arranged to visit them on Monday evening. I figured I wasn't going to have to look much farther than that for my front page lead story.

My first Monday was even busier than I had imagined. I started early with a round of potential advertisers. I'd known most of them since I was just out of nappies, and I made no bones about why I'd quit the *Observer* for the *Outlook*, taking care not to denigrate my former paper or its owner in any way. I'd long ago decided I was going to play fair, go straight down the middle, and be totally impartial and businesslike.

Perhaps I did better than even I expected. I had my share of refusals, and maybe a few traders were generous enough to do the new boy a favour. Whatever, by the time my new editor and I set down to lunch in the Kilmorey Arms I was able to tell him that round of the shops had already netted us just shy of £50.

The look on his face was priceless. Then he smiled and remarked, "You mean I collect sixty percent of that?"

I smiled. "It's as good as in the kitty, and I have as many more calls to make in the afternoon. I'll give you the details on Thursday so that bills can be sent out."

He stroked his chin. "But that would cover your salary for a month and its only your first morning."

My grin widened. "I'm not complaining either."

We talked for over an hour and I furnished him with a list of my ideas. "I know it's going to mean a lot of work and it will take time, but once we get going I expect our circulation to increase steadily."

He inched forward in his chair. "I intended raising that point with you, Brad, and I have a proposition to put to you. Starting today, I want to offer you ten percent of all increased sales resulting from your efforts, after printing costs. I'll do the sums and let you know when you come up on Thursday."

I was touched. "Mr Brady, you don't have to do that. You've been more than generous already. I'm more than happy with our present arrangement."

He waved my protest aside and ordered two more coffees. After taking his first sip, he looked me straight in the eye, grinned hugely, shook his head and said quietly, "And Hawthorne was paying you just £4.10 a week!

Painter's progress

Charlie picked me up in his car after tea and we drove out to Glenloughan. I knew he had links to the Orange Order and, as an architect, had played a part in the design of the new hall, which was to be officially opened on Saturday afternoon by a prominent MP.

I did the rounds of the officers and the bandsmen, recorded their accounts of the attack on them and took several photographs. I told them I looked forward to reporting the opening ceremony and promised to give them a good spread. To put the icing on the cake, the lodge secretary ordered me to place a double-column advert for the opening in Friday's paper.

I was in no hurry home and asked if I could lend a hand with any work that was going on. Charlie appeared and told the secretary I was a dab hand with a paintbrush and was the very man to put on a coat of clear gloss paint to finish off the sign over the entrance. What could I say?

So there I was, up a ladder, wielding a paintbrush, when a familiar van pulled in and my old boss stepped out.

"Mmmm," he called out, "I see you've got a new job!"

"The pay's an improvement too," I couldn't resist re-joining.

He'd obviously come to do a story on Saturday's fracas so I

carried on painting and left him to it.

As dusk was settling in, everyone was invited inside for a cup of tea. Charlie said he needed a chat with the committee and could I possibly cadge a lift back home with my old boss. I was sure he was having his own little joke, but I asked Hawthorne if it was all right.

"Certainly, he replied. "Hop in."

I suppose we both felt the irony of sharing that old van again. I know thoughts of Smithy flashed through my mind.

"Mmmm, I didn't know you were a member of Glenloughan Lodge," he enquired.

"I'm not. As I thought you knew, I'm not in the Orange Order at all."

"It was just when I saw you up that ladder with a paintbrush, I thought you must be."

"Not at all. I was only lending a hand to some old friends."

Happy in my work

I worked like the proverbial beaver all that first week, probably logging more hours than I had in the *Observer*. The big difference was I felt I was working as much for my own future as for the *Outlook*. Brady had been more than fair with me and I was determined to do as much for him.

I did the rounds during the day and typed up columns of copy, working well into the small hours. We'd already arranged for my copy to be collected by someone from Rathfriland or to have it picked up off the bus. I picked up the van, a year-old, shiny Ford Thames, on Tuesday evening and visited Newcastle and Castlewellan on the Wednesday. As this was the *Observer's* heartland, I wasn't able to repeat the success of Kilkeel, but still managed enough to make it worthwhile.

I'd known some of the local photographers for years and Nicky McConville in Kilkeel, Tom and Isaac Smyth and Ronnie's' Studios in Newcastle were delighted to provide wedding and presentation photographs in return for a mention. I also made good use of my own camera. That first week alone I garnered enough wedding pictures and reports to make a double-page spread. Weddings were a brilliant circulation booster and the brides' and grooms' families would purchase dozens of newspapers to send to relatives and friends all over the world.

I returned the van on Thursday afternoon, at the same time

delivering more stories and pictures. I was introduced to the staff, including E T's son, Alan, and the paper's *Girl Friday*, Vera McDowell, who seemed to fulfil every chore from advertising manager and proof-reader in chief, to accountant and tea-maker. She was delighted when I presented her with the details of the adverts I'd collected. I was surprised and delighted to find the advertising revenue amounted to almost £100. I insisted on not taking my share of that revenue until all bills had been settled.

In my time in Rathfriland I'm happy to say that every single advertiser paid up on the nose. It took me a long time to rationalise that I would have had to work for three months in the *MO* to earn the sum I took home in my first week.

My new boss drove Alan and me to their home, just outside the town, where I was introduced to and welcomed by Mrs Brady, a delightful woman. After we'd enjoyed a truly wonderful meal, Brady called me into his study, shook me warmly by the hand and insisted we shared a toast to our successful enterprise.

"I was confident our little arrangement would work well to our mutual advantage, Brad, but I have to say I couldn't have imagined anything like this. Long may it continue. And it's high time you stopped calling me Mr Brady. It's E T or Edward to you from now on."

"Thank you," I responded. I can scarcely believe it myself."

"You and I should have got together years ago."

"Amen to that," I smiled. "Here's to carrying on as we've started."

Openings and opportunities

The official opening of Glenloughan Hall on the Saturday afternoon was a splendid affair. Alan Brady and his girlfriend Rita Shields picked me up at home and drove me out there before heading off together. I said I'd find my own way home. In the manner of these affairs, there was plenty of copy and I took a number of photographs.

I was pleased that several officials came up to congratulate me on my report, which had appeared the previous day. "You certainly gave us a good show, Brad," the WM said, and sticking up a thumb in the direction of the sign over the entrance, added with a wink, "and that wee bit of painting you did sure looks well."

I typed my report of the opening on Sunday afternoon and sent it, together with the spool of film I'd taken, on the bus to Rathfriland before starting my rounds on Monday morning.

I was back in Glenloughan again on Tuesday night, as a guest at an official opening dance. Charlie had also been invited and picked me up in his car. A large crowd turned up, including many familiar faces.

Quite late in proceedings my attention was drawn to one of the dancers, an attractive, blonde girl whose golden tan was accentuated by a sleeveless ivory-coloured cocktail dress. I invited her on to the floor at the first opportunity and quickly discovered that her name was Norma Hanna. Although I couldn't recall meeting her before, it turned out that I had been to school with her brothers, Bertie and Cyril.

We danced together and chatted pretty much for the rest of the evening. As the dance was coming to a close I apologised for not being able to offer her a ride home, as I had come in a friend's car. She smiled and said I wasn't to leave her home in any case. However, she did agree to meet me the following Tuesday and gave me her address. Slightly surprised by her ready acceptance, I thanked her and said I looked forward to seeing her then.

I found her final remark intriguing. "I look forward to seeing you too," she said as she turned to go. "But if you're looking for any sort of permanent relationship then I think you'd better find someone else."

"How enigmatic is that?" I confided to Charles as we drove home.

Another first date

My second week in the *Outlook* followed much the same lines as the first and I was gratified that almost all the advertisers supported me again. I also found myself looking forward to Tuesday evening with increasing anticipation.

My knock on the Hanna front door was answered by my old school chum, Bertie. He was glad to see me, and when I enquired about Norma, explained that she'd gone out half an hour earlier to call on their married sister, who lived in a bungalow half-a-mile farther down the road. He stepped forward to point out the house.

I thanked him, and after a brief chat, was on my way. This time my knock was answered by a woman who looked about five years' Norma's senior. On learning the purpose of my visit she stood aside and invited me in. Norma was in the sitting-room and rose as I entered. "Hello. So you did come?"

"It rather looks as though you thought I wouldn't. When you know me better you'll find I always keep my promises."

Perhaps sensing a slight atmosphere, her sister asked if I'd care for a cup of tea, or a drink. I declined politely and Norma performed the introductions. "Where are you two off to?" her sister said.

"I don't mind at all," I replied, looking at Norma.

"Well, wherever you end up do have a nice time."

In in end we decided on the cinema in Warrenpoint. The movie was called *Lost* but, at this distance in time, I can't remember a thing about it.

As we drove along I referred to her closing remark at the dance. "So, you're not looking for a permanent relationship? That's fairly conclusive."

"It's no more than the truth. I wouldn't want you to think otherwise."

"Well, Norma," I said lightly. "A fellow likes to know where he stands, and now you've made that pretty clear."

She actually smiled. "I suppose that did sound a bit stark. The thing is I wouldn't want you to have any false aspirations. I could tell from how our conversation was going in Glenloughan that you might want to head in that direction."

"And you're saying I shouldn't, even before we've got to know one another properly?"

She paused for a moment and then it all came tumbling out.

"Look Brad, you seem like a very nice fellow and I enjoyed talking and dancing with you the other night. If I hadn't, I wouldn't have agreed to our date. The thing is, I've just made up with a fellow I used to go out with some time ago, and we've started dating again. I haven't quite made up my mind about him yet. His name's John Little, you may know him?"

I nodded. "Not very well, but I've seen him around. Now, accuse me of having a vested interest and I'd have to agree with you, but if this is your second time around and you've yet to make up your mind, then he's not for you. All I can say is that I would like to see you again, so it looks as if the ball's in your court. Would you like to think about it?"

"Thank you, I would. John is taking a fortnight's holiday starting Monday, so I wouldn't be able to see you anyway. We're not going anywhere, so you may see us around. If you'd like to see me after that then that's fine."

"Fair enough, Norma. Let's leave it like that. I'll be in touch the week of the 23rd. I think I'd like to see you again, but not as part of a threesome."

I dropped her home, shared a warm kiss, and drove back to Kilkeel.

A long, hot, busy summer

Work was progressing well and a routine was beginning to form which enabled me to enjoy much more free time. I joined the Newcastle Tennis Club, which, happily, enabled me to retain contact with Derick and Clifford Mills from the *MO,* and many of my friends. I was useless at tennis, but typically, persevered to the extent that it led to trouble. More of that in a moment.

Charlie was kind enough to drive me to a few dances, at two of which I bumped into Norma and John Little. I kept well away but once, as we passed on the floor, she flashed me a dazzling smile over her escort's shoulder. I returned it, but only after poking out my tongue and treating her to a huge wink.

In those days it was the custom for most weekly newspapers to shut down for a week in summer, usually the week of the Twelfth of July. While the time off was welcome, it meant I was deprived of my midweek transport. That was one reason I spent hours at the tennis club every day, with only a short break for lunch. There weren't many signs of improvement, but I consoled myself that, at least, I was keeping fit.

In bed on the Saturday night I felt a severe stabbing pain in my right shoulder and upper arm. It grew worse on the Sunday and eventually I called to see Dr Craig, my local GP. He was typically good about it and insisted on driving me to hospital for injections and an X-ray. They put my arm in a sling and took my temperature, which was high. They wanted me to stay overnight but I elected to go home and straight to bed, where I spent a restless night.

The doctor called next morning to find the pain much worse and my temperature even higher. "It's back to hospital for you my lad," he said. "to be admitted this time."

I didn't argue. Before being put to bed and injected with what I presumed was morphine, I was allowed to ring the *Outlook* and my folks in Newcastle and inform them of my plight. ET said not to worry and that Alan would do my rounds and cover for me until I was discharged. "And don't be concerned about money," he added, "your pay will continue as usual." So typical of the man. I asked my aunt in Newcastle to tell the gang I'd be laid up for a while.

Although the pain persisted, regular injections kept it bearable. The hospital staff were tremendous - a relaxed, cheerful and friendly lot. I was touched by the number of folk who came to see me, once word of my incarceration had spread.

On the Thursday I was taken by ambulance to Daisy Hill Hospital in Newry for another X-ray. Dr Baker, a genial specialist, put the film on an illuminated screen and talked me through it. "Your problem is a classic case of bursitis," he explained, waving a fountain pen at the image of my innards. "It's an inflammation of a bursa and occurs principally in the shoulder and upper arm. What happens is the fluid between the layers of fibre crystallises and forms little granules which can cause intense pain when you move. The condition is usually attributed to overuse of those muscles. I can tell you the worst is over and it's clearing up. What it needs is rest for a week or so. A little gentle swimming is good too if you can manage it, but avoid anything too strenuous."

I couldn't help grinning. "You're certainly right about the pain. I have been playing quite a lot of tennis lately. I suppose that didn't help?"

He shook his head sagely. "That explains it. Cut it out for a few weeks and when you start again don't overdo it."

I thought of telling him about all the months I'd spent wielding a hammer and cold-chisel channeling tracks in concrete walls in the service of Davy McConville, with no ill-effects, but let it pass. I was just relieved to be given the all-clear.

Having passed my final medical inspection on the Friday, I was told I could leave the following day. On my last evening I was honoured to be invited into the hospital's common room where the nurses threw a little party for me. I felt it ought to have been the other way round. Then next morning I was off home, feeling almost as good as new.

Back on the circuit

Back in Newcastle. I phoned ET and explained that normal service would resume on Monday morning. I also thanked him for last week's pay packet which Alan had already delivered. I dropped by the tennis club, but only as a spectator. It was good to be back in the swim. Quite literally in fact, for I followed doctor's orders and had a few gentle lengths in the pool Monday morning before heading for Kilkeel.

I was given a further boost when I reached Kilkeel and bumped into Jim McCulla, who ran a comprehensive business in Greencastle Street which incorporated a large hardware and general store. He'd been one of those who'd declined to advertise with us when approached in my first week. "If you call in the shop later I'll have an advertisement for you," he said. "I've decided to use your paper and the *Observer* in alternate weeks."

I thanked him and said I would. I was certain his change of heart had been prompted by the fact that his great rivals, Sam and Jim Knox, who ran a similar business, and had given me adverts from week one, had clearly been benefiting from it. I had to admit that this would also be a particular thorn in the side of Jim Hawthorne. He would hate having to share a client and especially, losing half the income.

A profitable morning was completed when I met Jim Annett, the town's principal auctioneer and estate agent. He asked if I would be prepared to offer a cut-price rate for advertising in all his forthcoming business. Over a cup of tea in his office, he proposed 15 per cent. I suggested 10, and we settled on 12.5. This was huge, steady business for the future and I knew ET, who had been rebuffed by Jim several times in the past, would be delighted.

Advertising was going well, but I knew I had to produce lots of news, sports coverage and features to attract readers and boost circulation. My weekly chat column was already arousing interest and the editor and Alan were augmenting it with items from Rathfriland. I launched a similar kind of column in the sports section. It's commonplace in daily newspapers nowadays, but it was something of an innovation in 1957. Gossip and behind the scenes comment from football, cricket, GAA and other sports quickly became a talking point in those circles.

Weddings continued to attract readers and most weeks we had anything up to two pages of pictures. So much so that the *Observer* was compelled to follow suit. As often as not though, we managed to beat them to the punch. By the end of my fourth week a delighted ET informed me that sales had gone up by more than 500 since I'd arrived.

Absence makes the heart . . .

I hadn't spoken to Norma in more than three weeks, so I was looking forward to our meeting on Tuesday evening and hearing how things were with her.

We had dinner in Newry and then strolled along by the canal. It was a balmy, late-summer evening and she sympathised over my brief sojourn in hospital. Had she known at the time she would certainly have paid me a visit.

"You couldn't be expected to know," I said, "but it would have been good to see you. I take it you saw lots of John during his holidays?"

"I saw you keeping an eye on us at a few dances," she smiled.

"I'd no intention of inviting him outside to settle our differences," I rejoined, "He's much bigger than me for a start. I presume you two are still an item – and, if so – where does that leave us?"

"Actually, I wanted to talk about that. I've got a feeling John knows about us. Nothing concrete, but he hasn't been in touch for a while, which isn't like him."

"I suppose I ought to say I'm sorry, but I'd be lying if I did."

"You're dreadful, but I suppose that's an honest thing to say."

"Are you going to get in touch with him?"

"No."

"Why not?"

"Because it's not my place to. He has my phone number if he wants to use it. I don't chase anyone."

"I can understand that all right. So, what about us? Do you still want to see me?"

"Do you want to keep on seeing me?"

"Norma, you're a dab hand at answering a question with another question. Of course I want to see you. I'm here tonight, aren't I?

A broad smile. "I see you know how to answer a question with a question yourself. But yes, you *are* here – and I'm glad."

She stopped suddenly, flung her arms round my neck and gave me a resounding kiss.

"Good answer," I said and returned her kiss with interest.

Dirty work at the crossroads

So far, affairs between Jim Hawthorne and me had been conducted in an upright and professional manner. Both of us seemed prepared to play by our own Marquis of Queensbury type rules. Sadly, that was to change.

Unknown to me, while making some changes in the Rathfriland edition of the paper last week, a page containing a number of adverts from Kilkeel shops had been omitted. Although they had appeared in all other editions, including Kilkeel, this was an unfortunate mistake. Worse still, it was immediately seized upon by Hawthorne, who marched round the shops in Kilkeel, brandishing the different editions and informing them that this was how they were being short-changed.

There's no doubt this was a potentially damaging matter and I wasn't best pleased when I had to draw Brady's attention to it on the phone. Neither was he when he heard the news and immediately apologised.

"I'm dreadfully sorry about this, Brad. It's entirely my fault and is no reflection on you whatsoever. Tell me, is there anything we can do to put it right?"

"Leave it with me, ET," I said, "just promise it will never be repeated."

The first thing I did was to visit every business concerned, apologise for what had been a genuine mistake and give them my personal assurance that it would never happen again. I explained that their advertisement had appeared in every single edition of the paper, apart from the late, local Rathfriland one, so they would still derive full local benefit from it.

"In the circumstances, however, you won't be charged one penny for this ad and we will repeat it in all editions in our next issue at no cost to you. I'm truly sorry it happened and I promise you won't lose out by it."

I'm delighted to say that every single trader accepted my explanation that an honest mistake had been made. This including those who had not been directly affected by what had happened. I shook hands with each one of them and several actually went so far as to suggest that it had been a rather vindictive action by our opposition. Not wishing to be tarred with the same brush, I contented myself by replying, "I think so too, but I'm glad it was you who said that."

ET was a much relieved man when I reported back and he complimented me on being able to smooth things over. Hawthorne and I never referred to the incident, but I do know it didn't cost us a single advertiser. I wondered, sometimes, what it might have done to his own reputation. I know it certainly went down a few notches in my book.

Still more changes

It appeared that Norma had been right in believing that John Little had found out about us. She still hadn't heard from him and clearly was determined not to make the first approach herself.

"Feeling sad about it?" I asked her.

She wrinkled her pretty nose. "I suppose I am in a way; a girl doesn't like being dumped, whatever the reason. I do think he might have told me so himself though."

"Norma, it's my fault and to that extent I'm sorry. But I'm not sorry for having met you."

She smiled that wide smile. "Thank you Brad. I think I needed that."

She raised her head and proffered a gentle kiss.

We drove to Rostrevor and took advantage of the warm evening to walk along by the northern shore of Carlingford Lough. She clung to my hand in a way she hadn't done before. Perhaps, for the first time since I'd known her, a hidden vulnerability was showing. A little farther on we sat on a summer-seat for a long time, huddled close together, not speaking, each of us simply thinking our own thoughts.

The last feature

Over a period of about six months while I'd been in the *Observer* I'd compiled a series of feature articles under the heading of Old Families of the Mourne Country. It had proved popular and I'd enjoyed interviewing the families and writing about their histories and experiences. Many of the people I talked to had rare tales to tell and some allowed me to borrow treasured old photographs to accompany my writings.

I remember travelling to Mourne Park, outside Kilkeel, to talk to the Earl of Kilmorey for the first of the series and noticing, as the butler admitted me and led me down the panelled entrance hall to meet his Lordship, a tiny mouse poking its nose out from behind one of several suits of armour, its whiskers quivering as we paraded by. If he was aware of its presence, the butler certainly didn't divulge the fact, but continued serenely onwards.

Dorothy Grace Waring, who was popularly known as D G, was a fascinating interviewee. One of the last in line of an old upper-class Protestant family from County Cavan, now resident just outside Kilkeel, she had written a number of historical novels, many of them set in Ireland, and was a regular panellist on BBC Northern Ireland quiz and talk shows.

We chatted in her book-lined sitting room while, clad in an ornate kaftan, she reclined on a chaise longue, surrounded by no less than a dozen assorted cats, all of whom had quite ridiculous exotic names. They either ignored me completely, or, with arched backs, hissed complainingly at my intrusiveness. Our talk may well have been longer but for the fact that I was almost overcome by the acid stench of cat urine which pervaded the large room.

One of my most enjoyable encounters was with Mr Archie Gordon, a unique and remarkable old gentleman, who was the closest that Kilkeel had ever got to having its own squire. Always impeccably attired in smart hacking-jacket, jodhpurs and black riding-boots, he was a familiar figure as he rode through the town on his magnificent chestnut gelding. He was a splendid raconteur and claimed he had done everything from prospecting for gold in the Yukon, to herding cattle in the Argentine pampas and running a sheep station in Australia. It was both a pleasure and a privilege to have interviewed him.

Occasionally, after I'd left the *Observer,* one of these features would appear and when I read the last one I suppose I knew the umbilical cord had been finally severed.

Out in the open

Now that the liaison between Norma and John Little had finished, there seemed no good reason for keeping our relationship under wraps. There were other places to go besides Newry, Warrenpoint and Rostrevor. We had no wish to confine our meetings to Tuesday and Wednesday evenings either, but the absence of a car of my own was becoming a positive hindrance.

Charlie, who strongly approved of my relationship with Norma, had himself acquired a new girlfriend, the charming Jeanie, whom he introduced to us one evening with proprietorial delight. By way of celebration he drove the four of us to Newcastle, where, after a coffee in the Broadway, we enjoyed a night's dancing in the Central. While I was relieved to have everything out in the open, I sensed that Norma was always figuratively looking over her shoulder in case we should bump into John. As it happens we never did.

Over dinner at his home one Thursday evening, ET, who I'd discovered enjoyed his little ceremonies, solemnly presented me with a cheque representing my first 40 percent share of advertising revenue. Up to that time it was probably the largest amount I'd ever held in my hand.

"If you don't already have a bank account," he said, "I strongly advise that you open one and start it off with that."

He waved aside my thanks and said he was certain it was the

precursor of many more. Turning to the subject of transport, he continued, "I believe it's high time you had your own car. Why don't you look out for one, and if you see one you fancy we'll discuss it. It would be much better all round, and if you like, I'll help out with the finances and it can be insured through the firm so that you won't have to pay for that. You're already on the books anyway in respect of the van."

I thanked him warmly and assured him I would. He was one thoroughly decent man and I admired him tremendously. "In any case," he laughed, "Alan will be pleased to be able to have the van midweek to drive to Annalong and see that girl of his, Rita Shields."

Everything in the garden . . .

Looking back on that period of my life it seems like a fairytale, a dream come true. Of course I was working hard, but I was doing a job I loved, I had a beautiful girlfriend, good friends, an understanding boss and I was about to get my own wheels. Everything in the garden was lovely. Things couldn't get any better – or could they?

My cousin, Bobby Crutchley, who owned the newsagents and bookstore where I used to help out and read comics and books in the back office, hailed me one day.

"You're just the man," he said. "I've a gentleman inside who would like a word with you. Come on through."

I followed him into the drawing room and was introduced to Capt Henderson, owner of the *Newsletter*, one of Northern Ireland's four daily newspapers. Over a cup of tea he steered the conversation towards newspapers and the *Newsletter* in particular.

"Bobby here tells me you've been doing great things with your local paper. I know you have improved it greatly and have increased the circulation. That's excellent. Now, as it happens, I have a little proposition for you. In short, I intend appointing a special correspondent to cover the Mourne country, and if I may so, you come highly recommended."

This was a total surprise, but I thanked him, while Bobby gave me a surreptitious wink from behind his eyeline. The Captain immediately got down to business. He suggested I write a feature article on a topic of local interest, which would appear under my own by-line as a special correspondent. I would also be expected to cover the courts, councils and all important news events. He handed me a business card containing all the telephone numbers I would need, including his personal contact number and the number I should use for sending through news copy.

All calls would be reverse-charge. If all went according to plan, the question of a monthly retainer would be discussed in due course. Payment would be a penny-halfpenny a line, the standard rate for correspondents at the time.

We shook hands on the deal, and once Henderson had departed, I thanked Bobby for the introduction. "This is only the start, Brad," he declared. "I don't know about the *Irish News,* but I know the editors of both the *Telegraph* and the *Northern Whig* and I'm sure we can make the same sort of arrangement with them. No doubt there are openings for the Fleet Street newspapers as well."

My head was in a spin; things were moving too fast. It was almost too much to take in. There I was, blandly assuming I knew everything there was to know about the newspaper business. In actual fact I was nothing more than a rank amateur.

Shadow over Mourne

My half-page feature appeared in the *Newsletter* a fortnight later. It was headlined *Shadow over Mourne* and hadn't needed much in the way of research, for it was about the slump the area was going through at the time. The fishing industry was in decline, farmers were having a hard time and ongoing attempts to attract more industry had met with scant success. A check with the Stormont Government and local MP's predicted better things to come – but that remained to be seen.

A letter from Captain Henderson, containing congratulations and a cheque for three guineas, was my reward. It was still fashionable in those days to pay in guineas – that's three pounds-three shillings for those of you who weren't around then.

True to his word, Bobby furnished introductions to the editors of the *Telegraph* and the now defunct *Northern Whig.* I had interviews with both of them and we shook hands on arrangements similar to that I already had with the *Newsletter.* When I called to thank Bobby I told him it was approaching the stage where I might have to take on an assistant! I felt obliged to apprise ET of these developments and assure him the *Outlook* would always be my first priority. Typically, his reply was, "Don't give it a thought, Brad, but thanks for telling me. More power to your elbow."

I knew Nicky McConville sent the occasional item to the Belfast papers and the last thing I wanted was to step on his toes. I took him out for a coffee and put him in the picture. He too wished me luck and was delighted when I said he could represent the *Irish News* and I would happily share any of my copy which was of interest.

The *Observer* strikes back

One Friday morning the *Mourne Observer* carried a front page announcement that it had acquired the Mourne Printing Works in Kilkeel and was opening an office and job-printing department.

"Just think, all of this could have been mine," I joked to ET when we discussed the news. "I'm not unduly concerned, but I'll have to think of a response that will ruffle his feathers."

I knew that Hawthorne had taken on a new man as replacement for me. He was a former colleague from Dromore by the name of Ned McCartney. I'd met him a couple of times and he'd been curt and uncommunicative. Derick, never one to mince his words, described him as "A total gobshite. A self-proclaimed jack of all trades who knew bugger all about any of them."

"I'm sure he speaks well of you too D," I told him.

Later in the day I bumped into Paddy McConville, brother of my first employer, Davy, in the town and he stopped for a chat. I knew that, shortly after I'd moved on from the electricity business, Paddy and another local businessman, Thomas Murphy, had launched a small printing operation in a workshop behind Davy's shop. I'd actually called in for a look and a chat a couple of times. They combined part of their names and christened it the MurMac Printing Works. Rumour had it that it was barely paying its way.

Paddy was in an untypically black mood. "What do you think of the bloody *Mourne Observer*? "he said by way of greeting. "As if business wasn't bad enough without them starting up on our doorstep."

I sympathised. "I wouldn't worry too much, Paddy. I expect it will mostly be an office to collect news and adverts. There used to be a couple of platens and a small press in there when the Heaney's had it. They used to produce letterheads, invoices and small posters."

"That's exactly the type of work we do. It's going to hit us hard."

Suddenly I had what I believe, nowadays, they call a lightbulb moment. A bright idea. "Wait a minute, Paddy. How would you and Thomas like to join forces with the *Outlook* and sort out a deal that would be to our mutual advantage? It sounds like a plan and it would certainly be one in the eye for our mutual friend, Hawthorne."

I could almost hear the cogs grinding round in his head. Then his eyes lit up and he chortled gleefully, "Let's go and talk to Thomas."

Thomas liked the idea too, and so did ET when I phoned. He told me to set up a meeting for the following week.

ET and Herbie, the chief printer, drove down for the meeting on Monday and I performed the introductions and left them to it. I rejoined them to find that a deal had been struck and all that remained was for the fine details to be worked out.

Back in Rathfriland, ET confided that MurMac's equipment wasn't up to much. Any serious print jobs would have to be done in Rathfriland, but the amalgamation should show a small profit. "At the very least," he smiled, "it will irritate our mutual friend from Newcastle. And that's always a bonus."

Lots of irons in the fire

A mobile phone and a laptop computer would have been invaluable during those extremely busy weeks, but both inventions weren't even pipedreams in the fifties. I had the house phone in Newcastle, but Dad had never felt the need to have one installed at home. Consequently, I made considerable use of the public call-box not far from our front door.

Because the majority of my calls were reverse-charge, I had to go through the operator and I got to know the switchboard crew very well indeed. Quite often I had to break off between calls to allow other folk the use of the phone box and resume when they'd finished. It was a far cry from today's high-tech world.

This upsurge in work activity meant I was missing out on lots of social activities. I rarely got to the table tennis club in the Slieve Donard Hotel, or to attend many dances. I missed meeting up with Norma and not seeing friends like Charlie, Derick, Clifford and Brian as frequently as I had. The last time I'd spoken to Brian he mentioned that he was moving soon to take up an appointment in Scotland.

On the plus side, the deposit account I'd opened in the Ulster Bank was moving steadily in the right direction.

Norma and I had gone out for a meal one evening and she said in all seriousness, "You know, Brad, you're becoming a proper workaholic. If you're not careful, you'll be turning into a carbon-copy of that man Hawthorne you're always on about."

"Perish the thought," I cried, but deep down, I began to wonder if she might not have a point.

Later in the evening she said. "Oh, I almost forgot, but I mentioned to my brother Bertie that you were looking out for a car and he said to tell you there's one for sale in Speers' Garage on the Newry Road. He thinks it might be worth a look."

"That sounds promising, love. What do you say we drive out that way tomorrow evening and take a look at it?"

So we did. At least it meant I was out with Norma on two successive evenings.

I knew Robert Speers reasonably well and he took us to have a look at the car, a dark blue Morris 8 that seemed in fairly decent order. "Take her for a spin up the road," Robert said. "I'll be open for another hour or so. You can leave your van round the back. It'll be all right."

We drove out the familiar road in the direction of Newry. The little Morris seemed fine and I liked the feel of it. Norma said she liked it too. I gave her a kiss but she declined with a laugh when I suggested we should try out the back seat to make absolutely sure.

We drove back to the garage and Norma sat in the van while I had a chat with Robert. He explained that the car had just been serviced and that it was taxed and insured for ten months. We discussed terms, bartered and bantered for five minutes and finally shook hands on the deal. I agreed to collect it the following Friday.

I ran Norma home, thanked her and asked her to pass on my thanks to Bertie as well. We arranged to meet the following Tuesday and I said I'd take her for a drive then.

ET was delighted when I told him of the deal that Thursday night. So too was Alan as he drove me down to Newcastle.

"At least you'll be able to take Rita out on Tuesdays and Wednesdays now," I joked.

"About bloody time too," he smiled. "I'm sure you and Norma have the Thames well broken in by now. Good luck with the new Morris."

A tape from Tony

There was a package waiting for me when I got back to the house and even before I opened it the postmark and the scrawl of bright green ink was a giveaway. It was the promised tape from Tony, all the way from Down Under.

He'd written a note as well which concluded, "I'll bet you a quid you haven't even bought a recorder yet. I know what you're like, Fleming. So nip across to Neesons and buy one right away. Enjoy this and then start recording and get it back here ASAP."

He was right of course. I hadn't bought a recorder, but I rectified that omission immediately after breakfast by hurrying over to the shop and buying the latest Grundig machine. It was great to hear Tony's familiar voice again. The double-sided tape ran for 45-minutes on each side and was packed with interesting accounts of his voyage out there, their new family home in Melbourne and his new job in a weekly paper. He instructed me to record The Walton Programme, his favourite music show on RTE before returning the tape.

I recalled how we used to laugh about this 30-minute show that featured traditional Irish music, including many old rebel songs, and the host's standard and heavily accented opening, which ran, *"Greetings everyone and welcome to da Walton Programme, yer weekly remoinder of da grace and da beauty dat loies in our heritage of Oirish songs; da songs our fadders loved . . ."*

I played it a couple of times and invited a bunch of our mutual friends down the following Saturday to hear it and help record a reply. I made sure to add that day's Walton Programme to round it off. It was the first of many tapes we exchanged during his sojourn Down Under.

Goodbye Norma, hello Mollie

I collected my new car that Friday afternoon and drove to Newcastle. It handled well on the thirteen-mile journey and the garage had given it a good wash and shine. That didn't stop my aunt giving it a good going over with the Hoover and presenting me with a new sponge and cleaning kit.

I took them for a little drive and intended taking it to Castlewellan that night where there was a dance. However, Charlie and his girlfriend Jeannie called and invited me to go with them. I'd been looking forward to driving up there under my own steam, but, in the circumstances, I could scarcely refuse.

Midway through the evening I had a dance with a pretty black-haired girl in a powder-blue long-sleeved blouse and an Elvis rock-and-roll skirt. She asked where I was from. I told her Kilkeel.

"Oh," she said, "I've never been there. Is it nice?"

"It's not bad, I suppose, slightly bigger than Castlewellan and just about as quiet. As a matter of fact, I hope to drive up there to a dance tomorrow night."

We chatted on and one thing led to another. She told me her name was Mollie Foster and in no time at all I had arranged to take her to Kilkeel. I was slightly amused when she asked if her cousin, May, might go with us. Safety in numbers, I thought Sure, bring your chaperone along.

I picked up the girls in Castlewellan as arranged and we drove to Kilkeel. Mollie hadn't been there before, so we took a tour of the harbour and had a walk around the town before going to the dance. We met up with Charlie and Jeanie and I was acutely conscious of a few stares and knowing looks from some of my usual dancing partners as Mollie and I mostly danced together. All in all though, it was a most pleasant evening.

When I dropped Mollie home afterwards it seemed the most natural thing in the world to ask if she'd care to go for a drive the following afternoon. This time she didn't suggest May should accompany us.

My aunt made up a picnic hamper for us and I called for Mollie after lunch. We visited Clough and Ardglass, and walked along the beach at Tyrella, fed the seagulls and talked for a long time. She told me we'd met briefly four or five years before when I was with the *Observer,* and I vaguely recalled stopping to ask a group of young girls directions to the home of the McCracken family where I had scheduled an interview. She had been one of them.

"And you remembered that?" I asked in wonder.

"Oh yes," she said. "When I saw you at the dance on Friday I said to May, "Look, there's my little reporter!"

I couldn't help laughing. "But you were just a kid then."

"I suppose I was, but I'll be eighteen next birthday."

I'd only just turned 23 myself, but *almost eighteen* seemed ridiculously young.

Mollie and I met in Newcastle the following day, took in a movie and walked and talked the length of the promenade and back. I knew instinctively I wanted her to be my steady girl. When I tried to explain, she simply smiled and said that was all right with her.

I had arranged to see Norma the following evening and I knew she would have to be told. It wasn't a task I was looking forward to. We went to the Vogue to see a Mario Lanza film *Serenade,* and there was an actress in it so like Mollie it made me gasp. For the first time, I didn't put my arm around Norma as usual, and when we drew up outside her home afterwards she clearly didn't need to be told.

"I assume you've met someone else, Brad?" she said matter-of-factly. "I sensed it in the Vogue when we didn't have our usual cuddle."

I nodded. "I'm sorry, Norma. I truly am. I'd no idea this was going to happen."

"Oh. As quick as that, was it? Surely not since the last time we met?"

All I could do was nod again. "As I say, it came out of the blue. I wasn't looking for anyone else."

She turned her head to look through the windscreen and I could see her biting her lower lip. "Do I know her? Am I allowed to know her name?"

I don't think you do. Her name is Foster. Mollie Foster. She's from Castlewellan."

Norma turned towards me again. I couldn't fathom the look in her eyes. She didn't say anything, only stared at me. I had to break the silence that was building. "I needn't have told you, I suppose. I could have gone on seeing you, could have let things drift, but that wouldn't have been fair. To any of us."

Her smile was touched with bitterness. "At least you didn't just slope off without a word the way John did. Maybe I should be grateful for that."

"Gratitude doesn't come into it, Norma. Not on your part anyway. But I know I have a lot to thank you for, and that I do. I hope you and I can still be friends."

She gave a small shake of her head, gathered up her handbag, and said simply, "Thank you, but I doubt that would work; certainly not for me. But I do pray this will work out for you. I wish you and your Miss Foster well. Be happy, Brad."

"You too Norma. Good luck!"

Quite suddenly my thoughts flew back down the years to an almost identical conversation I'd had with a girl years before. Mildred and I had parted and she'd gone off to get engaged to another fellow. This time the roles were reversed. Recalling how I'd felt at that moment, I realised I could have been kinder, less abrupt, more sympathetic. I ought to have broken the news more gently. Old Willie Shakespeare surely knew what he was on about when he penned the line *"Parting is such sweet sorrow."*

I would have got out and opened the door for her, but she climbed out and I heard the staccato clicking of her high heels on the driveway as she strode towards her front door. I waited until she was safely inside before driving away.

Another year turns

If 1957 had been a happy and successful year for me, 1958 promised to be even better. I thoroughly enjoyed working in the *Outlook* and a steady return from my correspondence work for the Belfast papers was boosting my savings. There were busy days and slack days, and I made the most of both.

Periodic chats with ET revealed that he was equally content. Advertising revenue was steady, and circulation had increased by over 1,300 since I joined, and was still rising. As he handed me a handsome Christmas bonus, we drank a toast to an equally profitable New Year.

My relationship with Mollie was blossoming. Her parents, Sam and Margaret, and younger sister Jean, had always treated me like one of the family and I was a frequent visitor to their home. I liked the whole family enormously.

It was good to keep in touch with old friends in the *Observer* and I saw Derick, Ken, Clifford and the others regularly. For some time, I'd had a warm relationship with Malcolm Crichton, owner and editor of the Downpatrick–based *Down Recorder,* whose circulation area bordered our own in towns like Newcastle, Castlewellan and Dundrum.

It became something of a ritual for Malcolm to invite me for lunch after a court. "My old shorthand's a little weak, you know," he would say, "and perhaps you wouldn't mind if I checked a few things with you?"

Of course I didn't mind, and I enjoyed his company very much. He had a great love of boating and sailing, especially on Strangford Lough, and I had several outings with him there, and later with his son, Colin, who was equally fond of being on the water.

The Munich disaster

It was the habit of reporters covering Kilkeel Rural Council's monthly meeting to meet afterwards for tea and chips in the Harbour Café. Ken, Hal O'Brien of the *Newry Reporter,* and I had just arrived there one day when the news broke of the dreadful air crash in Munich, Germany, involving members of the Busby Babes, the first of the great Manchester United teams.

Returning from a European match, their Elizabethan charter aircraft had just taken off in a gathering snowstorm when it crashed at the end of the runway. Of the 43 passengers on board, 23 were killed, including stars like Eddie Coleman, Liam Wheelan, David Pegg, and Roger Byrne. Duncan Edwards (21), hailed as potentially the best player of his generation, passed away from his injuries 16 days later.

Famous sports journalists, Henry Rose, of the *Daily Express*, Frank Swift, himself a former England goalkeeping great, and Don Davies, *Manchester Guardian,* also lost their lives.

Manager Matt Busby, grievously injured, survived to win the European Championship with the club a decade later, Jackie Blanchflower (24), brother of Northern Ireland captain, Danny, also recovered, but was never quite the same player again. Bobby Charlton, then just 20, also survived to enjoy a stellar career and win a World Cup in 1966. Irish international goalkeeper, Harry Gregg, performed heroics in helping injured passengers and continued to play at club and international level for many years.

Later that year a severely depleted United team lost the FA Cup-Final at Wembley Stadium 2-0 to Bolton Wanderers.

Domestic news

As the winter progressed, Mollie joined the busy news team of Fleming and Foster and often helped out by phoning copy through to the daily papers while I continued typing. She seemed to quite enjoy it. She was also happy to act as telephone operator in chief.

One day Bobbie told us that he was being transferred to work in a Civil Service post in Norwich and he and Ethel would be moving out, He wasn't sure when, but promised to let me know immediately he heard. I made sense for them in lots of ways. Ethel hailed from Diss, near Norwich, and they'd met and married while he was based there with the RAF during the war.

A few days later he took me aside and made a suggestion that really set me thinking.

"Why don't you talk to Bob next door and see if you can continue to rent the house?"

Of course I had known Bob Dalzell and his wife, Betty ever since coming to live in Shimnavale and we were on excellent terms. He and Bobbie were respectively chairman and treasurer of the local Newcastle and District Football League and I had contacted him many times for the newspaper. And not having a television set of his own, he would invariably call round to watch a game in our house.

I thanked Bobbie for the suggestion and then, as I usually did in these situations. I took the dog for a long walk and put in a lot of serious thinking.

Just a few months before I'd been working all the hours God sent in the *MO* for a mere pittance. Now I had a new job, a car, an expanding freelance business with prospects and a helpful and understanding girlfriend. Now, looming on the horizon, was the prospect of acquiring a home of my own. Was I lucky or what? I wondered what my fairy godmother or guardian angel had in store for me next. I needed to talk to Mollie and my Dad, in that order, without delay.

Mollie was as surprised by developments as I was. We'd already tentatively discussed the possibility of getting engaged on her eighteenth birthday – St Patrick's Day, March 17. Of course, her parents had not been informed of this master plan, but neither of us thought they'd object.

"It looks like a real gift horse, if ever I saw one," she said. "All I can say is I'm up for it if you are."

When I drove up to Kilkeel to talk to Dad he too was encouragingly enthusiastic. Asked if he might consider moving down to Newcastle to join me, he drew on his pipe before shaking his head.

"Maybe one day, but not just yet. I'm happy enough where I am. But it could be a good move for you. As you say yourself, Newcastle is more central for your job than up here is. Besides, it a good step nearer Belfast, where I expect you'll finish up one day."

A move to Belfast hadn't been in my immediate plans, but, looking back, he had a much clearer idea of my possible future than I had.

Bobbie and I called to see Bob Dalzell a few evenings later. He said he was sorry to see my uncle go, but saw no reason why I shouldn't continue the tenancy of the house.

However, a potential storm cloud loomed on the horizon when we spoke to him a week later. "I've been thinking it over," he told us, "and I think I'll let the place go to the highest bidder."

A while after that he beckoned me into his house as I was going out to the car. He sat me down and asked a direct question. "Brad, tell me straight. Are you holding the house for Bobbie to come back to sometime in the future, or do you really want it for yourself?"

The look of surprise on my face must have told him all he wanted to know, but he continued.

"Betty and I were just wondering about that. I'm sorry I had to ask you. I suppose you and that wee girl of yours will be getting married one of these days? It will be a nice wee place for you, and handy for your work."

Slightly embarrassed, I managed "We'll, we hope to get engaged on her birthday, St Patrick's Day, but we haven't told anyone yet, and marriage is a long way off."

"Congratulations," he said. "It will be good to have you and Mollie for neighbours. If you call up to see Mr McSpadden, the solicitor, in his office on Friday he'll have all the papers for you to sign."

We shook hands before I left.

I called to see George McSpadden, whom I knew well from seeing him at local courts, and he confirmed what Bob had said about the house. The rent was only £5 a month, which seems utterly ridiculous when one considers today's prices.

The house had a good-sized, comfortable lounge with a large bay-window, three bedrooms, a kitchen, annex and bathroom. There was a store and garden shed to the rear, beside an apple orchard and a low wall bounded a lawn which ran the full length of the property. On the other side of this wall a tinkling stream meandered by on its way to join the Shimna River. It would have been hard to imagine a more idyllic spot.

We want a union

Meanwhile, while I was engaged in things domestic, storm clouds were gathering in my old stomping ground in the *Observer*.

I received regular bulletins from Derick, Clifford and Ken that my old workplace was far from a happy camp. The lads had at long last united in a determined bid to force the paper to become a union house. A union representative had called and engaged in an angry slanging match with the Boss, which concluded with his being almost forcibly ejected. In true militant style, he threatened to call a full-scale walk-out if his demands weren't met.

Hawthorne reportedly declared a union would be established only over his dead body. I understood one or two of the more militant lads would have been happy enough to arrange that!

In some ways I almost wished I was still working there so that I could have enjoyed the craic. Well, not really. Wild horses couldn't have dragged me back to that slave shop.

Rules of engagement

Picking my moment, I drove Mollie's Dad up to Castlewellan one evening and we repaired to Savage's Bar, his local watering hole. Biding my time until he'd a Guinness and a Powers' Whiskey inside him, I broached the subject of his daughter's upcoming birthday and how she and I had decided, as it was also St Patrick's Day and all, it would be a grand time for us to become engaged.

Having said my piece, I sat back and awaited the outcome – not without a certain flutter of trepidation.

Sam swivelled on his stool, stuck a forefinger in the air to attract the attention of the proprietor, and pronounced "Two more of the same when you're ready, Pat. This man and I have something to celebrate!"

Immediately my hand was swallowed in his massive farmer's grip as he shook my hand warmly.

"Let's drink to the engagement, Brad," he exclaimed. "I'm delighted for the pair of you. I know Mollie couldn't wish for a better man!"

Pat Savage had overheard. "Gentlemen, if congratulations are in order, as I believe they are, then the drinks are on the house."

I was relieved to find his grip a lot less powerful than Sam's.

Mollie and I drove to Belfast a few days later and visited a number of jewellers before she found an engagement ring that met with her approval. I hovered dutifully in the background, content to let her make her own choice.

We had lunch in my favourite little restaurant, the *Val Dor*, in Wellington Place, and did a round of the shops. Mollie maintained she wouldn't show anybody the ring until the night of the birthday/engagement party.

That particular event was quite a do. I'd no idea how so many of our friends managed to cram into their small house but it was virtually standing room only. At one point Mollie's cousin, Olive, keeled over in a dead faint and had to be revived.

There were eats and drinks of every description. All the ladies admired the ring and Sam, God bless him, insisted on making a little speech welcoming me into the family.

There were cries of "Reply. Reply." I mumbled a few words, thanked Mollie's folks and everyone for coming. In response to Sam's remarks, I said while I wasn't quite a member of the family yet, I hoped it wouldn't be too long until I would be."

I wasn't much for making speeches. Even then, I think I

preferred the written word to the spoken one.

Takeover at No. 27

The next couple of months flew by. Bobbie and Ethel eventually left for Norwich, but not before Mollie and I arranged to buy some of their furniture. No. 27 had been home to me for a while now and I was delighted that I could continue living there.

Mollie was a tremendous help. She was as thrilled as I was to have a place of our own, and while the proprieties decreed that she continued to live at home with her folks, she would often come down to clean and tidy up while I hammered away on the old typewriter. She was especially in her element when we were able to entertain her folks, and my Dad, whenever they came down. My Gran and Uncle Jim, who also lived in Newcastle, were also frequent visitors

I was delighted to see that Mollie and Betty from next door began getting on like the proverbial house on fire. They were always nipping back and forth for a cup of tea and a chat, or going shopping to buy things for the house.

The only blot on the horizon was that my old Morris car was beginning to show signs of wear and tear. No shame on it, for I'd really been logging up the miles. When the clutch plate started to slip I was told it was only a matter of time before a replacement would be needed. With summer approaching and the prospect of a wedding looming on the horizon, I decided to exchange it for, of all things, a Vespa scooter.

Of course I should have got another car, but, being young and foolish, I reckoned a nice little scooter would be more adventurous. Mollie could always ride pillion, and besides, a Vespa would be much more economical to run. There will be more of the Vespa later.

Sad tidings

With summer fast approaching two events occurred which were to change my career – and my life, forever. One evening I attended a Young Farmers' Club social and guest tea in Seaforde. The entertainment was excellent, and the company even more so, because I shared a table with Malcolm and Mrs Violet Crichton, of the *Recorder*. Both were in excellent form, which made it even more distressing when I heard the following day that Malcolm had died suddenly in the early hours.

It was a double blow for the family, because Malcolm's father, the venerable W Y Crichton, who had been associated with the paper for well over half a century, passed away soon afterwards at the age of 89.

I wrote immediately to Mrs Crichton and Colin, offering my condolences and assuring them of my willingness to help in any way I could.

Colin phoned and asked if I could possibly report a forthcoming meeting of Dundrum Town Committee a few days later. He said he would try to drive over and have a word immediately the meeting finished.

Of course, I assented immediately. The meeting was short and contained nothing of note. Colin appeared just as it concluded and we sat in his car. He was obviously quite shaken and I felt for his grief.

He was silent for quite some time, then thanked me and said, "Brad, a heavy load has just fallen on my shoulders. As you can imagine, this has come as a great shock to us, Mum and me. We both appreciate your writing to us more than we can say. We've talked about it at great length and both of us would appreciate it very much if you could see your way to join us in the *Recorder.*"

This came as a total surprise. I had fully appreciated his circumstances, and been more than ready to give what help I could; but I was well established and happy in the *Outlook* and had never entertained any thoughts of leaving. Besides, Downpatrick was a long way from Kilkeel, where the majority of my work was centred. There was also the little matter of my loyalty to ET, who had shown me nothing but understanding and kindness in the past year.

Sensing my hesitancy, Colin continued. "I realise I've sprung this on you out of the blue, and from what you've told me in the past, I understand you're settled and happy in Rathfriland. Take time to consider if you wish, and if necessary, I've no doubt we could come to an accommodation with Mr Brady. A lot of our area overlaps and I'm sure we could exchange reports of most events like courts, councils and other meetings. Copy could be altered and headings changed to make reports read differently."

I thanked him for his offer and said I'd think about it and have an answer for him by the weekend. He offered a generous salary and petrol allowance and had no objection to my continuing as a correspondent for the daily papers. I would, of course, be losing my advertising commission, which had been coming along quite nicely. It was a case of swings and roundabouts.

I called at Mollie's on the way home and brought her up to speed. Typically, as I knew she would, she was content to leave the decision to me.

That Thursday evening in Rathfriland I asked for a private word with ET and told him the news. He had, of course, heard of Malcolm's death.

Upon hearing me out, he said, somewhat wryly, "You know Brad; I always thought it wouldn't be too long before you moved on. You're a hard worker and a good newspaperman. I'll be more than sorry to lose you, but the *Recorder* is a bigger paper than ours and it's a chance for you to spread your wings."

I forced a smile. "You make it sound as if I've left already. So, you want rid of me, do you?"

"Not at all, not at all, but I'm simply stating the facts. As I say, I realised you wouldn't stay with us forever."

We talked for a long time. I admired this man so much. He'd always treated me fairly and had been as straight as a die in all our dealings. When I told him of Colin's suggestion about sharing certain reports, he thought it a good idea and was sure something could be worked out.

Somewhat relieved by his attitude and acceptance of the news, I said, "At least you'll be getting a full hundred per cent on all the advertising now. I'll do everything can to make sure those firms continue to use the paper."

He smiled. "That's another thing I'm grateful to you for. It was remarkable how all those businesses supported you."

"It takes a Mourne man to know a Mourne man," I told him. "But they're not fools, they wouldn't have advertised if they weren't getting value for money. The same goes for Nicky McConville and all the sports correspondents I've fixed up. I'll talk to them too and make sure they continue. Alan can do the rounds in those towns and keep things ticking."

That friendly little talk with him had virtually made up my mind for me. I would accept Colin's proposal, but he would have to wait a month before I joined him. I certainly wasn't going to hold ET to the statutory weeks' notice!

It's a funny old world

My final month with the *Outlook* was a busy time for me because, as promised, I was also doing what work I could to help the *Recorder*. I didn't actually go over to their office in Downpatrick, but

154

a table tennis teammate, Bertie Hill, who worked in the town, kindly dropped my copy off for me. The Belfast papers, particularly the *Newsletter,* were also making demands on my time, so I didn't have much scope for relaxation.

However, I did manage to take in one dance in the Central Ballroom, with Mollie, her cousin May, and her boyfriend, Tom Bingham, with whom I had become increasingly friendly.

Well into the evening I almost literally bumped into John Little. I hadn't seen him in months; in fact, not since I'd inadvertently pinched his girlfriend, Norma Hanna. I suppose I might have expected a chilly reception. Instead we exchanged simultaneous grins, which quickly developed into a bout of hearty laughter. We stopped, right there in the middle of the crowded dancefloor, while introductions were performed. Not that introductions were strictly necessary, for John's dancing partner was none other than Rita Shields, who was still the girlfriend of my friend and work colleague, Alan Brady!

John and I both clearly appreciated the irony of the situation and found it highly amusing. In fact, although we had scarcely spoken in all that time, I liked him a lot; he was the sort of bloke who could easily have become a good friend. Not so Rita, who was plainly embarrassed at having been caught red-handed. A little later she drew me to one side and entreated me not to spill the beans to Alan, as she put it.

I had my own view of the matter, of course, but I said it was none of my business and I could see no reason to mention it to Alan. Someone else, however, obviously didn't share my discretion, for, just before I left Rathfriland, Alan confided in me that he'd broken it off with her. He didn't give his reasons, but I couldn't help but think he had made a wise choice.

Third time lucky?

I honestly believe there was a fair measure of regret on both sides on the day I left the *Outlook.* I had been happy there, enjoyed the best of times, and had made a host of new friends. It was comforting to know I wouldn't be severing all links. More than that, I'd come to appreciate that those twelve months marked a huge turning point in my personal fortunes.

I'd moved on from being an underpaid and unacknowledged hireling to mature into someone who appreciated the value of a decent reward for an honest day's work. It hadn't been an easy road but, in hindsight, I had to concede it had laid a good solid foundation.

Derick called down and we had a long chat that weekend. He acknowledged how things had changed for the better for me and wished me well in my new job. Things were still not good in the *Observer*, he said. Hawthorne was still digging in his heels about the Union, Ken and McCartney had had an enormous row over it which led to Ken walking out. He was only persuaded to return when the Boss hot-footed it up to Annalong and agreed to a settlement Ken wouldn't tell the others about.

"You're well out of it, Brad," Derick said. "If there isn't a clear resolution soon, I'll go myself."

I offered to have a word with Brady on his behalf but he said he'd wait and see.

It was against this background that I reported for duty at the *Recorder* office on Monday 2 June, 1958. To put it mildly, the difference between it and my two previous papers was startling.

While my first two newspapers had been of comparatively recent vintage, the *Down Recorder* had been founded in 1836 and was steeped in history and tradition. Strong family bonds had existed down the years and certain standards had been maintained proudly by Colin's grandfather and father. Indeed, the paper had changed little in appearance since its inception, and while Colin was a progressive and wanted to turn it into a publication more in keeping with the Twentieth Century, he was minded to proceed with caution.

At the time of my arrival it was a big broadsheet of about eight pages, not dissimilar in appearance to *The Times* or *Daily Telegraph* of the period. Long grey columns of type were relieved only by the occasional single- or double-column headline. Photographs were something of a rarity and quite a lot of advertising was carried on the front page. While there were three Linotype machines, much of the type was still set up by hand by a team of compositors. All in all, the building and what was inside it had changed little in more than 120 years.

The premises were situated prominently in the centre of town and were the first thing one saw when driving up Market Street. The ground floor was taken up by a shop in which the redoubtable Miss Mary Carson reigned supreme. Immediately above were the editorial offices and the photographic department and darkroom. This floor had formerly housed the Down County Club. Behind this stood the printing works, which could be reached only by an alleyway at the side of the building. To this day I can recall the strong odour of printing ink which permeated everything.

Colin took me on a little conducted tour where I had the chance of saying hello to some folk I would be working with for more than the next fifteen years. I'll introduce you to them in due course as this little tale unfolds. For now, let me say simply that in that time we shared a lot of laughs and jokes, and frights and blind panics, and - with apologies to old Rudyard Kipling – met with some small triumphs and disasters too.

I was told that I was in effect taking over from old Jimmy Reynolds, who had recently hung up his pen after more years as chief reporter than anyone could remember. I'd met him a time or two and could vouch that he was a scribe of the old school.

Over a welcome cup of tea, I met Leslie Daws, who ran the sports department. In fact, we were to share an office, although his section of it was cordoned off by a glass-topped partition and I could only glimpse the top of his head through a kind of serving-hatch contraption through which we could pass small items. Leslie was on the taciturn side, and until he loosened up a while later, a man of few words. I reckoned he would take a bit of getting to know, and I was right. Eventually though, we became quite good friends.

Much of the morning was devoted to sorting out my work routine and in the afternoon Colin drove me to Ballynahinch and later Killyleagh. Crossgar and Saintfield. I met some of the paper's correspondents in these towns, looked in on the police stations and talked to most of the local clerics.

Without going into too much boring detail, it was agreed that I should cover the local magistrate's courts, of which there were nine each month – Newcastle, Castlewellan, Ballynahinch, Killyleagh, Saintfield, Ardglass, Portaferry and two in Downpatrick. I'd also look after Newcastle Urban Council and Ballynahinch, Castlewellan and Dundrum Town Committees. Added to that would be the Down Assizes and Quarter Sessions whenever they came round and the occasional inquests.

There was enough there to keep me busy, and when the various political and farmers' meetings were thrown into the mix, I reckoned my cup was as full as it needed to be.

I happily agreed to use the Vespa whenever possible and I was told to use the firm's fuel checking account in Stewart's Garage. This arrangement suited well because I could drive straight from home to most of the courts without stopping by the office first. My little scooter would be okay during summer, but I realised I'd have to get a car when winter set in. On wet days Colin said I could use the office Morris shooting-brake.

The last thing I did that first day was to nip up to the house to see Mrs Crichton and to personally convey my regrets on the death of her husband. She seemed to be bearing up very well and was certainly putting on a brave face. She thanked me for the letter I'd sent and voiced her delight that I'd joined the paper.

She was taking an active interest in affairs herself by fulfilling the late W Y's role of personally checking all the proofs. We talked for quite a long time and I was quite touched when she asked me to keep a friendly eye on Colin.

"I know you two are about an age," she confided, "but you have more experience and have been around newspapers longer than he has." She gave a huge wink. "But don't tell him I mentioned it. It will be our little secret."

Settling in

Old W Y Crichton, whom I'd never met, had by all accounts been something of a tradition-list, a strict disciplinarian and loath to change. If something had been good enough to last for his lifetime, he saw no reason to alter it. Malcolm had managed to introduce some improvements, notably in the layout and presentation of the paper's content, and I was delighted to learn that Colin wanted to continue this trend.

I liked Colin enormously and found him one of the mildest, most easy-going men I'd ever known. As the new kid on the block, so to speak, I was reluctant to mention what I considered to be too old-fashioned about the paper. Let me put it this way – Ken Purdy would have been perfectly content to continue to report the courts and councils in the manner that had held sway for more than half a century. Long columns of grey type, starting at the point the gathering was called to order and finishing when business concluded.

To be fair, Colin often sought my opinion on these matters, and when he did, I was glad to give it to him honestly and straight from the shoulder. I felt the long history of the paper, and the family connection with it was a heavy yoke around his shoulders. Although I never mentioned it to him of course, I began to understand why his mother had encouraged me to keep a friendly eye on him.

Colin was never a boss in the mould of Jim Hawthorne. He was a gentleman in the true sense of the word, always requesting rather than ordering. In all the time I knew him I can never recall a snide remark or cross word. As a consequence, there wasn't much I wouldn't have done for him, or for the *Recorder*.

As the saying goes, the working routine in the paper was so laid back as to be virtually horizontal. I think Colin saw himself more as a manager than an editor, a role he was to assume in later years. When I arrived I was amazed to discover there was no formal system of editing or sub-editing copy. Everyone simply produced their own reports and stories, which then found their way into the paper, more or less at the whim of the compositors and printers.

The galley-proofs of type were read and corrected before being sent up to Mrs Crichton who conducted a final check. Several times every day she would phone the office to query a point, seek clarification, or make a suggestion. I quickly recognised this was a throwback to W Y's time.

Andy Campbell had been taken on as the *Recorder's* first photographer only a few months before I arrived, and it was unusual to find more than half-a-dozen pictures in a single edition. Most of these depicted a posed group of stern looking individuals sitting ramrod straight with their gaze fixed firmly on the camera. I'm not being critical here, that's simply the way it was. As often as not the bottom half of the front page was filled by an assortment of advertisements.

Gently, during my early days, I encouraged Colin to make some changes. More pictures, more news stories on the front page – and instead of two columns of dull, grey type, how to split a report and move the bulk of it to an inside page. Gradually the number of advertisements on Page One was reduced to give the paper a newsier look, and if anyone insisted on his ad being placed on the front page he had to pay more for the privilege. This last almost caused Mary Carson, who handled the accounts, to have a fit, but we stuck to our guns.

I've mentioned that Colin, like his father before him, enjoyed nothing more than heading down to Quoile Yacht Club to motor about Strangford Lough in the family cruiser, or perform heroics on his prized GP14 sailing dinghy. Often, during that long first summer, he would catch my eye, wink and suggest "Fancy a wee jaunt on the Lough?" Of course, it was no hardship to obey orders and we talked a lot about developing the paper during those impromptu outings.

Meanwhile, back on the home front

Mollie and I had been working hard most weekends, buying more furniture and bits and pieces for No 27. With the willing assistance of Betty from next door, we papered and painted the entire interior of the bungalow during successive weekends. We thought it all looked rather well.

Of course, I was impatient for Mollie to move in permanently, but such things would have been frowned upon back then. In any event, both of us were keen to get married. We had many a long conversation about it and agreed that Saturday, 13 September, the anniversary of our first meeting, would be an ideal day for the event. The task of sending out invitations and making a multitude of arrangements fell mostly to her.

Now this presented a few possible difficulties, not least informing our respective families. I knew there would be no problem on my side, and encouraged by her dad's reaction to our engagement, I hoped to secure his approval for this further step.

As custom now dictated, Sam and I repaired to Savage's licensed premises and I broached the subject. Having been a frequent visitor at No 27 and being aware of the improvements we'd carried out, I doubt my application was any great surprise to him.

"Is it a year already?" he exclaimed. "Boys-a-boys, but it scarcely seems like it." Then, quite solemnly, he went on, "Brad, as I've said before, you're one of the family now. I know Mollie loves you to bits and Maggie and I are sure you'll look after her for us. "

Another firm handshake was followed by a toast, Pat Savage again doing the honours.

Accidents, mishaps and soakings

As summer waned I came to realise, that while the Vespa was an ideal form of transport in fine weather, its shortcomings were highlighted by heavy rain and sleet Two incidents confirmed that it had had its day. I used it to go to my first Portaferry Court, which necessitated a long ride from Newcastle to Strangford and a ferry crossing of Strangford Lough.

On a bright, sunny morning I imprudently decided not to take my wet-weather gear and sallied forth in sports jacket and flannels. For the duration of the return journey it lashed out of the heavens and by the time I arrived in the office I must have resembled a drowned rat. Trying unsuccessfully to stifle a smile, Colin generously provided me with a complete change of clothing.

The die was finally cast a week later when I was transporting a number of wedding presents to Mollie's after work one night. It was raining heavily but I had my wet gear on and was balancing the parcels on the little platform between my feet. Just short of Castlewellan there was a dip in the road at the foot of Hanna's Hill. In the conditions I failed to notice that my way was blocked by a couple of feet of flood-water.

I rode straight into it, the Vespa stopped abruptly and I somersaulted over the handlebars, landing on my back in the middle of a lake that hadn't been there last time I'd used the road. Worse than that, as I lay half submerged, with my precious parcels bobbing merrily all around me, I realised the handlebar had gouged a 12-inch gash in my thigh.

A helpful motorist helped me gather up the presents, park the Vespa and ran me home. Bob Dalzell drove me to the doctors, where I collected a line of stitches and a huge swathe of sticking plaster running from knee to crotch. Later another neighbour and I brought the largely undamaged Vespa home in his van.

As I said to Bob afterwards, while the floodwater had caused the accident in the first place, had it not cushioned my fall, I might easily have broken my back or sustained a skull fracture if I'd landed on the bare tarmac.

Those two salutary lessons, however, were enough to convince me that my little scooter was not ideally suited to travelling in winter. Within days I had sold it and Dad stepped into the breach magnificently and gave me a spanking new Ford Popular car as a wedding present!

The stag party

Tradition dictated that I should have a stag party, which many friends from the three papers I'd worked in attended. For the lads from the *Observer* it also served to mark their victory over Hawthorne, who had finally, with ill grace, capitulated and accepted the formation of a branch of the union, the NGA, in his premises. Derick told me this triumph meant that he had decided to continue working there, at least for the foreseeable future.

The party was held in No 27 on the Saturday night before the wedding. It was largely organised by Derick and Tom Bingham, who was to be my best man. The guests were no doubt thankful to Mollie and Betty who had prepared lots of sandwiches, cakes and other goodies, but the lads saw to it that there was no shortage of alcohol in assorted guises.

I'd prudently apologised to Bob and Betty in advance in case they became alarmed by any sounds of revelry from next door. I have to say they were both very good about it, Betty going so far as to promise not to breathe a word to Mollie irrespective of how noisy or badly behaved we became.

As stag parties go, I believe it was tolerably successful. It certainly went on well into the small hours and copious quantities of drink were consumed. I was certainly glad I had a full week to recover before my journey down the aisle. One by one, my guests took their leave, the more prudent of them having arranged to be picked up by friends or in taxis.

By 2am only five of us remained. Clifford Mills had gone to sleep and was snoring contentedly on the settee; Andy Campbell was smiling beatifically in an armchair. Derick and Tom, hardened drinkers both, were engaged in a learned debate about something I couldn't understand and I was in another armchair surveying the wreckage of what at the start of the evening had been a relatively clean lounge.

A pall of dense grey cigarette smoke swirled from the level of the ceiling to three feet above the carpet and the carpet itself was littered with empty beer bottles, assorted glasses and spent lager cans. Numbly I reflected that something would need to be done to clean up this battlefield before Mollie and Betty conducted the inevitable inspection later in the day.

For some unfathomable reason I felt nothing like as hungover as I ought to, or deserved to have done, for I distinctly recall Andy rising to his feet and announcing solemnly that if he didn't get some fresh air he was going to be sick. After opening as many windows as we could, Tom, Derick and I manhandled him outside and walked him all the way to the top of Shimnavale.

There, he straightened up, shrugged us off and insisted he could manage perfectly well on his own. Ignoring all our well-intentioned entreaties to the contrary, he said he could walk an absolutely straight line without support from anyone.

So he did, but unfortunately his straight line took him up the driveway of the house belonging to Mr McGrath, one of my neighbours. He careered into the garage door with a resounding crash, loud enough to awaken half the neighbourhood, before sliding down to the ground in an unsightly heap.

Somehow the three of us gathered him up and frogmarched

him back to No 27, where we put him and a slumbering Clifford to bed in a spare room. Tom, Derick and I exchanged a number of fond adieus before they left, Tom in his van and Derick on his familiar large bicycle. Tom reached home without mishap, but Derick confessed afterwards that he had lost his bearings and inadvertently ridden into the town dump, He had then gone round in circles for ten minutes before managing to find the exit.

On the following Monday Colin and Leslie, who had prudently given the party a miss, insisted on hearing a verbatim account. Upon learning of Andy's encounter with the garage door they decided to have a little fun with the hapless photographer. Leslie went down to the shop and had Mary put a call through to Andy on Colin's phone.

Then Colin and I listened as Andy picked up the phone and we watched him turn pale as Leslie, in the guise of an irate Mr McGrath, berated him for several minutes with threats of legal action unless his badly damaged garage door was put right. In the end we all started laughing and put the poor fellow out of his misery. The little party I had before taking a break for my nuptials was an altogether more genteel affair.

Wedding bells

There was a lot to be done in the week leading up to the wedding and it didn't help that I developed a severe head cold. On the Friday, however, probably because of a heavy nosebleed, it cleared up. I was still waiting to collect my new car, so I hired one of the recently manufactured Morris 1000s for the honeymoon, which we intended spending on a drive round the entire coast of Ireland.

What can I say about the wedding? Everything seemed to go according to plan. Well briefed by the Rev Frank McCullough, of Castlewellan Parish Church, Mollie and I remembered our lines and best man Tom and bridesmaid May, who were currently on something of a roll in their rather on and off relationship, did all that was expected of them. The church choir, of which Mollie had been a member, were in attendance.

A surprising large crowd of guests and onlookers attended the ceremony or assembled outside to pelt us with confetti. I was delighted to see friends and colleagues from all three newspapers where I'd worked. I thought Mollie looked positively radiant – I know we were both ecstatically happy. It was exactly a year to the day since our first meeting, in the little dancehall only a few hundred yards from the church.

The reception, in Newcastle's Donard Hotel, was equally harmonious and pleasant and a lot of kind folk said nice things about us and wished us well. After thanking everyone, Mollie and I nipped off to No 27 to change, collect the car and leave the keys with Betty, who was keeping an eye on the house until our return.

We were waved off on our journey to Dublin, if not exactly into the sunset, at least into a calm, pleasant evening. We were fortunate that the weather had remained constantly good all day.

In those days there was a Customs' checkpoint on the border with the Republic. I had my driver's licence and insurance documentation ready, but we were waved through with a chorus of "Good luck" and "Have a great honeymoon." Another yelled "God bless the pair of you. Have a wonderful life."

Mollie looked puzzled. "But how do you think they knew we'd just been married?"

Picking a couple of bits of confetti from her hair – the inside of

Lots of friends turned up to see Mollie and I tie the knot in Castlewellan Parish Church.

the car was covered in the stuff – I smiled, "This is a bit of a giveaway, don't you think? Or perhaps it's because we have a bit of a newly-married look about us!"

We both burst out laughing. It was an ideal beginning to what turned out to be an ideal honeymoon.

Beautiful Ireland

Typically, we got lost in Dublin. I'd brought along a road atlas, but Mollie's map-reading skills were even worse than mine. I guess it didn't help that we hadn't booked in anywhere and intended finding a likely hotel on our travels.

We'd earlier noticed a little figure of St Christopher, the Patron Saint of Travellers, hooked on the rear-view mirror, and he was surely on duty that evening. We stopped to ask directions from a passer-by. She introduced herself as a Mrs Boylan and said she owned a guest house close to Phoenix Park. She'd be delighted if we stayed with her. She hopped in the back and we were there in a thrice. Our accommodation was ideal and she insisted on making us tea and sandwiches after our journey.

It was a mellow evening, and before turning in, we went for a leisurely stroll in the famous park, so steeped in the country's history. I'd read a little Irish history and regaled Mollie with a short précis of the Easter Rising of 1916, the siege in the General Post Office and the events that followed, including the executions by the British of Patrick Pearse, Thomas Clarke, James Connolly and other leaders of the Rebellion.

Although my singing voice leaves much to be desired, I followed this up with a complete rendition of Kevin Barry, the poignant ballad commemorating the death of a young Irishman who was hanged in 1920 for his part in the deaths of three soldiers. Thanks to my Uncle Bobbie, who was wont to sing it when in his cups, it's one of the few songs I know all the way through.

I'm not sure if Mollie was surprised that I knew it, or that I attempted to serenade her with the complete version, but it was probably just as well her father didn't hear me.

After breakfast and a quick look around Dublin we headed south, hugging the coast as much as possible. I was quite pleased with how the Morris performed, so much so that I eventually bought an identical model when the time came to change the Ford. We drove through Wicklow and Wexford before stopping for lunch in Waterford. There we met a man driving a Volkswagen Beatle who announced that he was the Mayor of Waterford. We took him at his word and he bade us follow him around the scenic route

The sun was out and it was a beautiful day. It was our first time in this part of the world and we thoroughly enjoyed the breathtaking views. After a pleasurable couple of hours drive we stopped and had a nice chat with his Worship before parting company. He was another who'd twigged on that we were honeymooners for he wished us a blessed and happy life as he indicated the best way to Cork. "We'll definitely have to get rid of all traces of that confetti," I said to Mollie.

We booked into the Country Club, overlooking the river, and after dinner got into conversation with a nice couple who were on their way to Newcastle the following day. We exchanged tips on the best places to see in both locations. The weather took a turn for the better on Monday and we spent a couple of days drinking in the delights of County Cork, Kerry and Killarney. This included a pony trek to the Gap of Dunloe and a jaunting car ride around the famous lakes.

We slowly worked our way west and north through Tralee, Limerick, Sligo, Castlebar and Donegal, agreeing that the last named county's Atlantic Drive had to be one of the most spellbinding coastal drives in the world. After Bundoran we crossed back into the North and took in Derry, Strabane and Enniskillen before sweeping round the Causeway Coast and back home by way of the Glens of Antrim and Belfast.

Back home again, everyone was glad to see us; Betty had done a super job in filling up the fridge and larder and laying in enough stores to more than see us through our first week. Dad, Mollie's folks and Gran and Jim came to Sunday tea and we spent much of the evening fielding seemingly endless questions about our adventures. When everyone had gone Mollie and I sat down on either side of a blazing log fire, with a contented Randy lying on the floor at our feet.

The next day I had to leave the hire-car back to Belfast and catch a bus to Downpatrick to resume work. Mollie would be busy boxing up slices of wedding cake and writing thank-you letters to everyone who had given us presents. In the words of the old saying – the honeymoon was over and life as a married couple beckoned,

Once more into the breach

After the inevitable bout of leg-pulling and near-the-knuckle jokes, I quickly settled back into the familiar routine of work. Slightly shamefaced, I begged off early as I had to travel up to Kilkeel to collect my new Ford Popular. It would be good to have four wheels under me again after my recent experiences with the scooter. My injured thigh was a reminder, but happily, the scar had almost healed.

Colin asked if I would call into the *Observer* before coming over in the morning to collect a proof he'd arranged to get from Hawthorne. I found my old boss in typically surly form, mumbling something about him being the perpetual victim of a one-way traffic system and wasn't it about time that favours started coming the other way for a change.

Making certain I had the proof firmly in my possession, I said it had nothing to do with me and I'd pass on his complaint. He kept chundering on as I opened the office door. I know it was naughty, but I just couldn't resist. "By the way," I asked mildly. "How are you getting on with the Union? I believe you've finally joined. Pity it hadn't happened in my time!"

Noting the expression on his face and hearing him build up with his regular "Mmmm . . ." I didn't wait for a reply.

I think it was the following week that we had one of our occasional blind panics in the *Recorder*. It didn't concern me directly, but I couldn't help but overhear an anxious conversation between Colin and Johnny McQuoid one day. It seemed that John Rea, the doyen of the big printing press, had come down with a dose of 'flu that was likely to keep him in his bed for at least a week. There was no way he would be able to handle that week's print run.

Worse, his assistant, the only other chap on the premises who could handle the press, had left for a job in Belfast a few weeks previously.

"What the hell are we going to do?" Johnny appealed, spreading his arms plaintively.

"We'll have to try to get someone in temporarily, but it won't be easy at this short notice."

It was clearly my big moment to come charging to the rescue. "No need to worry," I said modestly. "I'll do it."

Their expressions were something I won't easily forget. "But you're not a printer," Johnny managed eventually.

"In the *Observer* I had to turn my hand to most jobs," I replied. I used to take my turn on their Cosser. I'll have a look, but I can't imagine your machine is much different."

The three of us headed downstairs and I gave the big, black beast of a machine a quick onceover. "There are a few differences, but none that I can't handle," I told them.

I winked at Colin. "You'll have to do Downpatrick Court on Thursday while I'm otherwise engaged."

I walked back upstairs, leaving the pair of them staring after me in wonder. I suppose I ought to spin out this tale and build it up into something really huge. But why bother. It's enough to say that the print run ran like clockwork. I think we even finished about an hour ahead of schedule.

Of course I was the hero of the hour and I believe I managed to glean a measure of unaccustomed respect from the print crew. Mrs Crichton thanked me warmly and handed me a five-pound-note. But the most cherished accolade came from John Rea when he reappeared the following week.

As he shook my hand, he declared loudly, "By God boy, but you're not tied to the one profession!"

It was a saying he'd trot out periodically for years to come.

Contentment

The months slipped by and I found myself easing into a steady routine. That said, one of the great things about working on a newspaper is that, within that routine, there are peaks and troughs, small triumphs and disasters and a fair share of shocks and surprises. The thing is to always expect the unexpected.

Mollie decided to go back to work for a while and our joint account in the bank kept moving steadily in the right direction. Although we were largely content with life in No 27, we started to think more and more of owning a place of our own. A construction firm called Taggart was developing land in Tullybrannigan, on the foothills of the Mournes, and we decided to make enquiries.

I'd known Lindsay Graham, a local estate agent, for years and he agreed that a new bungalow in that location would be a shrewd investment, particularly as there was a generous government subsidy available at the time. We signed the papers, picked a site in Ben Crom Park, which afforded a pleasant view of the town and the sea beyond. Over the next few months we walked up there periodically to watch our little investment grow. No 5 cost us £1,875, including the £275 subsidy. It's hard to believe the valuation has increased virtually a hundredfold since.

We moved in in September, 1960 and that same weekend I headed off to Croke Park in Dublin to watch Down make sporting history by defeating kingpins Kerry in their first ever All-Ireland Final. The *Recorder* produced a free supplement to mark the occasion and the subsequent celebrations were something to behold.

Now, what I knew about the finer points of Gaelic football wouldn't have filled the back of a postage stamp, but I was friends with many of the players. Maurice Hayes, clerk of the town council and secretary of the team, provided us with a generous quota of tickets and I was delighted to be given a photographer's pass which allowed me access to the pitch with my camera.

This came close to causing my downfall. A dignified looking Bishop, whose name I've long forgotten, in his full regalia, was escorted to midfield to take what I imagined was a mock throw-in before the game got underway. In actual fact, it was the real thing! Players on both sides hurled themselves at the ball as I was still clicking the shutter. The Bishop and his retinue managed to escape unscathed, but I was bowled over in the scrummage before scurrying for safety behind the goal.

Back home in Newcastle, Mollie was recording RTE's commentary on the match by the ebullient Michael O'Hehir. I listened to it later and heard Michael scream: "The ball is in. Kerry have it. A Down man is on the ground. No, it's not a player. A photographer has been knocked flying ..."

As I explained to Mollie afterwards, the commentator got it half right. I was the cameraman in question – and if only I could find that bloody Kerry midfielder I'd . . . Even worse than that, he'd only gone and buggered up my potential prizewinning picture of the year!

As everybody knows, Down triumphed in the end. I got some smashing pictures and I remember crouching behind the Down goal, counting out the final minutes on my fingers to an anxious Pat Rice, the big fullback from Castlewellan.

Afterwards I wrote what we call a colour piece for the supplement, trying to put across what it all meant to the team, their supporters, the county at large, and especially to me. Ten years later I called at the home of GAA enthusiast H Hogg, in Ballykinlar, to collect a report. Imagine my surprise when he brought me into his living room and pointed to my article, mounted and framed in a place of honour on the wall. I felt humbled. It seems that not all our scribblings are fated to finish up as fish and chip wrappers.

Two arrivals

I especially remember two happy events of 1961. First, Mollie presented me with a beautiful baby daughter, Valerie Louise.

Second, my old friend Tony arrived on a visit from Australia. Val was two weeks late in putting in an appearance, but duly arrived safe and sound and was delivered in Hardy Greer House, Downpatrick.

Since moving into Ben Crom, we'd become friendly with an English couple, Frank and Sylvia Whittaker, who had taken a similar bungalow to ours close by. They kept tabs on how Mollie was progressing and when told that she was likely to be induced on the night of 8/9 July, Sylvia insisted that poor Frank come up and keep me company. By 2:30am we were talked out and the poor chap kept nodding off in his armchair, so I thanked him and packed him off home.

There was no way I could sleep and so I was still wide awake and becoming increasingly anxious when the hospital phoned at just after seven o'clock. "Congratulations," a quiet voice informed me. "You are the father of a lovely baby daughter – and both mother and baby are doing well."

I hadn't realised I was so tense. I fell to my knees on the carpet and sobbed my heart out.

Later that morning I brought a camera into Hardy Greer, hugged my two girls and took some photographs. I chatted to Mollie for a long time before calling at the *Recorder* where Andy developed my film and ran off a number of prints. I spent the rest of the day running round my folks and friends, giving them photos, accepting congratulations and drinking numerous cups of tea. In the evening I called back at Hardy Greer.

Tony and I had been keeping in touch since he'd left for Australia and I was delighted when he wrote to say he was coming back to Ireland for a spell. He wasn't sure how long he'd stay but his plan was to marry Patsy, the Kilkeel lass he'd been going out with, before returning Down Under with her.

I drove to the border to meet him and he rolled up in a huge Chevrolet limousine he'd bought on arrival in Dublin. "It does about eight miles to the gallon," he announced airily, "but who cares? It makes a good impression, don't you think? I'll flog it again before I go back."

I had to admit it did look the part all right. He kept on pronouncing it Chevro-let, with the stress on the final "t". In vain I tried to tell him that the "t" was silent, as in Hercule Poirot, but he would have none of it. It was some months later when he finally admitted, "Fleming, you were right, as usual, the final "t" is silent, as in fart!"

Tony divided his time between stopping with us in Ben Crom and in Kilkeel. In due course he introduced us to his mysterious girlfriend. Patsy Marks was a lovely girl and the four of us remained firm friends for the rest of their lives. We were guests at their wedding in Massforth Chapel, outside Kilkeel, later that year and were genuinely sorry when they returned to Melbourne soon afterwards. It was a happy reunion several years later when they returned to take up permanent residence, first in Dungannon and later in Kilkeel. Tony and I resumed our friendship as if he'd been around since yesterday.

Quite a birthday present

Mrs Crichton always remembered my birthday. Each year she'd call and invite me up to the house for a chat, a glass of something, and a little envelope containing a card and a ten-pound note.

In 1961 it was different. At close of play on the day in question, Colin said "Mum would like to see you before you head off home. I'll run you up. I don't think she'll keep you long."

She rose from her armchair to greet me as Colin and I entered the sitting room. "Good of you to come, Brad, Colin and I wanted to thank you for all you've done for us since you joined the *Recorder*. It's three years this month is it not?"

I confirmed that it was indeed three years and that no thanks was necessary. I was totally content and happy to be with the paper and couldn't have wished for better or more understanding employers.

She smiled. "I'm delighted to hear you say that, and I understand that Mollie is due any day now?"

I nodded in confirmation and she went on. "As a little token of appreciation, which I hope you and your family will enjoy, we have a small gift for you. I'd better let Colin explain."

Colin rose and shook my hand. "Brad, I endorse everything my mother has said. You've been a great asset to our newspaper and we are deeply appreciative. I know how much you've enjoyed our little outings on the lough and I also know you've especially liked the few runs you've had on Neville Walsh's cruiser *Snowgoose*. Well, Neville's family is growing and he's decided to get a bigger boat. In short, I've bought *Snowgoose* from him and would like formally to present it to you. My mother has added a new Evinrude outboard as an acknowledgement of all you've done for us."

I was completely overwhelmed as I somehow managed to

thank them both. What a marvellous gift and so typical of a family I'd come to respect and admire more than I could say. All I could do was to give Mrs. Crichton a huge hug and invite Colin to accompany me on *Snowgoose's* maiden voyage as soon as it could be arranged. That he did, and accompanied by half a dozen tinnies, we had a memorable first voyage down to Castleward and back.

My family, friends and I enjoyed many happy days exploring all around the Lough, especially picnicking in the lovely setting of Castleward. Another special treat was joining a flotilla of Quoile Yacht Club members to cruise down to Killyleagh to enjoy fish and chips on Saturday nights.

More arrivals and departures

The years ticked by and change came to the *Recorder*. Leslie Dawes, after doing more and more freelance work with Ulster Television in their sports department, eventually moved there full time. He was replaced by Mick Drake, who had just been fired by the *Observer*.

Interestingly enough, on the day of Mick's departure a 'friendly' one-off cricket match had been arranged between our two papers. I think it owed more to the Marquis of Queensbury Rules, or Fred Karno's Circus, than it did to the laws of cricket, but Hawthorne appeared to take it with his usual seriousness. Other than being determined to give them a good stuffing, the rest of us simply wanted an afternoon's fun.

We were secretly hoping the happy occasion might lead Hawthorne into giving Mick a late reprieve, but it was not to be. I can't remember the scores but I do recall we gave them a severe walloping. I had a quick word with Colin and suggested that, with Leslie leaving, it might be a notion to have Mick joins us. He assented readily, I spoke to Micky and the deed was done.

Colin and I held a council of war over a steak dinner in Rea's Hotel and it was decided that I should take over the sports desk and he and Mick would concentrate on news. In practice this meant I was responsible for sport, in addition to my share of courts and councils, but I didn't mind unduly. I'd always been keen on sport and I thoroughly enjoyed this new challenge.

Around this time there were other important changes and the *Recorder* upped stakes and moved from the old premises it had occupied since 1836 to its present headquarters just across the street. It was definitely a move in the right direction and further sweeping changes were soon to follow.

The paper appeared in danger of becoming something of a *Mourne Observer* old boys' club as Derick Moore transferred to join us in Downpatrick. He proved to be a tower of strength, especially when helping with the switch to web-offset printing in September, 1966. It was largely through his insistence that the front page of the first new issue was dominated by a huge aerial photograph of Downpatrick which virtually filled the page. It certainly demonstrated the sharpness and clarity of the new printing process.

In many ways, I consider myself fortunate that my fifteen years with the paper spanned the end of the old hot-metal printing and the advent of lithography. I saw many changes in that time, but this was by far the greatest and most significant. It was good to see the paper continuing to progress after I moved on, and when opportunity permitted I liked nothing better than to call into the office for a chat with my old friends and the new editor, Joe McCoubrey.

I remember taking Joe on in a freelance capacity, principally to help us cover local sports. He was in the Civil Service at that time, but I realised his heart was in writing and journalism. He was a natural, and it was no surprise to me when he joined the paper full time and ultimately became editor.

I was always made welcome when I would occasionally call into the paper afterwards and was delighted to renew my friendship with Joe years later when the pair of us entered the world of authorship and fiction writing. But, as they say, more of that later.

Time flashes by

It's tempting to write in a lot more detail of those days, but my story must be kept within reasonable bounds. I would be remiss, however, if I didn't mention a few personal recollections.

Like being granted a world exclusive interview with our local MP, Brian Faulkner, on the steps of Stormont on the day he resigned as Prime Minister of Northern Ireland. It was a good thing my shorthand was working well, for, as Andy Campbell's photograph confirmed, I was given enough copy to fill our entire front page.

We published next morning and carried the interview a full 24-hours before any other paper. The scoop was undoubtedly gratifying, and my sole regret was that, while my piece was copied by practically every daily paper in Britain and Ireland. I wasn't able to claim a single penny as a freelance. It did, however, bring a

My *world exclusive* interview for the *Down Recorder* with Northern Ireland Prime Minister, Brian Faulkner, on the day he resigned from office.

telephone call from Cowan Watson, then editor of the *Newsletter,* inviting me to join the paper. I subsequently turned down a number of similar requests before accepting an improved offer two years later and joining his paper as a sub editor. A personal letter of thanks and congratulations from the ex-Prime Minister was typical of the man.

Then there was the day I took a call from Malcolm Kellard, BBC Northern Ireland's Head of Sport, inviting me to lunch. After congratulating me on the *Recorder's* improving sports coverage, he asked if I'd ever considered going into broadcasting. I told him I supposed I had, but not too seriously.

After asking which sports I covered – all of them except Gaelic football and horseracing, I declared cockily – he invited me to prepare a two-minute account of any match I fancied and come down to Broadcasting House for lunch and a voice test the following Friday. He was clearly not a man for hanging about.

I redrafted a report I'd done on a recent Senior League cricket match between Downpatrick and Waringstown, which was still fresh in my mind, and trimmed it to precisely two minutes. Malcolm and a sound engineer watched through a glass panel as I was put through my paces. Although my throat was dry and I felt decidedly nervous, I was given the thumbs up and booked to cover Downpatrick's home match the following day for the 6.00pm Sportsound programme, which immediately followed Alistair Cooke's Letter from America. I was treading in exalted footsteps.

Determined to do a decent job, I got a note of the teams and checked their history and current standings. I even drafted a possible intro. Imagine my chagrin, therefore when I took a call from Malcolm at home at 9:30 next morning. He sounded a worried man.

"Glad I got you, Brad. I'm in a bit of a hole here. You said you covered golf among your other sports, didn't you?"

"That's right."

"Thank God for that. The thing is, Jimmy Magee, our golf correspondent, who was due to cover the Irish Amateur Open which starts today at Royal County Down, has cried off with some dreaded lurgy. Could you cover it for us by any chance?"

"Sure, I'll be happy to. It's right on my doorstep." I replied, hoping I sounded more confident than I felt.

"Good man, you're a lifesaver. I appreciate it. I'd like you to phone through a one-minute live piece for inclusion in the 12:55 lunchtime news and be down in the studio by six at the latest ready to do two minutes first up. I'll talk to you when you get here. For God's sake don't be late! Transfer charge calls to the number I gave you."

As a five-day member of the club, I knew the course well and was on good terms with the Secretary, Squadron Leader Jones and senior professional, Ian Murdock The former readily offered the use of his office for my call and Ian gave me some useful tips on how the course was playing and which players in particular to look out for.

I phoned in good time and was put on hold before being cued when to begin. I rattled off my little piece, finishing with a quote from Ian about the condition of the famous course. This brought an off air "Well done" from Malcolm and a further entreaty not to be late at BH."

It was a glorious afternoon and I walked round the course watching a number of the matchplay contests. I especially enjoyed a short chat with the famous Joe Carr, already the doyen of amateur golf in Ireland. Finally, I arranged with a friendly official that I'd phone him in the secretary's office soon after six to get an update. He seemed delighted at being involved.

I arrived in the Sportsound office in good time to find what I later discovered was the usual organised chaos. I explained to Malcolm about my prearranged call for an update. He looked slightly worried before nodding and waving me to a desk with a phone. "Make it snappy," was all he said.

My man at the course had some exciting news for me which changed the whole thrust of my report. He told me that Mark Gannon, a young 20-year-old from Bettystown, had just set a unique record by becoming the first golfer to record birdie twos at each of County Down's four difficult par-3 holes. This was clearly going to be my new intro. I was still on the phone when Malcolm came up and beckoned me to come with him. I knew there was still more than five minutes to go.

Hand over the mouthpiece, I said. "Give me a couple of minutes please. I'm getting a great story here."

He stalked off, looking over his shoulder anxiously, as I finished my call and jotted down a shorthand note of my new opening. I'd have to ad lib the rest while keeping an eye on the big studio clock with its remorseless sweeping second-hand. Malcolm grabbed my elbow and steered me into a chair at a circular desk opposite anchor-man Ira Milligan, who gave me a reassuring smile.

Malcolm sidled off after whispering "Listen to Ira and don't speak until your light comes on. Then shut up while Ira introduces the next man. When you finish get up quietly, without tripping over anything and slip away to your left and take a seat with the rest of the lads. And good luck!"

I nodded numbly and clutched my notebook. I could hear the familiar soft tones of Alistair Cooke concluding his *Letter,* and then Ira was introducing me.

"Brad Fleming is just back from the Irish Amateur Golf Championship in Newcastle and I hear he has something exciting to report. Tell us all about it Brad."

And tell them I did, reading from my Pitman's notes. My throat wasn't dry. I wasn't nervous. On reflection, I believe not having time to think about what I was about to do was a help rather than a hindrance. My two minutes flashed by. After telling my audience of young Gannon's heroics, I launched into an account of how Joe Carr and the other leading contenders had fared. When the big clock showed ten seconds to go I concluded with Ian Murdock's predictions for the rest of the championship, finishing on the stroke of my allotted 120 seconds. I even remembered not to fall over anything as I slid out of the hot seat.

Back in the anonymity of the shadows, I got a couple of slaps on the back from my colleagues on either side, and glancing through the long window into the control room, logged a vigorous thumbs up from Malcolm. It was only then the shock hit me and I breathed a silent sigh of relief.

The programme went off air and Malcom marched in, accompanied by a continuity girl who was tasked with collecting our scripts. In those days it seemed the BBC had to maintain a written record of every word spoken on air. I never asked why, I simply handed her my notebook and watched her look of incredulity as she saw my hieroglyphics.

"I can't make head or tail of this," she shrilled.

Malcolm looked over her shoulder and he seemed to pale visibly. "My God Brad, Is this a copy of what you just put out on air?"

I nodded. "It's Pitman's shorthand. I've always used it. I hope my report was okay. I had to make that change I told you about. I'm sorry but there wouldn't have been time to type it up or use longhand."

He asked if I would tear out the relevant pages from my jotter and passed them to the gaping girl. "It's all right love," he consoled her, "we can type up a copy from the tape."

We all repaired to the BBC's 69 Club, round the corner in Bedford Street, and had a few beers. The Beeb still paid their contributors in guineas in those days and the going rate was six guineas a minute. So I received £18.18, plus generous travel expenses, for my day's work. Times had certainly changed from my thirty bob a week pay-packet in the *MO*.

It wasn't until a long time afterwards that Malcolm confided why he'd been so anxious to get me into the studio early. "As it was your first time, and a big story, I was going to have you do a trial run," he said. "If that went okay I'd have used it on the show and you could have sat back, relaxed, and got the feel of the studio. I know what the first time live can be like. Your updating phone call put the kibosh on that and almost gave me heart failure."

He waved my apology aside. "Not at all. It was a bloody first class report. You're going to do well."

Rain stops play

I covered sports for the Beeb for over two years and enjoyed every minute. I also worked intermittently in News and Current Affairs but sports, and particularly Sportsound was always my favourite. Malcolm Kellard and his assistant producer, Joy Williams, who was later to take over from him, headed a happy and skilled team of regular contributors, household names like Harry Thompson, Stuart McKinney, Eddie Gordon and Hugo Patterson.

Hugo, an executive with the Northern Ireland Electricity Board, was doyen of our cricket coverage, a kind of Ulster John Arlott or Brian Johnstone. He was later to win even more fame (perhaps notoriety would have been a better word) as the Board's chief spokesman during the Loyalist Workers' strike of 1974 when the province almost ground to a halt and power had to be husbanded carefully to keep homes and businesses going. He presented regular bulletins through each day when "supplies were always on a knife-edge," or the entire country "was teetering on the brink of collapse."

Happily, his cricket coverage was more palatable and light-hearted. Strange to say, some of our more memorable broadcasts occurred when rain washed out play and Malcolm would ask the pair of us to natter about cricket for five minutes to fill the gap left by the absence of match reports. Hugo would take the lead and we would chat about what he considered to be the chief talking points of the day.

Arlott and Johnstone we were not, but I learned a lot about broadcasting from Hugo, as well as having tremendous fun. From what Malcolm told me, it seems our little Test Match Special-style blatherings were even more popular than the usual match reports. As Hugo once whispered, "I'd happily talk away all day at six guineas a minute." There was no way I was going to argue with that.

In my time with Sportsound I was privileged to have many on- and off-air chats with my past and present sporting heroes. Particularly in the 69 Club afterwards, the craic, as they say, was mighty. I wish I could recall even half of those stories today, but I'll never forget listening to Rugby legends like Willie John McBride and Mike Gibson, golfers Christie O'Connor and Peter Alliss and soccer's Terry Neill and Danny Blanchflower.

Life is never dull

Around that time changes were coming thick and fast. It came as quite a shock when Derick told me one evening that he had accepted a job in Norwich and would be handing in his notice. We'd been firm friends and had our fair share of adventures for more than fifteen years. He promised to keep in touch and would be sure to look me up whenever he came home on holiday. Coincidently, my Gran and Uncle Jim announced they were also moving to Norwich to be close to Bobby and Ethel.

Colin and I had several lengthy steak and chip dinners in Rea's discussing our options. He himself had been helping Derick in making up the paper with the assistance of a new apprentice, Gerry Carson, who was shaping up well. The obvious thing was to bring in an experienced make-up man.

Of course, we didn't do the obvious. Instead, I undertook to rejig my work schedule, largely forget about court and council reporting unless I was needed, and take on the dual role of sports editor and make-up man. This meant I would physically design and paste up the sports section as well as some inside pages. Jerry would split the inside pages with me, leaving Colin to finish off page one.

I really threw myself into the new task. It meant I would work through the night on Wednesdays, with an hour's break for supper, and then often carry on until both the paper and I went to bed at whatever time we finished on Thursday evening. It was interesting and I won't pretend it wasn't challenging and exhausting. I loved it. Colin and I never discussed money as such, but I did receive a generous hike in salary. I appreciated this as my new schedule precluded my doing a lot of my work as a correspondent for the Nationals.

Up to that time not a lot of thought had been given by any of us to planning and laying out the paper. The front page lead would be chosen and the page built up around it. The back sports page followed similar lines. Inside page stories were spread out among the advertisements. To put it bluntly, it was all rather Heath Robinson and amateurish. I decided to do something about that, at least as far as the sports section was concerned.

I had some page-planning sheets printed off and filled them in for Jerry and myself. Jerry thought it a great help. I offered to do one for Colin as well but he preferred to do his own thing. I like to think the style and content of the paper continued to improve. We certainly received no complaints and one or two people actually remarked upon it. Gradually we became more proficient, developed a workable system and slowly but surely reduced Wednesday night work. We were also winding up earlier on Thursdays and were often able to read copies of the paper, fresh off the press from our Lithoforme Printers in Portadown by the time we finished our customary group dinner in Reas.

As compensation for my heavy midweek workload, I usually had Fridays, Saturdays and Sundays free. I was still receiving occasional approaches to join the BBC or *Newsletter* full time. An old friend, Pat Carville, editor of the recently introduced *Sunday News*, invited me to lunch, and on learning I was now free on Fridays, offered me an eight-hour subbing slot. I gave it a trial, and after a few weeks, decided to make it a permanent arrangement. Later, Derek Murray, the sports editor, roped me in for a four-hour shift on Saturday afternoons when I wasn't otherwise engaged with doing a Saturday match for the Beeb.

The tax man commeth

I was working ridiculous hours – shades of my beginnings in the *MO* all those years before - but I was raking in considerably more than thirty bob a week. I was also logging up a lot of miles, but, thanks to Colin's insistence that I use the *Recorder* fuel account, all it was costing me was travelling time.

While Mollie was appreciative of our increasing spending power, she wasn't happy that we seemed to be seeing less and less of one another. Repeating almost the exact words Norma Hanna had said years before, she chided "You're becoming a proper workaholic. Valerie and I scarcely see you anymore."

I had to admit to the truth of this. There was no question that I'd been overdoing it. A letter I received the next morning underlined the point. It was a demand from the Inland Revenue claiming £824 in unpaid income tax. In the old days I'd have had to work more than a decade to meet that particular bill!

Happily, Colin suggested a possible source of aid. "Have a word with old HEG Dickson, the firm's accountant, down Market Street. He's a dab hand at tax matters and I'm sure he'll be able to pare that down a good bit."

He arranged an interview with the man that very afternoon. Dickson tut-tutted when I told him I'd dealt with previous tax demands by filing them away in the wastepaper basket. "You can't do that," he chided. "They just pick a figure out of the sky and if you pay up without complaint, they'll probably double it next time until you're forced to do something about it. I want you to go home and bring me every bit of relevant correspondence you can find."

He then took notes as he fired a string of questions at me. Did I use my car for work? How many work miles did I travel? How much of my phone and electricity bill was down to work? How much did I pay my wife for her secretarial help, etc., etc.?

"In future pass all such correspondence directly to me. I'll let you know when I have this sorted."

About two months later the Inland Revenue wrote to me again. I glanced at it briefly. £416 it said. Still steep, but at least the bill had been reduced by almost half – a huge step in the right direction. I called to see him and passed the envelope to him with my thanks. An almost fifty per cent reduction wasn't to be sneezed at.

He shook his head sadly. "Read it again," he said.

I did and did a quick double take. It wasn't a bill at all. They were paying me £416 because they had been paid too much tax – a turnabout of exactly £440. This man was a miracle worker. I could scarcely believe it. I shook him warmly by the hand and asked how much I owed him.

"Drop me in a bottle of Black Bush next time you're passing, and in future you'd better let me keep an eye on your tax for you."

I dropped off two bottles on my way home. I liked the man's style. There's nothing, absolutely nothing, like dealing with a professional.

A son and heir

In October, 1971, Mollie presented me with a son and heir. Unlike his sister, Barry came into the world more or less on time, and thankfully, on this occasion Mollie had a trouble-free birth.

I eased off work for a while to adopt the role of proud father, and Val, now a lively ten-year-old, was a dutiful sister and a great help to her Mum.

Mollie's parents were delighted at having another grandchild to spoil. The one sad note was that Dad had passed away after a short illness three years previously and never had the chance to see his first grandson.

Val and Barry

Columnists

Good, well-informed columnists are a vital part of any newspaper. While news reporting should be factual, accurate, and non-opinionated, a columnist has a lot more latitude, within reason, to pronounce his personal view and opinion about whatever he likes.

Indeed, if he isn't outspoken, and even provocative, then he isn't doing his job properly.

In my early years in the *MO,* this task was performed by Willie Morgan, a chirpy little Glaswegian, who wrote his *Man About Town* column in his small tailor's shop in Railway Street. It was probably the most popular item in the paper. Always written with tongue firmly in cheek, he saw himself as the voice of the little man, the man in the street, a kind of latter-day Don Quixote tilting his verbal lance at every bureaucratic windmill in sight.

I used to call every week to collect his copy, which was usually written in Biro on the back of whatever scraps of paper came to hand. As often as not he'd put the kettle on and we'd have a cup of tea while we sorted out, if not the entire world, at least our own little part of it.

I started a similar sort of column in the *Outlook,* although I'd be the first to admit it wasn't nearly as good.

One of the first things I did on arriving in the *Recorder* was to persuade Colin and his mother to engage a good columnist. I had the very man in mind too, Willie Hunter, my daughter's headmaster, a Newcastle urban councillor and a good personal friend. With a twinkle in his eye he agreed to take on the job, on the strict understanding that he would remain anonymous.

He himself came up with his own by-line, appropriately and amusingly – *Nimrod* – which, of course, means the great hunter. He was, in turn, humorous, acerbic, caustic and entertaining. Many tried to suss out his real identity, none succeeded. He retired sometime after I left the paper and only then did he allow his identity to be disclosed.

Wilfred McNeilly, known affectionately as the *Bard of Ardglass*, was one of nature's larger than life characters. I admired and liked him immensely and enjoyed nothing more than a run out to the little fishing port to share a pint and a chat with him in The Anglers' or Linehan's Bar. He wasn't a regular columnist but made occasional contributions.

He and his wife Jean lived in a quaintly-shaped little house, once owned by Colin Middleton, the noted artist, on the edge of the village. They'd met and married while Wilf was a serving officer with the Indian Navy during World War Two, and Jean was a Queen Alexandra's nursing sister.

When UTV launched in 1959, Wilf made regular appearances as a sort of homespun philosopher, a role he could play to the manner born. His London agent had apparently secured the franchise for the populist Sexton Blake novels and Wilf churned them out for years. When he was in need of drinking money, which I have to say was most of the time; he would lock himself away for a fortnight with his electric typewriter and a copious supply of coffee, and emerge with a new Sexton Blake paperback ready for publication.

Wilf surveyed the world benignly through a pair of heavy, horn-rimmed tortoiseshell glasses and often, it must be said, through the bottom of a pint glass of the amber liquid. I remember an occasion when I needed a Christmas feature to accompany a page of advertisements. I phoned Wilf. "Have someone call to pick it up in half an hour," he replied. I called myself, smack on time, and he was finishing it off on his typewriter as I arrived.

A lovable, charming, eccentric man, I read of his death, somewhere in England, a few years ago with immense regret.

Here's a typical Wilf McNeilly story. The famous group, *The Dubliners,* were appearing at a pub in Killough one winter's night and Wilf, who knew them well from somewhere or other, was in tow. He phoned the office and Colin and I took a couple of hours off to drive out to see their show.

As I recall, they were paid £200 for the gig, a tidy sum in those days, and loathe to drive all the way home at that ungodly hour, were glad to accept Wilf's invitation to doss down in his place for the night. Colin and I stayed for the start of the celebrations, but discretion dictated that we head back to Downpatrick while we were still in a fit state to navigate. It was as well that we did.

By mid-morning next day the bulk of the £200 had disappeared in some kind of alcoholic haze and the party decided to indulge in some less-expensive sport before the band finally headed south. Who suggested a game of leapfrog down by the harbour is open to question, but all present agreed it was a sporting way to work off a hangover.

It seems that all went well until, according to several witnesses, the gravel-voiced Ronnie Drew straightened up just as Wilf was vaulting over his back. The Bard went lurching off to leeward before disappearing over the side of the quay to plunge some fourteen feet into what little volume of muddy water was in the basin.

The alcohol in his system no doubt went some way to preventing serious injury, but, nevertheless, Wilf announced that his wellies, now filled with salt water, were stuck fast in the ooze. From what we were told, it required the full might of the Dubliners, plus the assistance of a couple of hefty locals, to hoist him back onto the concrete with the aid of a stout rope.

This mishap would surely have been enough for most mere mortals, but the author of Sexton Blake was made of sterner stuff than that. Instead of returning home via the safe tarmacked road, he insisted on a shortcut, leading his intrepid band of adventurers across the treacherous slippery rocks to his home in the teeth of the fast incoming tide.

After a journey that would have proved a stern test for Scott of the Antarctic in his prime, they collapsed for several hours, awakening to discover that Wilf's and Ronnie's wallets were missing.

"Fear not," asserted Wilf with a great show of confidence. "This sort of thing has happened before. Chances are our wallets will be trapped in a rock pool when the tide ebbs and we can recover them then." We just have to wait an hour or two for the tide to turn."

They waited, no doubt with increasing impatience and scepticism, for Mother Nature to take her course, and returned to the shoreline to search. I have it on Wilf's personal authority that they did, indeed, find both wallets, slightly waterlogged, but with their contents intact and largely undamaged, nestling coyly in a sheltered rock pool.

I haven't seen Mr Drew since, and as poor Wilf is sadly no longer with us, I'm just going to have to take his word for it. It may sound an unlikely tale, but after all, he was the *Bard of Ardglass.*

Advertising . . . what advertising?

In the run-up to Christmas one year I asked Colin why the paper didn't have an advertising department as such and why wasn't an attempt made to solicit advertisements from local traders, especially at this busy, seasonal time?

"It's not something we've ever done," he said, "and I can't say I've ever thought about it much. I suppose old W Y believed that if people wanted to advertise they'd come to us. He would never have condoned actively seeking adverts."

I accepted the *Recorder* was old-fashioned and loath to change, but this was plainly ridiculous. "Colin, I doubt there's another paper anywhere in the world which doesn't try to get advertising, particularly at this time of year. You're missing a great opportunity. For instance, just look at the amount of Christmas advertising the *Observer* and *Newtownards Chronicle* carry compared to us."

He shrugged. "I suppose you're right." After a short pause. "I tell you what. If you want to have a shot at it, then go ahead."

He smiled and added. "I know I couldn't do it, but if you want to you can have ten percent commission."

I smiled. "Is that all? I got forty percent in the *Outlook!*"

I don't think he realised what he was getting himself into. "Okay," he grinned. "Call it twelve and a half percent, that's half-a-crown in the pound. I'll be interested to see how you get on."

I set to work at once. In the three weeks leading up to Christmas we had to print first four and then eight extra pages to accommodate the ads. Traders needed no coaxing and were practically falling over themselves to advertise, the majority of them running ads in all three weeks. Colin couldn't believe it. I was quite happy myself, collecting well over £200 in commission.

It was a one-off though. Before the following Christmas came around the *Recorder* had established a proper advertising department, which has continued to expand down the years.

Belfast bound

I bumped into Malcolm Brodie, the ebullient sports editor of the *Belfast Telegraph,* one day in Havelock House when we were both doing a short piece for Ulster Television. We hadn't met previously but knew one another by reputation – his, of course, carrying much more weight than mine.

He asked if I'd be interested in doing a weekly sports column for *Ireland's Saturday Night,* the *Telegraph's* sports paper, Of course, I said I would and the feature ran for a long time. It was another guineas' transaction. I got £3-3s per column. It was published under my own by-line, which certainly didn't do me any harm.

I was now spending almost half my working week in Belfast. Malcolm Kellard called me aside one day and suggested I join the BBC as a contract freelance, covering news and sport. About the same time Cowan Watson, of the *Newsletter,* invited me to lunch in Kelly's Kitchen, one of his favourite watering holes.

He'd heard some good things from Pat Carville and Derek Murray about my subbing in *Sunday News,* and if I couldn't be persuaded to join his paper's reporting staff, how would I feel about becoming a sub-editor? He offered an attractive salary and added that I could continue working at the *Sunday News* if I wished. With a fetching smile, he stressed that, as subbing would involve a regular shift five nights a week. I would be free to continue reporting sports for the BBC, as well as any other freelance work I fancied.

All I could say was "Thanks very much Cowan – and I suppose you wouldn't object if I snatched a bit of sleep now and then?" In the end I said I'd think about it and get back to him.

There was certainly a lot to think about. For a start, I'd always been happy during my time at the *Recorder*. I liked the work and liked the people and it was only a 20-minute run from my home to the office. I also felt I owed Colin and the family a great deal. An added consideration was that the Northern Ireland troubles were gathering momentum at this time and driving to and from the city in the small hours could pose certain risks.

I talked it over with Colin. We'd always been frank with each other, and I wanted him to understand that I wasn't applying pressure in order to be given a pay rise. As usual, Mollie was content to let me decide this one for myself.

In the end we reached a compromise. I'd take the job in the *Newsletter*, but would help out in the *Recorder* by making up the pages on Wednesdays and Thursdays before travelling on to Belfast.

Newsletter nightlife

The transition from daytime to night-time working came easily enough. After all I hadn't had a nine-to-five kind of job for years. I had a relatively fast run into work as I was going against most of the homeward traffic and driving home in the early hours, with the roads virtually deserted, was a doddle.

A routine soon established itself. I'd leave home in Newcastle around 5:30pm to arrive in Donegall Street in time to start work at 6:30. Normally we'd finish about 1am, and I'd usually be home and tucked up in bed before two o'clock. About one night in seven I'd have to stay on as late sub and supervise any changes which might be needed to the final edition.

With the troubles now at their height, there was rarely any shortage of hard news. I liked the subbing crew and got on well with all of them, especially chief sub, David Kirk, and his deputy, Mike Chapman.

The job of sub-editing is rather like that of a schoolmaster tasked with marking and correcting students' essays. The down-table subs are thrown a pile of copy, with instructions to prune it down to a precise number of column inches, before adding a headline and making any other additions and corrections required.

Each newspaper has, or ought to have, what's known as a *Style Book*, to ensure that reporters and subs use similar spelling and grammar. For instance, the *Newsletter* insisted on spelling Tokio like this, instead of the more usual Tokyo. Don't ask me why, that's just how it had to be. We also had to write "in Page 4" rather than the more conventional "on Page 4". We soon got used to it.

Our first chore on arriving for each shift was to consult the Editor's comments on the previous day's issue. This usually consisted of a couple of A4 pages drawing attention to points he considered to be good or bad. Everybody rather irreverently referred to it as the *Beano* and it usually provoked a good deal of mirth.

There was a great deal of easy-going banter, especially as the night wore on and home time approached. A favourite pastime of about half the night crew was known as an *'interlude for war.'* This rather childish pursuit involved the participants arming themselves with rubber bands and using them as catapults to hurl paper pellets at one another while the rest of us got on with the serious business of producing the paper. It was perhaps surprising that nobody lost an eye during these hostilities.

Davy, the long-suffering printing shop foreman, would enter our room several times a night to complain about a headline that didn't fit into the column space allocated, or ask about some cryptic instruction he wasn't able to decipher. Blame was usually laid at the door of Richard, our university entrant, whose handwriting would have exasperated the most experienced chemist, however used he may have been to reading doctors' scrawled prescriptions.

Our chief sub-editor, popularly known as *The Bear*, would shake his head sadly, admonish the culprit and declare "For God's sake, Richard, watch that letter count or we'll have the whole engine room going on strike!"

One night, shortly after my arrival, Mike Chapman, standing in for the absent *Bear,* threw perhaps three-quarters of the total night's work in my direction, while most of the other guys sat twiddling their thumbs. Twigging on to what he was about I said nothing, kept my head down and got on with it. Our eyes met towards the close of the shift and we exchanged huge grins. We both recognised I'd passed his little test without demur and he never tried it again.

Telling it like it is

There were some huge news stories during my time with the *Newsletter*. One night I was late sub and tasked with preparing the front page lead, or *'the Splash'* as it was known in the trade. A massive IRA bomb had exploded in Great Victoria Street, causing widespread damage. We had a graphic picture with the story and Mike wanted to use the biggest headline type available which would have permitted a count of just eleven letters and spaces for the single line.

Not a lot to convey what I wanted. After thinking for a while, I asked him to reduce the point size fractionally to permit twelve letters. He agreed and I wrote

HEARTSTOPPER

I revamped the story to emphasise how the terrorists had tried, and failed, to bring the heart of Belfast to a permanent halt. How the people, shops and businesses were repairing and restoring and getting back to work, etc. etc.

You should have seen the write up I got in Cowan Watson's *Beano* the following day. It was almost better than a pay-rise!

Paisley in the news

Unlike the occasion mentioned above, there were times when the assembled brainpower of the subs-room failed to produce the perfect headline.

That was the year in which the Rev Ian Paisley, erstwhile leader of the Free Presbyterian Church, had been sentenced to two months' imprisonment in Crumlin Road Jail for refusing to pay a fine, imposed for having been found guilty of disorderly conduct during one of his habitual protest rallies.

He declared he would not pay up and would serve the entire sentence if need be. Some of his supporters, however, coughed up the amount required and he was discharged. One of our photographers had taken a splendid picture of the big man, then at the height of his considerable powers, framed in the doorway of the prison, chin thrust forward, chest puffed up, shoulders back, as though glaring defiantly at the entire world.

Clearly it was going to be the lead story next morning and demanded an equally powerful headline. The *Bear* passed it round the subs' table. The line just would not come to any of us. It was passed round again. Still nothing.

Deadline hour was fast approaching and we were no nearer a solution. Suddenly the door opened and Ray Managh, one of our reporters, rolled in, fresh from a visit to a local hostelry. He picked up the photograph and studied it for a moment, before declaring: "The Free Presbyterian."

That said it all. We had our headline.

I'd had a few run-ins with the reverend gentleman prior to this and had suffered the rough edge of his tongue more than once. This was during the days, long before he linked up with Martin Maginness to become one of the so-called *Chuckle Brothers* in the recent Stormont administration.

On one occasion, though, I thought he had gone a tad too far, even by his own peculiar standards, when he and a number of his Free Presbyterian Church supporters, staged a rowdy protest during an ecumenical service in Belfast's St Anne's Cathedral in honour of Cardinal Jozsef Mindszenty, the highest representative of the Roman Catholic Church in Hungary who had been imprisoned for years because of his outspoken criticism of Fascism and Communism.

Although it was somewhat outside my usual bailiwick, I wrote a short editorial highlighting the incongruity of such crass behaviour by a group whose own clarion call was "Freedom and religious liberty," in seeking to deny the same privilege to others.

I was immediately besieged by a delegation from Crossgar Free Presbyterian Church demanding an instant retraction and apology. I heard them out before telling them, politely but firmly, that in my view, an apology was not warranted as I had simply made a legitimate observation as editor, which I had every right to do. I added that, should they wish to protest further, they were welcome to make use of our correspondence columns.

"And will you publish any such letter exactly as written?" I was asked.

"Of course," I told them, "Providing it doesn't contain anything libellous or of a defamatory nature. Having said that, as editor, I will of course reserve my right of reply."

There were more howls of protest, coupled with a threat to withdraw all their advertising from the paper.

I made it plain that was a matter entirely for them. As was the case with correspondence, our advertising pages would always remain open to them, should they wish to use them.

They stormed off in high dudgeon and for the next few weeks they did, indeed, stop advertising with us. I knew that Colin was worried about it. In time, however, all their advertisements returned as realisation dawned that they needed us rather more than we needed them.

There was an interesting little sequel to all this a couple of months later. I was reporting an Orange service and parade in Dundrum at which Paisley was guest speaker. During a reception afterwards, the Worshipful Master of the Lodge escorted him across to introduce him to Ken Purdy, of the *Observer*, and yours truly.

Paisley was actually stretching out a hand to shake mine, but immediately upon hearing my name, swung away abruptly, cut me dead, shook hands with Ken, and bellowed in his rich baritone "Ah, Brother Purdy. How are you today and how is the excellent *Mourne Observer?"*

I was left standing, as we used to say in Mourne, with my two arms the one length! At least I could see the funny side of it. The big bully had encountered someone he couldn't bully.

Bomb stops play

Work was progressing as normal around 9:30 one night in the subs' room when the telephone in the middle of the long table that served as our work surface rang out shrilly. This was unusual, as external calls were normally routed through the main switchboard.

I was nearest so picked it up.

"Hello. May I help you?"

"Is that the *Newsletter?"* A shrill young female voice said.

"Yes. What can I do for you?"

"Yiz have ten minutes till get out!"

"What"

"Yiz heard me. Ten f...... minutes to clear the building before the bomb goes off!" There was a click as she rang off.

This couldn't be real. Was some idiot playing silly beggars? Instinctively and unnecessarily, I put my palm over the mouthpiece and spoke to the *Bear,* who was looking at me with curiosity.

"That call just told me there's a bomb in the building due to go off in ten minutes."

"Bomb alert!" snapped the *Bear.* "Quick. Everybody out."

I bent forward and slowly replaced the phone in its cradle. When I looked up a second later I had the room to myself. The swinging door into the corridor was the only indication anyone else had been here. Without bothering to grab my coat I scurried after them.

Printers, comps, machine men, drivers, clerks, telephone

operators, reporters and sub editors assembled in the back yard amid the delivery vans waiting to head off on their rounds. We stood in small groups, talking animatedly, speculating if it really was a bomb this time, or just another hoax. That's how it was in Belfast at the time.

"At least it's not raining, chaps." This from Richard. "And it's nice to get a breath of air, isn't it?"

"Every minute we spend out here means we're a minute later winding up," the *Bear* observed sagely. "If we have to hang about too long it's going to bugger everything up."

"If it really is a bomb and it goes off there might be no paper to put out tomorrow," opined Maurice Hawkins, another sub.

There was a screech of brakes and the sound of slamming doors from the other side of the yard gate and four khaki-clad figures sprinted past and into the rear of the building.

"Rather them than me," said Jack Midgley, the elder statesman of the subs room. "I say, *Bear,* instead of hanging about here for God knows how long, what about going round the corner for a little drink?"

"We all know you like your wee dram, Jack. But nobody leaves. We're waiting here until we're told differ . . ."

He was interrupted by an ear-shattering, gut-wrenching - B-O-O-M!!!

I glanced heavenwards. A dense pall of foul, black smoke was covering the roof like a giant umbrella. Broken slates and pieces of assorted debris were turning lazily in the air as though in ultra-slow-motion.

"Brad, get yourself down here. Pronto."

I recognised David Kirk's voice, and in precisely the same split second, realised that, for the second time inside a few minutes, I was the last man standing. I dived under the delivery van and huddled down beside David as, all around us, large chunks of debris were thudding into the concrete yard.

A couple of windows were shattered and the roof of one van carried a large dent for a long time afterwards, but thankfully, nobody was hurt. After a thorough search the Army bomb-disposal team announced the all-clear and said we could go back inside.

We were told the bomb had been planted in a narrow alleyway between our offices and the building next door. Most of the blast had gone straight upwards, hence all the flying debris from the roof.

As we made our way back indoors Jack exclaimed wryly, with the merest touch of gallows' humour. "Well boys, at least we don't have to travel too far for this little story!"

The paper appeared next morning, same time as usual. We even had a new front page *Splash!*

Winter comes

I'd been in the *Newsletter* for about a year when the long hours I was working began to take their toll. Sure, I had a nice house, a new car and a few quid in the bank, but I also had a wife and two growing kids I wasn't seeing as much of as I'd have liked. I hadn't played table tennis or enjoyed a round of golf in months.

I still loved my work of course; it was just that sixty-plus hours of it every week was a bit over the top, and with something of a shock, I realised I'd been doing that for close on twenty years. Too much work and not enough play could turn me into another workaholic like Jim Hawthorne, and with all due respect to him, I didn't want that.

What really tipped the scales, however, and prompted me to do something about it, was the approach of another winter. It was one thing driving into Belfast from Newcastle against the flow of outgoing traffic on a pleasant summer evening,; quite another to do it in the gloom of winter, squinting into the unceasing glare of approaching headlights. I never got to use full headlights on the journey.

Mollie and I talked it over at length. With the troubles intensifying, particularly in Belfast, we immediately ruled out all thoughts of moving too close to the city. We considered a number of likely towns before deciding on Lisburn. As well as reducing time spent commuting, it was within comfortable reach of Mollie's folks in Castlewellan and our old haunts in Newcastle.

With considerable reluctance, I decided that my Wednesday and Thursday stints in the *Recorder* would have to end. As ever, Colin was extremely good about it and fully understood my situation. I left on excellent terms, with a pledge that I'd keep in touch and help out should the need arise. Happily, my services were never called upon, although I did drop into the old place for a cup of tea and a chat whenever I passed through Downpatrick.

We sold the bungalow in Ben Crom Park – thanks to inflation – for more than four times what it had cost us, and bought a house in Manor Drive on the fringe of Lisburn. We didn't know it then, but it was soon to prove a propitious decision.

Good old Maurice

As everyone is only too well aware, the Seventies was not a great time for Northern Ireland. The troubles have been well documented, so there's no need for me to go into them in detail here, except to say that Ken and I had played our own small part by logging a couple of years' service in the RUC Reserve.

My jobs in the daily papers kept me in close touch with the horrors and tragedies of those unhappy years. My work for BBC sports was a welcome relief. True, I had a couple of close calls when driving home from work in the small hours of the morning, but by that time the streets were usually deserted. On a few occasions though, I had to venture into uncharted territory to avoid trouble.

This was the time of the Watergate Inquiry in the United States, and my homeward journey from Belfast was often enlivened by listening to the BBC World Service reports of President Richard Nixon's travails as he endeavoured to squirm out of the noose that was tightening about him and which led to his eventual impeachment.

One night Maurice Hawkins, a colleague in the subs room, pushed across a copy of the *Belfast Telegraph* with a double-column advertisement circled in red marker ink. "You've moving to Lisburn, Brad. Here's the very job for you, right on your doorstep!"

I glanced at the ad. It seemed the Ministry of Defence was looking for a civilian Information Officer to work in the Army's Northern Ireland Headquarters.

"They want someone with media and PR experience, as well as a good knowledge of the province. You know where their HQ is – you'd be able to walk to work in the morning. The salary's good too; a damn sight better than this place."

I tossed the paper back to him. "So you want to get rid of me Maurice, do you? Well, no, thanks very much. PR? I'll stick to the devil I know, if you don't mind. Why not have a go yourself?"

He leaned forward and whispered conspiratorially. "I live too far away. Anyway, I might be moving to Downtown Radio soon, but keep that under your hat."

I shook my head and smiled. But he wouldn't give up and kept on at me about it for the rest of the night, even going so far as to fill out the application coupon with my name and address and stick it in an envelope, which he addressed. He handed it to me as we were leaving with a trite, "Here, you can put your own bloody stamp on it if you want."

I shoved it in the pocket of my old raincoat and promptly forgot all about it until the following Saturday morning when I was in our local newsagents settling up for the week's papers. I put a hand in my pocket and pulled out Maurice's envelope. After almost a week it was crumpled and grimy.

By rights, I should have dumped it in the waste bin, but instead thought what the hell? I asked George, the newsagent, if he had a stamp and slid the envelope into the post-box outside his door. Then I promptly forgot all about it again.

Surprise, surprise

It must have been three weeks later that a letter arrived informing me that I had been selected for interview for the post of Information Officer with the Ministry of Defence. Would I please confirm that I would be available to attend an interview in Command Secretariat, HQNI, Lisburn, later in the month? I won't say I'd forgotten all about it, but it hadn't exactly been in the forefront of my mind. I acknowledged the letter and reckoned I'd better do a little research.

I re-read the Ministry's letter, which gave an outline of my principal duties and responsibilities. The main one would be to advise and support the Brigadier who commanded the Ulster Defence Regiment, his headquarters' staff and the eleven Battalions throughout Northern Ireland in all matters pertaining to public relations. I noted the bull points.

The successful candidate would become a member of the Defence Staff, working out of MOD Main Building in Whitehall. I would be joining a mobile grade, which meant I was liable to be posted anywhere in the world where the Government had Defence interests. As a member of Army Information Services (AIS), I would be responsible to the Chief Information Officer (CIO) HQNI, and through him, to the Director of Public Relations (Army) (DPR(A)).

If I got the job, I could see I was going to have to make myself familiar with a whole new world of titles and abbreviations. My starting salary would be within the scale £2900 – £3850 pa and I would receive an additional £1200 pa tax-free London Weighting Allowance.

All this sounded fair enough, I suppose, but as the day of the interview drew nearer, I was still undecided if this was a job I really wanted. I'd been in journalism most of my working life – and had thoroughly enjoyed it. If I were offered this post I'd be stepping across a line, and in a manner of speaking, would become a kind of poacher turned gamekeeper. Also I wasn't sure that Mollie, with her strong family ties to home, would relish the thought of a possible move abroad sometime in the future.

As a working journalist, and someone who'd lived in Northern Ireland for most of his life, I reckoned I had fair background knowledge of the place, not least the current troubles and the British Army's and UDR's role concerning them. A search of Google would doubtless have improved this, but that search engine had still to be invented.

Since initially applying for the job, we'd completed our house move from Newcastle to Lisburn. I was now living less than a mile from HQNI, and when the day of the interview arrived, I took advantage of the bright, sunny morning and decided to walk there.

The interview

I arrived just before the appointed time of 12 noon and was shown into a bare waiting room. After about ten minutes I was called into an adjoining room which was, if anything, even more austere than the one I'd just left. The best description I can give is that it was a slightly smaller version of the court-martial room in the Humphrey Bogart film *The Caine Mutiny*. All that was lacking was old Bogey himself, twitching spasmodically and twiddling his chrome ball-bearings in his fingers.

Four men were seated behind a long deal table, one of whom rose to greet me, announce himself as Peter Broderick, Chief Information Officer, and introduce me to his colleagues. A solitary chair stood in the centre of the room directly in front of the table.

For some reason I had a flashback to an old Z Cars TV programme I'd seen on TV years before, when a prospective candidate had failed because he'd taken a seat before being invited to do so. I remained standing until the chairman invited me to be seated.

I recognised one member of the panel from his photograph as the UDR's Commander, Brigadier Harry Baxter, who, some years earlier, as a major, had won the George Medal for removing an IRA bomb from Gough Barracks in Armagh. He cut a formidable figure in his uniform and black monocle, which concealed an old injury unconnected to his military service.

My other two inquisitors, whose names I no longer remember, were the Northern Ireland Command Secretary and a senior civil servant from the MOD in London who epitomised the archetypal government mandarin in his pearl-grey pinstriped suit, imitation Guards' tie, gold Rolex (which may or may not have been imitation) and matching gold heavy-linked chain on his other wrist.

It was he who initiated the questioning. Studying a slim folder in front of him, he began, "Ah, Mr Fleming. Good of you to come. Now, I perceive from your application form that you reside in Newcastle, in County Down. On consulting my map, I discover that is some miles from Lisburn. As this post is likely to entail a considerable amount of travelling and having to be called out in what I might term some irregular and uncertain hours, do you not consider this might be all rather arduous and difficult for you?"

My first thought was: Here's a man who won't be satisfied with using one word when an entire sentence will do. He was a verbose and long-winded character who wouldn't have got very far in journalism. Indeed, if I'd been sub-editing his opening statement it would have contained a lot more red ink than black, and would have been considerably shorter. However, I sought to put him at his ease.

"Thank you," I replied, "but, please don't be concerned. Since sending in my application, I've moved house from Newcastle to Lisburn. As a matter of fact, I walked from home to this interview this morning!"

He sat back in his chair and assumed an askance expression. "Have you indeed, Mr Fleming? Even before you've been interviewed? I must say I admire your confidence!"

What a pillock! As succinctly as possible, I explained that I had moved house to be nearer my work in Belfast and the transfer had been finalised well in advance of submitting my application. I noticed Peter Broderick doing his best to stifle a smile before taking up the questioning himself.

He asked a number of probing and pertinent questions about my career to date and my reasons for wishing to switch from journalism to public relations.

Without implicating young Maurice Hawkins, which I felt would not be the wisest move, I explained, honestly enough, that having taken a fair shot at most forms of journalism, I felt the time was perhaps right to try something new.

The strange thing was that, having gone into the interview with a kind of laissez-faire attitude, I thought why not give it a go and see what happens. A few minutes later, I thought, for the first time, that here was a job which was clearly, challenging, interesting and totally different from anything I had experienced so far. I began to sit up and pay attention, hoping I hadn't done anything thus far to scupper my chances.

The Brigadier, who had been watching me intently throughout, entered the fray for the first time.

"Mr Fleming, why did you join the RUC Reserve as opposed to the UDR?"

"When I joined the Reserve the UDR hadn't been formed. In any case, because of the nature of the work I was doing at that time, especially the irregular hours, the Reserve suited much better."

He switched tack. "Do you believe it's possible to persuade more Roman Catholics to enlist in the Regiment?"

I'd been expecting a question along those lines. I was also aware that Baxter had his roots in an old Catholic family.

"It's possible, but as things stand at the moment, it's not going to be easy. I'm aware that eight of the first 21 soldiers of the Regiment to be murdered were Catholics; for no better reason than that it didn't suit the aims of the IRA to have them serving in a British Regiment."

He nodded. "I see you've done your homework."

"Not really. Sadly, such unfortunate statistics are part and parcel of my present job."

"Do you have any suggestions to offer as to how this state of affairs might be improved?"

"As I've already said, and as I'm sure you know, there are more questions than answers. With respect, I'd begin by tightening up on the way some of your soldiers behave, both on and off duty. Every time one of them transgresses its damaging propaganda material for your detractors. Again, I'm sorry, but, on the subject of attracting more Catholics, the very name of the Regiment does you no favours."

He bristled slightly and said stiffly. "What do you mean by that exactly?"

I knew I was treading on dodgy ground, but I'd started, and as old Magnus Magnusson used to say, I'd better finish.

"I'm sorry Brigadier, but I'm certain you appreciate how sensitive both communities here are to such niceties. It shouldn't matter, but it does. When the majority of Catholics speak of Ulster they mean the old province of nine counties, not just the six of Northern Ireland. The Protestant community is more ambivalent about it and seem happy to use either description. It probably wouldn't have pleased everyone, but it would have made things a lot easier if it had been called the Northern Ireland Regiment from the start. The same thing applies to the RUC. The fact is neither the

Army nor the police have jurisdiction in the one-third of the old province of Ulster that lies south of the border in the Republic. It's always going to be a sore point, a kind of red rag to a bull, not least south of the border."

I saw that Broderick was listening to this little exchange attentively. If I wanted this job – and I was becoming increasingly certain in my own mind that I did – he and the Brigadier were clearly the two people I had to convince. The other two would fall into line and follow their lead.

It was Broderick who asked the next question. "It's an interesting point, Mr Fleming. While we're on that particular subject, do you have any more suggestions to offer?"

"Only that perceptions count for a great deal in Northern Ireland. We're the best and friendliest folk in the world, but most of us see things through either orange- or green-tinted glasses. There are a few neutrals about, or some folk who simply don't care one way or the other, but they're a small minority."

"And your point is . . .?"

"For a start, you could stop shooting yourselves in the foot about so many things. In your news releases and when your spokesmen give interviews, stop making references to the Regular Army, or worse, the British Army and the UDR. Be proud of the fact that the UDR is a regiment of the Army, and not some separate entity. Of course it is a unique amalgam of regular, full-time and part-time soldiers, so make that a virtue rather than a fault. Stress their dedication, their local knowledge, and the fact that Northern Ireland is their own special part of the UK and they know and love it better than any outside ever could."

"In addition to that, you might consider stopping your regular officers and spokesmen using demeaning phrases like they'll be glad to get back to the UK. I know there's a tendency for regulars to look on a posting here as an overseas tour. The fact is Northern Ireland is part of the UK. If it wasn't they wouldn't be here in the first place."

"Finally, I believe it would help the Regiment's image considerably if the phrase 'UDR man' was banned. Full-time or part-time, they're soldiers. The phrase UDR man is too similar to UDA man, or UVF man – or even IRA man. Half the people on the mainland won't know the difference and some will tar you all with the same brush. You wouldn't talk about a Royal Anglian man, or a Parachute Regiment man, so UDR personnel should all be treated in the same way – and referred to as soldiers."

Peter Broderick leant forward and let out an audible "Phew."

"Well Mr Fleming, I suppose we asked for that. Thank you for expressing it so forcibly."

Brigadier Baxter nodded. The other two members of the board looked as if it was time they were sitting down to lunch. Plainly the interview was almost over. I figured I'd either get the job, or be chucked in the brig. If I'd been in uniform, I may well have been court marshalled. At least no one could say I hadn't given an honest opinion.

Finally, Broderick thanked me for attending and asked if I there were any questions I would like to ask.

I didn't have any, but there was one which might possibly indicate which way the wind was blowing. I rose to my feet, volunteered my warmest smile and said. "Thank you gentlemen for your patience in giving me such a fair hearing. If I'm fortunate enough to be successful, please be assured I shall do my best to warrant your confidence."

What a bloody crawler. I couldn't walk out of the room on a note like that, so I added. "I apologise for mentioning it, but I believe it's only fair to tell you that, much as I would relish this job, I would be taking a considerable drop in salary if I were to start on the bottom rung of the pay scale mentioned in the advertisement."

I fancied Peter Broderick was struggling to hide a smile as he shook my hand for a second time. "Have no worries on that account, Mr Fleming. If the board agrees and you secure the appointment, there would be no question of someone of your experience starting at that level."

I reckoned a nod was as good as a wink. Sure enough, less than a week later a letter bearing an MOD motif arrived confirming my appointment, subject to security vetting. My starting salary would be one rung off the top of the pay grade.

Early days

"Welcome aboard," Alan Graham beamed pleasantly, as he shook my hand.

An ex-regular soldier, now on the staff of Army Information Services, he had come down to help usher me through the permanent checkpoint which guarded the entrance to HQNI when I arrived to take up my duties on that first Monday morning. A personable, middle-aged Yorkshireman, he explained that he had been filling my new post on a temporary basis and would be working with me for a couple of weeks while I settled in.

He showed me where to park my car before escorting me to UDR headquarters to find my well-appointed office and be introduced to Cathy, my PA, a charming young lady who promptly made us both a cup of tea. I was to discover that the military, rather like the Press, existed on frequent cups of tea or coffee.

Alan explained the HQ routine, adding that I would be given a number of briefings both there and across the road in HQNI in the early part of the week. It would also give me a chance to get to know the rest of the staff. I would have a staff car at my disposal and in due time we would drive to visit the Regiment's eleven battalions and meet the respective Commanding Officers and Unit Press Officers.

First things first though, I had to have my mug-shot taken for my security passes and sign the Official Secrets Act. Although a lot of water has gone under the bridge since that day, I am still technically bound by it. Consequently, I cannot be quite as open as I might wish to be about certain matters. Sorry to sound so mysterious, but that's how it has to be.

I had been pencilled in for a private tete-a-tete with Peter Broderick at eleven o'clock and I was looking forward to that and to having the opportunity of thanking him for confirming my appointment.

Peter greeted me with typical warmth when Alan brought me to his office in the main HQ building across the road and left us alone. Peter asked for two coffees to be brought in. I quickly discovered that the phrase *"NATO Standard"* referred to tea or coffee with milk and two sugars.

Once we were comfortably seated I thanked Peter for selecting me for the post and for his courtesy during my interview.

He waved a deprecating hand. "Don't think I did you any favours. You were the obvious choice."

He went on to say that most of AIS, and indeed the entire HQ staff, were from outside Northern Ireland and lacked detailed local knowledge. "Your remarks about UDR personnel being soldiers, not just men, and our lot going home to the UK certainly struck home with me and with Harry Baxter too. We also liked your thinking on a number of things.

"Thank you," I said.

"Make no mistake," Peter went on. "You have a king-sized job on your hands across the road, and you're lined up for a lot of hard work. But, sparing your blushes, I'm convinced you're the man to do it."

I mumbled something to the effect that I'd do my best, and he went on to outline the bull points of what he expected of me. I would have comparatively free rein in handling all UDR PR-related matters, although he would expect to be kept informed, especially of anything contentious. "Remember, my door is always open to you, day or night. Don't hesitate about coming to see me if you need to."

I'd also be expected to work closely with the Press Office next door and to go on the rota to do a regular eight-hour shift as duty watch-keeper. "It will give you a chance to chat to your old colleagues when they ring in," he smiled. "And, now you're a gamekeeper rather than a poacher, they'd better not expect any favours!"

I pictured my old colleague, Harry Robinson, on the news-desk in the *Newsletter,* making his usual hourly check call and asking, "Well, what's happening? What have you got for me today?"

I was taken aback when Peter confided that I'd been selected from a total of 84 applicants, and a final short-list of six. Apparently, it had been a unanimous choice by the panel. I probably shouldn't have, but I owned up and told him of Maurice Hawken's part in the story. He shook his head and laughed. "Well, I'm sure Maurice has done both of us a favour."

When we'd finished Peter led me across the corridor to meet his civilian Number Two, Colin Wallace, whom I'd met previously on a few occasions, including once when I'd spent a week with the Ist Battalion, Royal Irish Rangers, then based in Haemer in West Germany, producing a series of features for a number of local Northern Ireland weekly papers.

As we left his office, Peter laid a finger along his nose and remarked wryly. "Colin largely does his own thing. As far as possible I let him get on with it, without asking too many questions. I suggest you do likewise."

In those days, with sometimes dozens of terrorist-related incidents occurring every day, most of the newspapers, TV and radio stations checked in with the office on an hourly basis, day and night, and even more frequently if there was an on-going incident.

As the army was leading from the RUC at that time, the Press Office was manned by a team of watch keepers on a 24 x 7 basis 365 days a year. There were banks of TV and radio monitors and recorders and a viewing room for the Top Brass and visiting VIPs to watch bulletins of particular interest.

Alan led me round to be introduced to my military colleagues, an assortment of majors and captains who had been posted in for tours of duty ranging from six months to two years. They were a friendly bunch and I kept bumping into some of them for years afterwards as I saw service in many corners of the world. The morning ended with visits to the photographic and printing departments, and the *Visor* Offices, where the soldiers' very own NI weekly magazine was published. Later I'd become a regular contributor.

Lunch in the Mess

I'd had quite a lot to take in on my first morning and it was a pleasant interlude when Alan invited me down for lunch in the Officers' Mess. On the way there he explained that all civilians of a certain seniority were accorded an honorary rank, or status, which equated to that of their military counterparts. As an example, he and I were categorised as majors. At first I found this faintly ridiculous, but, as I grew more familiar with the system, I found it made good sense.

For a start, it meant that any officer of equivalent rank or above could address me by my first name and he knew exactly where I fitted into the general scheme of things. Never too strong on undue formality, I much preferred being called Brad rather than Mr Fleming. Even more practically, it meant that on overseas postings, my family and I were entitled to be allocated married quarters commensurate with my grade. Perks of the system if you like.

While there was a strict dress code in the Mess – uniforms or ties and suits to be worn at all times, that sort of thing – by and large, hats and ranks were left at the door. This suited me admirably. I'd never felt comfortable calling anyone sir, unless he was of pensionable age, or I thought he'd earned it. So, from day one, the General was the General, the Brigadier was the Brigadier and so on. This was my rule of thumb for over twenty years in MOD. I never received a single complaint – and if I had, I'd have ignored it.

There must be some truth in the old adage that an army marches on its stomach, for in all that time, I can't recall being served a single indifferent meal. In fact, the general standard would not have disgraced a five-star hotel. So it was when I first lunched with my new friends in Lisburn.

It was good to have proper introductory chats with the team. For the most part, civilians and military blended together seamlessly, and it wasn't all shop talk either. So many of them endeavoured to ply me with alcohol that, if I hadn't been careful, I'd have slept throughout the afternoon, instead of going back to work. And that would have been no way to start my first day.

I particularly enjoyed talking to my fellow information officers, Mike Taylor, who hailed from Birmingham, and Gordon Shepherd, from Edinburgh. As soon as they decently could, they buttonholed me about my background and demanded to know how I'd fared at my initial interview. Having fielded their enquiries as best I could, I contrived to switch the conversation to how they reckoned I could best fit in to the HQNI mix. Some of their advice was to stand me in good stead.

As an aside, I should mention that money never changes hands in an officers' mess. Instead one signed a bar or meal chit and the bill was settled at the end of the month. I found both drinks and food ridiculously cheap, only a fraction of prices in civvy street.

Briefings galore

Alan had given me a comprehensive printed schedule of my first week's itinerary. That afternoon and all the next day were devoted to briefings and introductions with the HQ staff and in Command Secretariat. I had a particularly pleasant half-hour with Brigadier Baxter who warmly congratulated me on being appointed. He looked forward to implementing a number of things we had discussed on the day of my board.

The Deputy Commander, Lt-Col Paddy Ryan, gave me a thorough briefing on the Regiment's history, development and modus operandi, using a map to show the areas covered by the 11 battalions. Essentially two of these, the 7th and 10th, were based in Belfast, the remaining nine spread throughout the country, essentially on a county basis.

The other senior members of staff were a mixture of Regular officers on one or two year deployments, full-time UDR officers and a handful of retired officers who were employed in various civilian capacities. They were known as ROs (retired officers).

Each working week started with Commander's Prayers on Monday morning. It was a throwback to bygone days when a Chaplain would actually say a short prayer. This had long been dispensed with but the name lingered. In fact, it largely amounted to a diary conference at which everyone was brought up to speed on recent and forthcoming events.

This brings me to the military's style of writing. There is, indeed, a weighty style book, which is in effect a much more elaborate version of the kind used by most newspapers. At first reading by a civilian it seems unnecessarily detailed and pernickety, but it actually has a lot going for it. A couple of examples may illustrate the point. For instance, all paragraphs are numbered, enabling a relevant passage to be found quickly at meetings, or in telephone or radio conversations. Particular problems are presented and dealt with under headings such as Background, Problem, Conclusion and Proposed Action. Such brevity was dear to the heart of an old sub-editors and I quickly adopted the system.

I also had to become familiar with a whole string of abbreviations, particularly when doing my stints on the Press Desk. Just a few examples will suffice.

CWIED – Command-wire improvised explosive device. A booby-trap.

FUIP - Follow up in progress. A response to a terrorist incident.

PVCP - Permanent vehicle check point.

VCP - A temporary movable check point.

PIRA - The Provisional Irish Republican Army.

There were scores of others. I suppose it was the military's own form of Pitman's. It certainly saved a lot of scribbling in longhand.

Tragedy strikes

I didn't have long to wait for my first taste of terrorist action, and it was a particularly sad occurrence. An IRA home-made mortar attack on a UDR company base in Clogher resulted in the death of Private Eva Martin. Women had only recently been admitted to the Regiment and had become popularly known as Greenfinches.

Eva, a pretty 28-year-old schoolteacher, was the first woman soldier to be killed by terrorist action in Northern Ireland, and her death was all the more poignant by the fact that she was only in the base that evening to have an ID photograph taken. The photographer was actually her husband, a corporal in the same company.

When the attack began she was ordered to take safety downstairs. The blast caught her as she was passing a window and she tumbled down the stairs to land at the feet of her husband who was coming to fetch her. That last photograph of Eva went all around the world, but in the most tragic of circumstances.

Alan and I attended the funeral at her little church in Tyrone a few days later. We would have wanted to go in any event, but we had to help deal with the huge media presence. There were TV crews and photographers everywhere. Alan brought along one of his young daughters and I vividly remember how she turned, buried her face in my chest and clung to me as the final salute was fired over Eva's coffin. I will remember the photograph of that beautiful young woman until my dying day.

Northern Ireland on the brink

As I've said, these were turbulent times in Northern Ireland and my proposed two-week handover from Alan Graham was disrupted by a province-wide strike called by the Ulster Workers' Council, made up of delegates from the entire spectrum of Unionist/Loyalist/Protestant groupings, in protest against the proposed Sunningdale Agreement, specifically what many Protestants perceived as the sharing of power with Nationalists and the proposed involvement of the Irish Government in running Northern Ireland affairs.

Within a matter of days, the strike had imposed a virtual stranglehold on the life of the entire community. Assuming complete control of the electricity generating system, they effectively rationed power supplies and threatened a complete shutdown of the grid if their demands were not met. Hugo Patterson, my old colleague from my days in the BBC, held the whole country in thrall with his daily bulletins on how the service was teetering on a knife-edge.

Illegal roadblocks sprang up all over the province, and many workers who wanted to defy the strike were prevented from doing so. The protest also called into question the integrity of the RUC and the UDR, for both forces were caught between the community and the British Government in a conflict of loyalty. The reality was that both local forces were, like the British Army itself, largely impotent to deal with the escalating situation. The outcome was inevitable. On the fourteenth day of their campaign, the UWC strikers forced the resignation of the Northern Ireland Executive.

Alan and I found ourselves involved in a series of top-level meetings during this period. There were daily demands from politicians, press and public to put the Army into the power stations. In the end it had to be pointed out that it was impossible, due to insufficient manpower, to protect the grid from sabotage. In effect the Security Forces could do little but keep their heads down until things returned to normal.

Patrolling my little empire

Plainly, my new job was going to lack nothing in excitement. Alan and I eventually completed our rounds of all eleven UDR battalions and I introduced myself to the Commanding Officer and Unit Press Officer of each one. At that early stage I had only one point to put across. As well as reporting all incidents up the operational chain to HQNI, it was imperative that my office was informed separately, especially if it were likely to have unwelcome or damaging consequences. In other words, if the Press asked a question I needed to have the answer ready without having to go scratching around for it.

I also paid courtesy calls on as many weekly newspaper offices as I could within each battalion area, introducing myself and giving them details of how I might be contacted. I promised to give them all the information I could and hoped to set up a series of meetings over lunch before too long. In this connection I was delighted to find that I had at my disposal a generous sum of money for Press entertainment. I intended seeing it didn't go to waste. I knew well what my former brethren were like.

In the midst of this busy schedule I had my first eight-hour shift in the AIS Press Office, learning the routine from the Duty Press Officer, a Captain on a six-month detachment. I was on from 4pm until midnight and the time passed quickly enough. At that period the office was dealing with in excess of a thousand calls in a 24-hour day.

We had a direct phone line and secure radio link to the main Operations Room, directly above us on the first floor, and received regular updates to ongoing incidents. Apart from the banks of TVs, monitors and recorders mentioned earlier, the walls were lined with maps, charts and statistical information of every kind – running totals of terrorist related deaths, attacks, explosions and weapon finds etc. There was a direct line to the RUC Ops Room at Knock and Northern Ireland Office at Stormont. We also maintained a running logbook of all incidents and media enquiries.

Time would fly by and when things got particularly hectic, one or two other staffers would join us to field incoming calls.

I was amused that first evening to take a call from Harry Robinson, my former colleague in the *Newsletter's* newsdesk. The two other occupants of the office downed tools to listen in, one of them going so far as to reach over and switch it to loudspeaker.

"Army Press Office," I said.

"Robinson, *Newsletter* here . . . wait a minute, I know that voice. That you, Brad? I see you're still on nights then."

"Night and day, Harry. Nothing changes. It's all go here."

"What about you, man? Settling in there all right? How's the new job going? Getting on okay with all those military types, are you?"

"It's going just fine, Harry, thank you." I essayed a broad wink at my two companions. "I'm enjoying working with an altogether better class of bloke here. Not like you scruffy lot in the paper."

Long silence. "Hmmm, you've changed your tune since you moved. I don't remember you complaining when you were here."

"I never complain, Harry, it's a sign of weakness. Now, my son, what can I do for you?"

"What's happening? Have you got a story for me?"

"Sorry, Harry. Nothing doing at the moment. It's ten to seven and all the boyos have gone home for their tea. They'll probably be out again in an hour or so. You know how it is."

"Anything more on that arms find outside Cookstown?"

"Nothing new, Harry. I take it you have the details from the last time you called?"

"Okay then, I'll ring again in a wee while."

"Fair enough my man, talk to you later. Give my regards to the *Bear* and the boys next door."

My fellow watch-keeper smiled. "So that was the great Harry Robinson, was it? I think you handled him very well."

"Harry's just a pussycat," I told them. "His heart's in the right place."

Not quite routine

I was going to say that once Alan had returned to his old post in HQNI, I settled quickly into the routine of my job. But that wouldn't be totally accurate. There was a more or less set routine, of course, but one never knew what each day was going to bring.

Most days would start with a read through the local newspapers and I'd mark up any stories of interest to the Regiment for Cathy to cut out, photocopy and distribute to the rest of the HQ. This would be supplemented by a more comprehensive resume of relevant news from AIS. I'd make sure the Commander or his deputy were notified of anything of importance before going across to HQNI to ascertain what was new in their world.

I started a log book of incidents and media enquiries which

Cathy updated when I was out of the office. I also put down a marker with Peter that the UDR shouldn't be overlooked when the steady flow of national and international journalists visited for briefings. He readily agreed to this and saw to it I was included to add my tuppence worth. He also encouraged the media to come to my briefing room at every opportunity.

To be frank, I didn't think much of the briefing material I'd found in the HQ when I arrived and set about preparing a proper presentation with slides and other visual aids. In addition, each visitor received a press pack in a neat folder bearing the Regimental Crest, complete with a potted history of the Regiment, a list of the Roll of Honour and its finds and successes.

At that time the Regiment produced a quarterly in-house tabloid newspaper which was intended largely for internal distribution. I reckoned it could be improved considerably, circulated more widely and the current issue included in the press pack.

I suggested to Brigadier Baxter that all recruits to the Regiment should be briefed on the importance of public relations and how presenting a fair and impartial image to both our communities could help make their task easier and safer. He readily agreed and I had talked my way into another job.

The Army held at least one study period annually at which the officers were briefed on all aspects of service in Northern Ireland. While the UDR was included in this, why shouldn't the Regiment have its own study day? Once again I got his agreement.

I tried to visit all eleven battalions at least once a month, making a point of seeing the CO, the UPO and as many company commanders as I could. I also encouraged them to hold a local press briefing and lunch at least annually. I would see to it that this would be financed through AIS.

I seemed to be adding to my own work-load every day, but I loved the job and felt it had to be done.

A political football

The year 1974 was a grim one for Northern Ireland. The troubles showed no signs of abating; indeed, the number of terrorist incidents continued to grow. The Ulster Defence Regiment was very much at the centre of these developments and this brought both good and bad news.

Having begun as predominantly a part-time force, a decision was taken to expand its full-time cadre, giving it more responsibility and a round-the-clock capability. While this was welcomed in some quarters, it did not go down well in others.

The toll was a high one. By the close of the year 46 soldiers had been murdered by terrorists and many more wounded. The majority of the deaths occurred while the soldiers were off duty, in their homes or places of work, when they were at their most vulnerable. If their enemies believed this would deter men and women from joining, they were mistaken. The strength of the Regiment soared to more than 7,000.

I listen in as UDR soldiers brief Northern Ireland Secretary Merlyn Rees during a patrol near the border with the Republic.

Of course this did not go unnoticed by the IRA and the UDR's political detractors who seized every opportunity to blacken its name and reputation. When a small minority of soldiers overstepped the mark and engaged in unlawful reprisals, usually under the umbrella of the UDA or UVF, it did the Regiment immeasurable damage. A classic example of this was when two off-duty soldiers were involved in the ambush and murder of members of the Miami Showband on their way home from a gig.

The two were later convicted and sentenced, but their actions presented the IRA and some nationalist politicians with a huge stick with which to beat the entire Regiment. In Army parlance it was a classic case of shooting oneself in the foot.

In terms of any PR rebuttal there was little we could do to defend the indefensible, other than to point out the obvious – that the vast majority of those serving in the UDR totally denounced such unlawful actions. It didn't help when several well-meaning supporters referred to "a few bad apples." Everybody knows what a few bad apples can allegedly do to a barrel!

When Unionist politicians in their turn accused their Nationalist opponents of unfairly criticising the UDR, the spiralling acrimonious debate did the Regiment no favours. The IRA and the republican propaganda machine must have rubbed their hands in delight when the likes of the Rev Ian Paisley heaped praise on the UDR and condemned its critics. The die was well and truly cast: the UDR had become a political football.

Indeed, when briefing politicians and the media, I would frequently use that expression to illustrate my point. Years later, at a high-level meeting in Stormont Castle, a chinless Whitehall mandarin told me that the SDLP MP Seamus Mallon, a long-time critic of the UDR, had asked that the phrase should not be used.

I told him I'd be happy to comply with Mr Mallon's request the moment he stopped referring to Northern Ireland as 'the North of Ireland.' I doubt the mandarin had a clue what I was on about, but I hope he passed on my message.

Reinforcements

I was now logging up more working hours than in my early years in the *Mourne Observer* and the strain was probably showing. It wasn't uncommon for the phone to ring in the small hours and I'd have to make my way into the Ops Room to deal with a problem. I didn't mind; it came with the territory, but it was hard on Mollie and the kids to have their sleep disrupted perhaps several times a week.

There was lots of weekend work as well, as this was generally the best time to visit the part-time companies. David McDine, Deputy Director of Army Public Relations, (DDPR(A)) flew in from London on a three-day visit and spent a lot of in talking and travelling round with me. Tall and easy-going, he was later to become my line boss and a close personal friend. He was quick to size up how things were and acted immediately. Soon another Information officer was dispatched from London to assist me and a

UDR major also joined my little team shortly afterwards.

I've worked with some great people in my time and Bill Moore, my new colleague was one of the best of them. A former deputy editor of the *Daily Mirror,* and the author of several books on military subjects, he settled into the job immediately and was a pleasure to work with.

I'd already met Major Tom Agnew, formerly of 10 Battalion in Belfast, and Bill and I were delighted to welcome him on board. He was completely new to public relations but his military knowledge and experience quickly proved itself. The three of us were able to spread the load more evenly and also share on-call duties.

I'd been in post over two years when David McDine summoned me to MOD for a five-day visit. Typically, he insisted I stay with him and his family at his home in Herne Bay on the south coast. Ostensibly I was to learn something about the inner workings of the Government's vast Information Service, particularly as it related to the three Services, Navy, Army and Air Force. While I did pick up a lot of useful knowledge, I discovered that David's real aim was to help chart the course of my future career. That's the sort of man he was, and I came to understand that I wasn't the only member of staff to benefit from his personal interest.

The first thing I noticed was the time taken by his daily commute. After breakfast at 5:30am, we had to leave the house not later than 6:10 to catch the 6:30 train into London. Usually his wife dropped us off at the station and collected us on our return. It was a slow train and the journey took two hours, with stops at every station along the way. On arrival in London we'd grab a tube to Charing Cross or Embankment and scurry across the park, with luck and a fair wind, to arrive in Main Building just before 9:00am. That's a round trip of almost six hours on a good day!

"The good thing is," David quipped with a smile, "that I live so far out in the sticks I'm always guaranteed to get a seat."

When everything ran like clockwork and he hit every connection smack on the dot, he'd make it home in time to say goodnight to his two children and grab a quick shower before sitting down to dinner at nine. He needed a six-day rail ticket as he often had to work Saturdays.

He explained that normally he'd read a paper or a paperback on the train before grabbing forty winks. Gallantly, he'd given up his naps when we travelled together and instead we had a series of long chats, usually about my plans for the future.

Theoretically, as London was my base of operations, Lisburn

was regarded as an away posting. This meant that I should serve there for a year, or at the most, two. Having just started my third year, I was on borrowed time.

"In the normal way of things you'd come over to MOD for at least a year," he said, "then it would be a posting overseas. How does that sound?"

One look at my face gave him all the answer he needed. "I'd have to take digs in London and leave the family back in Lisburn, getting back at weekends whenever I could. But if that's what I have to do then so be it."

He nodded understandingly. "Not too keen on that, and I can't say I blame you. Don't worry, Brad, we have any amount of people keen to shuffle through the portals of Main Building. I think we can let you pass on that one, at least for the time being."

My relief must have been evident for he smiled that slow smile of his before continuing. "There are a couple of possible openings coming up, but not for about nine months or so. Would you be happy to continue in Lisburn until then?"

I nodded, trying not to appear too eager. He wasn't fooled in the slightest.

"Okay Brad, if you can carry on as you are doing until next January, how would a three-year accompanied posting to Hong Kong sound? Do you think Mollie and the kids would fancy that?"

Hong Kong was regarded as AIS's plum posting. I certainly fancied it and I had little doubt Mollie and the children would be equally delighted.

David waved aside my thanks. "No need for that. I recognise the work you've done in Northern Ireland and how hard it's been. You've earned Hong Kong."

On our final journey into London the following Friday David let me into a little secret. "Keep it under your hat for now. It won't be announced for a month or so, but I'll be joining you in Lisburn shortly. I'm doing a swop with Peter Broderick, so I'll be seeing you again soon."

Changing scenes

I expected the family to be overjoyed at the prospect of spending three years in Hong Kong. I was wrong. Barry was far too young to have a view on it, I think Valerie was keen enough, but Mollie, who was very much a home bird, had reservations about leaving her folks, who were now getting up in years. In any event, no decisions had to be made immediately and I was soon busy enough with other things.

I'd become good friends with a Royal Tank Regiment Major called Mike Pavitt, who'd been attached to AIS for almost a year and was on the point of being posted to Germany. He was a charming, gregarious character who had taken a fancy to Mollie's strong curries.

She agreed to make him an extra-hot one for his last visit to 4 Manor Drive. Although his face and neck reddened perceptibly and he loosened his collar, he displayed no other signs of distress and consumed two generous platefuls, pausing only to enjoy what he described as his habitual inter-course Rothman's cigarette.

The rest of us had enjoyed our curries at a more reasonable temperature and Mollie couldn't resist asking Mike if the meal had been hot enough for his liking.

"Excellent my dear," he replied, shooting a quick glance in my direction. "Pretty fair, pretty fair. Perhaps just a trifle on the cool side!"

We all burst out laughing and I said "Mike, you're a hero for swallowing that."

"Serves you right for demanding a really hot one," Valerie chipped in.

As we all relaxed afterwards, Mike produced a bright red bandana handkerchief from his pocket and asked if we'd like to see a little party trick. Of course we all said we would and he opened the bandana to reveal a set of Tarot cards.

"The least I can do after such a splendid feast is to tell you all your fortunes," he said. "Are you all up for it?"

Of course we were. None of us had seen a Tarot reading before, but Mike explained he'd been a devotee for years and his readings were uncannily accurate. He began with Mollie, then Valerie and finally me. Barry, aged five, was excused.

We listened good-naturedly as Mike ran through his little spiel. All fairly standard stuff which could easily have come from his knowledge of the family. The one surprising revelation, which was common to all three of us, was that we would all meet up again in the future when we were posted to Germany!

I protested. "But Mike, you know we're off to Hong Kong early next year. You're having us on."

"Can't help that, Brad. I'm only telling you what the cards say. And they never lie!"

When Mike had gone, Val said "I think Germany would be all

right. I wouldn't mind that."

Mollie said "At least it would be a lot closer to get back to Ireland than Hong Kong."

Mike left shortly afterwards and I didn't think a lot more about his prediction.

The fight against terrorism continued and the UDR was playing an increasingly more prominent role in it. For the first time it was decided that the Regiment should train outside Northern Ireland and several battalions embarked for an intensive week's course in Warcop, a large training area in the north of England.

I accompanied 2 UDR on the first of the camps and was kept busy arranging facilities for the National press and media, as well as a large contingent from Northern Ireland. A lot of MPs also jumped on the publicity band wagon. Apart from the opportunity of being able to train in unfamiliar areas, perhaps the main benefit for the soldiers was that they could relax and stop looking over their shoulders so much when they were off duty. The camps proved a great success and would continue.

The training area was spread out over a considerable area and I was glad to have a little Morris Mini placed at my disposal for the week. I managed to get a whole day off and was able to drive across to the Lake District and follow the tourist trail round Kendall and Windermere and some of the most beautiful country in the British Isles.

I think everyone thoroughly enjoyed the experience. I know I certainly did, and since then I've have made a number of return visits to that idyllic part of the world. I saw to it that both Bill Moore and Tom Agnew were each able to enjoy a visit to Warcop before the season ended.

That same summer we accepted an request from the BBC to make a thirty-minute *Spotlight* programme on the UDR and I met Jeremy Paxman for the first time. In later years he was to make quite a name for himself as chief inquisitor on the hard-hitting *Newsnight* programme. At that time he was cutting his teeth in Belfast, covering the troubles for BBC Northern Ireland.

The new Commander UDR, Brigadier Mervyn McCord, who had succeeded Brigadier Harry Baxter, and some of his senior officers were understandably concerned at subjecting the Regiment to what might well turn out to be a hatchet job and provide a platform for detractors to vilify the Regiment.

Both David McDine, who had taken over from Peter Broderick as CIO, and I argued strongly that the programme should go ahead.

Of course the critics could have their say. But we had nothing to hide, and furthermore had a good story to tell that the people of Northern Ireland had a right to hear. Our argument prevailed. In the end I was left holding the baby. If the programme was deemed to be alright, I'd have proved my point. If it didn't my credibility would be shot and I'd better pick up my bed and walk.

As a first step, David and I invited Paxman to lunch in the Mess. He was all sweetness and light. He expanded on how much he personally admired the UDR and indicated that would be reflected in the finished programme. Bearing in mind that his own career had yet to blossom and he was by no means the vicious interviewing Rottweiler he was to become later with *Newsnight*, both David and I were sceptical.

I took him back to my office after lunch and got down to sorting out the bones of the programme. I told him he'd be given every facility to film the Regiment in action and to interview the Commander and other officers and soldiers. Within reason, he could ask whatever questions he wished, although I couldn't guarantee that they'd all be answered to his satisfaction. He smiled at that.

"Look Jeremy," I said, "We both know what *Spotlight* is about. The UDR is a controversial subject and I know you want to reflect that controversy. All I'm asking is that you give us a fair shake."

He grinned. "Are you suggesting I won't."

"In the Mess a little while ago you spoke of your admiration for the Regiment. It would be nice if that was reflected when the show goes on air."

"You understand that my personal feelings don't come into this, Brad. I have a job to do and I intend to do it."

"That's totally accepted, Jeremy. I have a job to do too, so let's agree to compromise."

I believe we understood each other. In the next half-hour we agreed a set of guidelines, and to be fair, he stuck to them throughout. He accepted that only the Commander could speak on policy and that others he interviewed would only be questioned up to the level of their own responsibility. If that wasn't adhered to I'd stop the filming.

There would be no filming of interviews or operations unless I was present and his crew would not wander off and engage in any unsupervised filming. The team could film in all areas, including sensitive ones, providing there were no close-ups of operational maps and mug shots of people of interest.

Finally, I accepted the fact that he might want to talk to critics of the UDR and that was perfectly fair. All I asked was that in his final interview, Brigadier McCord should be given an opportunity to respond to this. Jeremy thought for a while, then stretched out his hand.

Filming took more than a week, and as I recall, Paxman was granted every facility he asked for. In return I got a sneak preview of the programme.

It's for others to judge its fairness or otherwise, but from my point of view, an opinion shared by David McDine and Brigadier McCord, *Spotlight* gave us a fair shake. Where criticisms were expressed – and there were a few – the Brigadier answered them. Officers and soldiers made some telling points and the operational shots were excellent. Paxman had played fair and I told him so in a phone call afterwards.

Perhaps spurred on by the *Spotlight* programme, David talked to me about making a proper film about the Regiment. Occasionally he'd ring and ask when I was planning a night out with one of the UDR companies. It gave him a chance to escape from the headquarters for a few hours and I know we both enjoyed these outings. We would talk a fair bit about our film project. He saw it as providing a comprehensive account of the UDR's history and development, something that would provide both an historical record and briefing aid in the years to come. It would be a major project.

He had already sounded out the Central Office of Information who had agreed to provide a producer and film crew.

"I'd like you to write the script, select the locations, supervise the filming and escort the team round. It will be a nice farewell present for you to leave behind before you head off to Hong Kong."

The best laid plans . . .

A week before I was due to take the COI team on a preliminary reconnaissance prior to the start of filming, David phoned and asked me to step across to his office. Immediately I saw his face I realised something was wrong. He waved me to a seat and said gravely "Brad, I owe you an apology."

"Whatever for?"

I'm afraid we have a problem. You know you're due to fly out to Hong Kong in February, don't you?"

"Yes of course. What's up? Has there been a change of plan?"

He shook his head sadly. "I'm afraid so. I have to ask you to let me off that promise, if you will."

"That's all right, David," I replied. "No worries. I fancy Mollie will be quite relieved; she's still having doubts about it." I had a sudden thought. "You're not sending me to London, are you?"

He grinned for the first time. "No, it's not quite as bad as that. How would you and the family feel about spending the next three years in Germany?"

I hadn't expected that. I'd been to Germany before and had quite enjoyed it. I'd be happy enough to spend three years there and I appreciated that Mollie would relish being close enough to fly back to Ireland and visit her folks whenever she liked. Hong Kong would have been good, but Germany was preferable to a long spell in London.

David seemed to be following my train of thought. "You don't have to make your mind up right away. Think about it. Talk it over with the family and let me know in a week or so. But I'd take it as a big personal favour if you'd agree to take this on."

In the next few minutes he spelled out the reasons for the change of plan. "You'll have heard that the three services are all staging special events to mark the Queen's Silver Jubilee next summer?" I nodded and he continued. "The Army is planning probably the biggest parade in its history next July – the 7th of the 7th, 1977. It's at a place called Sennerlager in West Germany; the Queen, Prince Phillip and God knows how many top brass and VIPs will be attending. It will be a massive logistical exercise and the world's press and media will be covering it."

I nodded again, wondering what was coming next. "The parade will be on the 4th Armoured Division's patch and I'd like you to go over there and look after PR on the ground."

Seeing the expression on my face, he rose and put a hand on my shoulder. "Don't worry, there'll be a massive PR team involved in this and everyone will muck in. But we need an experienced man in situ to handle all the preparatory work and help run things on the day. I think you're just the chap!"

We threshed it out for another half hour and he convinced me that I could do it. I'd always enjoyed a challenge, but this one looked just about as tough as it got.

I broke the news to the family who took it very well. As I'd anticipated, Mollie was pleased that making holiday trips home from Germany would be easier than travelling all the way from Hong Kong.

In any event, I didn't have a lot of time to dwell on the matter. I had to take the COI film crew round on their recce, plan their programme and write a script for the one-hour project. There was never a dull moment in those days.

As it happened, the crew had a short sharp shock on the night of their arrival in Northern Ireland. There were four of them in total and I booked them into the White Gable's Hotel in Hillsborough as a handy base of operations. I bought them a drink and left them to have dinner, arranging to collect them the next morning.

Sitting at home an hour later, I took a call from the HQNI Ops Room. A tip-off had been received that the Gables was a potential target for an IRA bomb. There was nothing for it but to alert the team and move them to another hotel. It was suggested that the Beechlawn Hotel, in Dunmurry, would be a safer bet. So I rousted the team out of Hillsborough and transferred them to the Beechlawn, trying as best I could to make light of the warning.

Another call from the Ops Room just after 2:30 in the morning informed me that a bomb had gone off in the Beechlawn and the hotel had been evacuated!

I got down there to find the crew, and other guests and staff, huddled outside in their night attire. Happily, no one had been injured and the bomb had been a small one, causing only minimal damage. Once bitten twice shy, however. I had the crew moved into the Mess for the remainder of their stay. No wonder some folk claim that military intelligence is a contradiction in terms!

Another door opens

After that indifferent start, filming went well. I thoroughly enjoyed working with the crew and taking them to a number of locations. After *Spotlight*, it was good to be involved in an entirely positive project, free of criticisms and propaganda.

I flew to London for the final editing and enjoyed writing the commentary which was added later by Don Anderson of the BBC. The film was premiered – if that's the right word - a few weeks before I departed for Germany. The COI boys had done a fine job. I liked it and reckoned that it was as fitting a legacy as any to my work of the last three years.

About that time, I was involved in one more pleasant job. The Regiment commissioned a painting by the accomplished English artist, Ken Howard, and I had the pleasant of escorting him around while he completed the work. He was an affable companion and one evening, when I invited him home for dinner, he delighted my daughter Valerie by adding a pen and ink sketch of her in her autograph book.

Ken was concerned about being able to encapsulate the work and worth of the Regiment in a single canvas. "Why not do a vignette?" I suggested, "In that way you could show a number of facets."

So it was agreed, and the final painting showed five scenes of the UDR going about its varied work. When I left for Germany I was presented with a signed print of the painting. Nothing could have pleased me more. It's on the wall of my study as I write.

Once I had positive confirmation that I was Germany bound, Bill Moore advised that I should take advantage of the opportunity to buy an export model tax-free car. I was able to save around £3,000 in tax provided I didn't return it to the UK inside two years. It was too good a deal to pass up and I flew to London and came home with a gleaming red top-of-the-range Audi.

It was only afterwards I realised I ought to have gone for a left-hand-drive model, especially as I intended changing it before I returned to the UK. Still, it was a smashing car and I enjoyed driving it.

There was one piece of sad news shortly before my departure. Mike Taylor and his wife Maureen hosted a dinner party for the AIS staff in their home just outside Antrim. It was a typically jolly affair until about halfway through the evening when David McDine took suddenly ill, complaining of severe pains in his chest. Our worst fears were realised when he was diagnosed with acute angina and hospitalised for a time. It meant his tour in Northern Ireland ended prematurely and he was ordered home to Herne Bay for a period of rest. We had lost a first class leader, and in my own case, a close personal friend.

I couldn't help but recall a conversation we had on one of our long train journeys into London about the length of time he spent commuting. All those long hours must surely have taken their toll. David was replaced by Robin Goodfellow. We barely got to know one another before I was off on my travels.

There was another development around that time which could easily have taken my life in a totally different direction. It came about quite by chance. I'd done a small favour for a Mr Lowry, a high-ranking official attached to the Secretary of State's office in Stormont. It was nothing special, but it did require an input from someone with a good background knowledge of Northern Ireland.

A few days later I received a letter of appreciation from him, together with an invitation to come and see him in Stormont. What he had to say came as a total surprise. Over a cup of tea he explained that the United States was continuing to take a keen interest in Irish affairs, particularly with regard to the ongoing violence and unrest.

A post was being created in Washington which would need to be filled by someone with a firm understanding of Irish affairs, coupled with an up-to-date grasp of the Government's information policy and experience of public relations and briefing the media.

"From what I've seen in recent days and from some enquiries I've made, you seem ideally suited to the job," he said. "Initially it would mean an 18-month posting to our Embassy in Washington, with the possibility of an indefinite extension, depending on developments. I appreciate it would mean a significant career change for you, but I need scarcely say the financial and other benefits would be considerable. We can discuss these in detail later if you wish."

I hadn't been expecting anything like this. Lowry's offer had come totally out of the blue. In one sense the opportunity seemed too good to be true; on the other hand, arrangements were virtually finalised for me to take up my post in Germany. Talk about being spoilt for choice. If ever I needed to take advice from David McDine it was now. But he was seriously ill in hospital and there was no way I would burden him with this problem. Besides, He was depending on me to help with the Jubilee parade and celebrations in July.

My prolonged silence caused Lowry to raise an enquiring eyebrow. I snapped out of my daydreaming. "I'm sorry," I said, "it's all very flattering, but this has come as quite a surprise."

I told him about the forthcoming Sennerlager parade and my proposed part in it. A lot of arrangements had already been put in train. There was the matter of the Audi and I'd also arranged to rent out Manor Drive on a three-year lease.

Lowry was understanding, but said he'd need an answer inside seven days. I thanked him again, said I'd discus it at work and with the family and let him know in a day or two.

Perhaps not surprisingly, Mollie and Val, having already come to terms with the idea of moving to Germany, declined the Washington move out of hand. Figuring there was little point in discussing it with the newly arrived Robin Goodfellow, I confided in Bill Moore over a couple of beers in the Mess.

"You lucky sod," he responded, "Fancy being confronted with a couple of options like that. It's a tough choice, I know, but if it were me, I'd be inclined to stick with the devil I know and plump for Germany. Besides, you wouldn't really enjoy hobnobbing with all those Yankee fat cats and politicians in Washington."

Next morning I telephoned Lowry, thanked him again for thinking of me for the post, but said I'd decided to stay with MOD. I can't help wondering though what life would have been like if I'd gone for the other option.

GERMANY BOUND   PR colleagues (back row from left) Terry Stockton, Henry Bodjys, Roy Hart, (front) Bob Crooks and Bill Moore at my farewell party in HQNI.

Pastures new

My last couple of weeks in Ireland flew by. There was a hectic round of farewell parties and lunches – many of them of the liquid variety - in HQNI, HQ UDR, the Police Press Office and the NIO. The BBC, UTV, Downtown Radio and many journalists entertained and said some nice things about me. I think the media appreciated that, even if I hadn't always been able to give them all the information they wanted, I'd helped them as best I could and had never knowingly misled them. Lose your credibility with those boys and you never win it back.

I drove round to bid personal farewells to all eleven UDR Battalions and wish them safe and productive futures. I admired those men and women tremendously and had seen at first hand their courage and fierce sense of duty. I'd forged many enduring friendships in their ranks and, sadly, had attended far too many of their funerals.

I was scheduled to have gone on a six-week course to learn German, but we were far too busy. The next best option was to take a seven-day crash course to learn the basics, but I missed out on that too.

Recalling my days learning Pitman's shorthand, I remembered a booklet by a woman called Emily D Smith entitled *Six-hundred Common Words*. This system was based on the fact that 600 commonly used words make up almost 80 per cent of colloquially-spoken English, A lot of my early shorthand studies had involved learning the outlines for those 600 words.

Okay I reckoned, what if I were to memorise the German equivalents of those frequently used words? It probably wouldn't make up 80 per cent of a different language, but it would be a start. I wrote out my list, appended the Deutsch equivalents alongside and began learning them parrot fashion, resolving to master at least thirty every day. I completed my task on the eve of my departure.

My grammar was rubbish, but at least I could grasp the thrust of what people were talking about, as well as being able to make myself understood in a kind of monosyllabic fashion. Over time I became a little more fluent, but must have sounded fairly pathetic to a native German speaker. I quickly discovered, however, that once I'd made the effort to learn their language, most Germans were only too happy to demonstrate their own good English.

It was going to take about six weeks before I could secure a married quarter and the family were able to join me. In the meantime, I would be billeted in the officers' mess of the 4th Armoured Division's HQ complex in the picturesque old Westphalian town of Herford, on the banks of the River Weser.

Bill promised to keep an eye on the family for me and to drive them to the airport when their flight was organised. He and several other friends from work came down to see me off.

I'd mapped out my route and loaded the Audi with as much personal gear as I could manage. I'd even made a cassette tape of my 600 German words to reprise on the journey. The February weather was unusually kind as I headed for Larne and the ferry crossing to Stranraer. The ninety-mile drive to Dumfries was uneventful. I spent the first night there with some old friends and continued on to Hull the next day, arriving in time to catch the night sailing to Rotterdam.

The Audi was handling beautifully but I was quite relieved when I'd safely negotiated the busy rush-hour traffic in Rotterdam and pointed its nose east in the direction of the West German border. As an aide memoir I pasted a sticky label bearing the words *Think Right!* on the steering wheel to prevent me falling into bad habits.

As it happens, I experienced little difficulty in driving on the *other* side of the road on the continent. The only problem was having to pull out a little farther than usual when overtaking in order to get a better view of the road ahead. As I recall I got it wrong only once.

I'd stopped at a filling station to top up and discovered the attendant was English. An ex-soldier, he'd married a German girl and had settled over there. We chatted away, passing the time of day, pleased to enjoy a conversation in our own language. Possibly because of that, I waved him goodbye and promptly pulled out in the wrong direction, straight into the teeth of a line of oncoming traffic!

Mea culpa. No question about it. Confronted by a cavalcade of flashing lights, blaring horns and shaking fists, I scuttled for the safety of the hard shoulder and awaited my opportunity to head in the proper direction. I never made that mistake again.

I came to quite enjoy driving on the autobahn. Soon I was talking glibly about it taking an hour to Hanover and three hours to Hamburg, rather than listing the miles or kilometres. It was certainly a speedy and efficient way of getting from A to B.

Back to my first morning. After a couple of hours, I pulled into a service station for a coffee and sandwich. On my way back to the car I was accosted by a gaudily dressed individual who had conman written all over him. Loud jacket, louder tie, and a slick line in patter. He'd obviously sussed out from my registration plates that I was British, for he immediately launched into a pre-rehearsed spiel.

He said he was a Romanian who had been working in Holland and was hurrying to get home where his poor mother was dying. He had left his job on hearing the sad news and had no money. All he owned was his dead father's old watch, a valuable Rolex. It broke his heart but he needed to sell it to get money for food and for his fare home. I could have it for a giveaway price.

I waved my wrist to show I already had a watch. He could

scarcely conceal his scorn. That was not a watch. His Rolex was a proper watch and never missed a second. It pained him to let it go. Only this dire emergency had forced his hand. I declined again and suddenly the price decreased by 25 per cent.

I finally got rid of him. What use had I for a fake Rolex case and a Timex mechanism? He shrugged. I was missing the bargain of a lifetime. Finally, he flounced off in search of another sucker.

Three years later almost to the day, my daughter and I were making the return journey to Ireland - Mollie and Barry were flying back separately - and we stopped at a service station in the same area. Sure enough, there was my old Romanian watch salesman. Only now he was Polish and was rushing to England to the bedside of his dying mother. Would I come to his aid by buying his dead father's valuable Rolex?

I wondered how many folk he'd conned in the years since we'd last met. I shook my head sadly, said I was sorry for his trouble and suggested he should come up with a new sales pitch. That one was showing signs of wear. He clearly didn't remember me and obviously hadn't a clue as to what I was chattering on about.

Hello Herford

Arriving in Herford shortly after lunch, I had little difficulty in following the signs to 4 Div. HQ. I knew the PR Office was fourth in a line of grim, greystone barrack blocks which had all been erected for Hitler's Wehrmacht back in 1936. They had outlasted the Thousand Year Reich and were now home to the British Army.

The front door was open so I strode in and continued down a long corridor to an office at the far end. The door stood ajar but I knocked politely.

"Come on in," said a well-remembered voice. "What kept you? I told you we'd all be meeting up here again, didn't I?"

Rising from behind his desk, hand outstretched, was Major Mike Pavitt, my new military opposite number, with a smile as wide as the Shannon River and that same mischievous twinkle in his eye. "Welcome to Germany, mate. I told you the Tarot never lies! Have a good trip?"

I hadn't forgotten his card reading feat in Manor Drive all those months before, but it hadn't been in the forefront of my mind.

We shook hands warmly and I asked him how he'd known of this meeting all that time ago.

"I didn't know," he answered, "but the Tarot obviously did. I only ask the questions and spell out what the cards say. It doesn't mean I have the answers."

Two good German friends, Michael Neumann (left) and Col Ewe Schrader get close up and personal with a World War II Tiger Tank at a military museum.

In the months that followed I saw Mike perform some amazing feats with that pack of 78 cards he kept hidden in his red bandana. It was his regular party piece. Later, when he was ill in hospital for a spell, he let me borrow his cards for about three weeks and I performed a number of readings myself. I still don't pretend to understand how it works; all I can say is that I achieved some remarkable results.

Later Val bought me a pack for my birthday, together with a little guidance manual. I lost them some time later during a house move. As Mike himself put it, "The Tarot has been around for more than 2,000 years. I can't see it surviving that long unless there's something in it."

Knuckling down

We had a little round-table welcoming confab over coffee and Mike introduced me to the rest of the team.

Inge, tall, blonde, slim and typically Germanic, was a native of the Hanover area and had been in the job of office clerk, secretary and interpreter for about nine years. She was highly efficient, spoke and wrote excellent English, and was, like many of her race, almost totally lacking in humour. Inge took her job – and everything else in life – extremely seriously.

In sharp contrast, Kit, our sergeant-photographer, was a huge, good-humoured man who hailed from Yorkshire. He was a skilled cameraman and he and I were to spend many hours cruising the autobahns, roads and byways of Germany, usually driven by Wally, our lance-corporal driver and general handyman. Like many soldiers, Wally had a German-born wife and spoke the language fluently, although he contrived to keep this a well-guarded secret. When it came to speaking German, Kit and I were well down the office league table. I was, however, determined to improve in that regard.

The last but not least member of our little crew was another German lass, Crystal. A strikingly pretty girl, with a shock of flaming red hair, she tended to keep herself much to herself, As well as being Kit's back-up photographer, she ran the darkroom and photo-processing department.

Each of us had a large office to ourselves. Although I'm bound to say the males among us were a fairly gregarious lot and spent a fair amount of time in one another's offices, as often as not simply to share a coffee or a chat. I'm glad to say we ran a happy ship.

Briefed up to the eyebrows

My first week was much like when I'd begun back with the UDR. Mike conducted me on a tour of the HQ and introduced me to the GOC, General Nigel Bignall and his staff. Almost without exception, they impressed on me the importance of the role our little PR department would play in the Queen's Jubilee Review at Sennelager on the Seventh of the Seventh, Seventy-seven.

"You'd think it was the most important event to happen in West Germany since the end of World War II," I said to Mike as we trooped back to the office.

"As far as they're concerned that's exactly what it is," he replied.

"They fancy a lot of their reputations are at stake and they're probably right. If all goes well a whole fistful of gongs are going to be handed out. Not that you and I are likely to figure in that particular list."

"No problem there then, Mike," I said confidently. "You and I can crack this little gathering, no bother!"

"Tell that to Col Hoyle, down at Corps HQ in Belfield. We're off to see him for lunch and a full briefing on the big show tomorrow."

Belfield was about half-an-hour away and it was a journey I was to repeat many times during my stint in BAOR. I liked Col Keith Hoyle at first sight and reckoned he and I were going to hit it off just fine. He was the best sort of senior officer, the kind who left rank on the other side of the door when you were with him. The same went for his 2iC, Major Bob Stewart, and their German civilian Information Officer, Gerd Schaefer.

Back in the office after lunch, Col Hoyle got straight down to business.

One wall was covered with a large-scale map of Sennelager Training Area. It was vast, a fitting amphitheatre for what was to be produced there in a few months' time.

He waved a pointer at the map. "This is the only place big enough to cope with the show we're putting on here in July. It will be the biggest demonstration the British Army has ever mounted, or is ever likely to mount. Practically the entire 4th Armoured Division will be on parade. Some 3,000 men, about 600 tanks, guns and other support vehicles and Army Air Corps helicopters, not to mention the massed bands, comprising over 600 musicians."

"God knows how many TV crews will be turning up, but I do know that the BBC are planning two hours of live coverage. The same goes for the German stations. There has been interest from the Japanese and the Americans too, although they will probably end up taking the BBC feed. We're expecting blanket radio coverage too."

He looked directly at me. "Your first job will be to prepare a comprehensive press pack, with descriptions and potted histories of all the regiments and units taking part. Your girl Inge will translate this into German as necessary. The British newspapers will be here in numbers too, but at least London is handling their arrangements and accreditation. Gerd here will assist you with the German side, and here too there will be huge interest."

The briefing continued for the better part of an hour. Then we broke up, having agreed to reconvene at Sennelager the following morning to walk the course and familiarise ourselves with the set-up.

Quite an amphitheatre

I'd been on a few parade grounds in the previous three years, but I'd never seen anything like this. It was vast – a huge, flat area of the North German Plain which normally served as one of the BAOR's main training areas.

"It looks pretty bleak at the moment," Col Hoyle said, "but it's all going to be very different next July. It's going to be a damn sight hotter for a start!"

We stood in a group and surveyed the arena. Although it was mid-February, the ground was dry and dusty and almost devoid of grass. Several squads of fatigue-clad soldiers were already engaged in assorted clearing-up tasks.

We walked up to the only building on site, an old disused windmill which stood sentinel over the square. Keith waved a hand. "The saluting base will be directly in front of that, and once the Queen and Prince Philip have inspected the troops, they will take their positions there to take the salute at the drive past. Seating will be erected on either side to accommodate some 25,000 spectators. TV crews and photographers will be confined to certain designated areas. We can't have any of the perishers being run over by a bloody Chieftain tank, now can we? Each group will be in charge of a dedicated PR officer."

Although there wasn't much else to see, we continued our little tour of inspection for another half hour before heading off for the inevitable cup of tea. Mike and I drove back to Herford with a lot to think about, but with a clearer idea of what the battlefield looked like.

Other business

While the Jubilee Parade was undoubtedly the focal point of my first year in Germany, there was also a fair amount of what might best be called routine public relations work to be carried out.

The British Army of the Rhine spent the bulk of its time training to deal with any possible threat from Russia and the Warsaw Pact countries on the eastern side of the border between the two Germanys. That threat was perceived to be very real in the 1970s, and both sides guarded and patrolled their respective sides of that fortified border with grim seriousness.

To that end, large-scale military exercises were held regularly, focusing in the main on resisting and combatting any possible incursion from the Eastern Bloc until reinforcements could be brought in. Sometimes these manoeuvres involved our NATO allies, particularly those from West Germany, the United States and Denmark.

These affairs were realistic in their scope and elaborate measures had to be set up to deal with complaints from the German community with regard to such things as accidents and damage to property. A squadron of Chieftain tanks can make quite a mess if it crosses a field of potatoes or sugar beet, or collides with someone's new Mercedes. Where possible, compensation was sorted out on the spot and a tidy sum was set aside for this purpose.

Of course, most Germans weren't too pleased about this, but mindful of the threat from the other side of the border, appeared to accept it with typical Teutonic stoicism. Locals I spoke with during these exercises appeared genuinely in dread of a Soviet invasion and of being consumed by the Warsaw Pact countries.

The West German press and media covered these exercises as a matter of routine and to that end each Division would establish an information centre in the exercise area to brief them, answer enquiries and provide facilities for them to cover events. These regular occasions did much to improve my Deutsch. As I explained earlier though, most of the reporters were pleased with the chance to demonstrate their usually excellent English.

An enjoyable and routine part of our job was to provide facilities and briefings for the UK-based media to visit their local regiments and units serving in Germany. We were also expected to churn out what we called Home Town and Local Boy stories on serving soldiers for dispatch to weekly newspapers in the UK.

This was deemed necessary labour, but it could be boring and repetitive. I quickly discovered that my opposite numbers in the other divisions weren't skilled or interesting in broadcasting work, so it was tacitly agreed that I should look after it.

Our office was equipped with a couple of high-quality Uher reel-to-reel tape recorders and a functioning editing suite, and I enjoyed nothing better than making good use of it. Harking back to the old days with the BBC in Belfast, I was delighted at the opportunity of being reporter, interviewer, producer and broadcaster all rolled into one.

I still remember my first little foray abroad with the Uher. Major

John Prendergast, an officer friend of Mike's, was something of a tame inventor. He had constructed a miniature hover-craft and he intended making an attempt on several world speed records on a measured course on the River Weser a fortnight after my arrival in Germany.

Kit took several pictures of the intrepid speedster and I did an interview and brief commentary as our hero reeled off the laps. I edited it all together and sent a copy to the BBC in London and BFBS, the British Forces Broadcasting Service, in Germany. It was broadcast on Radio 4 and the BBC World Service as well as on BFBS.

Mike was especially tickled by my introductory sentence and talked about it for days afterwards. It ran something like: "It isn't every day that you see three world records smashed on a sleepy Sunday afternoon, but that's what a British Army major did on the River Weser in West Germany today."

I did a quick edit, put it through to BFBS in Cologne, who linked up with the Beeb and it was transmitted that night and the following day. BFBS were delighted with it and demanded more. I did a lot of work with them over the next three years.

Happy reunions

I quickly settled into life in the Mess. It was only a three-minute walk from the office and, as I'd expected, the quality of the food was excellent. It was a large, well-appointed building and the story had it that Hitler himself and a number of his Nazi cronies had stayed there on more than one occasion. I attended a number of formal dinners and other functions there. At one end of the main banqueting room there was a wide minstrel gallery, set high on the wall, where a regimental band would entertain us from time to time.

UK television only arrived during my second year in Germany, but the mess boasted no less than three television rooms, each showing a designated German channel. Close by the mess, a large cinema screened fairly modern films, usually within two or three months of their general release.

Soon after my arrival I was delighted to receive a phone call from my old friend, Alan Graham, who was now my opposite number in the 1st Armoured Division and based in Verdun, about seventy miles north of me. On hearing that the family wouldn't be joining me for some time, he promptly insisted that I drive up and spend my first free weekend with him, his wife Doreen and the kids.

All smiles as the family move into our new married quarter in Herford West Germany.

My improving navigational skills proved up to the task and I spent a thoroughly enjoyable couple of days with the Grahams. It was great to see them all again and to catch up on the gossip.

While I was there Alan put through a call to Berlin and I was able to have a chat with another couple of old friends, Mike and Maureen Taylor, who had just begun a three year posting in Berlin.

This resulted in another invitation and I promised to come up and see then once Mollie and the kids arrived from Northern Ireland.

In that regard, I was in constant touch with the family back home and they were understandably anxious to come over and join me as soon as possible. I became friendly with the divisional housing officer and he promised to move us up the waiting list for a married quarter as soon as he could. In the meantime, would I be prepared to move into a private German-owned apartment in the town?

Of course I would, and the deed was done inside a week. Mollie supervised the handing over of our house to a young newly-married couple, and Bill Moore was kind enough to collect the family and deposit them at RAF Aldergrove for the flight to Gutersloh, the nearest RAF base to Herford.

It was grand to be reunited with them again after six weeks and we quickly settled into our temporary accommodation. This was an ultra-modern, two-bedroom apartment, equipped with all mod-cons, overlooking the river and about a seven-minute drive from the office.

I'd already made arrangements for the kids' schooling. Barry was to attend the military primary school, just across the way from my office. His class teacher was Mike's wife, Hilly, and he quickly settled in. Val had the option of being a boarder or a day-pupil in Prince Rupert School in Rinteln, about an hour-and-a-half away from Herford by school bus. Not unexpectedly, she chose the latter option, although it meant her having quite a long day. She too settled in quickly and told us the curriculum, which was based on the system then in force in England, was at least a year behind what she'd been used to in Northern Ireland.

In spite of her earlier misgivings, Mollie coped well with the new environment and soon made lots of friends. Service families, well used to a variety of overseas postings, were a gregarious lot and looked after their own. Often when I arrived home for lunch a lively coffee morning was just breaking up.

With the Mess, school, cinema and a vast and well-stocked NAAFI on our doorstep it would have been easy to ignore local community life altogether and spend our time within the British community. Many army folk did, but I felt to do so would be to miss out on a marvellous opportunity of getting to know Germany and its people.

One of the first things I did was buy a decent television set and have it installed in our apartment. All it could receive in those pre-satellite days were German-based channels, but the family appreciated it, not least because I was having to spend a considerable amount of time away from home. They especially enjoyed the music and variety shows where James Last, Boney M, Abba and other groups usually performed in English, which was certainly the international language of pop.

Everyone appreciated it though when, in our second year, BFBS began to broadcast about eight hours a day of British TV, minus the commercials. I enjoyed catching up with the UK sport, and Mollie and Val became addicted to Coronation Street. There were also lots of kids programme to keep Barry interested.

A couple of months later, when we moved into our permanent quarter - a huge, four-bedroom German house with a vast cellar - Barry and his Brit friends from our little exiles' patch in Eulenveg discovered a well-equipped children's playground nearby and they made regular visits. As kids will, they made friends with local youngsters and soon afterwards we noticed that Barry was using a lot of German phrases in casual conversation, often interchanging them in the same sentence.

As an example, he came up to me one evening brandishing a toy car and said *"Dad, mein auto ist kaputt!"* Smiling, I asked what was wrong with it. Pointing to one of the wheels he reverted to English and said "That wheel won't go round."

Sadly, just like the rest of us, he didn't persist with the language once we'd left Germany.

For convenience sake, we opened an account in a local bank and kept some cash there in deutschmarks. While we did most of our shopping in the NAAFI, we also made weekly visits to Markov, a large grocery and department store in the town. We especially appreciated their butchery and cooked meats department. We like lean meat and German shops are prohibited by law from selling products that contain too much fat.

I was still taking every opportunity to improve my Deutsch and carried a little phrasebook around with me all the time. Young Barry, mad keen on music even in those days, had demanded a mouthorgan for his birthday. I drove into town, parked outside a music store, and consulted my trusty guide. I quickly found the phrase I needed. *"Habt ihr ein mundharmonica bitte?"*

I got out of my car and walked into the shop to be greeted by a smiling assistant. "Good afternoon sir, and how may I help you today?" he enquired in perfect English. He'd noticed my British car registration, or perhaps my poor attempt at his native language, and was right on the ball!

Sad news from home

I got home from work one day and switched on the radio to hear the sad news that the former Prime Minister of Northern Ireland, and a man whom I'd long regarded as an old friend, Brian Faulkner, had died as a result of a riding accident.

It was quite a shock. By far the ablest and most professional politician I'd ever met, someone I'd admired and talked to and interviewed many times, he had contributed a great deal to Northern Ireland political life and undoubtedly had much more to give. My thoughts went back to one of our last talks together, when he'd given me an exclusive interview which had afterwards been copied all over the world. I felt his passing keenly.

But life goes on and I was busy at work and play, and coming to enjoy what life had to offer in Germany.

Much of my work centred around the preparations for the big Jubilee Parade in July. Usually accompanied by Kit and Wally, I did a round of the regiments and units who would be taking part. I compiled potted histories on each of them, highlighting their principal campaigns and battle honours. I found this part of it fascinating and I certainly learned a lot in the process.

Kit took photographs of some of the leading personalities and much of the weaponry and machinery that would be on display. Back in the office, I typed up copious amounts of material for the Press and Media Information Packs and passed it to Inge for translation. I figured it might not all be used, but I was determined that nobody could point the finger and say they weren't given enough information.

I was putting some notes together one afternoon when Inge walked in, carrying a sheaf of papers and wearing a puzzled expression. She placed the papers in front of me and pointed at a line. "Brad, I have no German word for this. What can I do?"

I glanced at the page. It concerned one of the regiments which had taken part in the Crimean War and there was a reference to the famous Charge of the Light Brigade, later immortalised in the epic poem by Lord Tennyson. "We have no word which means charging the horses in this way," she went on.

I smiled and couldn't resist pulling her leg. "You mean a warlike lot like you Germans don't have a word for charge? I can't believe it, Inge. You have donner and blitzen and blitzkrieg and all that fiery stuff. Surely you can translate charge?

"You mentioned blitzkrieg. Would that do?"

"Nice try, Inge, but it's not quite the same thing. Somehow the Blitzkrieg of the Light Brigade doesn't have quite the same ring to it."

In the end we settled for simply including the Charge of the Light Brigade in English. But I still find it remarkable that a warlike crowd like the Prussians, after taking part in all those cavalry charges, had never coined a word for the sport.

I was pleased when Colonel Keith and Kate Hoyle invited Mollie and me to lunch in their home in Bielefeld, together with Mike and Hilly Pavitt. It was a warm, social occasion and I was gratified that, for once, there was little or no shop talk.

Lots going on

HQ 4 Div. was a busy place and there was always a lot going on. Mike tended to look after the purely military business and I was largely left to do my own thing with regards to promotional PR. After my time in Northern Ireland, when most of my duties had been of a defensive nature, I found this refreshing.

In spite of what I'd said earlier, I did have to produce my fair share of local boy stories, but I also took every opportunity to concentrate on broadcasting work. I didn't keep count of these but the tally must have run well into the hundreds. BFBS in particular, which broadcast 24/7, were always on the lookout for offbeat and topical stories and I found a lot of good ones.

I became friends with two of their producers, Derek Hale and John Walker, who were helpful and used virtually everything I passed their way. My voice soon became quite familiar on the airways and this helped smooth my way on a number of occasions. It seems people think they know you when they've heard you prattling away while their eating their breakfast or dinner.

I produced all kinds of programmes, the more light-hearted the better. Most of them involved interviews, but I did a few little talks as well. The first of these came about during a skiing trip in Galtur, the beautiful little resort in the Austrian Alps.

Having strapped on skis for the first time in my life, and encountering some serious snow, I spent most of my first week crashing ass-over-tip and clawing my way out of deep snowdrifts. Of course I ought to have taken some lessons, but I couldn't be bothered with that. Time was precious. Looking back now at some distance, I was lucky not to have broken a leg or my neck.

Afterwards I did a little radio piece about it. Ski instructors had got it all wrong, I opined sagely. Ski lesson number one ought to be about how to stand up on the bloody things without toppling over. Lesson two should cover how to fall correctly, ideally without breaking a fetlock in the process. Lesson three could usefully deal with how, having fallen, one could regain an upright posture again. I kept sinking into the soft, powdery snow and it wasn't easy to get a purchase. Sadly, all of these essentials seemed to have been taken for granted.

The piece continued in the same vein, with graphic accounts of some of my more perilous adventures. I'm not sure I didn't enjoy preparing the broadcast more than I did the actual skiing. Anyhow, by the time I got back to base and put it all together, BFBS used it a couple of times and it also went out on BBC Radio 4. Sad to relate, I lost this tape, together with all the others I'd made during my time in Germany.

One of my more unusual interviews was conducted half in English and half in German, something I never dared to repeat. It was all quite light-hearted though and concerned a chat I had with the fabled Pied Piper of Hameln, a picturesque little town not far from where I was based.

A ceremony is held in the town each month, based on an old fable about a magic piper who was hired to charm all the rats away from the town. When he was refused payment by the city fathers he allegedly returned and spirited away all the children of the town. The story has been immortalised in a popular poem by Robert Browning. The pageant is re-enacted regularly and attracts many visitors.

BFBS asked me if I would do a piece on the event and I agreed. I took the family with me on a day out and arrived only to find the chap who played the Piper had even less English than I had Deutsch. Somehow we managed, with me acting as both interviewer and interpreter. It's probably no bad thing that the resultant tape was later lost with all the others.

One of the local Forces schools ran an essay competition where the kids, aged, five to eleven, had to write a letter to the Queen, congratulating her on her Silver Jubilee. The headmaster was so tickled by the results that he selected the best of them and had them mounted in an album for later presentation to Her Majesty.

Bearing in mind that many of these kids had never been to England, had no access to UK television, and could have had only scanty knowledge of the Queen, some of the results varied from touching to hilarious. I took my recorder along and persuaded a dozen or so of the children to read out their efforts.

One little girl thanked Her Majesty for "sitting on that hard throne for us for all that 25 years." Another "promised to give her a big wave when she visited Sennelager." Yet another asked "Will you please send me one of your Corgis as I need a dog."

I never did find out what Her Majesty made of them all.

A proper Wally

I had a bit of good-natured fun with Wally when he came into my office one day while I was editing some programmes. After he'd watched me splicing and packaging some tapes I asked if he'd like to do a short interview about his life in the Army just for his own personal use.

He was happy to agree and the tape ran something like this:

"Wally, how long have you been in the Army?
I've been in for six years altogether.
Have you enjoyed it?
Some of it wasn't too bad, but it can be dead boring at times.
How much longer do you expect to serve?
Probably three or six years next time, if I sign on again.
Where have you lived in England?
London and in Manchester for a spell.
I understand your wife is German. What does she think about you having to spend so much time away from home?
She doesn't like it much, but she's getting used to it now. She usually goes home to stay with her mother while I'm away for any length of time.
You must have driven a lot of vehicles? What sort?
All sorts really. Land-Rovers of course, 3-tonners and 10-tonners mostly. I drove the General's staff car once when I had the chance, as his regular driver was off ill.
What did the General have to say to you?
He wouldn't say much to the likes of me.
Did he thank you?
No way.
Finally Wally, what Army vehicles would you really like to drive?
I'd love to have a go at one of those Chieftain tanks or maybe a Scimitar armoured car, but I'm in the wrong outfit for that. All I can say is chance would be a fine thing.

Thanks Wally. Leave it with me and I'll have the tape ready for you by tomorrow."

When Wally departed I set to work with the editing suite, inserted a new set of questions and spliced in Wally's answers. The end product sounded something like this:

"Good afternoon listeners. My guest in the studio today is Wally, a young lance-corporal in the Army, who is hoping for a second chance, having had what one might call a less that distinguished career so far. Wally has just been released from prison, having served a lengthy sentence for illegally taking and driving away a number of assorted vehicles.

Hello Wally, thank you for joining us today. Now, to begin, can you tell us how much time you've spent in prison?

I've been in for six years altogether.

And where have you served your sentences?

London and in Manchester for a time.

How did you find your time in prison?

Some of it wasn't too bad, but it can be dead boring at times.

You say you want to go straight and we hope you do. You'd probably get a stiff sentence if you were to re-offend?

Probably three or six years next time.

I understand your wife is German. What does she think about you stealing vehicles and spending so much time in prison?

She doesn't like it much, but she's getting used to it now. She usually goes home to stay with her mother while I'm away for any length of time.

You must have stolen quite a few vehicles over the years? Did you have a preference for any particular kind?

All sorts really. Land-Rovers of course, 3-tonners and 10-tonners mostly. The General's staff car once when I had the chance.

Finally Wally, were there any Army vehicles you'd liked to have stolen, but simply never had the opportunity?

I'd love to have a go at one of those Chieftain tanks or maybe a Scimitar armoured car. All I can say is chance would be a fine thing.

I suppose the General wasn't too pleased when he realised you'd stolen his personal vehicle?

He wouldn't say much to the likes of me.

Well thank you for talking to us Wally and for being so open about everything. I sincerely hope you don't get into any further trouble with stolen vehicles.

No way."

Poor Wally's face was a picture when we ran the tape in the office the following day, but he took it all in good part and we presented it to him as a little reminder to be careful of how he expressed himself in future.

Ich bin ein Berliner

With apologies to the late President John F Kennedy for the above headline, I was anxious to take up the Taylors' invitation to visit them in Berlin as soon as possible. It had long been one of the cities I wished to visit, not least because it had been virtually sealed off from the world since 1948 by what Winston Churchill had referred to as an *Iron Curtain*.

Sadly, thanks to the existing protocol and the sheer bloody-mindedness of the Russians and East Germans, it took six weeks for our written application to go through the system and be approved.

Most people of my generation will recall those Cold War days when the curtain came down to divide Germany into East and West, and isolate Berlin so that it could only be reached from the West by an air-lift and later a narrow road and rail corridor running directly into the city through East Germany from near Hannover.

The Berlin run became one of the most famous train journeys in the world, second only, I suppose, to the Orient Express. As I've said, protocol was strict. All communications had to be conducted personally by the senior military officer of the train and he could deal only with the Russians. The East German state, its army and officials were totally ignored, much to their chagrin.

As we pulled into Berlin we were amazed to see squads of grey-uniformed East German guards diligently searching underneath the carriages with Alsatian dogs and high-pressure steam hoses. It was the same on the return journey. We were told this was a precautionary measure to prevent East German citizens escaping to the West. Shades of JFK's famous *"At least we don't have to build a wall to keep our people in,"* speech.

I regret to say that I was almost responsible for creating an international incident. While the passengers waited in the seats, the officer of the train collected our passports and marched under escort to an office to have them inspected by the Russians. He returned, ashen-faced, to report that my passport had not passed scrutiny and that no one would be permitted to proceed until the matter had been resolved.

It would have been laughable if it hadn't been so scary. The problem was simply that my passport had a black line drawn underneath my name on the front cover, while my entry documentation did not. What was the meaning of this discrepancy? In the end the problem was resolved quite sensibly by the British officer borrowing a ballpoint pen and solemnly drawing a line under my name on the document. Panic over, and World War 3 averted, we were allowed to proceed.

Mike and Maureen welcomed us warmly and saw to it that we all had a marvellous time in this fabulous city. To this day, although it is united now and there have been many changes, it remains one of my favourite cities in all the world.

In a jam-packed weekend we did all the usual tourist stuff, visited the Brandenburg Gate, the Blue Church, passed through Checkpoint Charlie, went skating in the splendid ice plaza, had a Guinness in two of the six Irish pubs, and viewed the dreaded Berlin Wall at close quarters. I particularly enjoyed the line of graffiti that some brave, or foolhardy, individual had paint-sprayed near the top of the wall. It proclaimed garishly in foot-high letters *"Come on over and join the party!"*

The real surprise for me though, and something I ought to have known in advance, was that Mike's PR office was in the main British HQ building, inside the impressive complex which had housed the 1936 Olympic Games. "I didn't know you operated in such splendidly historic surroundings," I exclaimed enviously, while he beamed with becoming modestly.

But it was young Barry, recently turned six years of age and not hitherto noted for any obvious signs of athletic ability, who put the clincher on our visit to the stadium. Totally unbidden and most untypically, he suddenly took off and jogged a complete lap of the track, where, more than forty years before, four times gold medal winner, Jesse Owens, had cocked a snoot at Adolph Hitler and his Third Reich buddies. I asked him why he'd done it and he had no idea, except that it had seemed a good thing to do. That lad constantly surprises me.

On the second day, while the girls went shopping, Mike and I paid a visit to the grim, grey edifice of Spandau Prison, which still housed Rudolf Hess, the last of the Nazi war criminals who were sentenced at the Nuremberg Trials immediately after the war. The place was operated by the Four-Power authorities who took turns at guarding that final inmate until his death in 1986.

The place was demolished the following year to prevent neo-Nazis from turning it into a shrine. To demonstrate how the once mighty had fallen, it was afterwards rebuilt as a shopping centre for British Forces.

The main event – 7th of the 7th, '77

If the final weeks leading up the Jubilee Parade were busy, the final week was positively hectic. By the dawn of that last week, the temperature was well into the red zone and Sennelager was sweltering. We based ourselves there virtually every day. I brought the family down on one occasion and poor Barry got a severe case of sunburn.

There were a number of rehearsals, culminating in a complete run-through on the 6th. Nothing was to be left to chance and I can vouch for the fact that a considerable number of fingers were firmly crossed.

The engineers were concerned at the possible affect the unusual heat might have on the many heavily-armoured vehicles taking part, and a number of recovery vehicles were stationed at strategic points to whisk any vehicle which might come to grief out of the way. Fortunately, their services were not needed. Clad in t-shirt and shorts, I felt sorry for the luckless bandsmen in their heavy uniforms and the boiler-suited Tankies in their Chieftains.

Inevitably there were some moments of comic relief, heightened enormously because of their potential seriousness. Not least among these was the antics of Dettingen, the massive dapple-grey drum-horse of the Queen's Own Hussars, which was earmarked for a prominent position in front of the massed ranks of bandsmen immediately opposite the Royal Box.

Dettingen, originally chosen by the Queen, and presented to the Hussars by Her Majesty the Queen Mother, was in many ways the centrepiece of the entire parade. Named after the famous battle of 1743, the great horse carried two silver kettle drums which had been captured from the French on that occasion.

Everything seemed in order until the massed bands struck up and began to play. Despite the best efforts of his rider, the great horse swung round a full 180 degrees to see what the hell was going on behind him. A couple of stout attendants were summoned and stood, firmly clasping the bridle, either side of the horse's head. Same result – the pair of them were carried round when Dettingen repeated his about turn.

Changes were made for the next day's rehearsal. Dettingen was moved forward a fraction and the bandsmen withdrew a couple of yards. Two even-stronger attendants were stationed by his head. It mattered not a jot. Dettingen turned about immediately the musicians struck up. Worse still, he repeated the manoeuvre when the 25-pounders of the Royal Artillery fired the Royal Salute.

There was mild panic in the ranks and genuine fears were expressed that the horse might have to be withdrawn from proceedings. But surely this was unthinkable and would be construed as an unforgivable affront to their Majesties? The veterinarians were called in and a calming sedative was proscribed.

With many sets of fingers firmly crossed, the full dress rehearsal got under way. Surely one last chance for the great horse to perform. And perform he certainly did – but in a totally unexpected and near-farcical way. I need to frame this as delicately as possible, but whatever medication the vets had administered caused the horse to display his reproductive tackle in a most spectacular fashion. Those of you who have visited a stud farm will understand what I mean. The episode was nothing short of hilarious. Those of us in the PR corps and everyone else in attendance – with the possible exception of the Top Brass – collapsed in a fit of hysterics. The solitary consolation was that Dettingen, no doubt with other things on his mind, paid absolutely no heed to either the efforts of the massed bands or the gunners' Royal Salute. Clearly his thoughts were somewhere far, far away in a mystical little world of his own.

It was one of the great, unspoken and unpublicised, behind-the-scenes questions of the Jubilee Review of 1977. How would Dettingen react on the great day? We all waited to find out, not without a fair degree of evil anticipation. Whatever was to happen would unfold in the full glare of the world's press and media.

In the event - no pun intended here – Dettingen's contribution to the great event turned out to be something of an anti-climax. He behaved impeccably throughout and the spectacle that unfolded that day will live with me as long as I have breath. I watched it again on Google the other day and the video took me right back to Sennelager as though it were yesterday.

The blistering heat of that sun-baked plain, the vast crowd of applauding spectators, the serried ranks of military might and machinery during that long drive-past while Her Majesty and Prince Philip stood in salute.

I'm thinking now of the official News Release I wrote for

distribution that day. In it I'd highlighted the fact that while there would be more than a quarter-million tons of horsepower on view that afternoon, there would be only one genuine flesh-and-blood equine – Dettingen, the Drum-Horse of the Queen's Own Hussars.

I can't help but wonder what might have happened if the vets hadn't been able to work their magic and found a way to subdue his baser instincts so that he could put in an appearance. Just as well he did – otherwise my news release would have required some explanation! Happily, that incident remained the untold story of the Queen's Jubilee Parade of 1977.

Swinging parties

Afterwards the plaudits for our efforts came flooding in, from both official and unofficial sources. I especially enjoyed the personal letter from David McDine, now well on the way to recovery from his bout of angina, and back in harness in MOD.

The Hoyles threw a sumptuous end-of-exercise shindig in their home in Bielefeld where the entire Sennelager PR team assembled, ate and drank far too much and warmly congratulated ourselves on the part we'd played in proceedings. I appreciated the moment when Keith beckoned me into his study, threw an arm around my shoulder, and offered his own word of thanks for my efforts. He had worked harder than anyone and richly deserved the gong he was awarded in the forthcoming Honours' List.

Parties were a major part of the social scene in Germany and Mollie and I were invited out at a rate of almost one a week. All we had to do was bring a bottle or two of something nice.

Over dinner one evening Mollie suggested that it was high time we threw a dinner party of our own. I gladly concurred and discovered that she had already been making plans. Most of the parties we'd attended had either been formal sit-down dinners, or informal, help-yourself buffets. Because of the likely number of guests in our case – approximately thirty – a buffet was clearly indicated. She'd obviously given it a lot of thought already and was firmly against the usual fare or curries, lasagnes, or assorted sandwiches and sausage rolls. "What if I make about three big pots of Irish stew, with apple tart and cream for afters?" she suggested. "We can lay in some Guinness and Irish whiskey and have some Pims or punch for the ladies."

"Sounds like a right old Irish hooley," I smiled. "It will certainly be different from what most of our guests are used to. Apart from the PR people and wives, and our neighbours, I'll invite a few of my Irish Ranger pals from Haemer. We can put up seven or eight who'll be incapable of driving home, and our neighbours can probably cope with any overspill. Pick a date and I'll start laying in supplies."

That party was talked about for a long time afterwards. It continued well into the small hours and Mollie's Irish stew went down an absolute treat. Brian Barton, my PR mate from 2 Div., after his fourth plate of stew, warmly complimented Mollie and said he'd never enjoyed anything so much.

As planned, there was total informality. Mollie emphasised this in a little speech of welcome. "I don't care what you do at work," she said, "but in our house all badges of rank are left at the door. You're all our guests and our friends."

I couldn't have put it better myself. Everyone gladly accepted our ground rules and everybody from Col Keith to L/Cpl Wally happily entered into the spirit of things. Val was a great help to her Mum in the kitchen and was in charge of playing a selection of Irish background music on our stereo. Barry was granted special dispensation to stay up an hour later than usual and behaved himself extremely well.

Some of our Irish Ranger friends stayed with us overnight and claimed the evening had reminded them so much of Ireland that they were quite homesick. Having been a frequent visitor to their Headquarters, and attended a number of their St Patrick's Day parades and celebrations, I'm sure this was a huge exaggeration. Next morning we provided them with a solid Ulster Fry breakfast to send them on their way back to base.

Michael Neuman

Of all the German folk I encountered during my time there, Michael Neuman was by far the most remarkable. Area manager of a large Mercedes showroom in Einbeck, a pretty little town about two-and-a-half hours south of us, he was fanatically enthusiastic about all things military, especially tanks and heavy armour. He had served for some time in the German Army and regularly turned up as a spectator at some of our field exercises, where he would drive around taking photographs.

Major Ian Henderson, one of our HQ Intelligence officers, called at our office one day and asked if we would mind taking this fellow under our PR wing. "We've had him checked out of course, and he seems harmless enough, but he's making a bit of a nuisance of himself. We'd take it as a favour if you could keep him out of our hair."

It was agreed and Michael came up to Herford to see us, full of enthusiasm and laden with gifts. It was the first of many such visits. He was an intense, but quite likable character. He stayed in our home on a number of weekends and both Mike and I and our families accepted the hospitality of his palatial home in Einbeck on numerous occasions.

Mike and I had several conversations as to whether Neuman was really a spy, or simply a somewhat eccentric tank enthusiast. The question was never resolved. His interest and fervour were palatable but we never knew him to overstep the mark. Over the years we all came to share many adventures.

On one occasion he phoned Mike to ask if he and I could come down to Einbeck for the weekend and perhaps bring along some weapons. "I have arranged a little shooting competition for you with some of my friends," he enthused, "I will provide a few German weapons and it will be great fun."

We agreed and Mike had to sign out the weapons from our armoury – a Stirling sub-machinegun, an SA80 rifle and a regulation Browning pistol. "We'll be lucky not to get arrested en-route," he joked.

It turned out to be quite a weekend, bitterly cold and with lots of deep snow on the ground. Michael's friends had already assembled and we joined them in a welcoming round of mulled wine. We were quickly introduced to Willem, Neuman's neighbour and the local doctor, Karl-Heinz, the area's chief forestry officer, Alfred, Einbeck's Chief of Police, and Colonel Ewe Schrader, of the Garman Army. I was to get to know the last two gentlemen very well in the months ahead.

Neuman couldn't wait to get the shooting competition underway. We were driven to a nearby forest where a number of contests and targets had already been set up. He took charge as we were put through our paces. I'd done a little shooting in my time, but didn't consider myself any great shakes. Mike was cold and was trying hard not to look too bored.

Neuman had produced a fair quota of armaments, including a WWII Mauser rifle and a vintage Luger pistol. While we were merrily blazing away for something like ninety minutes and expending God knows how many rounds, a couple of caterers arrived with a coal brazier, a barbecue grill and a huge selection of cuts of steak, venison and processed meats. All this was topped off with freshly buttered brochen (bread rolls) and lots of delicious sauces and dips. For drinks there was a choice of tea, coffee or mulled wine.

While we were getting stuck in to that little lot Michael, who had been keeping score, produced a notebook and solemnly read off the scores in reverse order. I half expected a local *Oompa-Loompa* band to appear out of the trees and provide a fanfare.

Each lucky marksman was presented with a handsome beer-stein. My name wasn't called for a long time and I was starting to think I'd been overlooked, or had missed every target completely. Mike took fourth place and Col Schrader third. I nearly fell over when I was declared runner-up, close behind Neuman himself. No way in the world this could have happened. For reasons of diplomacy or whatever, I'm convinced the crafty old sod had deliberately cooked the books. Whatever, with great good-fellowship and cordiality we shook hands all round and thumped one another on the back.

With night drawing in and more snow on the way it was good to get back to the house and cluster around a leaping log fire. As we would say in Ireland, the craic was mighty and the companionship brilliant. My German had improved to the extent that I could understand most of what was going on, but as I recall, the conversation was in a strange mixture of English and Deutsch.

Frau Neuman, a slightly meek and mousey woman, remained firmly in the background, coming forward only to serve dinner. Surprisingly, the main course was a wholesome fish soup, with small potatoes and vegetables on the side. It was first class. I found myself seated between Neuman and the doctor. Willem had little English but was a jovial soul for a German. Almost all the locals I'd met up to that time, who'd served during the War, had been at pains to point out how much they admired England, or how they fought only on the Russian front.

Most Germans never spoke of Britain as such. To them, everyone from Ireland, Scotland or Wales was English. After a time I just accepted it and stopped trying to correct them. Even Neuman would often jokingly refer to me as *du verdammt Englander* (you damned Englishman.)

The good Doctor Willem, however, was refreshingly and openly different. Yes, he had served on the Western Front and had fought many British. "Bloody good fighters they were too, not like the *verdammt* French and Italians."

Every time Neuman visited us in Herford he came armed with presents, most of them extremely expensive. He would always appear with a couple of large crates of his locally brewed Einbecker beer, to which I wasn't particularly partial. Not wishing to offend I would accept them and pass them on to Wally or Kit, who quite enjoyed the stuff.

He took a liking to Barry, who was growing up fast, and brought him loads and loads of scale-model tanks, accurate to the last detail. The pair of them would spend hours on the lounge carpet, re-creating the Battle of the Bulge and other dubious encounters. He would call Barry *"Mein bishen Kommander"* (my little Commander), much to that young man's delight.

However, several of Michael's unsolicited presents did cause Mike and me some measure of concern. They were invariably what you might call manly or very masculine gifts and were expensive enough to possibly be misconstrued as a bribe. First he presented me with an elaborate sheath-knife in a leather scabbard and, for Christmas, a superb pair of Carl Zeiss 10x50 binoculars, complete with tooled leather case. At the same time Mike was handed a powerful .22 air rifle by a leading manufacturer.

"These are all very nice," said Mike, "but we'd better let the security chaps know, just in case we land in trouble somewhere down the line."

I agreed, and clutching our trophies, we marched across to Ian Henderson's office, laid them on his desk, and asked his advice.

"Bloody nice toys," he acknowledged. "Ask him if he's got something for me. After all, it was me who put him on to you!"

Some months later Col Schrader invited me to be his guest on a German Army live-firing exercise by a squadron of elite Leopard 11 tanks on the ranges at Honer. Don't worry about driving," he explained, "I will arrange to have you picked up. Then we can have dinner and a few drinks in my home afterwards. Please stay with us overnight if you wish and you will be driven home the next day."

I thanked him profusely. "Not at all," I heard him chuckle. "It will give my wife Greta a chance to show off her English. It is much better than mine."

At that time the German Army's new Leopard tank was probably the best of its type in the world. Not as powerful or as heavily armoured as the British Chieftain, it was lighter, faster and more manoeuvrable. I was looking forward to the outing and it was everything I expected it to be and more. Not only did I see an exciting demo, but my friend arranged for me to have a high-speed run in a Leopard, an experience I will always look back on and treasure.

Frau Schrader was a charming and hospitable hostess and Ewe hadn't exaggerated in the slightest when referring to her English. It was perfect, virtually cut-glass BBC. Dinner was superb and the evening was one of the most enjoyable and relaxing I've experienced. We kept the shop talk to a minimum, but I did grasp the opportunity of sounding him out about Neuman.

"We've checked him out," I said, "and I quite like him, but what's your view, Ewe? Do you believe he's all right?"

Schrader smiled his laconic smile and poked a finger in my chest. "You've checked him out, my friend? "We've checked him out too. Many times. We will keep on checking him out. But who knows? Who can really say about these things? You and I are not paid to worry about the Michael Neumans of this world. So, tell me Brad, what do you think of our little Leopard?"

Holidays

One huge advantage of being based in Germany was the opportunity it presented to travel around Europe by car, without having to bother with booking flights and car ferries. All we had to do was grab a road-map, load up the car, and we were off. With the Jubilee Parade consigned to history, we took a week's family holiday in Holland – 180 miles away, but a mere three hours on the autobahn.

Holland is a great country, with fine people, and I always enjoyed visiting there. The long, hot summer was continuing and we booked into a small hotel in Eindhoven. The local language is quite similar to German and I had no difficulty booking us into a couple of comfortable rooms.

Trooping down to breakfast next morning, I was greeted by the owner-manager, a woman of formidable appearance, whose iron-grey hair was drawn back into a tight bun. We exchanged a few pleasantries in German, assuring her that our rooms were quite comfortable and that we had slept well, while she ushered us to a corner table.

Having ordered a light, continental breakfast, we were chattering away in English when the lady swept back to our table. "I beg your pardon," she exclaimed in excellent English, "You are English; not German?"

I assured her that indeed we were, but based in Germany with the British Army.

Her whole attitude changed immediately. With a beaming smile, she clapped her hands to summon a waitress. We were ushered to another, larger, table by a window, which afforded an excellent view of the town square, and watched in amazement as our table was re-laid with a staggering assortment of wooden platters containing every imaginable variety of cheeses and cold meats.

Asking permission to join us while we ate, Madame Crueff, as she introduced herself, apologised for having mistaken us for Germans. Memories of the War had lingered long in the Netherlands, she explained. The German occupation had not been good and their soldiers had murdered her husband, along with many other citizens.

Nothing was too good for us during the rest of our stay and I guessed our final bill was a lot lower than it might have been. We also made friends with her son Rudi, a bright and breezy thirty-something, who had picked up seven languages while working as a steward on the cruise ships. They were a charming, friendly couple. Not for the first time, I admonished myself for having virtually ignored modern languages at school. Old Harley Lyle Sleith would certainly never have approved.

We all thoroughly enjoyed our time in Holland, especially the kids, and were so glad we could stop pretending to be German! We spent an entire day exploring the fairytale world of the De Efteling Theme Park, really a forerunner of Euro-Disney, with its Dream Forest, Musical Dancing Waters and host of amazing sideshows. I captured several reels of movies on my 8mm camera although, sadly, these too have been lost.

With Val appointed map-reader-in-chief, we visited The Hague and many other of the major cities, receiving a warm welcome everywhere we went. Of particular appeal to me was an afternoon spent in the massive Philips Electrics Museum in Eindhoven, where we explored all sorts of gadgets, many of which had still to be introduced to the public.

There was just time for one more holiday before winter set in. "Where would you like to go?" I asked, rather fancying a trip to Italy.

"Let's go home to Ireland," Mollie and Val chorused in unison. I was clearly outvoted – not that I minded too much.

We planned to spend a fortnight with Mollie's sister Jean, husband Billy, and family in Annsborough, near Castlewellan, but this stretched to a month when the Audi had to go into workshops for repairs as the result of an accident. Happily, no one was hurt.

I phoned Mike to explain the situation and apologise. "Don't give it a second thought," was his response. "Get things sorted out and come back when you're ready. Make it an extension of your leave and enjoy yourselves."

Somehow, we managed a couple of weeks' break in Ireland every year we were away. The ties to home are strong. I didn't mind too much, as my work took me to a number of European countries, including Austria, Italy, Denmark and Luxemburg.

We had a mini-adventure on our journey back to Germany. Disembarking from the North Sea Ferry in Rotterdam, the Audi began to show signs of distress. The engine was overheating and I was losing power fast. Worse – I was in the centre of Rotterdam, on a four-lane motorway in the middle of the morning rush-hour! So much for the costly repairs carried out in Lisburn.

With some difficulty, and to the accompaniment of blaring horns, waving fists and spiteful glares from the surrounding drivers, we crawled to the first exit. I hadn't a clue where we were heading and had to pull over several times to refill the radiator which had developed a leak. After what seemed an age we limped into the forecourt of a tiny, back-street garage.

This, I thought, is going to push my little bit of Dutch to the limit. I shouldn't have been concerned, because the garage man spoke passable English. He grasped the problem right away too and poured some sealant into the radiator. The alternator had also packed in and this presented more of a problem. He explained it would take at least 24-hours to get a replacement. We'd have to find accommodation until the following day.

One look at our faces must have told him all he needed to know. "Wait a moment," he smiled encouragingly. "I have an old Volkswagen alternator here which I might be able to adapt. At least it should hold out long enough get you home."

What a player the man was! He worked solidly for an hour-and-a-half and when he'd finished we were back in business. The Audi was driveable. I gave him every bit of Sterling money I had in my wallet and we were both well content. A few hours later we rolled into Herford without further alarms and I had the alternator replaced the next day.

I recounted my little adventure to Neuman next time he came to visit and he clicked his tongue in vexation. "Bah! The Audi is okay, Brad, but what you need is a Mercedes. Now that *is* a car. I know, I sell them! Would you like one? I can fix."

I blanched. I might be able to accept a hunting knife and an expensive pair of binoculars, but Major Henderson and his intelligence mates would surely do more than raise an eyebrow if I suddenly appeared with a gleaming new Mercedes, courtesy of my mysterious German friend.

Michael must have sensed my hesitation, for he immediately waved a hand. "Not a present, Brad, you understand. Even I could not afford that. But I can get you a new, top of the range model for . . . let me think . . ."

He produced a small notebook and began scribbling with a ballpoint. After a few minutes he looked up and smiled. "I have a brand new Mercedes in my showroom at this minute. Its price is 49,000 D-marks (£12,250)." He looked down at his notes again. "If you wish, you can have it for 19,500 D-marks (less than £5,000). It is left-hand drive, of course, but that can be converted for about 500 D-marks."

To say I was gobsmacked would be putting it mildly. I was tempted; of course I was, but eventually sanity prevailed. I cleared my throat and said soberly "Thank you Michael. It's a most generous offer and I appreciate it. But I'm afraid I can't accept. The powers that be here might not understand."

He studied my face sagely for a long minute before nodding his head. "Okay, Brad. Don't worry. I understand."

I don't know, I really don't know. Perhaps I should have accepted his amazing offer – but, in the end, discretion won the day. Besides, a Merc would never have fitted into my little garage back home in Lisburn.

Old friends

Tony Heaney and I still contrived to keep in touch regularly. He had a good job and a nice house in Melbourne, but he and Pat, so typically and sentimentally Irish, were missing Ireland, their families and friends. Tony had suffered a couple of hard knocks when his parents passed away within a few months of each other.

For the first time, they began to entertain thoughts of returning to Ireland. "You never know, Fleming," he said in one of his tape-recorded messages, "we might even be back in Kilkeel before you finish your tour in Germany. And it would be great if you stopped your globe-trotting as well and come home to the old country."

I was still in the early stages of my time in Germany and had no idea where I might be posted next. The troubles were still continuing apace back home, but I was in no doubt what the family would want if the whereabouts of my next posting was left to them.

As events transpired, I had a chance to get a heads-up on my possible future a lot sooner than I'd anticipated. David McDine, whom I hadn't seen since he'd been invalided out of Northern Ireland with angina well over a year ago, had recovered and was back in harness in London. He phoned to say he intended making a tour of the PR staff in BAOR and I insisted that he stayed with us in Herford. I'd be delighted to chauffeur him round to see the other culprits.

I picked him up off the plane at RAF Gutersloh and was delighted to find him looking much like his old self. As we drove to Herford, however, he recalled the conversations we'd had while commuting from Herne Bay to London. "You were right when you turned down the chance of coming to Main Building," he said. "You were well out of it, Brad. I'm afraid that daily grind eventually got to me. It was all just too much for my old ticker."

"I know," I said sympathetically. "There's a lot to be said for living close to work. I've been fortunate both here and in Lisburn to be only a few minutes from the office."

He glanced across at me. "I'd like you to keep it to yourself for now, Brad, but I'm giving up the DDPR job and taking over the South-East District IO slot in Canterbury. We may even move up there from Herne Bay. I reckon it will save me about three days travel time every week, and it means more time at home with the family. It'll take a few months to arrange but it's on the cards."

"I'm glad to hear that, David, and I think it's a sensible move. I certainly wish you well."

He smiled. "That's one of the things I want to talk about while I'm here. Have you thought any more about what you'd like to do when your time in Germany finishes? I take it London is still a no no?"

I returned his smile. "If at all possible."

"I rather thought you'd say that. But first things first. Sparing your blushes, the work you've done here, and in Northern Ireland, hasn't gone unnoticed. You're more than qualified for promotion and possibly a move to another Ministry. How does that grab you?"

"To be honest, David, I haven't given it any thought. I suppose a move to another Ministry would ultimately take me to London in any event?"

"That's almost certainly the case, and rather self-defeating from your point of view. You still have your house in Lisburn and I know you like a short commute!"

I nodded and he continued. "I'll be long gone by then, of course, but a Senior Information Officer post should be coming up in HQNI around the time you're due to finish here, and if you're interested, I can't see you having too many serious challengers. There'd have to be a Selection Board of course, but you should sail through that."

"Thanks David, and especially for the vote of confidence."

Mollie and the kids were delighted to see David again and I certainly enjoyed whisking him around my colleagues in the other divisions.

Trouble on the home front

A letter from Mrs Bird, our next-door neighbour in our old house in Lisburn, alerted us to the fact that there had been a bit of bother involving the young couple who'd rented our house. I checked it out and discovered the newly-weds had split up and No 4 was lying deserted, with the front and back gardens overgrown and in a sorry state. A call to my bank revealed that no rent had been paid for six months.

This was all we needed. I made arrangements for a few days off and took a flight home. My friends in HQNI kindly put a car at my disposal and I set about sorting out the mess. First I called to thank Mrs Bird. She wasn't able to tell me a great deal except that the wife, Elizabeth, had had a baby and had gone back to her parents' home in Hillsborough. It seemed that husband, Robert, had moved out to whereabouts unknown.

I inspected No 4 and found that both lawns hadn't been cut for months. The grass was 2ft high and the back lawn was strewn with old tyres and assorted pieces of discarded machinery. I used my spare key to enter the house. It was dank and damp and clearly hadn't been occupied for some time. Thankfully, there appeared to be no substantial damage.

I tracked down Elizabeth's parents in Hillsborough and spoke to her and her father. She was in tears and full of apologies as she sat, cradling her young baby. I could feel nothing but sympathy for her as her sad tale unfolded. The facts were simple enough. Robert had had an affair and had abandoned her and their child. She understood he had taken up with a married woman but hadn't been able to find out where they were living. She confirmed that he hadn't paid any maintenance for the upkeep of her or the baby. She was sorry, but she knew nothing about the unpaid rent as that had been her husband's responsibility. He had worked at a garage in the village for a time, but had moved on.

I left, having sympathised with Elizabeth and her father,

promising I'd pass on any information I managed to find on her missing spouse. I checked with the garage in Hillsborough and discovered that Robert had left on short notice about three months previously. They believed he was working at a garage near Mallusk.

It pays to have good contacts, and a swift phone call to the local UDR Company confirmed that my late tenant was indeed employed in the accessories department of a local garage. I thought it best to have a word with my solicitor, Gordon Bell, of Rathfriland. He was sorry for my trouble, but felt I could wave goodbye to my unpaid rent. "From what you tell me about this character, I doubt you have a pup's chance," he sympathised. "Best you can do if you see him is demand the keys back and we'll terminate the tenancy agreement."

I was in no mood to wave goodbye to over £1,000 of unpaid rent, or to pay a gardener to put the grounds of No 4 to rights, so I wasn't feeling exactly charitable as I headed for Mallusk

I asked the receptionist at the front desk if I might have a word with my former tenant concerning a private matter. She put through a telephone call and in a few minutes I heard the sound of approaching footsteps and some discordant whistling. Both sounds ceased abruptly as the door opened and Robert saw me standing there.

"Oh," he said, and turned a few shades whiter. "It's you!"

"Indeed it is," I said. "I think we'll have a private word outside."

I nodded my thanks to the receptionist, opened the door and stepped out into the forecourt.

Robert followed, meekly enough, and I turned to face him. Before I could utter a word, he blurted out. "I'm sorry, Mr Fleming. I know why you're here."

"I'm sure you do. And I'm sure you know you're in big trouble!"

Now those who know me will tell you I'm a fairly easy-going sort of fellow, laid back and reasonable to a fault, someone who will go a long way to avoid trouble. But there's an old saying – beware the anger of a patient man. And I was really angry with this fellow, not only on my own behalf, for the trouble he'd put me through, but for what he'd done to his wife and baby, and her parents. He had behaved intolerably, and from where I was standing, deserved neither mercy nor consideration.

Endeavouring with all my might to stay stony-faced, I held out a hand. "First, I want my house keys back, all of them."

He fumbled in a pocket and handed them across.

"Second, you owe my £1,200 in unpaid rent."

He blanched. "I haven't got that sort of money. I'm broke."

"Tough," I said. "I will be at No 4 at six o'clock on Friday. Bring me the money by then, personally. All of it, every penny."

He said nothing; simply let his head droop forward.

"Second, you have left my house in a total mess; I expect it to be tidied up and left the way you found it by Friday. That's the grass and hedges cut and all that junk removed. Fair enough?"

He started to speak, evidently thought better of it, and nodded dumbly. "Okay."

Again I looked him straight in the eye. "Make sure you pay up on Friday. You won't get a second chance. And put my place in order. One last piece of advice for you. You know who I'm with. Fail to pay up or do what I ask, and it will come out of your hide. Don't think you can run away. Wherever you go you'll be found and it will go hard with you. That's a promise. Six o'clock Friday. Don't be late."

I turned away abruptly, climbed into my car and drove off, leaving him standing, a desolate, solitary figure in the centre of the forecourt. As I drove I became aware that I was literally shaking, with the emotion of what had just occurred. I can never remember being so tense. Had I really said all that? Really issued that threat? There was certainly no way I could have it carried out. Ah well, the proof of the pudding would come on Friday.

I spent a couple of enjoyable days visiting family and friends before going down to No. 4 on the Friday. I wasn't quite sure what to expect, but sure enough, a car was parked on the road outside and Robert climbed out and walked up to me. I noticed a woman in the front passenger seat. The lawn had been cut neatly and a walk round the back confirmed that the mess there had been tidied up.

"Good start," I said, beckoning him inside. Without a word, he handed me a bulging manila envelope. "You'll find the correct amount in there," he said shortly. "I had to borrow it from my Dad."

I figured his father would be lucky to see any of his money again, but I said nothing. That wasn't my problem. I counted the cash, which was in £10s and £20s. It was the correct amount.

"Fair enough," I told him. "We're done here. You and I are square."

He looked so utterly miserable and downtrodden I couldn't help but feel genuinely sorry for him, and for the threat of possible repercussions I'd issued a few days before. Yet this was tempered by the manner in which he'd so callously abandoned his wife and new-born baby.

"What on earth happened to you, man?" I said. "You had everything going for you. Why chuck it all away?"

He rose, shrugged and stretched out a hand, which I ignored. "I honestly don't know, Mr Fleming. It happened. Just one of those things."

Perhaps I should have left it there. I'd got what I came for. But I added one last thing. "As I said, you and I are square, but you have a wife and child to think about. They need looking after and that's your responsibility. You might like to do something about it. It's up to your conscience, but you should know I'll be telling them where you work."

And that's exactly what I did when I called to see them half an hour later. I also put through a call to my solicitor. "Thanks for your advice about the keys, Gordon, I got them back. You were wrong about the money though. I got all of that back too!"

The Christmas Panto

"They've talked me into producing the Christmas Panto," Mike said one morning over coffee.

"Good for you," I responded. "You're the very man. I know you have an artistic bent. Put me down for four tickets."

He peered at me hopefully. "I don't suppose you'd care to write the script for it?"

"What!"

"We don't want to pay for a professional script. Besides, half the fun of it is splicing in bits of local colour and cracking good-natured gags about a lot of the top brass. They all sit in the front rows on the last night, lap it up and think it's great."

"The last night? You mean there's more than one performance? How long does it run for anyway?"

"There are four evening shows and a Saturday matinee. All told, more than ten-thousand people will see it, including a lot of German nobs from the town. It's one of the great social events of the year you know. Go on, Brad, say you'll do it. Put it down as a special favour to me. Besides, it will be a big feather in your cap."

"Mike, I've never ever been to see a panto, never mind write one. I haven't a clue about them. Sorry and all that, but it's not really my cup of tea."

Fifteen minutes, and another cup of coffee later, he'd talked me into it!

"Good man," he beamed, "I knew you wouldn't let me down."

257

Of course I knew the essentials of the Cinderella story, - Little girl lost, Ugly Sisters, Glass Slipper at the Ball, Prince Charming and all that good stuff. "I'll give you an absolutely free hand," he said expansively. "As long as you follow the basic storyline, you can introduce as many characters as you like, within reason. It would be a good plan to have a few Jerrys in it for instance, as long you don't poke too much fun at them.

Mike called round to the house that evening and quickly got Mollie and Val on his side to clinch my agreement to write the thing. "Tell you what," he said. "Take next week off, stay at home and get down to it in peace and quiet. The rest of us will hold the fort in the office. It's a fairly quiet week anyway."

"Thanks a bunch," I said.

I accompanied Mike to a preparatory meeting in the Green Room, not saying much, just sitting in the background trying to work out which of the wannabes I could envisage in the different roles. I realised this was Mike's prerogative as producer, but the blighter had said I could have a free hand. Besides, I needed to glean as many ideas as I could.

I already knew many of the likely cast, so I jotted down a few notes to talk over with Mike afterwards. I was particularly struck by a chap called John Patch. A captain in Transport, he was a Robert Newton lookalike, and I reckoned he'd make an ideal Long John Silver-type pirate, right down to the "ohs" and "arrs" in his distinct West Country accent.

I half expected an argument from Mike about introducing a pirate in Cinderella, but he merely smiled, waved a dismissive hand, and told me to carry on.

I virtually locked myself away in the house, ignoring all interruptions, existing mostly on endless cups of coffee and typed like a maniac on my old portable. I left spaces for Mike to append whatever music and stage directions he thought fit. I finished in four days – all three acts and 250-odd pages of it - and presented it to Mike with one huge sigh of relief.

Retreating to my own office, I left him to get on with it while I caught up on my backlog of work. I was gratified to hear the occasional loud guffaw emanating from his office during the following hour or so, and eventually he came in with a beaming smile and clasped me warmly by the hand. "A brilliant job," he enthused, "We won't need to change a thing; just add the stage cues and sort out the music."

Over the next couple of months, I kept well away from the

rehearsals, but was pleased when several cast members came up and offered their congratulations. I told Mike I'd be happy to make any changes he thought necessary, but he said everything was fine. The family and I attended the final dress rehearsal and I was surprised and delighted at how well the performance came across.

We attended all of the four concerts, skipping only the Saturday matinee. Each performance was better than the last, and the concluding one on Saturday night almost brought the house down.

John Patch was a veritable Robert Newton/Long John Silver as the leader of his band of cut-throats. Graeme, a 6ft 6ins Guards' Major, and Jean, the petite wife of a colonel, barely 5ft in her high heels, were an unlikely pair of Ugly Sisters. Avril Duvaine, in the title role, was a beautiful Cinders, and her husband, Tony, a hilarious Buttons.

[Sadly, I next met Tony in tragic circumstances five years later, on 6 December, 1982. He was Commanding Officer of the Cheshire Regiment, then based at Shackleton Barracks, Ballykelly. I had to arrange a media facility for him to be interviewed after an INLA bomb destroyed the nearby Dropin' Well Inn, killing 11 of his soldiers, six civilians and injuring 30 people who were attending a disco. It was sad that we had to meet again in such circumstances.]

Isn't it strange how Fate can, as though on the toss of a coin, bring so much innocent happiness and such unspeakable sadness into our lives?

Christmas and New Year

Christmas in Germany was a special time. Not that it isn't anywhere else in the world, but that first year especially, we all found it quite an experience. The 4th Armoured Division didn't quite close down and shut up shop – its role was too important for that – yet everyone was given as much time off as possible, and we all did our best to make the most of it.

There was a non-stop round of parties and entertainment; often two or three on the same day. On our little patch in Eulenveg it seemed that every door was open and we trouped gaily from one house to the next, toting something seasonal such as a bottle or some mince pies. I expect it was because all of us were far away from our homes and loved ones; I know we certainly missed our wider family and friends in Ireland.

We found that the local population celebrated the Festive Season very much as we did. There was a general feeling of camaraderie and warmth, and everyone seemed in high good humour. Michael Neumann arrived laden with crates of Einbecker beer and an embarrassing amount of presents, and stayed overnight. I think many of our military neighbours didn't quite know what to make of him. Barry welcomed his visits though, and had been presented with enough model tanks and other military gear to start his own little World War 3.

One difference we noticed was that, while the town and local shops and houses were bedecked with Christmas lights, all of them were white. The locals didn't seem to go in for coloured bulbs as we Brits did.

The gaiety continued more or less unbroken to include the New Year, which is called Sylvester in Germany. The standing, rather sick, joke of the times was that, if the Russians were ever going to invade the West, then Yuletide was the ideal time to do it, as they would find us in no condition to offer much resistance

Because of the one-hour time difference between Germany and the UK, we were actually able to see the New Year in twice. First we had the German celebrations and sixty minutes later repeated them to mark the arrival of the New Year back in Ireland. In practice it was all just one huge party.

Off to the Alps

For ten days every January most of the 4th Division decamped to the snow-covered mountains of Austria for the Army's annual Ski Meeting. While there was a serious side to it, there was a fair measure of fun as well. We were based in the resorts of Ischgl and Galtur, two fairytale little towns about 16 kilometres apart. One of the best things about it was that we were all accommodated in top class hotels, with ample opportunity for lots of après ski entertainment.

Hotel Rossle, where we stayed, was equipped with every conceivable convenience – heated swimming pool, saunas and spa rooms, two bars and a splendid gamesroom.

At an altitude of just under 7,000 feet, there was certainly no shortage of good-quality snow, and although very much the novice, I joined in with the rest. Not quite possessing the nerve or expertise to tackle the harsher Alpine slopes, I was introduced to Nordic skiing, or *langlaufen,* as the locals called it. I found this easier in some respects, more difficult – and certainly more exhausting – in others.

MOONBOOTED Great friend and colleague, Major Mike Pavitt, and I enjoy the ski slopes of the Austrian Alps.

Nordic skis are longer (usually six feet or more) and narrower than their Alpine cousins, and bloody unwieldy things even when you more or less get used to them. There is a certain art to their use which I never quite acquired.

Have you ever tried making an about turn wearing two-metre-long flippers? It's akin to doing the splits! But I was younger and fitter in those days and persevered as best I could.

The routine was that we worked in the mornings and were free to do our own thing in the afternoons. Work, in the main, was collecting local boy stories, taking pictures, and doing lots of radio interviews. We got about the place either on skis or in *'Moon Boots'*, calf-high footwear with firm, treaded soles. The weather was crisp and invigorating and during our time there we had remarkably little snow. The sun appeared most days and the setting of dense green conifers and snow-crested peaks, starkly outlined against an azure blue, cloudless sky was breath-taking.

Christa makes a face at the hotel disco. Husband Carl Heinz appears not to be amused.

I made something of a small reputation for myself one day when, just after lunch, and without announcing the fact, I decided to ski down to Ischgl. The cross-country route was perhaps a couple of k's farther than by road. I figured the largely downhill route would be a fair test, and I intended calling at our ski centre there and begging a lift back to Galtur.

The trip was relatively straightforward and I only experienced a couple of minor mishaps. It was quite exhilarating in fact, and I arrived at the centre in reasonable nick. To my acute dismay, however, I found that the centre had been locked up for the day.

Foolishly, I hadn't brought any money with me, so there was only one thing for it. I had to hike back to base.

I quickly discovered that going uphill on langlauf skis is a totally different proposition from cruising downhill. I knew the accepted method was to point the toes of the skis out in a sort of herringbone pattern and take reasonably short strides, while adding well-timed thrusts with my ski-poles.

All well and good. Perhaps that's how the experts did it, but, as I've said before, I was no expert. A couple of hundred metres of this torture convinced me that to press on in this fashion would quite probably banjax my back and legs, not to speak of wracking unmeasurable damage to the Fleming family jewels!

It was clearly an emergency. The sun had already begun to disappear and I reckoned it would be pitch dark in about an hour. I could head for the road and try to beg a lift, or I could soldier on and adopt my own patented version of the Muhammad Ali ski-shuffle. For better or worse, I chose the latter course.

A few people flew past me, heading downhill, but I had the uphill trek all to myself. Plainly, the locals had more sense. For the first time I came to realise how Scott of the Antarctic must have felt on his final fateful Polar journey. And no doubt he was well used to it and had a few companions with him. I hadn't experienced anything like this since my days hacking down trees in Tollymore Park – and at least I'd then had a mate on the other end of the saw.

It was unimaginably hard going. I persisted with my Ali-shuffle, taking tiny steps, like the kind David Suchet did when portraying Hercule Poirot. At last I saw the lights of Galtur. They looked awfully bright, but I wasn't sure if this was because I was getting nearer, or the night was getting darker. I counted twenty shuffles, then twenty more; then started over again.

All told it must have taken another three hours, but I eventually reached the haven that was *Hotel Rossle*. I remember sitting on the entrance steps, brushing snow off my clothing, and unbuckling my skis. I never wanted to see the damn things ever again. Somehow I summoned the energy to return them to the equipment store before creaking up to my room and the luxury of a hot shower.

I donned a towelling robe and collapsed on the bed for twenty minutes; then changed and strolled down to the bar. My friends were there, wondering where I'd disappeared to. It's fair to say that the tale of my adventure lost nothing in the telling. Not that I had to embellish it all that much. I may not exactly have been the hero of the hour, but I didn't have to put a hand in my pocket to buy a drink the entire evening.

As a rule, our evenings were given over to disco dancing, chatting in one of the bars, or mingling with folk from a variety of countries, including Norway, Sweden, France, Luxemburg, Germany and Russia as well as our little party from the UK. There was a good number of talented musicians in our midst, all of whom did their party pieces. The nightly singalongs were superb, and thank goodness, English was the universally adopted language.

One evening I got into conversation with a young German couple. Karl-Heinz Rode was a pleasant enough, if rather solemn fellow, with whom I enjoyed several fairly intense games of table-tennis. His pretty wife, Crista, was precisely the opposite, fun-loving and free-spirited.

A small group of us took to playing a light-hearted little game which involved small pieces of wood of different lengths. We played in pairs and it soon became evident to me that Karl-Heinz was taking it in deadly earnest, and bending every effort to win. In contrast, Crista almost seemed to be trying to ensure that he didn't succeed. After losing two games in a row, he excused himself and stomped off in something of a huff.

Crista chose to remain with us and she and I got into conversation. I chided her gently. "That was very naughty, you know. Your husband was trying his best to win and you seemed to be doing your best to ensure that he didn't."

She flashed a smile that displayed her magnificent white teeth. "Ah, so you noticed that, did you? I think Karl-Heinz takes life much too seriously. We are on holiday; we must have fun."

"I suppose it's all right, as long as you don't upset him too much," I cautioned.

She looked at me steadily. "You are very observant, Brad; very perceptive. Is that the right word?"

"Thank you," I replied. "It is exactly the right word. Your English is excellent. I wish my Deutsch were only half as good."

"Your Deutsch is fine, Brad, you shouldn't apologise. For us, English is the second language in the schools, you know. I am happy to have the chance to use it this week. Please promise me that you and I will speak English together."

I was only too happy to acquiesce.

We continued to chat and she asked about my job and my family. She was charming, intelligent, and remarkably easy to talk to. In many ways, she reminded me of Smithy, all those years ago in Newcastle. She spoke about her own life and her two sons back home. There was nothing flirtatious about our relationship; we were simply two people from two different worlds getting to know one another.

"I am not skiing tomorrow," she told me. "I jarred my knee slightly on the slopes today. Karl-Heinz will go with the others, but I think I will stay in the hotel. Perhaps I will see you?"

"I have a few little jobs to do in the morning," I said. "It shouldn't take long. If Karl-Heinz doesn't mind, why don't you come with me? It's on level ground, not far from the hotel and it doesn't involve skiing. After that we can have lunch if you like?"

I was again treated to that beaming smile. "Thank you, Brad. I would like to do that very much, if I am not in the way. Karl-Heinz will not mind. He has his own things to do."

I explained to Mike and Kit that I would be bringing a guest with me in the morning. "You crafty beggar," Mike teased. "I wondered what you were up to last evening."

In vein I protested that it wasn't what they thought. I could scarcely blame them though. Crista was an attractive woman. I warned them darkly, however, that I expected them to be on their best behaviour, with no innuendo or snide comments to be made.

I collected Christa after breakfast next morning and introduced her to the team. She assured me her knee was much better, but she had elected not to risk any downhill runs. In any event, she said she was more than happy to spend the day with us.

We piled into the Land-Rover and Wally drove us the short distance to the ski area. With a sly wink, Mike volunteered to handle the local boy forms while Kit took the pictures. "The least we can do is to leave you free to escort Madam Rode around," he whispered. "Behave yourself now!"

I did behave myself, although I suppose you can't blame a fellow for thinking. Here I was, wandering round the Austrian Alps, with no work to do, nary a care in the world, and accompanied by a beautiful German fraulein. Life surely didn't get much better.

I explained to Crista that Mike had offered to carry out my duties for the morning in order that I could escort her properly. She smiled prettily and said, "I think you English are so wonderful."

After dutifully watching proceedings for an hour or so, I suggested we head back to Galtur for a coffee, or a glass of something warm. We took our leave of Mike and Kit, saying we'd catch up with them later, and Wally chauffeured us back to the village.

He dropped us outside a quiet little bistro, close by the hotel, virtually deserted as everyone was away on the slopes. We took time over a leisurely coffee and an apfel struddel, followed by a warming gluhwein.

We talked for ages, long after our meal was finished. Once I inadvertently called her Chris, instead of Christa. I apologised immediately, but to my surprise, she seemed both pleased and amused. "No one has ever called me Chris before," she said. "I like it."

From then on, she became Chris to me. Once again I was reminded of Smithy. The two, although widely different in looks, were strikingly alike in their personalities.

More than an hour passed pleasantly until I suggested it was probably time I escorted her back to the hotel. With a glance at her wrist, she said, "It is early yet, Brad. Might we take a little walk, up that slope beside our hotel?"

It was a fairly gentle incline, up one side of the valley. After half-an-hour or so we reached a small plateau, which provided a spectacular view of the valley and the narrow, winding road away down to Ischgl in the distance. I told her of my adventurous round-trip down there the previous day.

We gathered our breath and drank in the majestic scene. The shadows cast by the mid-afternoon sun had already begun their advance across the valley floor, almost fast enough to be discernible to our gaze. I'd rarely witnessed anything so wondrous.

I was aware of Chris taking my hand. I turned as she said softly, "You know Brad, I've never been kissed by an Englishman. Especially not on top of a mountain in Austria."

This was totally unexpected. Like a clot, I stammered, "What a pity I'm not an Englishman, Chris. Shall I run down and see if I can fetch you one?"

Looking momentary perplexed, her little frown quickly dissolved into a smile. "Did I say Englishman? Poof! Of course I meant Irishman."

We stood, close together on our own little mountain, surrounded by beauty on every side, and kissed. It was a kiss to savour. Austria holds many memories for me – but this was the best.

Chris and I met only once more, when I was a guest in her home months later, but, just like my old friend Smithy – and with apologies to Robbie Burns – we only ever shared *"One fond kiss."*

Several years later, back home in Lisburn, I was surprised to receive a little note from Chris. It had been forwarded on from my old office in Herford. She trusted I was well and still cherished sweet memories of Galtur, just as she did. One sentence lingers in my memory. "It is a sad thing that we lose touch with someone dear, because we are too passive."

I no longer had her address, and couldn't have replied, even had I wanted to. Perhaps it was just as well. Ships passing in the night again.

An impressive aerial view

One of the most enjoyable exercises I took part in was a joint affair with the American and Dutch Armies. I always got on well with my US counterparts and came to appreciate their efficient, but laid-back approach.

In fact, there was a US PX (the equivalent of the British NAAFI) near Hameln, about an hour south of Herford. We visited it quite often. The kids enjoyed the enormous scoops of soft ice-cream and I picked up a host of newly-released LPs, straight off the home market in the States. These cost four dollars each, as opposed to the normal stateside price of 20 dollars. We'd collected more than 2,000 records by the time we left Germany.

I was in the joint media-centre one morning when a report came in that one of our Scimitar reconnaissance tanks had blundered into a plantation of saplings, destroying many of the valuable young trees. This was bad enough, but, clearly, if it turned and attempted to extricate itself, even more damage would result.

"This sounds like a job for Superman," the US Colonel in charge declared in a deep Texan drawl. He barked a string of orders for a Chinook helicopter to be made available. "The Scimitar is only around six tons," he announced. "We could lift two of those babies at once, if need be."

I'd been in a Chinook and knew he wasn't boasting. They're huge beasts. He noticed me standing to one side with Bill Bain, camera strung round his neck, who had replaced Kit as divisional photographer, and yelled across. "Hey, why don't you guys grab a ride and get some good pictures?"

In seconds he'd ordered a Lynx to be put at our disposal. This was a new experience for me; the Brits were considerably more cash-conscious and prudent with their helos. In no time at all we were off and running. The Scimitar was spotted, bogged down in a fair-sized forest. What the driver had been playing at I can only imagine. He was surely in for a king-sized roasting when he returned to base.

But that was his problem. Bill kept clicking away merrily as the Lynx circled the scene and the Chinook lowered a grappling hook and fished up the tank, minus its occupants, clean as a trout out of a lake. I imagine the crew had a long walk back to base to face their bollocking!

As if that wasn't sufficient, I listened in amazement as instructions came through on the radio to "fly down the Rhine aways and snap a few nice shots of the rescue against a background of some of those picturesque castles." We kept this up for over forty minutes; so long in fact that the Lynx had to break off to re-fuel. Back we came to collect more shots on the homeward flight. I still have one of those pics, showing the Scimitar being hoisted over the battlements of a medieval castle. The Yanks certainly know how to put on a show.

That particular exercise was memorable for another reason. German IO, Gerd Muller, joined us from Dortmund and escorted us to a splendid vineyard he knew in the Mosel country. A friend of the owner, he had arranged a private wine-tasting evening for us. There were seven or eight of us present and we were each able to buy as much wine as we could carry away for virtually cost price.

As an example, I bought two cases of magnificent eis-wien (made from grapes gathered and crushed in the early morning with the overnight dew still clinging to them) for five marks a bottle. "They sell in London for the equivalent of 64 marks a bottle," Gerd confirmed. "Not a bad deal, eh?"

The stuff was like nectar, and was definitely best kept for special occasions. We reserved one bottle to celebrate our first dinner back home in No 4 Manor Drive.

Back to Blighty

My last two years in Germany were in many ways mirror images of the first. There were differences and changes, of course, but the overall pattern was the same.

Mike was transferred, to be replaced by a mild-mannered chap named Nigel Harris. Wally moved on too and Sgt Bill Bain, had taken over from Kit. It's the Army way. Old friends go, new ones move in.

To be honest, I think when the time came, we were all ready for a change of scene. I'd written another pantomime, visited Austria twice more, helped run the same familiar exercises, dealt with the same old problems, produced dozens more stories and radio programmes and watched a lot of water flow under the bridge.

David McDine had been true to his word and had taken a demotion to revert to being an Information Officer in his beloved Kent. In the autumn of 1979 I was summoned to Main Building in London to discuss my future. Forewarned by David, I was well prepared for what was on the table.

After an overseas posting, I could expect a spell in London. How did that sound? There was a knowing smile when I said "Thank you, but no thanks."

The next ploy was that I was ideally equipped to apply for a Senior Information Officer post anywhere within Her Majesty's Government. Was I aware of the opportunities in other Ministries? Yes thank you, I was.

Finally the wheel turned full circle. There was still a shortage of people prepared to serve in Northern Ireland. The troubles were ongoing and experienced hands were urgently needed. There were no SIO vacancies at present, but one would be coming up in the not too distant future. If I returned I would be ideally situated to apply.

Thank you very much. That seemed the best course of action. And so it was agreed. I had already been making what arrangements I could with precisely that in mind. I had sold the Audi, having ensured that it was exempt from tax, and bought a new Opel Cavalier. This had been made in Holland and was a distinct cut above its Vauxhall sister, manufactured in the UK. All I had to do was keep it in Germany for twelve months before it was imported into the UK and thus save myself a large chunk of income tax.

To be fair, we had taken advantage of the tax arrangements then in force to stock up with a whole range of duty-free goods. We would bring back with us a new dishwasher, washing-machine, spin-drier, stereo-system, television set, adapted to view both European and UK channels, fridge-freezer and one or two other luxuries. Service abroad certainly had its advantages. I assembled a well-documented file of receipts for all purchases, containing all essential dates and prices.

I had some regrets about saying goodbye to Germany; I think the whole family had, but in the main, these were far outweighed by the realisation that we were going back to Lisburn. For all its faults, for all the fact that the *troubles* showed no signs of abating, it would always be home.

Curious customs

We marched out and handed over 11 Eulenveg in good order exactly one year and one day after buying the Cavalier. I wasn't taking any chances about being caught inside the 12 months' limit. Val and I were travelling in the car, Mollie and Barry were spending the night with friends and flying over the next day.

The weather was good for driving and Val and I had a trouble-free trip to Rotterdam. I've already described how we encountered our would-be Rolex salesman. You really had to hand him top marks for persistence. It was likely to be the last time I'd have to drive on the *wrong* side of the road for a while. Pity in a way, as I'd got quite used to it after three years.

We had booked into an overnight cabin on the North Sea ferry and were sitting down to a reasonable dinner as the ship pulled away from her mooring. Although it was mid-February, we had an ultra-smooth crossing.

It was as we were preparing to disembark that we encountered our first problem, in the shape of an over-zealous Customs official. While other motorists were exiting the ship at regular intervals, it quickly became apparent that I had drawn the short straw. I handed over all my documents and stood by as this fellow went over them and the Cavalier with a fine-tooth comb. He appeared to check and cross-reference everything. We even had to move some luggage in order that he could verify some serial numbers.

We were driving all the way north to Stranraer and I reckoned we had a good hour to spare before catching the 7-30pm ferry. I knew the route well and was thankful for a mild winter. I knew all too well what the Pennines and the West of Scotland can be like in a heavy snowfall.

Precisely one hour and forty minutes from starting his examination, the official straightened his back, returned my documents and managed a smile. "I see you know the rules of importing a car," he said. "You do know, I suppose, that you had just one day to spare?"

"I do know that," I replied.

His smile broadened. "Some don't, and get caught out. Have a safe journey and good luck with the car. She's a beauty. I hope I haven't delayed you too long."

He had, but I didn't tell him that. Time was pressing. I also didn't tell him that I'd had the car back home during a fortnight's leave the previous summer, which would have completely invalidated my position. The man had clearly had a lot on his mind that morning. There was no point in worrying his head over such a trivial detail.

Things were going to be pretty tight time ways, and we didn't hang about. We made good time up the A1, stopping only twice for comfort breaks and to refuel. From Carlisle onwards we encountered dense fog, which slowed our progress. Not for the first time, I was grateful for the consideration of many lorry drivers, who signalled us to overtake whenever it was possible. We made the ferry to Belfast with scant minutes to spare and were glad to relax on the trip across the Irish Sea.

Home by 11-30pm, we hurriedly made up a couple of beds and tumbled into them, leaving the central-heating on all night to air the house. I think we both slept the sleep of the just before driving to Aldergrove the next day to collect the other half of the family. It was good to be home.

Back in the old routine

I touched base with the office, but took a week off to recharge batteries and put the house in order. There were a hundred-and-one things to be done, not least accepting and unpacking two-dozen MFO boxes packed with our possessions, which arrived midway through the week. The new kitchen machines had to be connected up and plugged in and space had to be found for the extra-large television and stacked Pioneer hi-fi system. That last part though was a genuine labour of love.

We'd already been in touch with the children's new schools and I'm glad to say these changes took place seamlessly. Mrs Bird was still in residence next door. She was glad to see us back and put us in the picture with regard to the new neighbours who had moved into the drive during our absence. We made our introductions to all of them over the next few days.

As I was taking a week's leave, the kids demanded the same privilege and were allowed time off school. I suppose it was only fair. One of our first outings was to Castlewellan to visit Mollie's side of the family.

I called into the office one morning to say hello and to meet the AIS staff. There were a few old faces, and some new ones. Not unexpectedly, things were changing both in HQNI and in AIS.

When I'd left, the Army had been running the show. Now the way was being prepared for the RUC to take the lead, both operationally and in PR terms. While this made a lot of sense, it didn't appear to have cut the workload to any great extent.

Around this time, a letter from Tony confirmed that Pat and he would be coming home from Australia in the summer. This was excellent news. It would be good to have my best friend back in the old country again.

When I resumed work the following week, I found I had a new and larger office and a new PA, Kathleen. Bill Moore had gone and I was saddened to learn of his death, not long afterwards, as the result of a sudden illness. I missed him greatly. He was a solid and dependable colleague and a great friend. In his stead I had a succession of serving officers from the Regiment as my assistant during the next few years.

I was fortunate in that I had worked with the Commander, Brigadier Pat Hargraves, on a previous occasion, and also that he had a keen appreciation of the importance of public relations. I quickly got to know the remainder of the HQ staff, several of whom I remembered from my previous service.

The Regiment was still being subjected to a high level of violence, both physically from attacks on its soldiers, and in terms of criticism and propaganda. During our first conversation, the Commander voiced his concern about both, and said he would welcome suggestions as to how best to deal with them.

We talked about it for a long time. I told him I realised everything possible was being done with regard to the personal safety of his soldiers. Ironically, they were often more at risk when off-duty in their homes or workplace than when actually serving. The terrorist will always go for a softer target.

The persistent and well-orchestrated smear campaign against the UDR was equally worrying, but there were a number of points to be taken on board. First, everyone in and connected with the Regiment had to be made aware that, if they weren't doing a fine job, and being a real thorn in the side of the terrorist, then their opponents wouldn't expend the time and effort they did to mount their campaign of vitriol and abuse.

"You're really hurting them." I said. "If you weren't they'd be more inclined to leave you alone. They don't have to authenticate whatever allegations they make against you, they simply have to make them, and they will find their way into the media. Every one of your men needs to be made aware of that and the fact that your political opponents are quick to jump on the bandwagon."

He nodded agreement and I emphasised the point. "You know as well as I do that every time one of your people steps out of line, and especially if he breaks the law, it's like a knife in the ribs to every decent guy who's doing his bit honestly. I know all your recruits go through intensive training before they go operational. I firmly believe that training should include some straight talking on PR. I know it's done generally, but here in Northern Ireland it needs to be specific."

He smiled grimly when I recounted my political football analogy. "In Army parlance, the UDR has shot itself in the foot far too often," I finished my little spiel. "If you don't make mistakes and give the opposition propaganda material on a plate, they'll have to invent it. And once they've done that it can be rebutted and shown up for what it is."

He rose and shook my hand, and I realised I'd just talked myself into another job. Well, I suppose that's what they paid me for.

First things first

As well as drafting my lecture for the recruits' training course, I worked my way round all the battalions, renewing many old acquaintances and introducing myself to the new COs and Press Officers. As the months passed, I met quite a few officers I'd got to know in Germany. That's one thing about working with the Army – one keeps bumping into old friends. No wonder someone once described the Services as the biggest club in the world.

I held the first of my PR courses in Ballykinlar Camp, encouraging the recruits to join in and ask whatever questions they liked. A lot of useful stuff emerged and I soon found myself looking forward to these regular encounters.

I was also dividing my time between my UDR duties and with AIS across in the main headquarters. The CIO liked the brief I'd prepared for the recruits and asked me to work on improving the press briefing notes normally given to foreign and UK mainland media visitors.

This had once been the preserve of Colin Wallace, but he had now moved on from MOD under something of a cloud. Without going into detail, I recalled the warning Peter Broderick had given me when he advised me to leave Colin to do his own thing. I doubt anyone knows the complete details of what happened there, but I can't say I was sorry not to have been involved.

In time, amid all the staff changes and comings and goings, the expected vacancy arose for the Senior Information Officer post as deputy head of AIS. I was firm favourite for this, but took nothing for granted. It was held in London and I knew most of the competition. Many of us went out for a liquid lunch in the old Sherlock Holmes pub nearby, and discussed our chances. A week or so later my appointment was confirmed.

Inevitably this led to a number of changes. I moved into a new office across the road in HQNI, and took on a new job description which broadened my responsibilities considerably. For a time I also retained my old office in the UDR building, but as the months passed, I handed over more day-to-day control to my latest assistant, Capt Caroline Arnold, whom I'd known for a long time as Adjutant and UPO of the 10th Belfast Battalion.

My duties were wide and varied, and certainly never dull. Without going into unnecessary detail, the scene in Northern Ireland was continuing to change. The RUC had by now assumed operational primacy, with the Army adopting a more secondary and supportive role. This transformation was supervised and driven in the main by Sir Jack Hermon, Chief Constable of the RUC, and Sir Richard Lawson, the new Army GOC.

My new job involved working closely with David Gilliland, head of the NIO Press Office, and later his successor, Andy Wood; and Bill McGookin, boss of the Police Press Office. I'd known all three for some time, especially Bill, a former journalist with the *Belfast Telegraph.*

There were regular meetings and discussions, and although I had no way of knowing it at the time, those years were to help provide much of the background which enabled me to write and publish my first novel, *Role of Dishonour.* More of that later.

Looking back on it at some distance, it scarcely needs stressing that those years marked a sad and grim period in Ireland's long and troubled history. It's not my task here to delve too deeply into the causes, or the rights and wrongs of all that occurred. Suffice to say it cost the country – and me personally – too many close and dear friends and colleagues.

Briefings

I've lost count of the number of people I've briefed over the years. These sessions didn't always follow the same pattern and I always tried to tailor each brief to the needs of the individual concerned. To ensure they got the information they wanted, I encouraged questions, and as far as possible within the constraints of security, I strove to be open and straightforward. If I couldn't answer a particular question, I'd spell out the reason why.

BBC NI were punctilious in ensuring that their newly-arrived reporters were sent along to be briefed. The Army considered this a good thing – the better informed they were, the less chance of their making a horlicks and upsetting everyone. I'm not sure all journalists totally accepted this.

I recall one obviously bright, but pugnacious young woman, who, fresh from London, had been in Northern Ireland for all of two days, demanding "Why should I believe what you have to tell me, rather than what the Sinn Fein press office has to say?"

I did my best to hide a smile, and replied not unkindly, "I suppose the short answer is that you don't *have* to believe what I say. But remember, I'm speaking on behalf of the Army, and ultimately the Government. If I lie to you, or mislead you, they aren't going to be best pleased, and the buck will come back to stop with me. In other words, I'm accountable. Sinn Fein are accountable only to themselves and aren't obliged to justify anything they say."

She took this in, then snapped back, "So you'd never lie to the Media?"

"Certainly not deliberately. Apart from obviously being wrong, it would be totally counterproductive. Think about it for a moment. Suppose I told you something today and you broadcast it, only to find out tomorrow that it was a whopper. Would you be likely to believe me next time? I don't think so. I'd have lost all credibility in your eyes, and once that's lost in this business it's gone for good."

I saw her again, six months later, shortly before she returned to London. I'd heard several of her reports. She was good and went on to make quite a name for herself nationally in succeeding years. She'd clearly learnt a lot in her time in Belfast, and I was pleased when she made a point of thanking me for my initial briefing.

Apart from working journalists and broadcasters, I always enjoyed briefing and talking to authors and writers who would come in search of background material for their forthcoming books. Having already made up my mind to write a novel based on the *troubles* once I'd retired from MOD, I was keen to pick their brains as much as they were mine.

Many of these one-to-one chats stretched over several hours and I have a shelf of autographed books in my study as a reminder of those days. Included are tales by Gerald Seymour, Edna O'Brien, Fergal Keane, Max Hastings, Chris Ryder, Martin Bell and Terence Strong to name but a few. Their visits certainly impressed on me the value of research.

Retracing old footsteps

Regular changes in the staff of AIS brought many new faces to Lisburn, too many to mention here. When Alan Percival arrived as CIO, he brought with him an engaging personality, a shrewd professionalism and a keen, analytical mind. We took to one another right away and his presence in the office made coming to work an absolute pleasure. We'd been friends for some time before that and our relationship was to continue long after he left Ireland.

Alan introduced a number of changes and innovations, one of which changed my routine significantly. Up until that time, Army units arriving for Northern Ireland tours had been briefed exclusively by military officers. Efficient as they might be, Alan felt they lacked the essential local knowledge to give incoming units a thorough brief on what serving here was all about.

Most of the young officers and squaddies landing here had never been to Northern Ireland before, and apart from their military training, needed to be given a more general background brief and understanding of how to behave, and especially what to avoid on these shores.

"It's going to entail a fair bit of travelling," he said, "both to the mainland and Germany. Will you take it on?"

Of course I agreed readily enough, and he went on to say it was probably time I eased off on my duties with the UDR. Caroline was settling in well and was ready to assume more responsibility. I set to work preparing another briefing pack, complete with a variety of slides and video clips.

During the next couple of years I made innumerable trips to England and Germany. Most of the latter briefings were conducted in the well-equipped lecture centre in Sennelager, and of course this brought back memories of the Jubilee Review of 1977. On one such trip I managed to make a quick visit to my old office in 4 Div. HQ, now managed by Maj Leslie Hutchinson, an old Irish Ranger friend. Inge was still there, efficient as ever, the only one of my old crew still in harness.

Speaking of the old crew, taking a flight to London one day, I bumped into Mike Pavitt heading in the other direction. We had only a few minutes to chat, but he mentioned that he'd left the Army and was now a rep for Rothman's, the cigarette company. I told him he was well qualified, having supported them as a forty-a-day man for as long as I'd known him.

We embraced and promised to keep in touch; but of course we

didn't. I'd warned him the smoking habit would be the end of him, and sadly so it was, a few years ago just after he'd celebrated his 70th birthday. I learned of his passing through friends on the internet. Poor Mike, we shared many wonderful times together.

Off to even farther fields

The Falklands War came and went. Alan was down there with the Task Force, and on his return, he followed David McDine into the DDPR(A) chair in London. We kept in touch and the decision was taken to maintain a strong garrison in the Islands. This required that a permanent Press Centre be established in the capital, Port Stanley, to deal with the increased workload that was expected.

I had a call from Alan one day. He had just bought a new house in a place called King's Langley and wondered if I'd like to come over for a few days. I could also travel up to MOD with him, meet a few old friends and catch up with developments.

We met up in the capital a ten minutes' walk from his home, for a couple of swift pints. As it turned out, the pints weren't so swift, and after a little small talk, he said he had a proposition for me.

"Not more lecturing and briefing?" I enquired.

"Not exactly," he said, "although, to be honest, I expect there'll be some of that involved as well."

"Go on," I said. "Where are you packing me off to this time?"

"Not all that far," he smiled. "Only to the Falkland Islands! You'll love it there. It's great fun. I know, I've been. Let me get another round in and I'll tell you all about it."

Falklands bound

Alan returned, shoved a pint in front of me, and talked for ten minutes non-stop. The gist of it was that the Mount Pleasant airfield, thirty miles from Stanley, had been extended and was nearing completion. The 2,500-strong garrison was being maintained for the foreseeable future. There was also a squadron of fighter aircraft, and a Royal Navy submarine would be kept on station permanently.

He resumed straight away. "As you know, the political situation in Argentina is extremely volatile at the moment. It's unlikely the Argies will try another invasion, but the possibility can't be ruled out. They've never officially declared an end to hostilities."

"I get it, mate. And you think if they hear I'm coming down there it will deter them! Thanks a bundle."

"It just might, if you take the UDR down with you. Seriously though, that's not the only reason I'd like you to go. You may have heard rumblings about talks between Westminster and the Falkland Islands' Government concerning the establishment of a 200-miles fishing zone around their shores. Permits will be issued and the Falklands are expecting to rake in millions from the likes of Russia, Japan and several European countries. This zone will be enforced by a fleet of patrol ships."

"There's more, but that's the gist of it. Our friends in the Foreign Office would like an experienced PR hand based down there for a month or two until things settle down. There will be some major facilities to be arranged. Panorama and News at Ten have already been sniffing around. We've been asked to provide a steady, dependable officer for the task. I couldn't think of one, so I wondered if you'd like to do it?"

"Thanks a bunch, Alan. A month or two you say. How long is this for - really?"

"I'd say four months, five at the most; starting next September."

I have to say the idea appealed to me. I'd never been to the southern hemisphere. And from what Alan had said, the job looked certain to be both interesting and challenging. I also appreciated that the family wouldn't like my being away for that length of time.

I accompanied Alan up to his office the next morning and spent much of the day being briefed and lectured on what lay in store for me. Then I headed for Heathrow and back home to break the news to the family. As I'd expected, they were not amused.

An eventful flight

The weeks passed quickly and in no time at all I had packed my bags and was on my way to RAF Brize Norton to begin my 8,500-mile journey to the far side of the world. In the meantime, I'd visited the library and read up everything I could on the Falklands. In any case, it was still fresh in everyone's mind following the Argentine invasion.

There are two main islands – East and West Falkland, with a population of just over 2,000, the great majority of them of British origin. The garrison had swollen this number to about 4,500. There are numerous small islands clustered round the main two. The nearest land to the east is South Georgia, over 850 miles away; the next stop due south is Antarctica and the South Pole. It's a lonely, desolate, wind-swept spot, yet in my comparatively short time there,

I came to love it - and it's hardy, fiercely loyal, inhabitants.

In the ninety-minute wait before boarding I had time to run the rule over my fellow-passengers and chat to a few of them. There were about ninety in all, mostly military personnel, but also a handful of Islanders, returning from a trip to the UK, and a dozen or so civilian workmen who were going down to complete the building work at Mount Pleasant.

I settled into my seat and began to read that morning's copy of the *Daily Telegraph*. One of the first items to attract my interest was a story that the body of an Argentine pilot, believed to be that of Capt Juan Manuel Giminez, had been discovered on the slopes of Blue Mountain, in the wreckage of his 1A-56 Pucara fighter plane.

He was believed to have crashed while heading back to base after an attack on British ships at Port Carlos. Nothing had been heard of him since and he had been posted as missing in action. I concluded that the incident was going to be one of my first PR problems – and I was right.

I relaxed as our plane prepared for take-off, then started down the runway. Everything seemed routine until suddenly a claxon sounded, all the warning lights flashed on as the brakes were applied, and we came to a juddering halt, uncomfortably close to the end of the runway. Later we were informed that one of the oil-pressure gauges had indicated a problem.

Not an ideal start to our long flight. There was a buzz of conversation as the calm voice of our pilot apologised for the false start. There had been a minor technical problem and we would be returning to the terminal while it was sorted out.

The delay lasted for four hours and thirty minutes, so we had ample time for a meal and several cups of coffee. We took off at the second attempt without further incident. Again the pilot apologised for the delay and assured us he would be keeping a watchful eye on all the engines on our way south.

All seemed well as we skirted Gibraltar and the Mediterranean and continued down the west coast of Africa. It seemed that the brief emergency had been resolved, until the pilot spoke again. Apparently he still wasn't entirely happy with the behaviour of the outer port engine, and while he could manage quite nicely on three, he was going to land in Monrovia, in West Africa, to have it checked and to take on more fuel.

We arrived at the splendidly-named Roberts Memorial International Airport at 6-30 on a swelteringly hot morning. The place belied its title. The dense jungle encroached to the edges of the two runways, which were in the form of a cross. We saw a control tower in the distance and to one side a concrete passenger terminal.

The place looked deserted and there were no signs of activity, apart from a small group of workmen in grubby overalls, loitering round an old 1940s Dakota that plainly hadn't been airborne for some time. There wasn't another aircraft in sight. I knew little about Monrovia, other than that it was a kind of port of convenience where much of the world's shipping is registered.

The pilot explained that we'd be more comfortable in the air-conditioned aircraft rather than venturing outside, where the temperature was already a steamy 35 degrees, and rising. He was having some difficulty in having the engine inspected, and the airport authorities were insisting that the fuel be paid for in US dollars. Negotiations were ongoing. An hour later matters were still deadlocked and we were told that we'd be going across to wait in the terminal, while the pilot sought advice from London. I've never experienced such heat as on that 200-metre trek across the concrete. There wasn't the semblance of a breeze and it was stifling.

It was a relief to get inside the terminal's reception area, which was air-conditioned and pleasantly cool. Unfortunately, at that early hour, none of the few facilities was open, so all we could do was take our seats and be patient. The RAF crew left us to our own devices and departed, no doubt to try to sort things out.

Nothing of note happened for perhaps twenty minutes. Then a door at the far end of the concourse opened and a man appeared. He must have been as close to seven-feet tall as makes no odds and he cut a majestic figure. He was attired in a peaked, military-style, cap, with heavy gold braid insignia around the brim, and an elegant chocolate-brown uniform, bedecked with gold epaulets and a row of matching buttons down the front. A tooled, brown-leather belt encircled his tunic and his long legs were encased in matching trousers, with a wide gold stripe down the outside.

Without a glance to left or right, he ignored our little party completely, and marched in stately fashion the length of the concourse, finally disappearing through a door in the opposite wall. There was a buzz of conversation as we speculated as to the identity of this regal personage.

Did Monrovia have a President, and if so, could this be he? Or perhaps he was a General, or Field-Marshal in their Army? He was clearly a personage of some importance. Had he been summoned to determine what was to befall us?

In a matter of minutes the matter was resolved and we couldn't restrain our amusement. Our friend returned, whistling tunelessly through his teeth, and armed with a mop and bucket, commenced to wash the terrazzo floor! What is it they say about clothes maketh the man?

After a lengthy wait, our little fuel problem was resolved to the satisfaction of the airport authorities and we were able to take off. Our next stop – the tiny speck in the South Atlantic that is Ascension Island.

It's hard to visualise a more isolated spot. Only 34 square miles in area, it stands 1,000 miles off the African coast and some 1,400 miles from Brazil to the west. It served as an important staging post during the Falklands War and the RAF shares its base there with the US Air Force.

During our four-hour stopover we were able to freshen up, have a meal, and make a short tour of this small equatorial paradise by Land-Rover. I recalled what someone had said to me shortly after I joined the Government Information Service. *"Join us and see the world."* I was seeing a fair bit of it on this trip alone – and there was more to come.

News filtered through of some inclement weather in the vicinity of the Falklands and there was some doubt that we would be able to continue. However, after our aircraft had been thoroughly checked once again, and we'd taken a new crew on board, it was decided that we should proceed.

We were heading into the prevailing south-westerlies, which meant a strong head-wing all the way, so this final leg of our journey took nearly nine hours. Even then, with cross-winds gusting to over fifty knots, it was touch and go whether we would be able to land at RAF Mount Pleasant.

The alternative was yet another diversion, this time to Chile, and a chance to see a little more of the world. Fortunately, our brave pilot elected to go for the landing and he made a superb job of it too, although he confessed on the inter-com afterwards that the gale had caused him to veer some fifty metres across the runway. I think there are some facts one is better not knowing.

The good-humoured staff did everything possible to speed us through the necessary arrival checks and a driver appeared to take three of us down the rocky road to Port Stanley. It was pitch black, still blowing a howling gale, and there was little to see of the route. It was a journey I was to make many times in the future.

We reached Stanley just before midnight to be told that we would be housed in temporary transit accommodation. This turned out to be spartan in the extreme. I drew the short straw and was billeted in a single hut which boasted one small convector heater and an iron-framed single bed with a pillow and two thin army blankets.

Although tired, I knew I wasn't going to sleep much. I turned the heater to maximum, kept all my clothes on, wrapped myself in the blankets and collapsed on the bed. I had been travelling for fifteen minutes short of 48-hours.

Four seasons

The Falkland Islands must be one of the few places on earth where it's possible to experience all four seasons in the course of a single day. The wind seems to blow all the time, perpetually from the South-West around Cape Horn. Over a twelve-month period the daily average is just shy of fifty knots. In my five months there I counted only five almost windless days.

As the seasons are reversed in the Southern Hemisphere, I awoke on my first morning to the equivalent of a brisk March day in the UK. Apart from the wind that is! The clawing fug inside my hut gave way to a stiff breeze immediately I stepped outside. In dire need of a shower and a shave, I asked directions to the nearest facilities. Half-an-hour later, feeling moderately better, I went in search of breakfast.

On my way to the Mess Hut I encountered Peter Simmonds, the officer I was replacing. He was full of apologies for not having greeted me on arrival and for his failure to arrange more convivial accommodation. He blamed the late arrival of my aircraft. As introductions go, I didn't think much of it. As he was returning to the UK two days later, it left little time for a proper handover.

The best part of that first day was a marvellous full-English breakfast in the Mess. The quality of the food was the best I've experienced. One thing the Armed Services seem to do is to provide A1 grub, even in such a far-flung outpost of Empire.

Peter's relief at going home was evident. He gave me a briefing of sorts, and said he would introduce me to the Commander and his staff the following day. After one uncomfortable night in the transit hut, I told him all that could wait. What I needed was for him to show me where I was to be quartered.

"Of course," he apologised feebly. "Immediately we finish

breakfast."

My new billet was a dull grey porta-cabin half way down a passageway of identical structures, 20 metres from the nearest ablutions and four times that distance from the Mess. These considerations were important because of the unpredictability of the weather. I was unfortunate enough to be caught in the open during a number of vicious hailstorms. It's akin to being bombarded with shovelfuls of gravel.

My quarters were comfortable enough, if a bit on the spartan side. I noticed that two stout hawsers were strung across the roof, their ends buried in oil-drums full of concrete. "It's to prevent the cabin from being blown away," Peter said somewhat unnecessarily. "The gales here are something else, as you'll soon find out."

He left soon afterwards to complete his packing, promising to meet up for lunch. I spent the next couple of hours unpacking and arranging my few belongings in the cabin. I'd had to travel light, of necessity. A couple of suits, a sports jacket and some slacks and an assortment of shirts and sweaters I hoped would cope with all weather conditions. Warm underclothing, socks, ties, shoes and a pair of solid army boots completed my wardrobe.

I'd also packed my Olympus OM10 camera, equipped with several lenses, a generous supply of film, a short-wave radio and a dozen paperback novels. I'd no idea what the social life in Stanley had to offer, but I'd come prepared to provide my own entertainment if need be.

After lunch, another thoroughly satisfying meal, Peter introduced me to some of my colleagues. They were drawn from all three Services, with only a handful of civilians, and in the main, seemed a friendly and sociable lot. I excused myself after a time, as I wanted to see something of Port Stanley while daylight permitted.

Our little camp, known as *Lookout Rocks*, was based on a promontory overlooking the town and the wide bay beyond The next stop due south was the Pole itself. It was a lonely, yet strangely beautiful setting.

Armed with my camera, I took one of several narrow streets leading into town and turned left along the crescent-shaped main street which ran parallel to the shore. The little dwellings and few scattered shops, most of wooden construction, somehow brought to mind the old Pete Seeger song *Little Boxes*.

The first building that I recognised from photographs was the little red-brick church with the famous whalebone arch outside. It overlooked the bay and although designated a Cathedral, was much smaller than most churches back in Ireland.

Almost opposite, on the sea side of the road was something I had been looking out for in particular. The sight of it took me back nearly forty years.

My little public relations domain on the other side of the world. The sign translates as British Forces Falkland Islands, our last outpost of Empire. Note what the prevailing wind is doing to what's left of my hair!

Anchors aweigh

Once, when I was a small boy in Kilkeel, my Dad took me on a Sunday afternoon bus trip to Newcastle. As I recall, we lunched on fish and chips, followed by ice cream, and afterwards walked along the promenade before stopping in front of a massive black ship's anchor *and chain.* A plaque beside it informed us that it had once belonged to the SS Great Britain, which had run aground in Dundrum Bay in 1846 and remained stranded for months before being refloated.

My Dad told me the story of the great ship, a tale that had fascinated me and sparked a lifelong interest. Briefly, the great ship, in its day the largest in the world, was designed by the famous engineer, Isambard Kingdom Brunel, and had a long and chequered career – which included transporting troops to the Crimean War and ferrying the first England cricket team to visit Australia - before ending its days as a burned-out wreck in the Falklands. In 1970. At considerable expense, it was refloated and towed back to Bristol, where it had originally been launched. Refurbished, restored and spruced up, it is on show there to this day, and has been visited by millions of people.

And so I stood there, by the windswept Southern Ocean, and stared at an exact duplicate of the great anchor I had first seen in a County Down seaside town all those years before. There was even a similar mounted plaque to confirm its identification. How I wished that my father, by then long dead, could have stood beside me at that moment.

There was yet one more coincidence I couldn't begin to explain. As my Dad and I turned away from the anchor in Newcastle that long past afternoon, a silver band which was entertaining people on the nearby bandstand, started playing the hymn *Onward Christian Soldiers.* Now, on the other side of the world, as I resumed my walk, I heard the sound of singing from the neighbouring Cathedral.

Yes, it was that same hymn – *Onward Christian Soldiers!*

Port Stanley

Continuing my exploratory stroll along the seafront, I came upon many buildings I'd read about. The first of these was the Falkland Islands Company Store, a huge square structure that I later discovered sold just about everything from a needle to an anchor.

Across the road was another large building which served as

town hall, library, courthouse, post office and dance hall. Both the Falklands and South Georgia have a well-deserved reputation for the sale of postage stamps. Later I became a member of the library, and as such, was never short of reading material.

Also to my left was the new War Memorial, which was diligently maintained and complete with the names of those who lost their lives in the recent conflict. A short distance beyond lay Government House, which still proudly displayed the bullet holes left by the invasion. One of the first items on my itinerary was to pay a courtesy call on the Governor and enjoy a pleasant chat while drinking tea from elegant china cups.

LYING DOWN ON THE JOB   Falkland seals and penguins are quite tame if you lie down like this and let them approach. I'm glad I brought my camera.

I passed by two other buildings worthy of mention. One was the headquarters of Cable and Wireless, with its massive satellite dish out front. This provided a valuable link with home. As I recall, I was able to buy phone cards which cost about £1 a minute. Reception quality was generally excellent.

To seawards I saw the little office of the Falkland Island Broadcasting Service, popularly known as FIBS. In fact, practically every service on the Islands was prefaced by the initials FI. I knew I would have to pay an early call on its manager and broadcaster in chief, Patrick Watts, who had actually been on air, describing the invasion when the Argentinians barged in and forced him to stop at rifle-point. But that, like so many other things, could wait until the following day.

At the far end of Stanley stood the array of small buildings that housed the headquarters of British Forces Falkland Islands, (BFFI), including the khaki porta-cabin which would be my main workplace for the next few months. It was the best part of a mile's walk from Lookout Camp.

I had a cursory look, but didn't venture inside. Time enough for that tomorrow.

Back in the swim

The following morning Peter and I enjoyed a hearty breakfast, before joining the little crowd making its way from Lookout down to the headquarters. I wanted to make an early start and have a look at the office before the first meeting of the day, which was scheduled for 9 am. I was introduced to Capt Dick Saunders, with whom I was to share the little cabin. He was a pleasant chap and I reckoned we would rub along nicely. Dick was essentially in charge of civilian liaison, so our jobs dovetailed neatly.

I also met Private George Philips, who had been assigned as my photographer. A tall, gangly young man, I found him efficient enough, if a little on the taciturn side.

I don't know how he and Peter had got on, but I told him I was happy for him to do his own thing when work was slack, but I would expect him to step up to the mark when push came to shove, as it surely would.

The office had a small porch, positioned at 90 degrees to our front door to provide some shelter from the prevailing south-westerlies. The equipment was fairly basic – two metal-topped desks, each with an internal and external telephone, and an assortment of filing cabinets. Half-a-dozen alloy-framed chairs and two small tables completed the furniture. One of these contained a Gezetner photo-copier and transmitter and a slide-projector, and I was glad to note the other held an electric kettle, some assorted mugs and a large jar of coffee. One wall was taken up by a large-scale map of the islands and two noticeboards for signals and photographs. It was all relatively bog-standard stuff.

Morning prayers was a brief affair. It was taken by the Assistant Chief of Staff, who welcomed me warmly and introduced me to everyone. He hoped I would be happy amongst them and also wished Peter a safe journey home. As we walked back to the office, Peter explained that, by and large, the rest of the staff officers had been content enough to leave him to his own devices. "They have their own jobs to do, and basically know bugger all about PR anyway," was how he put it. Once again, I sensed that his tour of the islands had not been a happy one.

We had half an hour to wait before I was due to have my first interview with Commander Falkland Islands, to whom I would be working directly. The post was held in turn by senior officers from the three Services, each of whom was in station for twelve months.

Admiral Kit Layman had assumed command about a month before my arrival, and Peter confessed that he didn't know him well, other than he was reported to be wary of the press and media. Fully aware that the Admiral and I were about to enter a busy period on the PR front, beginning with the visit of a journalist from the Leicester Mercury the following Friday, I reckoned that the Admiral and I were going to have to start singing from the same hymn-sheet from day one.

I studied Admiral Layman closely as Peter performed the introductions. He was slight and wiry, with the clear blue eyes so typical of a sailor, and a shock of steel-grey hair. I knew he had commanded a destroyer during the recent hostilities. He greeted me affably enough before offering us coffee, which we both declined. Instead of returning to his desk, he ushered us into two armchairs before taking a third himself.

We chatted in general terms for a few minutes, during which time he asked about my career in PR and how I felt about my present posting. Realising that he would already have been fully briefed about me, I was concise and said simply that I was looking forward to my tour of duty.

Turning to Peter, he thanked him for the work he had done and wished him well on his return to England. He surprised me then by asking if he and I might have a word in private. When a somewhat flustered Peter had excused himself and left, the Admiral and I resumed our seats.

The Admiral smiled, but his voice was grave as he said "Mr Fleming, are you aware of the old Chinese greeting, or toast, "May you live in interesting times?"

"Yes, I have heard the saying," I replied.

He nodded. "Well, with what lies ahead in the next few months, the imposition of this fishing zone, and a number of important visits, not to mention the funeral of this Argentine pilot who crashed on Blue Mountain, it's safe to assume that our time together will not be without interest."

I explained that I had already been briefed by the Foreign Office and MOD about the busy programme. "I read about the discovery of the pilot's body on the flight here," I said, "and I'll be talking to my people in MOD about it today. It will be for London to decide what is to be done about it."

"You do know there is a small cemetery here for the Argentinian war dead?" he said. "It's quite separate from our own military cemetery and I understand the islanders insisted that it be out of sight of the settlement of Goose Green. At this stage it's uncertain whether the body will be interred there, or flown back to Argentina. Either way, there is likely to be considerable press interest. It will present all sorts of problems."

I assured him that I understood the delicacy of the situation, especially as it affected the islanders, and would be keeping a close eye on developments.

With a somewhat wry grin, he continued, "You may have heard that I am, shall I say, more than a little suspicious of the gentlemen of the Press. Let me tell you that, from personal experience, I have good cause to be. That said, however, I realise that, with our immediate programme as it is, I have to accept them as a necessary evil."

So, his feelings were out in the open now. Good. It seemed clear that this was a make or break moment which would establish our working relationship in the future for good or ill. There was only one way to find out.

"With respect, Admiral . . . "I began, but was stopped by his upraised palm.

"Brad," he declared. It was the first time he'd used my forename. "When I hear that phrase I know I'm going to be told something unpalatable."

I smiled in return. This man had something about him. "I hope it proves more factual than unpalatable, Admiral. You've just used the phrase *'necessary evil.'* If I may say so, I think you've got that only half right."

He raised an eyebrow. "Go on."

I'd started, so like the old saying, I'd better finish. "It's correct that the Press are necessary. That is, a good press is essential to the job we have to do here. But I don't believe they are necessarily evil – at least not all of them. We won't always agree with what they write, but when all's said and done, they have the right of a free press to report it; just as we have the right to take them to task if they get it wrong."

He looked at me hard for a long time as if to say I hear what you say, but I don't necessarily go along with it. "All right, Brad, we'd best leave that one for now. What about this journalist who's coming on Friday? What will he want and what will he be writing about?"

"Essentially he'll do a general piece and concentrate on people from within his circulation area. He'll want to talk to you of course."

"Hmmm. I suppose that's one of the necessary evils we were just talking about. What will he want to know?"

I had an idea. "Suppose I gave you a list of ten questions he'll most likely ask. That way you'll have time to prepare your replies."

"You can do that?"

"Of course. They'll be on your desk this afternoon."

The press visit came and went. I sat in on it and it went exceptionally well. The journalist was a decent enough fellow, intent as much on enjoying his visit to the Falklands as on producing a good story for his paper.

The Admiral sent for me afterwards.

"Your list of questions was very useful," he said, "but how come he only asked seven of them?"

"Perhaps he wasn't sharp enough to ask the other three," I replied.

I fancy there was a twinkle in the Admiral's eye as he thanked me. I think we understood one another.

Patrick Watts

Peter's last chore with me was to take me along to the small wooden building that housed FIBS, the island's broadcasting service, and introduce me to the manager, chief broadcaster and general factotum that was Patrick Watts.

Patrick had made something of a name for himself by remaining on air, updating the islanders about the invasion, until the raiding soldiers had closed the station at gunpoint. A staunch Anglophile, and as I was to discover, a lifelong supporter of the English football club, Preston North End, he was happy to talk about anything and everything apart from the invasion.

With the help of three women, a sound engineer and a seemingly endless supply of willing volunteers, he ran a tight 24 – 7 operation. Of chief interest to me was the fact that he transmitted a 30-minute news and current affairs bulletin each morning and evening. The station also drew heavily on the BBC, especially its World Service, to fill the rest of its schedule. I was glad I'd decided to pack my portable radio.

Having checked with my London office, I was able to give him an update on the funeral of the Argentine pilot, Capt Giminez, and later that evening, as I was showering before dinner, I was gratified that it made lead item on the FIBS evening news. I was surprised to hear that my own arrival came in at item number three!

Coming to grips

Peter left for home the following day, plainly relieved to be returning to his usual haunts. Dick Saunders confided that my predecessor, although pleasant enough, had found life in the Falklands difficult and he had never really settled. He hoped I'd have better luck.

I found Dick an agreeable and helpful colleague and a good man with whom to share an office. He'd been in post for four months and was able to pass on much useful advice. He explained that his main job was to liaise with the islanders, to deal with any complaints or problems and to help them out whenever possible. He said he'd be happy to take me along any time I fancied a trip to meet some of the folk out in the Camp.

I'd only been in post a few days when I discovered that not having a dedicated vehicle at my disposal was going to make life difficult. This was another thing Peter hadn't bothered to mention. Dick, who didn't have his own wheels either, said it was a case of putting in a bid-form to the motor pool to request a vehicle as far in advance as possible. All bids were dealt with strictly according to priority.

Perhaps I'd been spoilt by always having a dedicated vehicle in my previous postings and had expected this tour would be no different. But it seemed to me that not having permanent transport in so diverse a location as the Falklands, especially with so many media facilities looming ahead, was out of the question.

Of course I could have taken my problem directly to the Admiral, or called on London to intervene, but that would have scarcely have earned me any brownie points with either the guys in the motor pool, or those of my colleagues who also had to make do with Shank's pony.

As it happened, the problem was resolved in a rather unusual way.

Pick up a Pizza

Over a drink in the Mess one evening, Capt Steve Bates, who ran the motor pool, entertained us by telling the story of the cheek of one of his young mechanics. The lad, from Mill Hill in London, on a farewell night out with friends, picked up a card in his local Domino's Pizza Parlour which proudly proclaimed that they *"delivered anywhere."*

"As soon as he arrived here he posted the card to them and demanded they fulfilled their promise and send him a pizza," Steve said. "Now, he's only got a letter from them saying they're prepared to make good their promise!"

My ears pricked up immediately. I drew Steve aside and arranged to see him and this young man, Cpl Andy Evans, next day. After a chat with them, I phoned the London press office and asked them to get to work on the story, suggesting it would make a great item for one of the big Saturday night TV shows.

Sure enough, London Weekend Television expressed interest in putting it on Michael Aspel's popular Saturday evening show. The snag was that it would be too expensive to send out a TV crew. Could I arrange something at my end?

I talked it over with Patrick Watts and he put me in touch with Alex Gordon, a Stanley resident who had a decent video camera. I invited Alex, a Scot's retired schoolteacher for dinner in the Mess and told him the tale. He thought it a huge joke and readily offered his services. It only remained for me to phone LWT and discover what sort of footage they'd like. Alfred Hitchcock eat your heart out!

I called a roundtable conference with Steve, Andy and Alex and outlined my idea for a likely film-script. All I had to do now was write the script, ensure that Alex could handle it, and make sure my actors knew their parts. I would direct the shoot, help Alex with the editing, add a commentary, and pack it off to LWT.

It was a hilarious day. First we faked Andy posting off his challenge and receiving the reply from Domino's. Then filmed the mailbags arriving off the TRI-STAR at the Mount Pleasant sorting office, before being transported by three-tonner along the thirty miles of rocky road to Port Stanley, Alex filming out of the window as I drove the accompanying Land-Rover.

Dominos had done us proud, sending not just one pizza, but two-dozen large packs. I fancy just about everyone in *Lookout Rocks Camp* got at least one slice.

The closing shot showed Steve and Andy, seated at a candlelit table, being served their pizzas by two attractive WRAC girls, decked out as French waitresses in spotless white blouses, short skirts and fishnet tights. Looking back on it now, it ought to have gone into the Guinness Book of Records as the longest pizza delivery the world had ever seen!

Everybody was a winner. Andy got his long-distance pizza, LWT got a classy item for their Saturday show, Dominos got ten minutes of national advertising for the price of a few pizzas, the MOD and the three Armed Services picked up a lot of kudos for entering into the spirit of the thing, and ace cameraman Alex received a big pack of pizza to take home to the family.

As a matter of fact, I didn't do too badly myself. I happened to be sharing a beer with Steve a few nights later. He said everyone had enjoyed the whole episode enormously and he thanked me for putting it all together. If ever he could do me a favour in return, he'd be happy to oblige.

"Funny you should say that, Steve," I said gently, "but I do have this little personal transport problem." I outlined my predicament.

"I'm sure the Commander would be sympathetic if you were to ask him," he said.

"I'd rather not trouble him with this, if it could be avoided."

He stroked his chin. "Tell you what, Brad. There's a battered old Mercedes jeep in the back corner of our workshop that the Argies left behind when they went home. It goes, but it has only two forward gears – second and fourth – plus reverse, but it's drivable and would get you around. We can always fix you up with proper transport when you really need it."

I shook him solemnly by the hand. "Thanks Steve, I appreciate it. That's a pizza I owe you when we get back to Blighty."

Next morning I picked up the jeep and drove round to the front of our office. I stuck my head through the door and saw Dick reaching for the kettle. "Coffee?" he asked.

"Do you fancy a little spin first?" I replied. "I'd like your opinion on our new office runabout."

Socialising

Once I had mastered the gearbox, our little jeep made a handy runabout for Dick and me and certainly scored us a few brownie points with other dwellers in the Mess. As many passengers as possible would scramble aboard to get down to HQ in the mornings and back after close of play. "We ought to hire it out as a taxi," Dick laughed, but of course we never did.

It certainly saved us a fair bit in boot-leather, and although it broke down a few times and had its share of punctures on the rocky road from Stanley to Mount Pleasant, it proved a real boon. It also meant that when I needed proper transport to ferry press visitors around, Steve and his lads in the motor pool were invariably accommodating.

As I've said, much of our day-to-day work involved contact with the islanders. Both Dick and I ran an open-door policy and encouraged them to drop into the office whenever they liked. In return, we were never short of dinner invitations to their homes. With well over a million sheep on the islands, the main course was invariably mutton. Never over-fond of it at the best of times, I promptly banned it from our household menu once I returned home. Small wonder our new friends relished invitations to the Mess, where they could enjoy a much wider choice of cuisine.

Patrick Watts, from FIBS, and Amanda, an enthusiastic young woman recently arrived from England to edit the *Penguin News*, the island's little newspaper, dropped by regularly to garner what morsels of news they could and to share a coffee. By far my most interesting visitor, however, was John Smith, who had visited the Falklands years before as a member of a British Antarctic survey team, and had married and decided to stay.

John, who hailed from the English West Country, was an intriguing character. On his first visit he admired a wall-calendar hanging behind my desk, containing pictures of British fighting vehicles. When I plucked it down and presented it to him his delight knew no bounds. He promptly excused himself, saying he would return in a few minutes.

True to his word, he reappeared and handed me a brown cardboard tube about four feet long. Sticking a finger inside, he unfurled a magnificent hand-drawn map of the Falklands, to which he had added miniature pen-and-ink drawings of some 286 ships that had come to grief on her shores over the centuries. Dates and the names of the vessels were appended where possible. It was beautifully done and remains one of my most treasured possessions.

I sat fascinated as he spoke of the history of these disasters. He explained how most of the old sailing ships had been driven onto the craggy coast by fierce gales after battling round Cape Horn.

John was an inveterate storyteller and could certainly spin a stirring yarn. He would tell us how the old square-riggers of long, long ago, northern-bound from Chile with cargos of guano for the UK and Europe, would have their seams sprung by the constant pounding of the huge waves of the southern ocean.

"Once the sea-water reached the cargo holds," he said, "it would saturate the loose guano, effectively turning it into a mass of concrete. Sometimes the cargo became so heavy it literally tore through the ship's bottom and she foundered. On other occasions the ships, dismasted by the gales and totally beyond the control of the crews, could do nothing else but crash onto the rocks."

John related how one ship, shorn of her two masts, managed to reach the safety of Stanley Sound. "The skipper sent word to England by means of a passing ship and new masts were sent out. The whole business took more than a year, but eventually the vessel was repaired. The ship set sail only to founder in a sudden squalls two days later, with the loss of everyone on board."

John took me to see the well-appointed Falklands War Museum he'd been largely responsible for creating when the war ended and the Argentinians had departed.

"The Argies left a lot of their gear behind," he explained, " and I figured it would be a good idea to gather as much of it as possible as a memento of those grim days. So I went to see Brigadier Thompson, the British Commander. He smiled, waved his arm, and told me "Certainly John, take as much as you want.""

Looking around at the imposing display of fighter planes, helicopters, uniforms, weaponry, landmines and k-rations, I told him he had done well. I might have added he was welcome to have my two-geared Mercedes jeep once I'd finished with it, but thought better of it.

Trapped in a minefield

"I have to nip out to the Camp and visit Kevin McNamara," Dick said one day. "He's a fellow-countryman of yours and quite a character. I think you'll like him."

There was no way I was going to pass up an invitation like that. The McNamara place was way out in the wilds and the only way of reaching it was over rough, cross-country terrain. "I think it might be beyond your little jeep, so I'll book a Land-Rover from the pool," he added.

It was one of the Falklands' better days weather-wise, and as we drove, Dick filled me in on the man we were going to visit. It seemed Kevin had owned a thriving law practice in Ireland before switching careers and opting to head for the far side of the world. He now owned one of the biggest sheep farms in the islands.

We had turned off the narrow track and were heading across an expanse of open grassland when Dick suddenly slammed on the brakes. I raised an eyebrow as he turned and said to me, "That's torn it, mate. I think I've made a boo boo!"

"What's up?" I asked, not having a clue what he was on about.

Pointing to a rectangular sign mounted on a post some thirty yards ahead, he said, "That's a warning notice. I think we're in a minefield!"

I recognised the sign well enough. It had its back towards us which meant we were on the wrong side of it – and any possible mines.

"I didn't see any sign back there," he said. "It must have blown down or something."

"So, what's the plan now?" I asked.

"You could always put your fingers in your ears and walk ahead of me while I follow slowly behind."

"Very droll, Dick. But as you're the one who got us into this mess I think you should walk in front while I drive behind at a respectful distance."

We both laughed, but we realised that we were in something of a pickle. As soon as they'd arrived, the Argies had laid minefields in many parts of the islands. Even worse, they either hadn't made any maps of their dispositions, or else had destroyed the details when they realised they were going to lose.

Periodically a mine would be detonated by a wandering sheep, or uncovered by the strong winds. It had long ago been decided it simply wasn't cost-effective and much too dangerous to have them all removed. These areas were fenced off and plainly marked. We ought to have paid more attention.

We held a brief council of war before following the maxim that the shortest distance between two given points was a straight line. We advanced slowly until we got past the sign, then stopped and exhaled deeply.

"Wouldn't fancy going through that again," Dick grated. "Seconded," I replied.

Keven McNamara laughed uproariously when we recounted our little adventure. "A right pair of bloody eejits," he declared. "Not safe to be let out on your own." He poked a finger at me. "You're from Ireland, like me, so that's some excuse, but Dick, you've been here long enough to know better."

We were seated round the table in his comfortable kitchen, sipping mugs of hot, sweet tea and enjoying homemade scones. Moving on from his good-natured ribbing, Kevin was happy to talk of his life in his adopted wilderness. "It's great out here," he enthused, "and I've no wish at all to go back to the rat-race and cow-tow to a bunch of bewigged judges."

Later he took us on a little tour of our immediate environment and I was struck by a loud cackling from inside the wreck of an old abandoned car. Several brown hens fluttered away at our approach, protesting at being disturbed.

"There's something of a history to this old banger," Kevin explained. "Let's go and eat and I'll tell you all about it."

Once we were re-seated at the well-laden table, our host began his story of the old vehicle which, it emerged, had once been a splendid Rolls-Royce.

"Back in the Fifties, the Queen and the Duke of Edinburgh paid a short visit to the Falklands on their way back from opening the then British Empire Games in New Zealand. Their official car was brought ashore and used on their official visits, not that they were able to travel very far in those days. Anyway, before they departed, Prince Philip presented the Roller to the Governor as a gesture of good-will.

"That worthy was, of course, delighted and romped about in it on every conceivable occasion for the next ten years or so. Eventually it was sold on to the local undertaker and it became the Port Stanley hearse. The back seat was removed and replaced by a more suitable platform. For long enough it was used to convey a long line of Falklanders to their final resting place.

"Some time later it came up for sale and I acquired it, partly as a joke and partly as a small status symbol. We used it to drive into Stanley to stock up with provisions, in some style. I was especially proud of the Royal Coat of Arms emblazoned on the front doors, but never quite ran to flying the Royal Standard. Eventually though, it became rather more trouble than it was worth. Now, as you see, it still serves a purpose – at least the hens seem to enjoy it."

A little while ago I watched a BBC documentary about the burgeoning tourist industry in the Falkland Islands. The place has become a mecca for rich United States and British visitors and the big cruise liners put into Stanley on a regular basis, allowing their passengers to spend a day on shore.

I watched it with interest, keeping a lookout for old, familiar faces. Sure enough, there were old friends, Kevin McNamara and Patrick Watts, amongst others, glad-handing hordes of visitors and shepherding them onto fleets of splendidly-painted coaches to commence their sight-seeing tours. Never the sort to miss out on an opportunity, the Falklanders – and who can blame them?

Home-grown entertainment

It might be timely to record a little of what off-duty life in the Falklands was like. I know it wasn't everybody's cup of tea, but, while I missed home, and family and friends, I suppose I settled into it quite well. In short, it depended on what you made of it yourself.

After a few weeks I was given the opportunity of moving to a slightly bigger – and certainly warmer, twin-cabin billet. It was a little farther from the main mess, but had its own bathroom equipped with a decent shower, wash-basin and toilet. I occupied one end of the building,, which provided slightly more space than my last. The other half belonged to Major Derek Matthews, a studious fellow with an abiding interest in the flora and fauna of our habitant.

One huge advantage for me was that, instead of having to attend to my own washing and ironing as before, I could now have my duds efficiently laundered in the civilian workers' hut next door. All this for the payment of one bottle of Scotch per month!

There were other compensations. Apart from the excellent fare in the Mess, which was heavily subsidised because of our so-called active service situation. Alcohol was ridiculously inexpensive, based on the fact that, like most other goods, it had to be flown down from the UK. As an example, a glass of whisky or gin cost only nine pence, while a can of coke cost 30p. Strange but true!

Everyone looked forward to receiving mail from home. This

usually arrived in the form of lightweight, folded sheets of paper, popularly known as *blueys.* These could be sent free of charge and were eagerly received hot off the TriStar on Tuesdays and Fridays.

My old office in Lisburn saw to it that Mollie and the kids had a steady supply of *blueys.* Mollie dished out bundles of them to our friends, so I was never short of news from home. I set aside an hour most evenings to write replies. Like most of the personnel down there, I found it an important and comforting link.

It would have been tempting to drift into the mess bar most evenings to share a drink and generally socialise, so I resolved to limit these pursuits. Fortunately, I was invited out for dinner in the town quite often, and enjoyed that immensely. The few senior officers who were accompanied by their wives were unfailing generous in inviting the rest of us to lunch or dinner from time to time.

One dinner in the Admiral's private bungalow was especially interesting. A modern prefabricated building, shipped out from England immediately post-war, it had been originally designed to face south, as is the practice in the northern hemisphere. The local firm charged with erecting it should, of course, have built it facing north in order to catch what little sun there was. Instead they had slavishly followed the original instructions and left the house facing the South Pole. Admiral Layman didn't seem to mind and claimed it made a good over-dinner talking point.

After dinner each evening some of us would gather in the television room to watch a video. I should explain that, after the invasion, the Argentines issued each Falkland family with a television set and VHS video recorder, to be paid for by instalments, in order that they could watch propaganda programmes and learn the language. When they'd been escorted back to their homeland, these sets remained, as an unintended parting gift.

Not folk to kick a gift horse in the teeth, the Falklanders were quick to capitalise on this uninvited generosity. Three video shops sprang up in Stanley, to be regularly replenished by imports from the UK. Similarly, loath to pass up the opportunity, we took turns to provide a video for our evenings in the mess. It's an ill wind.

One of the colonels, an avid bridge player, decided to launch a course of lessons over ten weeks. Having once played, intermittently and very badly, I put my name down. It was instructive and great fun, and I played two or three times a week for the duration of my tour.

Apart from keeping in touch via the *blueys,* I tried to phone home at least once a week and always kept a Cable and Wireless cash-card in my wallet. To avoid missing out, I'd write, telling them when I'd call. The line was always as clear as crystal, and as the BT phone commercial proclaimed, it was good to talk.

During one of these chats, coming up to Barry's birthday, Mollie whispered that the lad had his heart set on getting an electronic keyboard. What did I think?

"Go for it," I said promptly. "If that's what he wants. Tell him I'll be expecting great things when I get home."

We weren't to know it then, but that birthday present was later to launch Barry on his career as a professional musician, one he's pursued successfully ever since.

A military funeral

You've got to hand it to the military, when they bury one of their own – or a fallen enemy – they do it reverently and in style. A phone call from London informed me that a date had been set for the funeral of Captain Giminez and I could expect an influx of media visitors.

The political parameters had been established in London, no doubt after much head-scratching and soul-searching. Paramount to the proceedings was how to deal with the sensitivities of the islanders themselves, and their Council had been consulted at every stage.

A phone call from Alan Percival gave me a boost. "I told you we'd keep you busy down there, didn't I?" he observed. "You haven't dug up any dead Argies lately, have you?"

He told me the dead pilot's father, Senor Isaias Giminez and his sister, Maria, would be attending the funeral. Because of protocol and the restrictions still in force, they could not fly directly to Mount Pleasant. Instead they faced travelling from Buenos Aries to Paris and then to Mount Pleasant via Brize Norton. They would return home by the same route. A round-trip of more than 34,000 miles, whereas a direct flight would have taken just over 400 miles!

I learned that TV and radio crews from BBC, ITN and France planned to cover the event, the last-named on behalf of Argentine television. Patrick Watts intended giving blanket coverage on FIBS, and John Smith and others would be acting as correspondents for a number of newspapers in the UK and USA. I arranged to give them a special advance briefing and invite them to attend the main press briefing in the BFFI conference room. I also put together a number of comprehensive briefing packs.

It had been agreed that the Admiral would deliver a short statement to the media and answer a limited number of questions, steering well clear of anything politically contentious. I would chair the conference and do my best to ensure everyone toed the line. Layman was understandably nervous, but reassured somewhat when I advised him to keep tight-lipped and impassive if asked something he didn't wish to answer. "No list of ten questions this time then?" he smiled.

"They won't get a chance to ask even half that number," I said firmly, returning his smile.

In the best interests of all concerned, both the Giminez family and the visiting media would be doing a speedy turnaround and flying back on the Tri-Star, The media wouldn't like it, but I'd helped them out by arranging with Cable and Wireless that they could file their copy and transmit their pictures and film immediately.

It seemed to me that most of the islanders I talked to were totally ambivalent about the funeral. While sympathising with the Giminez family in their loss, they nevertheless couldn't dismiss from their minds that the man's death had come about while he was engaged in an attack on their homeland. While some councillors would attend, the vast majority of residents were content to give the occasion a miss.

Busy with the media, I didn't have a chance to meet Senor and Senorita Giminez until the actual funeral. He was a tall, rather stately man, who carried himself throughout with impressive dignity. He was said to be a stern critic of the prevailing regime in his country, which was alleged to be responsible for the unexplained disappearance of more than 20,000 citizens. His daughter Maria (24), tall and raven-haired, was equally striking.

They watched silently as their son and brother was laid to rest with due military honours alongside 237 of his countrymen in the Argentine military cemetery at Goose Green, where some of the bitterest fighting of the war had taken place four years before.

Everything went well from a PR point of view, apart from a ludicrously inaccurate story filed by Mike Edwards of the *Daily Mail*, claiming that two Argentine sympathisers who lived in the Camp had to take shelter to avoid the wrath of some of the islanders. It wasn't worthy of comment and, thankfully, I wasn't questioned about it. But everyone I spoke to viewed it with utter contempt.

Mount Pleasant

The main concentration of British personnel on the islands was in Mount Pleasant, thirty miles from Stanley and reached by a pebble-strewn, rough-surfaced track, with several traps lurking to snare the unwary driver. I had to traverse it several times a month and I became familiar with the rugged terrain. There were no houses along its length, and few buildings of any kind. Two distinct landmarks encountered on the journey were Mount Longdon and Mount Tumbledown, where some of the bitterest fighting of the war had taken place.

Apart from periodic calls on the senior staff, my main reason for visiting was to collect press and media visitors from the UK on their arrival at the airport and transport them to Port Stanley. I also produced a news release on the squadron of Tornado F3 fighter-planes based there at the time.

Mount Pleasant was essentially a modern fortress, designed both to deter any possible attack by the Argentinians and to provide a landing place for such reinforcements as might have to be brought from the UK. Like most service personnel I spoke to, I much preferred to be based in Stanley.

Much of the base was underground, and its construction had represented a considerable feat of engineering. Efficient it undoubtedly was, but I found it cheerless and unwelcoming. One of its dubious distinctions is that it boasts the longest corridor in the world – over 800-metres in length, with a number of shorter branches leading off it. With typical Service cynicism it's known by those who exist there as *The Death Star.*

Unlike *Lookout Rocks*, where we had at least some association with the locals, those based there had to resort almost entirely to their own devices, apart from the occasional trip to Stanley, or an outing on one of the Sunday *'bimbles'.*

As far as I know, the word *bimble* is unique to forces serving in the Falklands. A *bimble* is simply an organised walk, or hike to some designated part of the islands. Usually it takes in a battlefield tour, or a visit to one of the settlements out in Camp, or to explore one of the smaller outlying islands.

My own favourite island

I took part in a number of *bimbles*, and thoroughly enjoyed them. My favourite outing was to Saunders Island, off the far west of West

Falkland. It was enchanting - a fairytale place - and although as windswept as everywhere else in that part of the world, the sun always seemed to shine while I was there, and the sea took on that translucent, aqua-marine quality more typical of Hawaii, or the Bahamas. Appearances can be deceptive, of course, for although the water looked inviting, it was invariably bloody cold!

In all I visited Saunders Island four times, including once when I brought a television crew there to film some wildlife. Although measuring only 13 miles east to west, and less than that north to south, it positively teemed with wildlife, including several species of penguin, and a great many seals, together with some specimens of large and very ugly elephant seals.

I was glad I'd brought my camera and came away with hundreds of pictures. With patience, it was possible to get quite close to the seals, and although the penguins would waddle away if approached, I quickly discovered the best way to photograph them was simply to sit on my backside and wait. The little perishers were so curious they'd walk right up to where I sat, cock their heads to one side, and peer into the lens.

I saw Albatross with wingspans of up to four metres and several species of gull, and I was fascinated by the long-tailed Skuas, who persistently dive-bombed the large colony of penguins that occupied a long stretch of the shore, snatching the occasional egg, or baby chick in spite of the best efforts of the parents to protect them. It was a classic example of Nature in the raw. I was especially pleased to capture half-a-dozen colour photographs which now adorn the staircase in our home.

An adventure at Volunteer Point

Desperately keen to take some pictures of King penguins, three friends and I begged a lift in a helicopter one Saturday afternoon. The pilot dropped us off beside a large colony of these majestic birds on an isolated headland called Volunteer Point, promising to pick us up four hours later at 6 o'clock.

Of all the species of penguin we encountered, the King, or Emperor, is by far the most impressive. They can attain a height of about four feet, and with their bright orange and gold chests and jet-black plumage, they look for all the world like stately butlers in an English country manor. They are remarkably tame, providing one adopts the standard practice of hunkering down until they deign to approach. All four of us captured some marvellous photographs.

We'd brought sandwiches and a few cans of beer with us and were not unduly concerned when we weren't picked up on time. The first twinges of anxiety showed when seven o'clock arrived and there was no sign of our helo. Dusk settles quickly in the islands, even in summer, and all of us were booked in for a special dinner in the Mess at which everyone was to be presented with a personally engraved medal to commemorate our tour.

By 7-30 pm we were resigned to accepting that either we'd been overlooked, or our transport had broken down. There was nothing for it but to prepare for a chill night out in the bondo.

By good fortune we came upon an empty metal shipping container which someone had abandoned and left lying on its side. We were all wearing sweaters and warm anoraks, so things might have been a lot worse. Someone produced a packet of wine-gums and shared them around. Our main complaint was that the steel floor of our temporary home was bloody hard and uncomfortable.

An hour ticked by and our thoughts turned to the fine dinner we were missing in the warm and welcoming Mess. We had lapsed into a moody silence when, in the far distance, we heard the unmistakable throb of an approaching helicopter. Minutes later we had scrambled on board and were accepting the apologies of a chastened pilot.

"Sorry chaps," he explained, "but a last-minute commitment came in and mine was the only chopper available. "I know you've missed the main dinner, but I'm sure they've kept something hot for you."

They had indeed, God bless them, and we got our medals as well. I've just taken mine off a shelf as I write. It's a weighty thing, the size of an Olympic medal, bearing on one side the Coat-of-Arms of the Falklands and the motto *Desire the Right,* and on the obverse LOOKOUT ROCKS Officers' Mess 1986/7.

The following Saturday the four of us re-united for our own little dinner in the Mess, shared a toast to Volunteer Point, displayed our medals, and looked back on our little adventure. Charlie, one of our number, observed that in many ways it was rather a pity that we hadn't actually been marooned there overnight, as it would have added greatly to our story. He failed to find a seconder.

All at sea

The Capt Giminez funeral heralded the start of a really busy period for me, launching a succession of visits from television companies as well as the print media. George Younger, the Secretary of State for Defence, brought a gaggle of them with him when he came on a tour of inspection. Many of the reporters stayed on to cover the imposition of the new fishing restrictions.

When I spoke to Alan Percival back in London, I wasn't sure whether to thank him for all the activity or to give him a bollocking for dropping me in it.

Actually I was quite happy to be kept on the go. It would indeed have been a dreary posting if I'd simply had to hang around the office with time on my hands. There weren't too many dull moments when I was down south.

I'm glad to say I appeared to be establishing my point with the Admiral in that PR wasn't necessarily a bad thing, and that not all members of the Fourth Estate were entirely evil. I guided him through a number of live radio and televised interviews and he performed most creditably, even eliciting an approving nod from our lords and masters in Whitehall.

During all of this period I had to liaise closely with His Excellency the Governor and his advisors. Two enjoyable highlights for me were a visit to one of Her Majesty's submarines and escorting a TV crew out into the Southern Ocean to film one of our frigates patrolling the zone. They captured some exciting close-ups of the huge Russian and Japanese container ships which filled their holds with fish before returning home.

It was a bonus for them that they were also able to record a mercy flight when a Royal Navy helicopter transported an injured Russian sailor from his factory ship for treatment in Port Stanley Hospital. He was retained there for a week, under guard, lest he was on a secret spying mission.

It was a comparatively calm day when we were flown out to the frigate by helicopter, yet I was impressed by the sheer size and power of the South Atlantic rollers. There was a 20-foot gap between the crest to the trough of the waves and all of us passengers were in awe of the skill of her pilot as he picked his moment to touch down on the heaving deck.

Immediately he'd done so, a team of four crewmen raced out to clamp our helo securely in place. It was a masterly operation, rather like how a crew of mechanics operates at a pit stop in a Grand Prix – and a race-track doesn't gyrate in the way our little ship did! It was a relief when the crew bundled us under cover.

The film crew were delighted when a flight of Tornado F3s from Mount Pleasant carried out a mock strafing attack on our vessel and our gunners fought them off with blanks. All good action stuff and uncannily realistic.

I thanked the skipper, and the crew and we were taken to the wardroom and rewarded with mugs of strong tea, liberally laced with good navy rum. All in all a thrilling afternoon, not least when we were taken one-by-one across the heaving deck and thrust into our waiting helicopter. Once again the pilot had to pick his moment to take off.

Michael Bilton and his ITN documentary

I'd just waved off what I thought was my last television crew for a while when Michael Bilton arrived. He was one of ITN's leading news-documentary producers, and although we hadn't met before, I knew of him by reputation. Accordingly, I advised the Admiral that we were likely in for a challenge.

Michael was one of the most independent characters I'd ever met in my life. He arrived on a reconnaissance mission to suss out the lie of the land, prior to returning to complete the filming of a two-hour programme in the New Year. I picked him up off the Tri-Star, and on the drive to Stanley offered him accommodation in the Mess during his three-day stay. To my surprise he declined, saying he'd already booked into the *Upland Goose*, one of the small local hotels. I had intended inviting him to dinner, but he forestalled me by asking me to join him for a meal in the hotel.

I admired his obvious self-reliance, but explained to him how difficult it was simply getting about in the islands. "When the crew gets here next year I intend hiring a couple of Land-Rovers and using FIGAS, as far as possible," he declared. FIGAS was the Falkland Islands Government Air Service, which used a small fleet of Bristow helicopters (popularly known as *Erics,* after the world champion darts player of the time).

As though to prove his point, he confirmed that he'd arranged to be flown out to the settlement of Goose Green the following day. "I've booked a set for you as well," he added with a smile, in case you want to come along."

We set off bright and early next morning. It was my first experience of flying FIGAS and I found it utterly fascinating. Our *Eric* was a sturdy, dependable old chopper and we shared the tiny cabin with four locals and some assorted packages for delivery along the way.

Michael told me that he intended basing a large section of his programme around Goose Green, where some of the fiercest close-quarter fighting of the war had occurred and where Colonel 'H', of the Parachute Regiment had been killed. Once we touched down I was content to let him go about his business as he wished.

He met with a number of folk in the green-painted hut which served as a focal point in the tiny settlement. While he engaged the locals in conversation, outlining his intentions when filming began, I studied my surroundings. The main room, only slightly larger than my lounge back in Lisburn, had a tiny bar in one corner and two pictures on the walls – one of The Queen, the other of Margaret Thatcher.

There was also a framed letter of congratulations and support from the Prime Minister, who was absolutely revered in the islands. Although the war was acknowledged as a damn close-run affair, I was struck by the utter conviction of everyone I talked to that "Maggie would sort out the Argies." They had never the slightest doubt that a task force would be sent down to do the job.

Michael was also keen to have a look at the makeshift field hospital which Surgeon-Captain Rick Jolly had set up in a ramshackle barn at Ajax Bay. There was no way to get there other than by helicopter, and as it wasn't on a regular FIGAS route, he had to consent for us to be ferried there in one of our Lynx.

I was as nervous as he was as we donned our pink survival suits, which would keep us alive for no more than four minutes if we had to ditch in the icy waters. We scarcely appreciated our pilot's quip that *"they'll keep us afloat just long enough to boil an egg!"* and wondered afterwards how many times he'd cracked that sick joke.

The hospital, now derelict, was a gloomy and eerie place and it was hard to imagine that Capt Jolly and his team had tended the wounded and saved so many lives there, both Argentines and British, as often as not under enemy fire. A painted sign above where the door had been still displayed the slogan *"Welcome to the Red and Green Life Machine."*

I wish I'd been able to meet Jolly. He must have been quite a man and the stories about him are legendry. I particularly like the one of how he repaired the badly-mangled leg of Argentine pilot, Ricardo Lucero, who ejected from his fighter seconds before a missile blew it to pieces. The two became firm friends and Jolly even wrote to Lucero's wife, Cordoba, back in Argentina, assuring her that he was safe and in good hands.

The two entered into a wager that Lucero would never fly again. Jolly lost the bet. His patient stayed on in the Argentine Air Force, only to die in a mid-air collision three years after the war.

I rather got to like Michael Bilton during our short time together, and in a way, regretted that I wouldn't be around when he returned to do his filming. I'm sure he ruffled a few feathers along the way, but months later, I made a point of viewing his two-hour documentary when it was televised. I was doubtless in a minority, as I found it hard-hitting but fair, controversial in parts, yet scrupulously accurate.

CHRISTMAS DAY in the Falklands and Santa drops in by helicopter to meet Admiral Kit Layman and other revellers at a barbie on the beach.

When I called at the *Upland Goose* to collect him for the airport, I found him in his room, polishing the dust of the islands from his boots with a stylish-looking cleaning kit in a snazzy, brown leather zipped bag. When I admired it he insisted on leaving it with me as a little reminder of our association. I still use it today.

Christmas far from home

Christmas is celebrated worldwide – it's a time for family and close friends, for giving and receiving gifts, for eating and perhaps drinking far too much and for celebrating the person who gave it His name. So, for all of us who were parted from our loved ones half a world away, it was an emotional and poignant time.

Knowing my tour was coming to an end and that I'd be home early in the New Year, I'd urged the family not to go to the trouble and expense of sending presents. Nevertheless, some were sent, along with lots of Christmas cards and masses of the inevitable *blueys*. All my family and friends were well, I was being hugely missed, and Barry was having a ball with his new keyboard, and "improving every day."

My office-mate, Dick Saunders, was one of the lucky ones who would be re-united with his family in the UK. His replacement, Captain Willie Larkin, an engaging and likable character, settled in seamlessly and it was virtually business as usual. His first action, soon after arriving, was to procure a second-hand motorcycle from somewhere and shoot off on it to spend most of his spare time fishing.

I was touched by the number of gifts and cards I received from my civilian friends in Stanley, not to mention all the invitations to dine in their homes. There was a succession of formal and informal dinners in the Mess, together with any number of parties and special events.

The highlight of it all, however, was a unique barbecue and picnic on the beach on Christmas Day. Just about everyone attended and the weather was exceptionally kind. Looking through my old photographs of the occasion and noting the silver sand and cloudless sky, the setting looked for all the world like a South Sea island.

I'd made arrangements to call home at five o'clock UK time and knew that Mollie and the family would be waiting after dinner. When I got to Cable and Wireless, however, the queue of would be callers stretched for about fifty metres. I should have realised that everyone would have had the same idea. I called back later, by which time the queue had decreased significantly and I was connected in little over fifteen minutes.

As ever, it was good to talk, although they had been worried when I hadn't come through on time. As well as the family, some neighbours had called round and I quickly ran through the phone card I'd bought and the complimentary £10 one everyone in the garrison had been presented with. Barry thanked me profusely for his keyboard and promised to put on a little show for me when I got home. I said I'd let them know arrival dates and times as soon as they'd been finalised.

There was a succession of parties and dinners from Christmas through to the New Year and a pantomime in Stanley Town Hall. As 1986 gave way to '87, I left the celebrations in the Mess for a few minutes and stepped outside to look down over the lights of Port Stanley. From inside I could hear the strains of *Auld Lang Syne,* and far away in the town, the bells of the Cathedral ushering in the New Year.

Gozome

As expected, work tapered off a good deal as my departure date loomed. By custom and tradition, a dinner was held in the Mess for each homeward bound departee. These, sometimes rowdy affairs, were known as *Gozomes* (Goes home he) don't ask me why. I was going to share mine with two companions who had become good friends in our time together.

With a few days to go, news filtered back of an unfortunate incident concerning one of our colleagues who's *Gozome* we'd all attended some ten days previously. Captain Tony Hutton, of the Army Air Corps, had been a lively and popular member of the Headquarters, and when we heard what had befallen him we weren't sure whether to laugh or cry.

All RAF flights are dry – that is, no alcohol is allowed or served on board. Tony, not relishing the thought of a 8,500-mile trip without a glass of something, had devised a cunning plan. He bought a dozen large oranges and impregnated each of them with a shot of good Russian vodka by means of a hypodermic syringe.

We weren't informed how many oranges he'd managed to consume before the stop-over on Ascension Island, but he'd apparently decided to take a little stroll, during which he had staggered into a ditch and broken his leg!

"Typical Tony," somebody exclaimed. "Poor bugger. I hope they decide he's suffered punishment enough and he gets away with it." I never did hear the outcome.

I had a lengthy round of farewells, involving both the Falklanders and my colleagues and friends in the Garrison. Admiral Layman thanked me warmly and assured me London would be receiving a good end of tour report about my work. "Perhaps you're right when you told me that all journalists aren't necessarily untrustworthy," he smiled, "although at least one of them fell into that category. I've enjoyed working with you, Brad, and don't mind admitting I've learned a thing or two about public relations. You and I have indeed lived through an interesting time."

As I handed in my last library book and embarked on my final round of Stanley to bid farewell to the Governor and his staff, Patrick Watts and Amanda, John Smith, Alex Gordon and all the rest, I little thought I'd ever see them again. I certainly got that one wrong.

Back Home

Thankfully, the homeward journey from the Falkland Islands was a great deal less exciting than the outward flight had been. As opposed to 48 hours, this one took the standard 18. I was delighted to be invited up to the cockpit to spend an enjoyable half-an-hour with the Captain and co-pilot. Visibility was good and the views of a sunlit west coast of Africa were breath-taking.

As promised, Alan Percival had driven up to meet my Tri-Star. It was typically good of him, as it was a Saturday morning and he was off duty. We brought each-other up to speed on the drive to Heathrow where we had lunch and a couple of beers. Having checked the shuttle times to Belfast, I phoned Mollie to let her know when I'd be arriving.

Alan said my work in the Falklands had not gone unnoticed. I was now well in line for promotion to Chief Information Officer. There were a couple of interesting jobs coming up and he asked what was on my mind. I'd actually been tossing this matter around in my head for some time and had expected him to raise the topic.

He was well aware that I still had no wish to move to London, which really ought to have been my next logical career step. There was also the small matter of my personal finances. As an SIO, I was on the last rung of the promotion ladder that carried payment for overtime. Both in the Falklands and in Northern Ireland this amounted to a tidy sum and pushed my take-home pay well above the top rate for a CIO. As against that, overtime didn't count towards final pension entitlement on retirement.

Alan nodded understandingly. "The way things are going in Northern Ireland you'll be logging up a lot of overtime for the foreseeable future, certainly a lot more that you'd get on promotion. There's also the advantage of not having to move house. It's up to you of course, but in your shoes I'd be tempted to let the hare sit and stay as you are. Remember, you'll have more opportunities for promotion in the future if you fancy it."

I nodded in agreement. "My thoughts exactly, Alan," I said.

With that out of the way, Alan confided that there was a likely change of direction in the near future for him as well. He asked that

I keep it to myself for now, but Prince Charles was looking for a new Public Relations Officer and he was being considered for the post.

"Good for you," I said. "I hope you get it. Keep in touch,"

He accompanied me to the departure desk, where we exchanged a firm handshake before I went in search of the boarding gate for Belfast Aldergrove.

A happy reunion

Mollie and the family were waiting by the luggage collection point in the familiar surroundings of Aldergrove Airport. As we embraced I noticed streaks of grey in her hair which hadn't been there before. Noticing my glance, she chirped "I'm not dyeing it, so you can like it or lump it!" Running a hand through my own thinning locks, I could do little else but smile. Val and Barry seemed to have grown up a lot during my absence. It was wonderful to see them all again.

After taking a week's leave to get my bearings and catch up with things, I reported for duty at HQNI. Although some of the personnel had changed, many of the old guard were still there and it was very much a case of the mixture as before. Dermod Hill had recently been transferred in as CIO and was running a happy ship. In no time at all it was as if I'd never been away.

While terrorist activity had abated only slightly, there was still more than enough to keep us busy. I worked closely on a virtual day-to-day basis with the police Force Control and Information Centre (FCIC), still headed by Bill McGookin, backed up by his aides, Chief-Superintendent Bill Wilson and his civilian deputy, Dave Hanna. I also met regularly with Andy Wood, CIO of the Stormont Press Office, and his staff at Stormont.

I still did most of the press briefings and tried my best to keep in regular contact with the Belfast newsrooms and the weekly papers throughout the country. Although I had a nominal responsibility to work with the UDR, I was content to leave most of the routine day-to-day operations to Carolyn Arnold, who was now the HQ's permanent press officer.

Where has the time gone?

The weeks and months slipped by, friends and colleagues moved on, some to other posts, others into retirement. Some, sadly, were no longer with us. The ongoing troubles took their toll on too many good people. Faces are easily remembered; some of the names blur and fade over time.

Work, as hectic, interesting and unpredictable as ever, seemed to consume more and more of my time. Inevitably, family time paid the price. Seventy- and eighty-hour working weeks were commonplace. What is that old saw about work expanding to fill the time allotted to it?

Almost before I knew it, Val and Barry had grown up, finished school and begun to make their way in the world. In 1990 Val married a good man called John Crawford, an architect in the firm where she worked. In time they presented us with two lovely grandsons, Jonathan and Philip.

John designed and built a beautiful home for them just outside Lisburn. Fate dealt him a cruel hand, however, when, following a fall while working on his boat, he developed Parkinson's.

Through a good friend, I managed to secure Barry a job as a journalist on a weekly newspaper. He worked hard and was doing well, but one day he came to me and said, "Dad, please don't be disappointed, but journalism isn't for me."

I knew his great love had always been music, ever since we'd given him his first keyboard while I was in the Falklands. Even before he'd finished school he'd teamed up with a singer, Wilfie Higginson, to form the group *Keynotes,* and they were soon playing regularly all over the country. Better to follow a profession you love, rather than persist with one in which you have no real interest.

A couple of years later Barry met and married Stephanie Colgan who worked in the advertising department of the *Belfast Telegraph*. They bought a new house in Carrickfergus and had a beautiful daughter, Kerry Leigh. Sadly, as so often happens, the marriage didn't last.

Barry has persisted with his music and is now a solo artist. While he still regularly goes out on his gigs, his real interest lies in composing and song-writing. He has established his own studio, has released a number of recordings and made several appearances on radio and television.

Our great friends, Tony and Pat Heaney, back from Australia, lived in Dungannon for a time before settling in their old haunts in Kilkeel. We got together regularly, and as ever, picked up the threads exactly where we'd left them last time.

Retirement – well not quite

Sixty was the usual retirement age in my branch of government service and it seemed to sneak up on me quite quickly. To be truthful, I hadn't given the evil day a great deal of thought, content in the belief that things would slot into place when the time came.

I'm not a pipe and slippers kind of fellow, and I knew I would never be content to simply read the paper, walk the dog and watch the tele. I wasn't into gardening, and had even had the back lawn concreted over years before. I'd long had it in mind to write a book, I jokingly labelled it the GIN (my Great Irish Novel).

I'd catch up on a great many books I hadn't had time to read, take up bowls and maybe re-join the old chess and draughts club I'd once belonged to. Besides that, my golf clubs had been gathering dust in the garage for far too many years.

My plans were thwarted by a suggestion from MOD that I might like to consider staying on for a year or two as a paid PR consultant. I was assured that the duties would not be onerous and the annual stipend would mean a useful boast to the Fleming retirement fund. The State Pension was still a long way off. As Nigel Gillies, my last CIO put it, "You can give us all possible assistance – short of actual help!"

The arrangement provided a link with some of my old stomping grounds, not least a lunch in Belfast on the first Friday of the month with fellow members of our Liar Dice Club. This little institution had been running for years, and as well as allowing us to enjoy this harmless pastime, kept us up to speed with the latest gossip. By tradition, we also met for dinner in one of our homes once a year.

My consultancy role could scarcely be described as over-taxing. Instead, it provided several nice little perquisites, not least when I escorted a group of press and media to visit the Royal Irish Rangers in Cyprus and then a second group on the long journey down to the Falklands.

I'd never expected to return there again. It was still as beautiful and windswept as ever, but there had been many changes since I was last there, all for the better. Improved transport links with the UK had meant a wider selection of goods in the shops and jobs were more plentiful. But perhaps the most notable change was in a flourishing tourist industry, which has continued to grow ever since. The War had really put the islands on the map, in more ways than one and they were now a huge attraction for tourists.

I took a stroll up by *Lookout Rocks.* It was a veritable ghost town. My old porta-cabin office had gone and the headquarters was a pale shadow of what it had once been. Most operations were now conducted from the base at Mount Pleasant. Time changes everything.

Large cruise liners now call regularly at Port Stanley and hordes of tourists flock down in the season to visit the last bit of civilization before the South Pole. Old friends, Patrick Watts and Kevin McNamara, were there to greet them and ferry them on fleets of buses to surrounding penguin and seal colonies. It was good to see them both – and others – again. I regretted not being able to find John Smith, but was glad to see that his Falkland's War Museum was still going strong and attracting loads of visitors.

Checkers and bowls

"I hope you don't think you're going to sit around under my feet all day!" Mollie admonished firmly as retirement loomed. "I have things to do and people will be coming in for coffee and a chat."

"Perish the thought," I told her. " I have my own plans."

Some years before, when I'd built a new garage behind the house, I'd added an extra room at the back to serve as study, den and as a quiet retreat. It was a snug little spot, complete with a deep-pile Wilton carpet, convector heater and fluorescent lights. The walls were lined with purpose-built bookshelves. I was still determined to read as many of my accumulated books as possible and time was something I now had in abundance There was a desk for my computer and printer and a couple of comfortable chairs. Sheer bliss.

While in the den I dug out some old draughts books and started on a serious study of the ancient pastime. There's a lot more to the game than people realise. Like most pursuits I take up, I put a lot into it, but it was enjoyable. In all, I won two Northern Ireland Championships and five County Down titles, and played on a winning Irish team against England. For a time I made a holiday of attending various tournaments across the water and played against people from all over the world by correspondence and later via the internet.

My football and cricketing days long behind me, I took to outdoor bowls in the summer and played the indoor version at the Jim Baker Stadium outside Antrim, and Shaw's Bridge, Belfast in winter.

The Lagan Valley outdoor green was just around the corner from home and most weekdays in summer I would have a couple of hours' solitary practice in the mornings, when I generally had the place to myself, then return for more friendly practice in the afternoons, before a league or cup match in the evenings. There was usually a NIBA league match on Saturday afternoons. If the green hadn't been locked on Sundays, I'd probably have been down there as well.

Starting work on the GIN

Even before I'd quit work officially, I'd spent a lot of time thinking what my book should be about. From everything I'd read and been told, my story ought to be about a subject I knew and was familiar with. That seemed sensible enough. Like most old hacks, I reckoned I knew a fair bit about a lot of things, and probably not a lot about anything in particular.

On a succession of walks with the dog an idea began to crystallize. I'd been a newspaperman and broadcaster in the early days of the *troubles*. I'd been involved for years with politicians, the police and the army. I'd even had a few contacts with terrorists from both sides of the fence. Why not pull all these elements together into a stirring tale?

I liked the notion – now all I needed was a peg to hang it on. It had to be believable, yet different from all the myriad books that had already been written about the woes of this old country of ours. Why not aim high? Why not go for broke and produce a tale of a search for something that had so far proved unobtainable. My story would be about a search for peace – the equivalent of an Irish Holy Grail?

It was the one thing that everyone in Ireland wanted more than any other, and one which had eluded generation after generation. Peace! And not merely peace, but peace with justice.

The dog got quite a few more walks before the idea really began to take shape. I got into the habit of taking a small digital recorder with me on my rambles and logged ideas as they came to mind. Most were discarded, until one day something clicked.

Suppose a journalist, a soldier, a policeman and a politician became so appalled by yet another unspeakable terrorist atrocity in Ulster - and the authorities' apparent inability to deal with it and bring the perpetrators to justice – that they decided to take action themselves, even if it meant stepping outside the law?

The more I thought about it the more I liked it, and I spent the next few weeks giving my four lead characters names, identities and personalities. Then I fell to plotting the story, adding as many twists and thrills as I could come up with. I took advantage of the fact that I still had access to all departments in the Headquarters to check facts, figures and details and it was during this phase that I landed myself in trouble.

It came about like this. Part of my story involved the kidnapping of the Irish President, who was to be held hostage. I needed to find out if there was a drug with no harmful after-affects which would put her to sleep for a few hours. I put the problem to the Chief Medical Officer, who sucked his teeth for a while before saying, "I'll need to check up on this for you, Brad. There may be some new stuff they're working on which I'm not aware of. Tell you what, I'm due to attend a conference in Bart's in London next week and I'll check it out for you."

A week later I had a call from the Colonel who headed the G2 Security Dept. asking if I'd step up to his office on the first floor. He rose from his desk as I entered and waved me to a seat. I knew him fairly well, although our paths didn't cross often. We tended to leave the likes of him and his *spooks,* as we called them, to their own twilight world. A tall, serious-faced civilian in a dark, pin-striped suit and striped tie was seated in the corner. He made no response when I nodded to him and we were not introduced.

The Colonel didn't beat about the bush. "Brad, would you mind telling us what the bloody hell's going on and what you're up to!"

To say I was gobsmacked was putting it mildly. I had no idea what he was on about, and one look at his face must have told him so. "I'm sorry, but I'm afraid I don't know what you mean," I managed at last.

"I mean this business of looking for a drug to be used in the kidnapping of the Irish President. The shit has really hit the fan in London and I've been tasked to investigate you. So I say again, what in God's name is going on?"

The penny suddenly dropped. My MO friend had obviously ruffled a few feathers across the water when he relayed my question about a knock-out drug. I honestly didn't know whether to laugh or cry, but the stern faces of the other two plainly indicated that they didn't consider this was any laughing matter.

So I started at the beginning, explained that I would be retiring shortly and intended writing a novel about the troubles, part of which concerned the kidnapping of the Irish President by the Provisional IRA. I had tried to get information about a drug they might make use of to help accomplish this. I added that the book was at the planning stage and that I didn't intend to begin writing it until I was retired.

The Colonel relaxed visibly and even managed a terse half-smile. His companion, apparently unimpressed, leaned forward and spoke for the first time. "Mr Fleming, as a signatory of the Official Secrets Act, are you aware that any such book would require official clearance?"

I swivelled to face him. "Of course. As I say, I haven't started writing it yet. When it's completed, I intend submitting it for checking in the usual way."

His face devoid of all expression, he responded in clipped tones. "I shouldn't be in any rush, if I were you. You clearly have a vivid imagination. We wouldn't want to float too many bright ideas of this kind abroad at the moment. One never knows who might decide to act upon them. Might be a plan to wait a year or two."

They say a nod is as good as a wink. As it turned out, I finished the book within the year, then, for reasons totally unconnected with my *spook* friend's thinly-veiled threat, pushed it to the back of my desk drawer and more or less forgot all about it.

It lay there gathering dust for sixteen years until, having related the story to a number of friends, and having nothing better to do, I yielded to their appeals to have it published. So you see – it's their fault really. The story, titled *Role of Dishonour*, was published in paperback and e-book form, in 2012 and later by Master Koda Select Publishing, and is available in the USA and UK at Amazon and Amazon Kindle.

A parting of the ways

Life was drifting along its seemingly predictable orbit when, in 1997, an event occurred which swept me off on a completely different tangent and changed my life at a stroke.

Looking back, I believe that almost without realising it, Mollie and I had been drifting apart for some time. A good wife and mother, she had never shown any particular interest in my work. To be fair, there was a lot of it I couldn't talk to her about in any case. Long hours at work, and the likelihood of being called out at all hours, scarcely contributed to marital bliss.

When I finally stopped working, I remembered her remark about not wanting me under her feet all day. Although realising that, because of my other interests, there was little danger of that, there were many occasions in the future that I was to recall that comment.

A work colleague of Mollie's had helped kit me out with a set of bowling gear. I suggested she should join me in the bowling club and made her a present of some bowls, shoes and an outfit of her own. We practised together for a while, but it was never really her cup of tea. Eventually she said she didn't want to play anymore.

We would go out occasionally to listen to Barry and the *Keynotes* perform, usually in the company of friends. Other than that we seemed to have different interests. Nevertheless, it came as a surprise when one evening, as we were driving to the annual dinner of our Liar Dice Group in Ballynahinch, she said "You know Brad, I think the house is a happier place when you're not in it."

Thinking I'd misheard, I said, "Excuse me?"

She repeated the sentence, virtually word for word. I sat silently for a moment. This was totally unexpected. Eventually I said, "Well, if that's how things are, then perhaps I ought to leave."

That was all. Nothing more was said and we didn't raise the subject again, either during the dinner or as we drove home afterwards. That was it. There was no argument, no angry words. It was almost surreal.

I'd made friends on the internet with some members of a social group and we'd chat occasionally, usually in a small group, but sometimes on a one to one basis. One of them, Sara Morgan, a chartered accountant who lived in Earith, a tiny village half an hour's commute from Cambridge, had been particularly kind a few months previously when I'd had to fly to England at short notice to make arrangements for the funeral of my Uncle Jim, who'd passed away after a short illness at the age of 94.

Sara, whom I'd only talked to on-line and on the phone and had never met, insisted on picking me up at Stansted Airport and driving me to the crematorium in Norwich. She also invited me to stay at her home in Earith until all the funeral arrangements had been completed, before driving me back to the airport. I was enormously grateful and we'd kept in touch since.

Still at something of a loss at Mollie's comment, I suppose I needed someone to talk to. It's sometimes easier to converse online than face to face. Three or four nights later Sara and I were chatting and she must have sensed that something was amiss, for she asked me outright if anything was wrong. I found myself telling her the whole story.

We talked for a long while until finally she said, "You know Brad, if it helps at all, you're welcome to come over here and stay for a while."

This was an extremely generous offer. I thanked her and asked if I could have a day or so to think things out. As matters stood, there didn't appear to be a viable alternative.

I did some serious thinking in the next couple of days. After speaking again to Mollie and Sara, and putting Val and Barry in the picture, it was agreed that I should go to England for a period of three months, after which Mollie and I would meet to decide what to do from there.

The incredible thing was that I can't recall Mollie and I having a single cross word on the subject. As I remember, it was referred to only twice, once when she repeated her observation that the house was a happier place without me, and another time when she said "You really don't have to leave, you know."

I looked at her steadily and said. "I think I do, Mollie. Perhaps in three months' time we'll both have a clearer idea of how we stand."

Barry, who had returned to live in Manor Drive after his own marriage had ended, hadn't a lot to say on the matter, and it was Val who seemed more upset than any of us. I made it clear to both of them, that whatever the eventual outcome, their mother and I both loved them very much and that would never change.

Mollie was understandably concerned about what was to happen to the house and I assured her that it was hers to live in for as long as she wished.

Before packing a few things in the car and heading off to catch the ferry, I saw to it that all outstanding bills were cleared, the central-heating tank was topped up and the electricity and rates were paid until the end of the year. There were more than sufficient funds in the bank to cover the period I'd be away. In any event I could easily be contacted by phone or post should anything unexpected crop up.

We had already told everyone who needed to know what was happening, especially Mollie's sister Jean and husband Billy. We drove to Kilkeel and broke the news to Tony and Pat. It must have come as a huge surprise to them, as well as to our other friends and neighbours. I had a long private talk with Tony, who expressed the hope that this particular cloud would blow over quickly and that things would soon be restored to normal. We promised to keep in touch as usual and I said I'd call and see him when I returned.

A journey into the unknown

I had booked on an early-morning ferry to Stranraer and planned on reaching Earith around mid-afternoon. I made an early start, making as little noise as possible so as not to awaken anyone. I looked into Barry's room. He was snoring gently so I simply patted his shoulder gently. Mollie too was asleep. I stood looking down at her for a few moments, then kissed her lightly on the cheek and went out, closing the door softly behind me.

A good part of the journey was familiar to me as it had been a major portion of my route to and from Germany. I'd always done much of my thinking behind the wheel of a car and this was no different. My thoughts were jumbled and unclear. There were mixed feelings of regret, loss and sadness, as well as considerable uncertainty as to what lay ahead. I could only hope things would become clearer over the next three months. I'd just have to wait and see.

Sara had taken the day off and was busy hoovering when I arrived just before four o'clock. She downed tools and made us a cup of tea. Then we sat facing one another before both starting to speak at once. After a little time, we became more relaxed. She asked about Mollie and the family and how they felt about events, and if my journey had been trouble-free. I thanked here for putting me up and wondered what her parents thought of it all.

She said her Mum and Dad, John and Kathleen, had invited us for dinner that evening. They had a place in St Ives, the nearest town, about five miles away. I can't say I'd been looking forward to this first meeting and could not but wonder how they'd react to this complete stranger, some thirty years older than their daughter, gate-crashing their close family circle.

As it transpired I needn't have worried. Both of them were kindness itself and made me welcome. Whatever their private thoughts, they asked no questions and made no judgements. I liked them both very much for as long as I knew them. Sara had intimated that she'd simply told them we had met on the internet, had become friends, and that she'd invited me to come over and stay.

I didn't think it fair to leave it like that, so as soon as it could be arranged, I invited her dad, John, to lunch one day and put him in the picture as honestly and frankly as I could. I know how I'd have felt had our situations been reversed. We had a real heart-to-heart chat and I'm sure we both felt the better for it. A friendship began that day that lasted as long as I knew him.

Sara and I had agreed beforehand that all household expenses should be split evenly down the middle. With the typical efficiency of an accountant, she'd made a list itemising everything down to the last detail. We opened a joint bank account and deposited equal amounts each month. At the same time I opened a new on-line and telephone account in my own name with First Direct. I found them efficient and helpful, and I'm still with them today.

I explained to Sara that I intended returning to Ireland in three months for a final determination with Mollie. Beyond that, her guess was as good as mine as to what might happen.

"I hope you stay here with me," was all she said.

Sara

In many ways Sara Morgan was not an easy woman to read. She had a top job as a senior accountant and financial adviser to Cambridgeshire County Council, and drove into her office in the city every day, a journey of half-an-hour. We had a lot in common, not least a love of music and sports, and had both been followers of Liverpool FC for a number of years.

Thirty years my junior, she had made it clear from the beginning that she never wanted children, and that a conventional sexual relationship was not on the cards. In my rather peculiar situation, I was happy enough to go along with that. We did, however, share the occasional cuddle and enjoyed eating out, taking in a show or a movie once or twice a month.

On my first weekend we drove over to a Chris de Burgh concert in Stratford. He is one of my favourite artistes and it was the first time I'd been to one of his live shows. It was also good to see that part of the world again. I'd been there only once before. We also had an enjoyable week's break in the beautiful Center Parcs, near Sherwood Forest in Nottingham, swimming, playing tennis and exploring the forest on hired bicycles.

I was delighted when Val and Barry flew over for a short visit after I'd been in Earith for about a month. I think Val, in particular, wanted to reassure herself that all was well. As we drove them back to the airport I promised to come over in a few weeks. The last thing Val told Sara as they boarded their flight was "Be sure to look after my Dad for me please."

I think it was a difficult meeting for all of us and there were a few tears as they left. It was great seeing them though, and I insisted they phone to let us know they'd got back safely.

Mollie and I also kept in touch regularly by letter and phone, and I reiterated that I'd fly back for that clear the air talk as promised and hoped that we'd be able to resolve things.

Before that happened, however, a letter arrived from her one day informing me that she'd thought it over and wanted a divorce.

"What are you going to do?" Sara asked when she came home

from work that evening and I showed her the letter.

"Well, there doesn't seem much point now in waiting another month, "I said. "I'll book a flight asap, go back and try to sort things out."

She put a hand on my arm. "I'm sorry, Brad. You do know you're welcome to stay here as long as you wish, don't you?"

"Thank you for that," I said. "If you don't mind, Sara, I think I'll take a little walk. I won't be long."

"Would you like me to come with you?"

"No, thank you, not this time. I just need to think things through. As I say, I'll be back in a few minutes."

I suppose Mollie's decision wasn't entirely unexpected. Indeed, part of me had reasoned it would come down to something like this in the end. Her letter surprised me though. I thought we'd at least have a chance to talk things over face to face before a final decision was taken.

Divorced

I flew back to Northern Ireland a few days later. There was a lot to be done. I stayed with Val and John, both of whom were understandably upset at developments. John, himself, had been through a divorce before his marriage to Val, so he had a fair idea of how I felt.

I took Mollie out to dinner at one of our old haunts in Hillsborough and we talked through the whole thing amicably enough. After all, neither of us saw any need for recriminations. I told her I'd honour my promise that she could have the house, which I know put her mind at ease to a great extent. I appreciated the thought of losing it, or of it being sold, had worried her. I also said I would agree to as generous a financial settlement as I could manage. Apart from a few books and some personal effects, she could have all the furnishings and fittings in the house as well.

I saw my solicitor several times and he promised to set proceedings in train as quickly as possible. There would be forms to be filled in periodically and he asked me to send him a typed statement outlining my side of things. He estimated that matters should be finalised in about twelve months, and so it proved.

I closed our joint bank account, leaving it in Mollie's name and told her that if anything unexpected turned up she shouldn't hesitate to get in touch. Barry, and John and Val enquired if it would be all right to come and visit and I replied that of course it would. I also assured them I'd pop back to see them at regular intervals.

A new home and new friends

Sara was glad to have me back and I was pleased to note that she appeared much more relaxed and at ease now that there was no immediate prospect of my returning to Ireland. We became more of a couple than had formerly been the case. Perhaps it was because she felt she was no longer living with a man who was still married to someone else.

As if to put some sort of unofficial seal on our new standing, we decided to buy a dog. We travelled down to a kennel near Bedford and came home with a seven-week old golden Labrador we named Holly. Like all of her kind, she led us a merry dance until we got her house-trained, but she was a lovable, adorable, bundle of fun and was great company for me while Sara was at work. Holly and I enjoyed a couple of long hikes every day and she delighted in carrying my daily newspaper in her mouth while trotting by my side.

Sara's only sister, Alison, would call to see us periodically and at first would make great play of the age difference between us; but once she discovered that it didn't bother either of us, she let it drop. The same went for Sara's own social circle. Whatever they may have thought privately, I was quickly accepted as one of the gang.

I was delighted when Sara's dad invited me to join both his indoor and outdoor bowling clubs. Although he never said as much, I sensed he was quite relieved at the news of my impending divorce. The St Ives Bowling Club was steeped in history, and as well as fielding two teams, also had a lively social membership. After a couple of matches for the second team, I quickly graduated to the firsts.

The club had teams in the Huntingdon Indoor Stadium, which was some 25-minutes away, so I was well catered for all twelve months of the year. I still have a splendid collection of trophies and silverware at both team and individual level.

Most enjoyable of all, perhaps, was being invited into the inner sanctum of the St Ives Club's private domino league where the venerable old game was contested with a kind of cheerful, but cutthroat ferocity. It was tremendous fun and I shall never forget colleagues like Norman Pipe, Cyril Barret and Ivor Smyth, with whom I shared many memorable sessions. Unlike my old club in Lisburn, there was a well-stocked bar, so everyone could enjoy an after-match glass of beer.

John and I took turns at driving to and from the Huntingdon Stadium and we usually went out to lunch once a month. Norman Pipe, a retired police inspector, and I shared many a laugh and kept in touch for years afterwards. Sadly, both he and John died some time ago. It always leaves a huge gap when good friends pass on, and I seem to have lost more than my share over the years.

The new house

"I see they're building some new houses over in Bluntisham," Sara remarked over dinner one evening. "What do you say we drive over and take a look? I understand they have a number of fully-furnished show houses."

"Why not?" I agreed, although I was perfectly content where we were and we'd even had a few improvements carried out.

Bluntisham was little more than a cluster of houses two miles up the road towards St Ives, It had a couple of pubs, a few shops and a filling station. That was all. The new houses were being built in a quiet area close to the village cricket field, with a public right-of-way running all the way down to Earith. "Good walking country for Holly," Sara said.

There were three types of house and it soon became clear that Sara had set her heart on a four-bedroom two-storey, with a spacious entrance hall and wide staircase ascending to a wrap-around balcony-landing. There was a good-sized kitchen, an attached garage and the master bedroom had a well-appointed en-suite bathroom.

The agent who escorted us round wasn't in the least pushy and happily assented to our coming back to have a second look. "There's no question that it's a great house and a good investment," Sara enthused as we drove home.

Given our age-difference, she had every right to be more concerned about the future than I had. I didn't need another investment and was content to have things remain as they were. "You're the accountant," I said. "I'll go along with whatever you decide."

Sumerling Way was one of those developments, where once a deposit had been made, purchasers were able to choose their own fittings and interior design. It wasn't long until Sara was studying brochures and touring around leading stores in Cambridge looking at carpets, furniture, curtains and the like. I dutifully tagged along on a few of these safaris, and generally let her get on with it.

"You might show a little more enthusiasm," she chided me once, in what developed into our first real tiff. All I could do was repeat that, within reason, I'd back any decision she made.

To give Sara her due, she put her heart and soul into the project. She did her sums, had the Earith house valued, and talked her bank manager into agreeing a mortgage which she declared was more than favourable and a great investment for the future.

When she came up with a set of figures and handed me a copy of her calculations, I did some figuring of my own. From my own point of view, I could afford it – just. But did I really want such a commitment? Apart from anything else, the solicitors hadn't come up with a final divorce settlement yet.

One evening I asked Sara straight out "What kind of future do you see for us, long term I mean?"

She looked at me for a long time. "You're concerned about committing to the new house, aren't you, Brad?" she said. "I can tell, and I do understand. It's a big step."

"Put it this way," I said sombrely, "I'm not likely to be around by the time the mortgage is paid off!"

She rose at once and engulfed me in an enormous hug. Her eyes were moist. I'd never seen her cry before. Pushing me away to arm's length, she clasped my shoulders and said, "You mean a great deal to me, Brad. We began as friends, but you're being here has changed that. I love you. I want us to share this house together,"

Our embrace lasted a long time. It was an emotional moment.

A little later, when things had more or less returned to normal, I said, half in jest, "That wasn't a proposal back there, was it? I'm not sure I want to get married again – at least not until after a decent interval."

I smiled as I said it, hoping she understood the remark about marriage had been a joke.

She looked deadly serious as she replied. "I just want us to be together, and have a nice home of our own."

We signed the purchase documents a few days later.

Moving in

They say that moving house is one of the most traumatic experiences in life. Perhaps it is, but settling into number 21 Sumerling Way was relatively straight-forward. It helped that our new home was only a couple of miles away and we could move a lot of our clothing and smaller stuff by car.

A couple of friends, Jon and Jane, helped us and brought their large van to move furniture. He also helped me dismantle our garden shed and reassemble it in the new back garden. In no time at all we were sitting on our new lounge suite and enjoying four fish suppers and a celebratory drink.

Holly settled in immediately, having sniffed everywhere in sight and explored the large back garden. As already stated, there were any number of exciting walking trails within easy reach. She also loved retrieving her rubber ball on the expansive cricket field.

We embarked on a number of shopping sprees. I bought a few bookcases and was able to sort out the sizeable collection of books I'd brought from Ireland. There were many excellent bookstores in Cambridge and my library continued to grow apace.

One of the back bedrooms was transformed into a study-cum den, with twin desks for our computers and communal printer. Sara was a real whizz with computers, and having already built her own, soon put together a new purpose-built model for me. It was good to re-establish contact with internet friends I'd made in Ireland, and I was soon adding new ones almost every day from all parts of the world.

Candy van Olst

One of my new friends was Candy van Olst, a professor of English from South Africa whose on-line name was Shirley Valentine, from the popular film of a year or two before. She is one of the handful of folk from that period that I'm still in touch with today. By and large, internet friendships tend to be brief and as the old Irish saying has it, often fade away like snow off a ditch.

Candy and I seemed to strike a companionable chord right from the start, and as we continued to chat over time, it emerged that our situations were remarkably alike in a number of ways. I've said that it's often easier to confide in someone on-line than in the flesh and so it was with Candy. Perhaps it's because we inhabit different worlds, and in the normal course of things, are never likely to meet.

In Candy's case, as indeed with Sara, the exception proved the rule. I was in the throes of a divorce and, from what she told me, Candy seemed to be heading in the same direction. The coincidence went even farther. I had gone to England to meet Sara; Candy was contemplating flying to England to meet a man she knew on-line. But more than that, she intended visiting him for a brief weekend before returning to South Africa. Who said romance is dead? She promised to let me know on her return how the clandestine meeting had gone.

Relating the story to Sara, I said "There you are now, you and I aren't the only crazy individuals in the world."

She smiled. "That's interesting. Please keep me posted on developments."

Next time we spoke, Candy brought me up to date. She'd met this fellow as arranged, after he'd kept her waiting for several hours. The encounter had left her with mixed feelings and she wasn't sure what lay in store. I could certainly sympathise.

Candy and I continued to chat in the following months and her story gradually unfolded until the day she announced that she and her husband were separating and she was moving to England to live and find work. Uncannily, she and I had become kindred spirits. I wished her well and hoped she'd settle down as easily as I had. We agreed the very least we could do was to meet once she'd landed.

Nip and Candy finally meet during a holiday in England.

She sent word that she'd arrived and had taken a place in Royal Leamington Spa, near Stratford. We could meet there if I wanted to. We fixed a time and place and I asked Sara if she would like to accompany me. "No thank you," she said. "You can tell me all about it later. Drive carefully."

I was anxious to meet my fellow adventurer, and sure enough, there she was, tall and blonde in a full-length black coat. "Hello," she said after a welcoming hug, "do you think we're quite mad?"

"Absolutely," I could only agree. Neither of us realised it then, of course, but it was the beginning of an enduring friendship. We slipped into easy chatting mode, just as we had left off on line. Such things didn't occur often in my experience. It was reminiscent of the relationship I'd had with Smithy some forty years before.

As befitted a lecturer in English, she was a self-confessed lover of all things Shakespearian, and her familiarity with the writings of the Bard put my own scant schoolboy knowledge to shame. She'd already visited the town several times and took delight in acting as guide as we embarked on a leisurely tour of what every visitor to Stratford ought to see.

We walked and talked a lot, then talked some more over a delightful lunch. By the time we parted and headed for home, we probably knew as much of each-other's potted histories as it was prudent to know. I felt I'd made a good friend and promised to keep in touch.

Happy anniversary

John, Kathleen and Alison joined us for a housewarming dinner in Sumerling Way. Sara made no pretentions of being a master chef, any more than I did, but between us we managed to lay on a reasonable spread. Our guests toasted us and wished us well in our new home. I certainly hoped they'd be frequent visitors and said so.

At the coffee stage, John announced that he and Kathleen were coming up to a significant wedding anniversary. A booking had been made and we were all invited to join them in a fashionable hotel in York to mark the occasion.

We were delighted to accept. I'd never been to the historic town and looked forward to the occasion with keen anticipation. I wasn't disappointed and we had a fabulous time. Once again I felt so grateful for the warm-hearted way the Morgan family had accepted me.

While Sara and I were both fond of music, with a few notable exceptions, our tastes differed. After all, I was a generation or two ahead of her. While some of my Irish favourites were not exactly to her taste, we did share a liking for moderns like Elton John, Billy Joel, Abba and especially Chris de Burgh. Having gone to that initial de Burgh concert in Stratford on our first weekend together, we enjoyed several more of his performances over the years.

We travelled up to London to see *Mama Mia* at the Ambassadors and to Wembley Stadium for what was to have been a joint concert by Elton and Billy. Sadly, the latter had to cry off at the last minute because of illness, but Elton gallantly put in a double shift which delighted the large attendance.

We also saw our share of movies, but Sara had a horror of anything containing too much violence. She refused point blank to accompany me into Cambridge to see John Cameron's *Titanic* because *"all those poor people were drowned."* Alison, sensibly, had no such scruples however, and happily accompanied me. We both enjoyed the movie, and its special effects, tremendously.

Aided and abetted by her father, I tried unsuccessfully, more than once, to persuade Sara to join me in the bowls club. She almost threw up her hands in horror. "Perhaps when I'm a good deal older," she exclaimed. I pointed out that there were several members half her age, but she refused to budge.

We were both keen to watch Liverpool play in the Premiership. Sadly, we never managed to get to Anfield, but drove to Coventry several times before the Blues were relegated. In some ways I almost wished she supported another team and we could have exercised a bit more friendly rivalry, but like me, she was a Red through and through.

Strong bond

My links with Ireland remained strong and I visited my old haunts several times a year, sometimes flying from Stansted, but usually taking the car for convenience sake. I'd stay with Val and John, but always took Mollie out for a meal and a chat. It was good that, in spite of all that had happened, we remained firm friends.

I met up with a few old colleagues from work and especially enjoyed travelling to Kilkeel to see Tony and Pat. Sadly, although my old friend wasn't enjoying the best of health, we always seemed able to pick up the threads of a conversation virtually at the point we'd left off last time. We had maintained a flourishing correspondence for years, always finding something new or innovative to say.

One thing I did regret was that I could never persuade Sara to accompany me on these trips. At first I believed it was a not unnatural fear of not wanting to be caught up in the *troubles,* but as peace continued to break out, I began to think it was simply a reluctance to meet Mollie face to face. In the end I let it go and stopped trying.

To be fair, we shared a good few holidays in other places. I enjoyed particularly a trip to Sheringham, on the East Coast, a typically English seaside resort, with lots of outings to Great Yarmouth, Cromer and Sandringham. The next year it was the Lake District. We took a country cottage and used it as a base for taking in that wonderful scenery. An added delight was that we were able to bring Holly along and she seemed to enjoy it every bit as much as we did.

Calypso time

"Do you know, you and I have been together for almost five years?" Sara said one day. "What about doing something special to celebrate?"

"Celebratory dinner?" I suggested.

"No," she pouted. "I'm talking about doing something really special."

"Sure. What have you in mind?"

"I've always fancied going on a cruise. But not just any old cruise – one to somewhere exciting and out of the ordinary."

"Like?"

"I've always wanted to go to the Caribbean."

"It would certainly make a real change from anywhere we've been up to now, but can we afford it? I've no idea, but I imagine it won't come cheap."

"I'm going upstairs right now to check it out on the computer."

She was as good as her word and for the next couple of evenings practically lived on Google. She finally narrowed our options down to a 22-night cruise on the recently launched P&O luxury liner *Aurora* to the West Indies starting three months hence in November.

It was quickly evident that this was going to the most expensive holiday ever – and I'm not only counting the price of the tickets.

"We're both going to need several new outfits," she enthused, clearly warming to her theme. "I'll need an entire new wardrobe and you'll have to get a couple of suits, a Tux, some shoes, half-a-dozen formal shirts, new ties and some lightweight summer shirts. We'll also need two sets of matching suitcases. I'd better make a list."

"Phew," I said, stroking my chin, "perhaps we'd better think about re-mortgaging the house!"

"Don't be silly," said Sara. "Just think about it, we won't have to buy any more clothes for ages."

"I doubt we'll be able to buy *anything* for ages!"

During the next few weekends we embarked on a succession of shopping expeditions to Cambridge, by the end of which my wardrobe was beginning to rival that of Scott Fitzgerald's *The Great Gatsby*. Sara was indefatigable, and to be honest, I left her to her own devices as often as I decently could. Shopping is not my favourite pursuit. To be fair though, I haven't had to buy a new suit since, and I still have a fair selection of those elegant ties and dress shirts, not that I often get to wear them these days.

The great day finally dawned and John kindly ferried us and our luggage down to Southampton and waved us off. Moored at her berth, *Aurora* towered above us – all ten decks of her - like some huge leviathan.

I'd done my homework on Google beforehand; the ship displaced over 76,000 tonnes, was 270m in length, with a beam of 32m, and carried 1,878 passengers and a crew of 936. Her service speed was 26 knots. There was no shortage of on-board entertainment, with three swimming pools, two large restaurants, a cinema, theatre, casino, shops, a library and an assortment of cafes and bars.

In contrast to her maiden voyage to the Mediterranean the previous year, which had to be cut short after just sixteen hours because of an overheated engine-bearing, our own cruise was delightful and trouble-free, from the welcoming cocktail party to the closing breakfast.

Our suitcases had been delivered to our cabin by the time we arrived and everything appeared to be in order. The cabin itself was well-appointed, and lavishly furnished, with a television set, separate bathroom and shower, and our own Juliet balcony from which we watched the twinkling lights of Southampton as we eased out of port into the Solent.

We shared a table for eight at dinner - our six fellow guests proved a companionable lot – and afterwards embarked on a fact-finding tour of the ship. There was so much to explore that I reckoned we saw less than half of it in more than two hours. Still, as there were three clear days before our first landfall, there was going to be lots of time to explore the rest of it.

Sara discovered that Claire Rayner, the agony aunt and TV personality, was giving the first of a series of talks the next morning and booked in for the whole course. I enrolled for a course of Bridge lessons, given by an international husband and wife team, I was partnered with Bob Robinson, a retired farmer from Yorkshire, and to our surprise, we went on to win the end of cruise tournament, and were presented with matching silver salvers.

There was no shortage of things to do on board and we were spoilt for choice in the way of after-dinner entertainment. We took in a film one evening but generally opted for a cabaret or concert. The first land we sighted was the Azores and the following day we docked in Funchal, the rather quaint capital of Madeira. We went ashore for lunch and a look around and Sara tried unsuccessfully to purchase a Madeira cake.

The weather was quite magnificent throughout, and we made the most of it, taking every opportunity to tour as many of the islands as we could. I particularly enjoyed Saint Lucia and Barbados, where, despite the application of lots of sun-block, I managed to get sunburnt on a trip in a pirate ship. A complimentary glass of rum helped to ease the pain.

I suppose the highlight of the whole voyage for me was an undersea trip in the mini-submarine *Atlantis*, after which I was solemnly presented with a certificate testifying that I had reached a depth of 135 feet. It was a wonderful experience as we cruised past the occasional sunken wreck and watched shoals of gaily coloured fish streaming by in the crystal-clear water.

All too soon the cruise ended and we returned to the chill of mid-December in England, with winter just around the corner.

Break-up

It turned out to be a chilly winter in two respects. First, the weather took a turn for the worse, and second, so did my relationship with Sara.

To be fair, while we had always got on well enough in our relationship, we had never been what could be called particularly close. Indeed, while it had never been spoken aloud, I'd quietly entertained the hope that the long Caribbean cruise would lead to a closer understanding and a stronger bond between us. Still, over Christmas and New Year we soldiered on much as usual.

After my small success in the *Aurora* bridge competition, the instructors had urged me to consider taking up the game more seriously and suggested I play on the internet whenever possible, nominating Microsoft's Gaming Zone as a good place to start.

I dutifully logged into the zone one snowy day and found it fairly intuitive. There were rooms for beginners, intermediate and experienced players. I opted for the intermediate section and selected a quiet corner. My computer screen showed a small table and four chairs. The instructors had said it was best to play against robots to begin with before progressing to human opponents.

There was a slot at the bottom of the screen where one could chat to other players, irrespective of where in the world they happened to be. Later I was to meet players from every corner of the globe. A cursor blinked at the bottom of the screen and I was invited to choose a non-de-plume. I chose *Seafarer*. After my recent voyage it seemed appropriate.

I was about to take on the robots when there was a click and the chair opposite me lit up. The cursor flickered and a message appeared. "Hello. I'm *Nip and Tuck*. Most people just call me Nip. How are you today?"

I realised I should have closed off the room and concentrated on the robots, now it was too late. "Hello to you. I'm Br... Sorry, I mean I'm *Seafarer*. This is my first time on here and I'm afraid I'm not quite used to it yet. It's all a little intimidating.

"Oh don't worry Sea, we're a friendly lot on here and you'll soon get used to it. Where are you, by the way?"

"I'm in England, just outside Cambridge, near a little town called St Ives."

"Oh, I think I've heard of it. Isn't that where the man had seven wives, who each had seven kids, who each had seven kittens?"

"Actually, I believe that's another St Ives, on the far side of the country. It's an old riddle from way back."

"You say this is your first time in the zone. Have you played bridge before?"

"A long time ago – and not very well."

"I'm sure you're just being modest."

This last was accompanied by a little smiley face. I related the story of the cruise and the advice I'd been given to play on-line. I wasn't sure if I would.

"Oh I hope you do. It's good fun. I've made a host of friends on here."

"I'll certainly give it a go for a while, if I can work out the system. May I ask what part of the world you're from?"

"I live in Wisconsin. It's in the Mid-West. It's known as the Dairy

State. Lots of grass and trees.

"Sounds wonderful. I'm from Ireland originally, a little town in County Down called Kilkeel, where the Mountains of Mourne are said to sweep down to the sea."

"That sounds special too, and I know the song. I've never been outside the United States, but Ireland is one country I'd really like to visit."

"Who knows? Perhaps you will one day."

We continued chatting lightly until I said, "I've enjoyed meeting you Nip, but I must be keeping you from your friends. Thank you for the introduction. I'll stay on here for a while and see if I can make head or tail of it. Enjoy the rest of your day."

"Thank you Sea, but I'm not in any hurry. If you wish we can close the table and play a few hands against the bots. You'll soon get the hang of it. Then next time you can play with real people."

"Thank you. I'd like that."

The time flew by. Before I realised it an hour had passed and I had enjoyed the games – and the company of my new American partner. I'd seldom met anyone more patient and she'd taught me a lot. When it was time to say goodbye and go back to the real world, Nip typed that she'd be on-line at the same time tomorrow. If I could make it she'd be happy to introduce me to some of her friends and we could have some proper games.

"Thank you, I'd like that very much. Allowing for the six-hour time difference that's going to be three o'clock my time. Is that all right?"

"That's ideal. See you then. Bye Sea."

"So long Nip."

We played a lot in the succeeding weeks, sometimes several times a day. I came to look forward to our meetings. I was introduced to two of Nip's special friends, Doolots and Happily Retired, both from the USA, and they became our regular opponents. As we say in Ireland the craic was mighty. I wasn't sure I didn't enjoy that part of it more than the actual bridge.

Nip and I developed our own little bidding system, which was loosely based on ACOL, and gradually acquired that telepathy which is so essential to top-level Bridge. She was an intuitive player, with an uncanny knack for hitting on the best tactic. While still playing with our friends in the Intermediate section, we also tried out the senior rooms from time to time, and as often as not, held our own.

The months slipped by and a lot of the evenings took on a

distinct pattern. Sara and I sat side by side in the computer room, she busy playing *Age of Empires* with her own circle of friends while I was enjoying my bridge. She usually retired at around 9:45 pm as she liked her full eight hours before her early start in the mornings. I'd often stay up until midnight or later and she would be sound asleep by the time I got to bed. We were inexorably drawing farther and farther apart.

Changing times

There's anonymity and a certain intimacy, about talking to someone on-line that can easily lead us into discussing topics we probably wouldn't dream of raising in face-to-face conversation; not least when our confidant is thousands of miles away and the chance of meeting them is virtually non-existent.

Quite often after a game, Nip and I would stay on for a while, lock off the room, and talk about anything and everything. She had great patience and understanding and was an excellent listener. Over time it emerged that she was in an unhappy marriage and sometimes came on-line in a bid to escape her troubles. I suppose it was a little like telling tales out of school, but after a time, I found myself talking about my own situation.

The only other person who knew how things were in my personal life, was Candy, who herself had had her share of domestic travails. Sara and I had met Candy in Cambridge and she'd stayed with us for a weekend. I'd also met her for the occasional Sunday lunch, usually in Oundle, the half-way point between Leamington Spa and Bluntisham and we'd visited a few places of interest together. We also chatted on-line once or twice a week.

That Easter I took a week's break back in Ireland, again staying with John and Val and visiting old friends. Sara hadn't offered to take me to the airport, so I left my car in the long-stay park at Stansted. She was upstairs on the computer when I got home. I dumped my suitcase in the hall and shouted "Hello, I'm back."

All I got in return was a lukewarm "Hello," and she didn't come downstairs to greet me as she normally would. There was clearly an atmosphere.

Picking up a couple of presents I'd brought back, I ran upstairs and handed them to her. I attempted a kiss, but she turned her head away and it finished as a peck on the cheek. One of the presents was a box of her favourite chocolates. "Don't you know I'm trying to stick to a diet!" she said coldly.

After a couple more abortive attempts at conversation, during which she didn't look up from her keyboard, I said, "I'll just bring up my suitcase."

Without turning her head, she said, "You'd better put it in the spare room!"

"What's the matter, Sara?" I asked.

That didn't get a reply. Nor was there one the second time I asked.

Apart from a wildly enthusiastic welcome from Holly, it was like entering Charles Dickins' *Bleak House* for the first time. Conversation was virtually non-existent over dinner, and to be honest, I was glad to escape to the club for a couple of hours. When I returned, our bedroom door was shut and Sara had obviously retired for the night. In all our time together that door had always remained open.

I looked around to see if she'd left a note. She hadn't. Reluctantly I headed for the spare room and lay awake for a long time, doing a lot of thinking. I could only conclude that Sara must have gone through my e-mail correspondence while I'd been in Ireland. She was much more computer literate than I and could easily have done so. I'd made no attempt to hide anything.

I tried to remember what I might have said that could have caused offence. I certainly hadn't set out to castigate, or denigrate Sara in any way, but simply described my situation as it was. I'd told the truth, without embellishment. Still, I suppose I shouldn't have done so in the first place. On the other hand, what is it they say about eavesdroppers finding out no good about themselves?

As calmly as I could, I asked several times what I had done to upset her. She made no reply. Finally, I said, "Well Sara, if I have offended you I can only apologise. It was certainly not intentional, but if you won't tell me what it was there's not a lot more I can say."

She left for work next morning without saying goodbye. There was no way the situation could be left as it was. When she arrived home that evening I saw at once that there were no signs of a thaw. Without a single reference to what it was I was supposed to have done, she made it plain our relationship was over. I could either leave, or stay on; in either case we would go our separate ways.

I knew her well enough to understand that, once her mind was made up about something as serious as this, there was no way she would budge. Anyway, I saw no point in arguing about it. The idea of remaining there in the sort of climate that had existed in the last

36 hours was unthinkable. I didn't want to leave – but there appeared to be no way I could stay.

"It's a pity you didn't tell me this before I went to Ireland," I said somewhat tetchily. "At least I could have looked around for a place to live. Now I'm going to have to go back and start from scratch."

After a few seconds she said, "You could always take a place over here. That way you could see Holly every day. Your other friends too."

I could have told her that would have been too hard to take. I could have tried to explain that the relationship I'd hoped to build with her had never materialised, and now never would. Perhaps I'd been indiscreet with a couple of on-line friends, but I'd meant no harm by that. Whatever I'd said was nothing other than the truth. I might have added that, had things been different between us, there would have been no need for any of this. There were a great many things I might have said, but I doubt it would have changed anything.

Oddly enough, I had no wish to apportion blame. If Sara had delved into my private mails, as I suspected, and discovered more than she'd bargained for, then so be it. I hadn't tried to hide anything and had written no more than the truth. Perhaps, as Jack Nicholson had famously declared in the court martial scene in *A Few Good Men,* she "couldn't handle the truth."

If only . . . maybe there were too many *if onlys.*

Sorting things out

There were many things to be sorted out. Sara and I had purchased the Sumerling Way house as an investment as well as a home. We had a joint bank account and were continuing to split expenses down the middle. I think both of us, in our separate ways, tried to make the best of an unfortunate situation. Deep down though, the soft-cantered Irish part of me regretted having to move on.

I arranged another trip back to Lisburn and Val, plainly delighted that I was returning, busied herself in contacting local estate agents and e-mailing me lists of likely furnished accommodation. I marked off half-a-dozen of these for later inspection.

I finally decided on a modern two-bedroom apartment in Benavon Court within a few minutes' walk of the city centre. It was comfortably furnished, with a nice enclosed balcony leading off the lounge. I'd promised to phone Sara as a courtesy before actually putting pen to paper on the lease, but when I finally did so her reaction was as cold as ever. Any lingering hopes of a reconciliation were dashed when she said firmly "I think you should take it."

For John and Kathleen's sake as much as anything else, Sara and I agreed not to say too much publicly about our separation. I simply let it be known that I'd decided to return to Ireland for personal and family reasons, which was true enough as far as it went. I said goodbye to a lot of good friends and promised to come back for a visit whenever I could.

There was a wealth of stuff to be moved, mostly books and bookcases, over 2,000 LP records, clothes and other personal effects. Apart from loading the car until it groaned, I forwarded a pile of crates and boxes via Pickford's. All the house moves I'd made in the past had had a purpose, something to be looked forward to. This time I was stepping into a future full of uncertainty.

I didn't go out on the night before I left, just put the finishing touches to my packing. Sara retired early as usual, and when I came upstairs shortly afterwards, I looked into her room and sat down on the bottom of her bed. "I don't expect we'll be seeing each other again after tomorrow." I said. "Would you like us to spend our last night together, even if it's only for old time's sake?"

She was propped up on her pillows, a book open in front of her. She didn't look up, nor make any kind of reply. I waited for a few moments before standing up. "Goodnight then, Sara. And goodbye."

I went out, closing the door softly behind me.

The last morning

I was up bright and early the next morning, intending to make a prompt start. I was surprised to find Sara already downstairs, still in her pyjamas. Usually she'd have left for work by this time.

"Would you like some breakfast?" she asked.

"I can make mine, thanks. I'm used to it."

"The kettle's on. Would you like some tea? Toast?"

"Thanks."

We sat on either side of our small kitchen lean-to table. This was strange. We didn't usually share breakfast, apart from weekends.

The silence dragged. It seemed there was nothing left to say. After last night I certainly had nothing to contribute.

Finally she spoke. "Will you ring me tonight and let me know you got home safely?"

I shrugged and made no reply, my thoughts suddenly switching to the bed already made up in my new apartment in Lisburn.

The silence deepened, almost becoming a tangible thing.

I rose. "Thanks for the tea. I need to collect a few things from my room, and then I'll be on my way."

As I stepped around her chair to get to the door she reached out suddenly and clasped my hand, squeezing it tightly. I tried to pull free but she held on fiercely.

"Don't you think it's a little late for that now, Sara?"

Again I attempted to pull away, but she clung on even more tightly. "Brad, you believe you're losing someone you think you love. I'm losing my best friend!"

She released my hand, slumped back into her seat, and began to weep uncontrollably, her entire body convulsed by huge sobs.

I hadn't expected this. This was the very antithesis of everything I'd come to expect of Sara. It was as if the cold veneer of insularity had crumbled away to reveal a vulnerability I'd never seen before. Instinctively I reached out and folded her in my arms. It was a long time before the crying slowed and finally stopped.

She clung to me tightly, head buried in my shoulder. I managed to disengage one hand, fumbled in my pocket and reached her my handkerchief.

"I'm sorry," she managed finally, "about everything."

"I am too Sara, but, as I said, it's all too late now."

She raised her eyes. "I do care about you, in spite of what you may think."

There were many things I could have said, but I contented myself with a simple "I know."

"You will ring me later, please. Won't you?"

"I will."

Jumbled thoughts

The familiar journey to Stranraer seemed to take forever. I didn't fancy listening to anything that was playing on the radio. I tried to get interested in a couple of audio-books I'd brought with me, but gave up after a while. An hour-and-a-half up the A1 I pulled into a service station for a coffee and reached for my cell-phone. I couldn't find it. Don't tell me I'd left it behind in No. 21. I couldn't remember having seen it that morning.

I found a pay-phone. "Sorry to trouble you, Sara, but I wonder if I've left my mobile behind. I can't seem to find it."

"Oh hello. Hang on a tick, I'll have a look."

I waited. "Sorry Brad, I don't see it anywhere. If you like I'll have a proper look later, and if it turns up, I'll forward it on to you. Your trip going all right?"

"Thanks. Yes, I just stopped for a coffee and can't find my phone."

I recognised that chuckle. "Were you going to call me then? Missing me already?"

"I've been missing you for a long time Sara."

Damn! I wish I hadn't said that. Silence. Neither of us spoke. Then "You will keep in touch, Brad. Won't you?"

I wasn't sure how to respond to that one. Finally I managed, "I don't know, Sara. I'm not sure there's much point."

There was another lengthy silence. I ought to have hung up. Then she said "Well, you have my number if you want to. Goodbye for now. Remember, please let me know you got home safely. Take care."

"You too."

I checked again for my mobile when I got back to the car and found it had slipped down between the front seats.

Double damn! Now Sara would think I'd used it as an excuse to phone. I drove back onto the motorway, wondering if I actually wouldn't have phoned from the restaurant in any case.

A fresh start

I pulled up outside Benavon Court just before eleven. I was tired, but knew from experience that I never slept well after a long journey, and especially not in unfamiliar surroundings. That apart, I still had a lot on my mind.

I phoned Val. She said she'd got me some odds and ends and would call down in the morning. She wanted to know if I was okay. "Sure," I said. I think I may have been lying, just a little.

I called Sara who answered with what I thought was indecent haste. "I hope I didn't wake you?"

"No, no. I wasn't asleep, just reading, waiting for your call. I see you've made it all right."

"Thank you, yes. I had a nice run up to Stranraer and a smooth crossing on the ferry. Just arrived a few minutes ago."

"Well, thanks for letting me know. In spite of what you think, I do care."

Shut up Fleming. Let it go.

"Right. Thank you for that."

"I looked for your phone by the way. Couldn't find it."

"Oh. Sorry about that. I got it when I got back to the car. It had slipped down between the seats."

"Oh, good. I hope you'll use it now and then to keep in touch."

"We'll see."

"Holly's missing you by the way. She has been running round the place looking for you all day."

"I'm glad somebody does."

Shut up Fleming, for God's sake. Leave it.

"Stop fishing for compliments. Will you let me have your landline number when the phone's connected?"

"If you want."

"I do."

"Anyway, I've got to get some stuff in from the car and grab some shut-eye. It's been a long day."

"Right, I'd better let you go then. I'm back at work tomorrow and have the usual early start. Holly sends her love. Bye for now. Take care."

"You too. Goodnight."

Back to the bachelor life

I awoke and for a few seconds hadn't a clue where I was. Sunshine was streaming in the French-doors and the sound of a delivery van was just audible through the double-glazing. I lay blinking at the unfamiliar ceiling before the penny dropped. I was back in Ireland, had had a thumping good night's sleep and was about to open a new chapter in my life.

Untypically, I directed my thoughts towards the future, rather than the past. There were lots to do and I needed to get cracking. A quick shower, followed by tea, toast and scrambled egg, made me feel a whole lot better. My mobile rang. It was Val, to say she'd be down in about half-an-hour. Was there anything I needed?

Typical Val, I was certain she was relishing the thought of looking after her old man again. I told her I planned to do a round of the shops later and she was welcome to join me.

First things first, I needed to get the landline phone up and running. Apart from anything else, I wanted to re-establish contact with my friends in cyberspace. Isn't it odd how much we now depend on the computer and the internet in our daily lives?

The doorbell rang and I trotted down one flight of stairs to find Alan Flowerday, my new landlord, waiting, clutching a potted plant in his hands.

"Just popped down to check you'd arrived and were settling in all right, and to give you this as a wee welcome present. And speaking of welcomes, the neighbours have invited you to a little soiree this afternoon. It will give you a chance to meet them, and no doubt for them to run an eye over you."

He indicated the building directly opposite, across the flagged driveway. "It's at Hester's, around three o'clock. They're a friendly lot, mostly female. I'll pop in myself to perform the introductions. I hope you'll be very happy here, Brad, and if you need anything, anything at all, you have my card. Please don't hesitate to call."

The party was fine and everyone was quite nice. I became friendly with Hester, a widow in her eighties. I think she was lonely, for she had few visitors. Often, when I drove home in the evenings, she would rap her window and beckon me over for a chat and a drink. It was she who explained the real reason for my original invitation. Apparently, their little consortium had a right of veto over aspiring residents. I can't say I altogether approved, but was nonetheless pleased to have passed muster.

Val was a tremendous help during those early days. Not only did she pop in regularly and invite me up for meals, she also accompanied me on shopping trips for essentials. Although the apartment was more than adequately furnished, I think she felt it lacked the feminine touch. I called to visit Mollie quite regularly and was glad we continued to be on good terms. Barry had by this time gone to live in England and we kept in touch.

I rejoined the bowls club and happily found most of my old friends were still active members. It was good to be re-united and play again with Des Harper, Fred Reynor, Jim Spence, Eddie Rath, Ted Cairns and many others. Unlike St Ives, the club had no bar, and there was no dominoes school, but it was good to be back, I spent most of my summer afternoons and evenings down at the green. In the winter most of us switched to the indoor game.

Des, who lived not too far away, would drop in for an occasional yarn and I was always welcome to visit him and his lovely wife, Iris. Life could certainly have been a lot worse. Just about the only thing I didn't care for was returning to an empty apartment every night. I'm definitely not cut out to follow a monastic lifestyle.

Communications restored

I was delighted when the phone line was connected, my new television set was up and running and I was able to log on to the internet again. It's amazing how much we now take these luxuries for granted. Simply being able to check incoming e-mail in the mornings, and read the news and sport, was tremendous.

The first person to greet me when I rejoined the gaming zone was Nip. "Welcome back, Sea," she typed, adding a smiley face. "We've all missed you. Now tell me all about what's been happening in the past week or so."

We chatted for a long time and it was good to play some more bridge and to meet our other on-line friends. After thinking about it for a while, I talked to Candy, e-mailed Sara and we also had a chat. I'm by no means certain that she was missing me, but she explained that Holly certainly was. It seemed she'd found an old pair of my socks and had carried them into her basket to sleep on. She was such a loyal little dog and I missed her terribly.

Nip and I were chatting one day, and I was recounting one of my little adventures in the Falklands when she said, a trifle wistfully "You know Brad, you're lucky to have seen so much of the world. I've never been outside of the United States. I'd love to have seen Ireland, it sounds so wonderful."

"Well," I said, "if ever you're within a hundred miles of Lisburn, do make sure you drop in for a cup of coffee."

"Thanks very much," she responded, "but I don't even have a passport, so I don't think that's too likely."

"Well Nip, you never know. Neither of us is getting any younger. Just remember the offer's always open. It would be great to meet up with you."

It must have been three months later that she reminded me of that particular conversation. "Sea, did you really mean what you said a while ago about my visiting Ireland? Were you being serious?"

"Of course I was. You'd always be welcome. But remember, you don't have a passport."

"I didn't then – but I've got one now."

"Good for you. You off on a world tour then?"

"Not really, but if your offer of a coffee is still open, I might just visit Ireland and drop by for one."

I wasn't quite sure how to respond to that, but I soon discovered she was serious – serious enough to apply for a passport, the first one she'd ever had.

We talked about the prospect of her visiting at considerable length. Did she intend bringing her family, or a friend?

"No, I just want to see Ireland – and you of course."

"Well, I'm sure than could be arranged. How long would you like to stay?"

"I've really no idea; perhaps a weekend. What would you advise?"

"A weekend!" I couldn't resist laughing out loud. "You're considering a round-trip of 8,000 miles and you intend to stay for just a weekend. How do you expect me to show you Ireland in a weekend?"

"I'm afraid I've no idea. How long would you suggest?"

"Nippy, to show you round Northern Ireland would take at least a fortnight."

"All right then, I'll come for a fortnight – if that's all right with you."

I typed in a little smiley face. "That's fine with me, Nippy, a fortnight is much more like it."

An American visitor

In the next few weeks Nip and I played a lot of bridge and did a lot of talking about her planned visit. I was concerned about her travelling all that way, never having flown, or been outside America before. I was also worried about what her family might think of her going all that way to meet someone she'd only known through the internet.

"My sister thinks I'm utterly mad," she confided, "and my husband, Ed, just says it's up to me whether I go or not. My two grown-up daughters are also worried. Apart from being concerned about the *troubles*, they have a sort of *Quiet Man* image of Ireland, with pigs in the kitchens and drunks on every street corner."

"Tell her that's only at weekends," I joked, "for the rest of the week life is pretty normal."

"I tell them I run more risk of being murdered or kidnapped on a shopping trip to Milwaukee," she rejoined. "They don't seem to realise more people are murdered in the States in a day than in Ireland in an entire year. Anyway, they have your phone number and I've promised to keep in touch by e-mail."

When her flight tickets were booked, it meant a long-hop journey from Minneapolis-to-Chicago-to-London-to-Belfast.

Photographs were exchanged for purposes of identification. "You'll have no trouble picking me out, Sea," she confirmed. "I'll be wearing a two-piece, bright pink suit to make doubly sure. I should arrive in Belfast mid-afternoon, but I'll ring from London to confirm the time,"

That all seemed foolproof enough, but things didn't work out quite as planned. Nip had forgotten to bring some Sterling coins for the phone, and the tight turnaround in Heathrow didn't leave time for her to visit the bureau-de-change, never mind make the promised phone call. All I could do was drive to the airport and take up a position between the arrivals gate and the luggage carousel. Now it was a matter of scrutinising the disembarking passengers and zeroing in on anyone wearing pink.

Wouldn't you know it? Pink appeared to be the dominant colour that autumn. Lots of females came and went, but none of them remotely resembled Nip's photograph. The most likely candidate was certainly attired in a shocking pink two-piece, but she was carrying an enormous bouquet of red roses and accompanied by a striking black man who must have been close to two metres tall. An attractive blonde walked a pace behind them. All three were engaged in animated conversation.

As the influx of passengers slowed to a trickle, I retreated to a padded seat to await the next flight. I was about to go in search of a coffee when I became aware of the woman in pink handing the bouquet to the tall black man and approach my seat.

"Mr Fleming?" she enquired in a soft mid-western accent. Now I had no difficulty in recognising her from her photograph and rose to greet her.

"Nip," I finally managed. "I noticed you just now, but you seemed to be with that black man and the blonde lady. I wasn't expecting you to have flowers and was beginning to think you'd missed your flight. Welcome to Ireland."

Homeward bound

After we'd collected her other suitcase and located our car, she filled in the blanks. "I'm sorry Sea," she apologised, and went on to explain why she hadn't phoned me from London. "There was so little time and I didn't want to miss my connecting flight. I just hoped you'd understand and be waiting for me."

"I wasn't too sure it was you, when I saw you with the flowers and that big black fellow. For a moment I thought you'd brought your husband with you and had forgotten to tell me he was black."

She burst out laughing. "Ed wouldn't thank you for thinking he was black. No, what happened was that I hurt my shoulder in a traffic accident some time back and that man kindly put my case in the overhead rack for me and insisted on carrying it when we disembarked. He and his wife – that's the blonde lady – are just back from South Africa where she was bridesmaid at a friend's wedding. So, while they brought the hand-luggage I carried the bouquet. They were both very kind."

It was a beautiful sunny afternoon and we soon cleared the airport and were heading for Lisburn. "Not to worry, Nip. The main thing is you're here. Did you have a good flight?"

"Yes, I did, thank you. The flight across the Atlantic was fascinating, I spent so long watching the little screen which showed the progress of our flight that I eventually nodded off to sleep and missed dinner. Do you know, we flew directly over Lisburn? If I'd had a parachute, I could have used it and saved about 800 miles!"

"I think you did really well for someone who hadn't the right kind of money. But you must be exhausted. Your room's all ready for you and I expect you could do with a shower and a bit of shuteye after such a long trip."

"Do you know, perhaps it's the excitement, but I'm not the least bit tired. It may catch up with me later, but if it's all right with you, I'd much rather we took a little drive and you showed me some of this beautiful country of yours. It's such a glorious day and I don't want to waste it."

"The forecast says the weather is set fair for the next few days. We sometimes get a nice Indian summer in October, or else – as we say in Ireland – you've brought the good weather with you."

After a quick stopover in the apartment, we were on our way again, this time up into the majestic Mourne Mountains, which Nip had only heard about. We drove through the heart of the mountains, stopping to take in the view at Spelga Dam, before taking the coast road home through Kilkeel and Newcastle. Long before we reached Lisburn she had settled back in her seat and had fallen asleep.

The jet-lag had finally caught up with her. She almost sleepwalked into the apartment, snuggled under a duvet and that was the last I saw her for about three hours. I waved away her apologies when she finally resurfaced. I knew only too well the affect a long flight can have, not to mention switching to a new time-zone.

She wasn't hungry, but a black coffee went a long way to putting things in order, and she was more like her old self when Val and

Philip arrived a little while later. I was delighted when the first thing Val did was to throw her arms around Nip and engulf her in an enormous hug. That was so typical of Val – Nip was my friend, so now she was my daughter's friend too.

The two of them fell to chatting animatedly about the flight and what she thought of Ireland. This was followed by an invitation to lunch the following day so that she could meet John and Jonathan.

Philip didn't have much to say for himself, but when they left an hour or so later, and Val gave Nip another huge hug, I was delighted when he clutched his mum and whispered in her ear. With a wide smile, Val looked up at Nip and said "Phil wonders if it would be all right to give you a hug too?"

When they'd gone I fancied I saw Nip dabbing away a little tear. "What a wonderful family you have, Brad. They make a stranger feel so welcome."

"You haven't met them all yet, but I suppose that's a fair sample. I don't think you need have any concerns about that, Nip. My family and friends will love you."

Last item on the agenda that first day was a short spin up the airport road to park and look down on a panoramic view of the ribbon of lights stretching like a twinkling necklace all the way down the Lagan Valley from Lisburn to Belfast. "Beautiful," was all she said.

Touring and sightseeing

Methodical to a fault, I'd pencilled in a prospective itinerary that would enable Nip to meet my friends and see as much of Northern Ireland as time permitted. At least I had two full weeks to accomplish the task, rather than the mere weekend she'd originally suggested.

That October laid on the kind of Indian summer we see only a handful of autumns in a lifetime. The weather was settled and it rained on only one day, the last Friday before she left. "You told me it always rains in Ireland," she pouted. "You totally misled me."

"If only you knew the trouble I had arranging all this good weather you wouldn't believe it."

We toured all the usual beauty spots, heading somewhere different every day, eating out for the most part as I lay no claims to cooking. She especially enjoyed a drive along the Antrim Coast Road and up through the famous Glens, culminating in a visit to the Giant's Causeway.

She declined to believe my account of how Finn McCool had

put it there, but at least insisted on dipping her toes in the Irish Sea, inordinately proud that she could now claim to have paddled on both sides of the Atlantic. When I pointed out that it wasn't the Atlantic, she insisted on repeating the experiment when we drove across to Donegal a few days later.

With the leaves already beginning to turn from green to gold, I reckoned the countryside was already cloaked in its majestic best. "It's not bad," she acknowledged as we skirted the Fermanagh lakes, "but just wait until you see Wisconsin in the fall."

The world of culture wasn't forgotten either, with visits to Belfast, and trips to the Ulster Folk Museum and the American Folk Park near Omagh. Surprisingly enough, she enjoyed our outings to Hillsborough Park, right on our doorstep, as much as anything, and she asked me to take her there several times.

Although the Lagan Valley bowling green was closed for the winter, we had a peek over the hedge and I endeavoured to explain the game that occupied so much of my time during the summer months. "Judging by all those trophies I've seen back in the apartment, you must be pretty useful at it," she concluded.

We had lunch and dinner at John and Val's several times, and I thought it was an especially nice gesture when Mollie invited us to Sunday lunch. I have to say the two of them got on amazingly well. Now Mollie is justly renowned for the quality and quantity of the meals she provides, while Nip would not claim to be a hearty eater. So I was mildly surprised when, having consumed a generous-sized dish of home-made broth, she accepted an invitation to another.

The look on her face when Mollie produced the main course, a heaped plate of roast beef, Yorkshire pudding, mashed and roast potatoes, and assorted vegetables was something to behold.

Having made a valiant attempt, she finally admitted, that, excellent as it was, she really couldn't manage another spoonful. She was promptly forgiven, and the three of us broke into an uncontrollable fit of the giggles, when she admitted that she'd thought the broth was the main course. "If I'd known this huge feast was coming, I'd have settled for just one portion."

If any ice had to be broken – which I doubt – that certainly did it and the two of them have been firm friends ever since. They meet regularly and phone one-another every day.

Sunshine and shadows

One of the truly special days of Nip's visit came on the Friday before she left for home. It was the only time it rained and we drove up to Kilkeel at the invitation of my dear friends, Tony and Pat.

Sad to relate, Tony had been in failing health for some time, and had really gone downhill in recent weeks. It was vexing to see my lifelong friend so grievously ill. Nevertheless, he and Pat welcomed us warmly and we enjoyed the usual banter and repartee.

After lunch, Pat drove Nip into town on some sort of impromptu shopping spree, leaving Tony and I to one of our customary lengthy chats. I have to confess to not fully appreciating the gravity of his illness and I little realised it was the last time we would ever be together.

He seemed to rally a little before we took our leave and the last words he uttered were so very typical of him, and of what we had meant to one another down the years. Already aware of Nip's religious persuasion, he escorted us to the front door, shook hands, smiled, and said. "Keep working on him, Nip. We'll make a decent Catholic of him yet!"

How I hate goodbyes

"I can well understand how you and Tony are so close," Nip whispered as we headed for home. "I like both him and Pat enormously. She told me so much about you and Tony this afternoon. Do you think he's going to be all right?"

I shook my head. "I hope so, Nip, but I'm afraid it's not looking good."

When I went in to start breakfast the next morning – her penultimate day in Ireland – I found her standing staring out the kitchen window, a faraway look in her eyes. "Don't worry," I said, giving her a peck on the cheek, "It's all right to be homesick. Quite understandable in fact. But you'll be back home with your family in a couple of days."

She started, turned to face me and looked right into my eyes. "Brad, you don't understand, do you?" It was one of the few times she hadn't called me Sea.

"What's the matter, Nip? What don't I understand?"

She shook her head. Her eyes were moist. "Brad, I'm not in the least homesick. Quite the reverse in fact. I've been so happy here these past two weeks. You especially, your family and all your friends have treated me so well, made me feel welcome. I kind of wish I could stay here forever."

"Thank you Nip, that's a lovely thing to say. But you should know that you can come back to see us any time, and stay for as long as you wish. Why not come over again next year? We'd love to see you."

The thoughtful look was replaced by a pensive smile. "Not a chance, Mr Fleming. Next time it's your turn to come over to visit me. What do you say to that?"

She held my gaze, eyebrows arched slightly as though repeating the silent question. What could a fellow do in such circumstances except to say "I think that just might be an idea."

I drove her to the airport the following day, in good time, as she had to book in ninety minutes early because of the lengthy security procedures. After checking in her luggage, there was ample time for a last coffee. She reached across and put her hand on mine. "Thank you for giving me a wonderful time, Brad, and for being such a perfect gentleman."

I tried not to look embarrassed. "Not at all my dear. It was an absolute pleasure. We were all glad to see you. I loved your company."

Suddenly she was very serious. "Brad, I truly meant what I said yesterday about not wanting to go back. I haven't loved Ed for years. Maybe I never loved him at all. I know I shouldn't say this, but I think I've fallen in love with you."

I hadn't expected that. "Nip, please don't say that if you don't truly mean it and haven't thought it through. I've been hurt pretty deeply and I wouldn't like it to happen again. I've enjoyed your being here very much, but deep down, you know you must go back. Thank you for what you've said though; it means a lot. I . . ."

She clasped my hand tightly. "Brad, I know something of what you've been through, and I would never hurt you. I wouldn't have said what I have if I didn't mean it. I believe I was in love with you before I came over to Ireland; the last two weeks have simply confirmed it."

I leaned forward and kissed her. "Thank you for that Nip. I wish we could have had this conversation when you first arrived. It would have given us more time to talk, to decide what happens next."

"I know. I'm sorry."

"Please don't be. Look, we both have a lot of thinking to do, and we have time. Meantime, keep safe and call me when you reach home. We have to work out what can be done. I'm a free agent. You're not."

"You will come over next year? Promise?"

"I promise. If you still want me to then."

"You need never doubt that, Brad."

I know we both had tears in our eyes when we embraced at the boarding gate. Nip turned and waved just before she passed out of sight behind the screens. I remained standing there for some time before turning to leave. I did indeed have lots to think about.

Emptiness

The apartment seemed strangely empty when I got back from the airport. Nip's presence had made such a difference. I ought to have been used to departures and separations by now, but I found this one surprisingly hard to take. That final conversation at Aldergrove had certainly changed my perception about things.

There were lots of questions – no easy answers.

I stretched out on the settee and thought about everything that had happened over the last two weeks. Nip's companionship, good nature, and sheer congeniality had brought home to me what had been absent in my life for such a long time. Even while I'd been living with Sara I'd effectively still been alone.

I was a free agent, responsible to no one, but did I have the right to break up someone else's marriage, even if I accepted Nip's assurance that it was not a happy one? The fact that she was Catholic didn't bother me in the slightest, although I recognised it might well pose additional problems for her. Was there even a possibility that the two of us might have a future together, or was it simply another of my silly pipedreams?

After an hour I decided it was all too difficult, and I was getting nowhere. I was thankful that Val had invited me up for supper and I'd be able to escape the apartment for an hour or two. A solution, if indeed there was one, would have to wait until another day. An old Doris Day song popped into my head. *Que Sera Sera*. Whatever will be will be.

Keeping busy

Things gradually drifted back to where they were. For a couple of weeks, I'd kept as busy as I could and spent as little time as possible in the apartment on my own. I knew I was being silly, but it's true what they say – there's no fool like an old fool.

Des and I were on a winning run in the bowls up in the Jim Baker Stadium. We were top of the Pairs League and had notched up thirteen straight wins. We used our cars on alternate trips. One day he said "That was a nice wee American lady you had over a few weeks ago. I liked her. Will she be coming back again?"

"I certainly hope so Des. With any luck I hope to go over and visit her next year."

"Good for you boy. She's married, isn't she?"

"What's that got to do with it?"

He shook his head, laughing. "You're a bad egg Fleming, you really are. What am I going to do with you?"

Nip phoned. She'd got back safely and was missing me. She thanked me for the visit and passed on Ed's thanks for the book I'd sent him. We fixed a time to meet in the Gaming Zone later.

After an enjoyable game with *Doolots* and *Happily*, we stayed on for a long chat. She asked me to thank my family, Tony and Pat, and everyone else she'd met for their hospitality. We concurred that we were missing one another, that it had been wonderful meeting in person and that my trip over to the States couldn't come soon enough. In the meantime, we'd have to be content to talk as often as possible, play lots of bridge, and try to communicate every day.

Tony dies

My great friend Tony Heaney passed away on Christmas Day. It was typical of him to choose a special day to go. While it wasn't unexpected, his death hit me really hard. Pat phoned with the news and I said I'd come up and see her soon. Tony and I had known each other most of our lives, had shared the good and the bad times that life brings, had played, worked and laughed together with never an angry word.

The next day I dug out a lot of our old photographs, some of them still displaying the trademark blue dye of which he'd been so proud. I re-read some of the letters, all in his familiar green scrawl, that he'd sent from Australia. I knew I would never have another friend like him.

Mollie, Val, John and I drove up to Kilkeel for the funeral and I helped carry his coffin down the road from his little house in Dunavil. How many times had he and I walked that road together; or ridden along it on our bicycles? I ought to have told him how much his friendship had meant to me, and I hoped he understood. I found it unspeakably sad that this was to be our last walk together.

Afterwards we called in to speak to Pat and the family. I held her close and said I was conscious of her loss, even more than my own. She asked that I would keep in touch and come and visit often. She gave me a handsomely bound book she had given to Tony years before. It was all about the making of the film *The Quiet Man*. "He'd want you to have this," she said. "I know you both considered it your favourite movie."

We kept our promise and visited Pat often, but sadly not for long. Two years later she too was gone - a victim of cancer. As with Tony, it was a privilege to have known her.

Accepting an invitation

I'd always wanted to visit the United States, but somehow had never got around to it. Now Nip's invitation had given me all the incentive I needed. I thought my globetrotting days were long gone, now that I'd retired from work, but it seemed the old passport was going to get another outing.

So it was that in June, 2003, I packed my trunk and took a flight from Dublin to Chicago. I know most Americans pride themselves that what they've got is bigger and better than anyone else's, but I had to admit that O'Hare International Airport was impressive. I gather it's a toss-up whether it or Heathrow deals with more passengers. I'd passed on my flight number and arrival time, but couldn't have bargained for the fact that five aircraft landed in the space of eight minutes.

The resultant scrum of passengers heading for immigration and luggage reclaim must have given a fair approximation of the Israelites' flight out of Egypt. It was all right for the Yanks. A blaring tannoy directed them to two quick exit channels. The rest of us had to queue for one of the remaining eight desks, only four of which were manned.

It took over an hour for me to run the gauntlet and be allowed through. I thought of poor Nip, waiting expectantly somewhere on the other side of the barrier, wondering if I was going to show. One luckless fellow passenger, who had flown from England to be best man at a friend's wedding, was devastated because he'd missed his connecting flight.

"Business or pleasure?" the po-faced character enquired when I eventually reached the desk and he was preparing to stamp my passport.

"Definitely pleasure," I replied, hoping I was right.

And there was Nip, waiting patiently. I didn't need a shocking-pink outfit to recognise her this time. The welcoming hug spelt out how much we'd missed one another. "It's good to see you," we said simultaneously.

The trouble started after I'd collected my case. Nip's Ford Focus could not be found anywhere. "I'm sure I left it right there," she insisted, pointing to a vacant space in a huge line of parked vehicles. We walked up and down several times. No sign of it. "It couldn't have been stolen, could it?"

In frustration we found the information desk and explained our predicament. The woman in charge was kindness itself and accompanied us to the scene of the crime, if indeed crime it was. Nip indicated the still vacant parking slot. "I left it right there, about two hours ago."

We trooped back to the information office and Nip filled in a double-page form. The kind woman assured us she would make diligent enquiries about the car and inform us immediately she had news. In the meantime, she suggested the best thing to do was to visit Hettz and book a hire car.

About to telephone Hertz and give them advance warning, the woman suddenly snapped her fingers and said "I've had a thought. Would you like to come with me?"

She led us up one floor to an identical parking bay. There, in precisely the same spot where we'd been on the ground floor, was the Focus! A red-faced Nip was full of apologies. "Don't give it a thought," the kind woman smiled and returned the form to Nip. "I don't think we'll be needing this now. I hope the two of you have a wonderful vacation."

"How could I have been so stupid?" Nip apologised as we drove out of the car park. "I'm so sorry, Brad."

"Don't worry about it, love. No harm done . . . Watch out Nip, you're going the wrong way! You're going to hit those cars!" I screamed.

"Relax Brad. Relax. We drive on the right in this country!"

The penny suddenly dropped. "Who's stupid now?"

We were still giggling when we hit the freeway.

On the Bridge beat

After an hour's drive we had still only reached the outskirts of the sprawling city and Nip suggested we stop at a Holiday Inn before proceeding the next morning. She had sketched in a suggested programme for my visit and the first item on the agenda was a three-day Bridge Congress which was due to start the next evening in

Rockford, a city about eighty miles away.

Nip was disappointed next morning to discover the Inn didn't provide breakfast. The problem was easily resolved by our driving a short distance to a nearby restaurant for a typical American breakfast of coffee, eggs over easy, waffles and maple syrup. I was already beginning to realise why so many US citizens had bulging waistlines.

A leisurely drive brought us to Rockford where, after booking into a hotel, we drove to the convention centre and registered for the tournament. I was surprised to find we were two of more than 850 entrants. "You Yanks certainly don't do things by half," I whispered to Nip.

I wasn't used to bridge on this scale but Nip and I did moderately well. I was amused when the organisers, on discovering they had a visitor from Ireland, interviewed me and published an article and photograph in the congress news-letter.

"So much for travelling incognito," I joked to Nip. "Now our cover's well and truly blown!"

"I wouldn't worry too much," she laughed. "No one here is likely to know either of us."

She was wrong. An hour later, Tess, a friend from Nip's home town bridge club, who had come down to act as a director for the tournament, came across and introduced herself. When a blushing Nip hoped she would be discreet, Tess beamed conspiratorially and chirped, "Don't worry folks, your secret's safe with me."

We worked our way through the programme Nip had prepared, playing some bridge, motoring to different places to take in particular sights she wanted me to see. Wisconsin is a beautiful state, wooded and verdant and is in sharp contrast to the neighbouring Illinois, which seemed more industrialised and is certainly a lot dustier.

I especially enjoyed Wisconsin Dells, where we took a day's boat trip and learnt something of the history of the Native American tribes who had once inhabited the area. Another favourite was a tour of the *House on the Rocks*, the incredible building designed by the famous architect Frank Lloyd Wright, who had constructed many of the country's most famous structures. Erected on the side of a sheer cliff, it took almost thirteen years to complete.

Touring is my favourite kind of holiday and I was delighted to see something new every day. The usual plan was to stop in a hotel or motel for dinner and hit the road the next morning. The accommodation was invariably excellent, and as most of the places we stayed had a swimming pool, it was good to have a refreshing dip before breakfast.

As a lifelong devotee of fish and chips, I was delighted when Nip treated me to a real American Friday Fish Fry. The ranchhouse-style hotel known as *Don Q's* was reached by walking through a real-live World War II USAF Flying Fortress. It seemed the original owner had piloted one in the war and later fancied the notion of owning one.

Dinner was out of this world. Imagine the best fish you've ever tasted. Then add heaped side dishes of salad, corn-on-the-cob, cold-meats and several varieties of potato. Try as I did, I couldn't quite clear my plate. "Nip," I said, patting my swelling stomach, "if I lived in this country I'd be the size of the average Yank in no time."

Our room had a round sunken bath, and while Nip luxuriated in it, sending suds flying up to the ceiling, I reclined in a comfortable armchair and watched Lennox Lewis wallop Vitali Klitschko in a world championship boxing match on HBO. Had I been back home it would have cost me around £13 on Sky. Here it was all part of the hotel service.

All too soon our vacation was over. It had been as wonderful as our goodbye at O'Hare International was sad.

"I could leave the car and come with you," Nip said tearfully. "I brought my passport, just in case!"

It was a tempting prospect, but we both knew it was a non-starter.

"We couldn't do that, love. It wouldn't be fair, and it would be no way to start a life together. But I tell you this. If you ever come to Ireland again there's no way in the world I'll ever let you go."

A break in the clouds

The empty apartment was even more depressing than it had been after Nip's last visit. A whole new batch of memories had been added to our little stockpile. Whoever had come up with the line "Absence makes the heart grow fonder" had only told half the story. He should have added "Absence can break the heart altogether."

We talked by phone or on-line every day. When we played bridge we talked there too. Neither of us had the slightest doubt that we wanted to be together. I blamed myself for not going back with Nip and explaining things to Ed. Hindsight is good at that sort of thing. Now I didn't think it fair that she should take on that task alone.

We had just about decided that I would fly over and we would talk to Ed together, when my phone rang early one morning.

"What's wrong, love?" I asked anxiously. I hadn't expected a call, knowing we were due to meet for bridge as usual a few hours later.

"Do you want the good news, or the bad news?"

"Let's get the bad news out of the way."

"There isn't any bad news!"

"And the good news?"

"When would you like me to come to Ireland?"

"What!"

"You do still want me to come, don't you?"

"You know I do. But . . ."

"There aren't any buts."

"Of course there are. What about Ed for instance?"

"Are you sitting down, Brad?"

"Actually, I'm in bed. I haven't got up yet. It's just gone six in the morning here."

"Sorry it's so early, but I couldn't wait to tell you my news."

"Fire away then."

"Ed and I were talking a little while ago. I guess I was pretty miserable. Anyway, he suddenly asked me what was wrong and if there was someone else. I couldn't help it, Brad. I came right out with it and said there was. He asked who it was and I said 'You know who it is, Ed. Then he asked if it was you and I told him, "yes."

"I bet that went down well," I interjected.

"Actually, he was quite good and calm about it. He didn't seem surprised at all. Its little wonder, I've been walking about the place totally down in the dumps since you left. He couldn't help but notice."

"Well, I have to say that's a surprise, Nip. What happened next?"

"We just sat there drinking coffee and talked it over. I think he had already worked it out that you and I were getting pretty close. He knew, of course, that we played bridge and talked in the zone most days. I guess he just put two and two together and made four."

"I can't help feeling sorry for the man. I know how I'd feel if the situation were reversed."

"Brad, as I've told you, I haven't been in love with Ed for years. Maybe I never did love him. I got married way too young. He was always a good provider; I'll give him that, but I think we both just learned to tolerate each other."

"So, where do we go from here, love? Do you think I should phone him?"

"I don't think so, not yet anyway. He's suggested that we go downtown later this morning and start divorce proceedings, then start telling our family and friends."

"He's not wasting any time, is he? Nip love, I realise this isn't going to be easy for you. You shouldn't have to bear the brunt of this. I wish I could be there with you."

"Don't worry, honey. This has lifted a great weight of me. I can't tell you how much I'm looking forward to coming to Ireland for good."

From a distance

The next two months flew by for Nip and dragged interminably for me. She had a hundred-and-one things to do, while all I had to do was tell my family and friends what was happening.

As expected, her announcement was given a mixed reception back home. To his credit, Ed accompanied her on her rounds and they broke the news together. I respected him for that. It occurred to me, as I mentioned to Nip one day, that perhaps in his own way, he had been as unfulfilled as she was. Who can say?

Nip told me later that some of her erstwhile friends gave her quite a bad time of it. Thankfully, her real friends understood and stood by her in support. She took great comfort from a lengthy conversation she had with an old friend, Sister Kate, a local nun who was a qualified psychologist. "Marjorie, you have done your duty by your husband and family, and by your Church. Now it's time for you to seek a little happiness for yourself. God will understand." What a sensible woman, I remember thinking.

Apart from her clothes and a few personal items, Nip asked for nothing when the divorce petition was heard. The judge was surprised and went so far as to order a stay of six months in case there was a change of mind. There wasn't. She even left her Ford Focus behind.

I made it plain that all her family and friends were welcome to come and see us in Ireland and stay for as long as they wished. Some friends did visit, but sadly, for whatever reason, none of her immediate family ever did. We made a three-week visit to the States to see family and friends a year later, but while she doesn't say much, I know she still feels acutely the fact that they haven't come.

I gave the apartment a good vacuuming and an extra clean up on the day of Nip's arrival, before driving to Dublin Airport to meet her. She had one suitcase and a holdall, and explained that she had forwarded some other possessions by freight. "You could say I'm travelling light," she smiled, "my heart is certainly the lightest it's been in years."

Halfway home she said she'd fallen asleep and missed dinner on the flight. So we pulled into a little café in Dundalk for breakfast. Nip drew a baffled look from the waitress when she ordered coffee and eggs on toast with jelly. I knew that Americans refer to jam as jelly, but had no idea that she habitually added jam every time she ate eggs. There were many little peculiarities of that nature we were to find out about each other. It made such a difference having her in the apartment, which soon took on the homely features that only a woman's touch can bring. My little bachelor pad was transformed forever – not that I minded one bit.

Having travelled light, Nip needed lots of new clothes and various odds and ends, so regular shopping trips became the order of the day. She was outgoing and made friends easily. In no time at all she involved herself in local activities like bridge and bingo and said she couldn't wait until the outdoor bowls started next year.

Dr Ruddle, my local GP, was helping in having Nip registered immediately, rather than having to wait the statutory six months. We also checked with Social Services and were told that if she was to stay longer than that she had to sign an on-line application form. Otherwise she stood the risk of being deported. Dutifully we completed the form, sent it off, and promptly forgot all about it. That turned out to be a near disastrous mistake.

Panic!

"Do you know," Nip observed one morning, "in another ten days I'll have been here for six whole months. Doesn't time fly when you're having fun?"

"Doesn't it just?" I agreed. "Which reminds me, we'd better contact Social Services to make sure your application has gone through all right and there aren't any problems. I thought we might have had some confirmation from them by now."

"I don't think they'd kick me out now, would they," she laughed.

"Not a chance."

An hour later we weren't so sure and had good cause to be worried. The application had not gone through and had not been confirmed. Furthermore, there were only eight days left to sort it out!

We made enquiries on line. No joy. We visited the US

Consulate in Belfast. They were sympathetic but it wasn't their problem. They suggested contacting the British Embassy in New York.

We did. Immediately. They were helpful too – up to a point.

"Do you intend getting married?"

"Yes."

"In that case you'll need a marriage visa. That will cost £450."

"That isn't a problem."

"It must be paid by accredited banker's draft."

"Again, no problem."

"And it must be handed in to our New York office in person by the applicant."

"Ah. Can't it be sent by registered post?"

"I'm sorry; it must be delivered in person by the applicant."

Utterly nonsensical red tape, but there was no help for it. Nip was going to have to fly to New York with the draft. A bloody nuisance, but at least things could be sorted. Thank heavens we'd discovered this business in time. "Good luck," I managed, as I waved her off at the airport.

We were grateful that Linda Madden, a good friend and bridge-playing partner, who lived in Long Island, had graciously offered to meet Nip off the plane and put her up during her stay. Nip phoned to say she'd arrived safely and they were driving to the embassy the following day.

"Good luck," I repeated and thanked Linda for her help. "Don't worry, Brad," she said. "I'll look after her and have her back to you before you know it."

I should have known it wouldn't be as simple as that.

A frantic Nip was on the phone again next day. "Oh Brad, we're at the embassy. They say the bank draft isn't valid and is not acceptable."

"Use your credit card then. We'll cancel the draft later."

"I've already tried that. They won't accept it either."

"Hell's flames. Let me talk to them."

I heard a muffled conversation on the line before Nip came back on. "It's all right, love. Linda's a dear. She's going to pay and I will give her a cheque."

"Tell here I said she's a star and buy her the biggest bouquet of flowers you can find."

Nip came on the phone again a few hours later. "It's all right, honey. Everything's been sorted, and thanks to Linda, we've got our visa. Now I have a question for you. You know I had planned to stay on here and do some shopping, and wasn't due to catch a flight back until Thursday?"

"Yes."

"Well, I checked flight times a little while ago and I can catch one tomorrow if you like. It will cost an extra £100."

"Catch it Nip. Just come home."

Nip borrows a hat and joins a group of buskers in Cambridge

Happy New Year

New Year's Eve and the rain was coming down stair-rods. Nip and I were tucked up cosily in the apartment. "Thank goodness, we don't have to go out today. I don't think I could face it."

I coughed. "Actually I have to nip downtown for a few minutes, but I won't be long. No need for you to come."

"Can't it wait? Surely there's no rush."

"There is as a matter of fact. The shops are closed tomorrow. You sit tight, I won't be long."

Having already carried out a reconnaissance, I was as good as my word, and returned in half-an-hour,

Nip hung up my sodden anorak and handed me a towel. "Well, whatever it was, I hope it was worth it."

"I think it was, love, but it's for you to judge. Now go and sit down please."

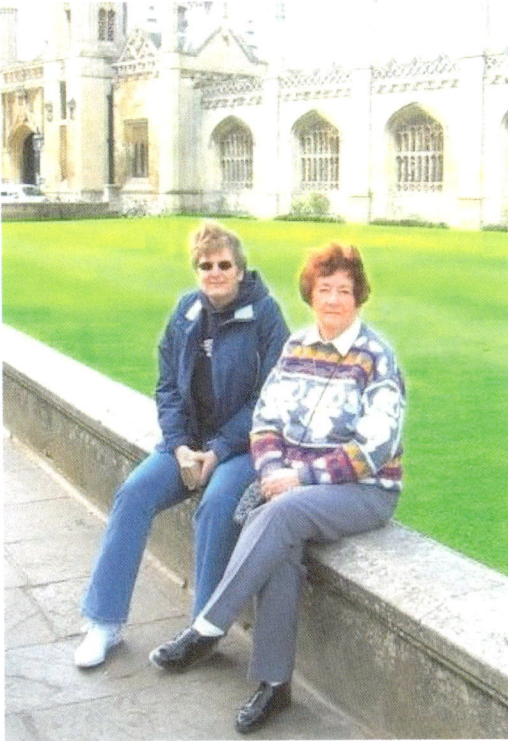

**Sara and Nip meet for the first time
during the same visit.**

As soon as she'd taken a seat, and feeling a total prat, I crossed the room and dropped to one knee in time-honoured fashion. "Nip, not only did you get a passport to come over here for a coffee a long time ago, you decided to come back again to stay. Now you've done another round trip to get a marriage visa. The least I can do is to make good use of it and ask you to marry me."

Wedding Bells

I produced a tiny square box from behind my back, opened it, and handed her a diamond engagement ring. "I reckon this was well worth getting wet for, and I hope you do too."

Her eyes were shining as she took it and slipped it on her finger. "Thank you so much, Brad, and happy New Year, darling."

"And to you, Nip, and many, many more."

Signing the register with Nip.

The outdoor bowling season had started and I'd introduced Nip to the ladies' section. She'd taken to it like a duck to water and was soon playing regularly on the team.

We were sitting watching one of their matches one afternoon, when Des remarked. "You know, that wee woman of yours is coming on great for someone who's only started. I've seen the two of you practising when you thought no one was looking."

"She enjoys it, Des. By the way, we plan to get married on the 18th of June. You and Iris are invited."

"Well done," he smiled, getting to his feet to shake hands. "I'm delighted with your news."

Ted Cairns and Eddie Rath came over to add their congratulations. "And you're invited too. You'll be getting your official invites in due course."

I was happy to leave Nip in charge of most of the preparations, chipping in only when required. We were out for a drive one day when she turned and asked "Do you think Mollie will want to come to the wedding?"

"I hope she does," I replied. "We'll certainly invite her."

She was silent for a few minutes before speaking. "You know, there's something I've never told you, until now. That first time I came over, Mollie and I had a long talk about you. I asked straight out if there was a chance that the two of you might get together again. I told her if there was I would accept it and back off."

"So, you had your eye on me way back then, did you?" I said, laughing.

"Of course. You didn't think I'd come all that way just for a coffee, did you?"

"And what did Mollie say?"

"She said the same thing you did; that the two of you were far better friends now than before, and she would be delighted if we ever got together. Of course, an awful lot has happened since then."

"Tell me about it," I said.

As Nip and I were divorced, a civil wedding seemed indicated. After some thought, we decided on the Island Centre in Lisburn. I have to say they did us proud and all the arrangements were first class.

Jeremy Brown, a Dubliner by birth, known affectionately to everyone as Toffee, a long-standing bridge friend of us both, insisted on travelling over from his home in England for the wedding, made an eloquent speech, gave Nip away and stayed with us for a week. My son-in-law, John, was my best man, and Sheila Buchanan, an old friend and fellow bowler, was Nip's matron of honour.

Nip and I were touched by a surprise gesture from the men and women's sections of the bowls club, who formed a guard of honour by each holding a bowling ball above our heads as we emerged as man and wife. Thankfully none of them dropped any of the heavy objects on us as we ducked underneath.

Toffee remained with us for several days and we didn't mind in the least delaying the start of our honeymoon proper. We took him on a number of sightseeing trips and I think he was genuinely sorry when the time came for us to drive him to the airport for his return

DON'T DROP IT! Lagan Valley bowling buddies provide a novel guard of honour for Nip and me after our wedding.

to Southampton. He and his charming wife visited us again the following year and later we spent a week as their guests. Sadly, he fell victim to Parkinson's disease and passed away some years later. He was a good friend and a wonderful man.

Day one apart, our honeymoon was blessed with glorious weather and Ireland was dressed in bright emerald green and looking at its best. I wanted Nip to see as much of my native land as possible and followed a coastal route for the most part of our journey.

We took in a delightful Percy French concert in Omagh and explored Donegal, Sligo and Mayo, before cruising down the west coast to Limerick and the Shannon. A look in on Blarney Castle was a must and Nip planted a smacker on the famous stone.

At the headquarters of Waterford Crystal, I bought Nip a handsome model of a rearing stallion and had it suitably engraved to mark the occasion. Among the other items on show was a handsome Cinderella coach and horses. It was priced at 24,500 euros and was beautifully done.

"Tell you what love; I'll buy you that for our golden wedding!"

DOWN AT THE BOWLS Sheila Buchanan, Nip's matron of honour, her husband, Sam. Ted Cairns and Des Harper watch the action.

It was a fairly safe bet, having just passed my seventieth a few days before.

Moving house

I came into the kitchen one day and was surprised to find Nip crying. She was standing at the sink, staring out the window, tears trickling down her face.

I hurried over and put my arms around her. "What's the matter, love?"

She pointed outside. "It's snowing. Just a little, but it makes me think of Wisconsin."

I hugged her tightly. "It's all right to be homesick dear, perfectly natural. I understand."

Nip and I have enjoyed many holidays in Scotland. Here we are on the west coast, with Ailsa Craig in the background.

"It's not that, honey. This is my home now. Back there the winters were hard, and the snow piled up really deep. This is only a dusting."

A little later she looked at me and said, "You know Brad, there are only a couple of things I miss here, apart from family and friends."

"What's that?"

"This is a lovely apartment, and I know we have a balcony and window-boxes for flowers, but I really miss my garden - and a dog."

The lease prevented our keeping a pet.

"Well, this is a nice convenient place, but we don't have to stay here you know. We could look for a house with a nice garden, big enough for a dog."

"Could we really? That would be ideal."

I mentioned it to Val and a few days later she called to say that a friend of hers was putting a house up for rent in Hillsborough, a pretty village three miles away. We arranged a viewing, liked it, and moved in two months later. It was a compact two-storey in Eglantine Park with a south-facing conservatory, attached garage and high hedges surrounding three manageable lawns. Nip fell in love with it right away. "Now all we have to do is find a dog."

We did – a bright, one-year-old rescued Border Collie she had already named Sparky in advance. He had apparently been dumped by his young owners when they divorced. He was nervous, wet the floor once, but settled down quickly. "That's it," said Nip. "We don't need another thing, except continuing good health."

Sadly, that wish was to be denied us both. Nip was diagnosed with breast cancer in the autumn of 2005, soon after we returned from a three-week trip to the US, this time to visit her family and friends. She was treated in Belvoir Park Hospital, Belfast, just before it closed down. Two years later it was my turn when I developed prostate cancer. This necessitated a course of thirty-seven treatments in the newly opened cancer wing of Belfast City Hospital. Thankfully, both of us have been in remission since.

I had just begun treatment when our home was broken into and our new Mazda 3 stolen from the driveway. We reported the theft to the police and it was recovered two days later. Unfortunately, because of a glitch in police administration, we were not notified that it had been found.

Needing to travel to Belfast daily for my treatment over a five-week period., we were put to the considerable inconvenience of having to buy and insure another car, only to discover the truth some time later when I received a bill for £1,136 from a car recovery firm who had been holding the Mazda in their depot for over six weeks.

After several complaints, the PSNI eventually apologised for their mistake and we were awarded compensation. But, all in all, it was a worrying and stressful time.

Over time, life settled down into what passed for normal in our little world. Mollie continued to live in Manor Drive and we visited her regularly. She had been joined by Barry, who returned from England and was pursuing his musical career. He was now composing as well as performing, writing what I considered to be really excellent material, based in my former retreat behind the garage, which he had transformed into a serviceable studio. Songs like Guiding Light and Household Honey were heard regularly on BBC and other stations.

**We've enjoyed many nights out listening to Barry
and his keyboard.**

Sadly, John's Parkinson's grew steadily worse, and he had to stop working. Val and the boys went through a really tough time, not least because she wasn't enjoying the best of health herself. To cap it all, Nip too was diagnosed with the early stages of Parkinson's. Talk about lightning striking twice!

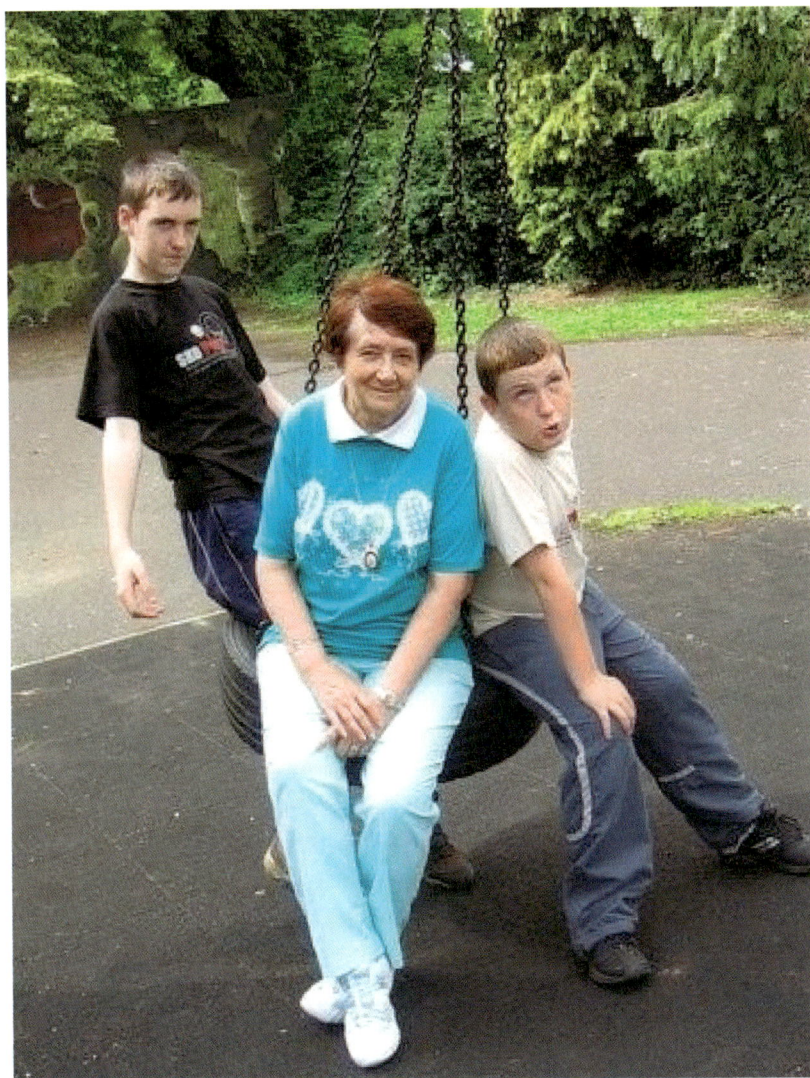

Nip gets to know grandsons Jonathan and Philip.

In February 2014 we moved house again, this time to Ashcroft Park, off the Hillsborough Road in Lisburn. It was more convenient in many ways, closer to the city centre and the shops and with good dog-walking facilities for Sparky down by the Lagan towpath.

Like most folk, we've had our share of ups and downs and been through some tough times, but, as we are fond of saying in Ireland, things could certainly be a lot worse. Of course, Nip has her own typical Yankee way of putting it. *"Life's a bitch – and then you die."*

I meet an old friend

My regular visits to the City Hospital led to one surprising development. Hurrying from the car park one afternoon I was hailed by a voice I was sure I recognised.

"Brad. Brad Fleming!"

Turning, I recognised the face immediately, although some years had passed since I'd last seen it. Joe McCoubrey, an old friend and colleague from my newspaper days, ran over and clasped my hand. I recalled that, years before, I'd given Joe an opportunity to do some sports writing for the *Down Recorder* and that he'd thrived to the extent that he'd eventually joined the newspaper and followed me into the editor's chair.

Both of us had lost some hair since our last meeting, but his smile was as warm and cheery as ever. It was good to see him. I was already late for my appointment, so there was time for only the briefest of chats and an exchange of phone numbers and e-mail addresses.

We made contact a day or so later. It was a fortunate encounter, and had it not happened, my life would have taken an entirely different turn. I wouldn't be writing this book now for a start!

During the course of several telephone conversations and e-mail exchanges we brought one another up to date with our respective lots. To cut a long story short, we'd both left the world of journalism behind us and had taken the first faltering steps at authorship; even if neither of us had yet to have a single word published.

By strange coincidence, our first attempts at novels had centred on the Irish *troubles,* and had followed remarkably similar themes

Joe was still working on his. Rather shamefacedly, I confessed that, after a gap of more than fifteen years, mine was still languishing in a box somewhere in my attic.

"You'll have to do something about that," he declared reproachfully. "Dig it out and send me a copy."

"Only if you send me a copy of what you've written so far."

That was the beginning. I revamped my GIN and he read it, corrected some typos and made a few suggestions. I did the same with his book, *Someone has to Pay.* We collaborated for months, editing, proof-reading, criticising, suggesting and encouraging. The great day came when his novel was published in e-book format and paperback. I congratulated him warmly. Shortly afterwards I released *Role of Dishonour* in the same two formats in both the UK and USA.

We exchanged mutual congratulations. It was akin to creating a child – well almost. We bathed in the warm glow of authorship.

"So, what's your next one going to be about?" Joe asked one day.

"What?"

I'd written a book – and had it published. That was it as far as I was concerned. Now I could go back to walking the dog, playing bowls, watching tele and reading someone else's books. Joe was having none of it. "I'm already making plans for my second," he said. "Don't tell me you're not going to keep me company?"

"Well . . ."

The cunning blighter talked me into it – thank goodness. I'd needed someone like him to give me a kick up the backside.

Since that day we've both written a number of novels and short stories, not to mention innumerable internet blogs on a wide variety of subjects. You could say it has given me a whole new lease on life.

I simply churn out the words, Joe is the technical man. He knows all about formatting, and publishing, and all that internet stuff that is virtually a closed book to me. He guides me through dealing with Create Space, and Amazon, and getting my books to the public. He's a wonderful friend, advisor and colleague, and I hope he realises how much that means to me.

About this book

This book came about quite by accident. I never intended writing it and it's certainly not meant for perusal by the public at large. It wouldn't interest them remotely in any case.

Some time ago my friend Candy Van Olst asked me to proofread a collection of short stories she'd assimilated from her days as a teacher and lecturer. It was an enthralling read and cast a fascinating and penetrating light on her profession and some of the folk she'd encountered in her career.

Now, I make no apology for cribbing her idea – although I did explain to her what I intended – but I figured it was as good a way as any of looking back over a long, and fairly rewarding life and jotting down a few memories.

It's not intended as the truth, the whole truth, and nothing but the truth; rather it's just a few scattered memories spanning almost eighty years. I've undoubtedly made mistakes and got some things wrong. I've forgotten quite a bit. I've certainly left a few things out, both intentionally and unintentionally.

I reckon I've quite enjoyed my time on this little planet. As Sinatra croons in *My Way*, *"Regrets, I've had a few, but then again, too few to mention."*

One obvious regret, of course, is that I've lost so many staunch friends along the way, and its small consolation that, hopefully, they're in a better place. There's far too many of them to mention here, and it would be remiss to leave anyone out. If there is an afterlife, they'll know who they are.

I doubt anyone will bother to read these reminiscences from beginning to end. That's fair enough; I won't feel slighted in the least. I hope there's a little time left to me yet, but if there is, I won't be recording it. Enough is enough. This is your lot.

In closing, I can do no better than quote a few lines from one of my favourite poets, Christina Rossetti, from her sonnet **Remember Me.**

But if you should forget me for a while,
and afterwards remember, do not grieve.
Better by far you should forget, and smile,
than that you should remember, and be sad.

Made in the USA
Charleston, SC
25 June 2016